D1227401

Praise for *The Common Sense Guide to Your Child's Special Needs*

"Dr. Pellegrino's book transcends labels with great clarity and guidance for parents. Like having your own developmental pediatrician patiently on call for your questions and concerns."
—Robert A. Naseef, Ph.D., psychologist, author of *Special Children, Challenged Parents*, and parent of an adult child with autism

"Offers a host of helpful guidelines of when to be concerned as a parent, suggestions for next steps in getting help, and recommendations for appropriate professionals who can be of assistance."
—Gail L. Ensher, Ed.D., Syracuse University

"This book really is a common-sense approach to helping parents understand their child's developmental delay or disability, and it affirms the parent's role as the expert on their child. The use of stories as teaching examples and eliminating or explaining jargon makes it very family friendly. I wish this book had been available when I first became concerned about my daughter's development. This is a must-read for any family experiencing concerns about their child and wondering how to take those next steps."
—Judy Swett, Early Childhood Coordinator, Parent Information and Resource Project, PACER Center

"Reading this book will be like sitting in a coffee shop and picking the brain of an expert on childhood disabilities. [Parents'] concerns about their developing child are expertly and humanely answered by Dr. Pellegrino in a way that is succinct and immensely helpful. A terrific resource for worried families!"
—V. Mark Durand, Ph.D., Professor of Psychology, University of South Florida St. Petersburg, Co-editor, *Journal of Positive Behavior Interventions*

"Dr. Pellegrino has truly hit a home run with this book! It is easy to use, easy to understand, and written in a refreshingly new and easy-to-use format. It is essential reading for all parents raising young children—disability or not!"
—Susan J. Moreno, President, OASIS@MAAP, MAAP Services for Autism and Asperger Syndrome

The Common Sense Guide to Your Child's Special Needs

When to Worry, When to Wait, What to Do

by

Louis Pellegrino, M.D.
The Upstate Golisano Children's Hospital
State University of New York
Upstate Medical University
Syracuse

·P A U L·H·
BROOKES
PUBLISHING C⁰ ®

Baltimore • London • Sydney

Paul H. Brookes Publishing Co.
Post Office Box 10624
Baltimore, Maryland 21285-0624
USA

www.brookespublishing.com

Typeset by Auburn Associates, Inc., Baltimore, Maryland.
Manufactured in the United States of America by
Sheridan Books, Inc., Chelsea, Michigan.

The information provided in this book is in no way meant to substitute for a medical or mental health practitioner's advice or expert opinion. Readers should consult a health or mental health professional if they are interested in more information. This book is sold without warranties of any kind, express or implied, and the publisher and authors disclaim any liability, loss, or damage caused by the contents of this book.

The individuals described in this book are composites or real people whose situations are masked and are based on the authors' experiences. Names and identifying details have been changed to protect confidentiality; real names and details are used by permission of the individuals described or their parents/guardians.

Cover photo copyright © iStockphoto.com. The photo on page x is used by permission of the individuals pictured and/or their parents/guardians, as applicable. Clip art on p. 149 copyright © 2012 Jupiterimages.com.

Library of Congress Cataloging-in-Publication Data

Pellegrino, Louis.
  The common sense guide to your child's special needs : when to worry, when to wait, what to do/by Louis Pellegrino.
    p.   cm.
  Includes index.
  ISBN-13: 978-1-59857-184-4 (pbk.)
  ISBN-10: 1-59857-184-2 (pbk.)
  1. Special education—Parent participation.   I. Title.
  LC3969.P45 2012
  371.9—dc23
                                                              2012011719

British Library Cataloguing in Publication data are available from the British Library.

2016   2015   2014   2013   2012

10   9   8   7   6   5   4   3   2   1

Contents

About the Author

Louis Pellegrino, M.D., is a developmental pediatrician who grew up in a suburb of New Haven, Connecticut, attended a small liberal arts college in New London, Connecticut, and completed medical school at the University of Connecticut, where he discovered his love of pediatrics. He then headed north to complete his pediatric training at what was then called the State University of New York (SUNY) Health Science Center in Syracuse, New York. There he met James C. Coplan, M.D., a dramatically bearded man with a booming voice who first exposed Dr. Pellegrino to developmental pediatrics. In a small room with a green carpet and a video camera, Dr. Coplan helped him to hone his skills at evaluating children with developmental concerns and laid the foundation for a career in what has come to be known as developmental-behavioral pediatrics.

Syracuse proved to be doubly lucky for Dr. Pellegrino in providing him both with a career and a spouse. He and his wife Joan next headed an hour and a half west on the New York State Thruway to the University of Rochester, where she completed her pediatric residency and he completed fellowship training in child development and developmental disabilities. With the enthusiastic support and inspired teaching of his mentors Gregory S. Liptak, M.D., Stephen B. Sulkes, M.D., and Phil W. Davidson, Ph.D., Dr. Pellegrino earned his certification in developmental-behavioral pediatrics and neurodevelopmental disabilities.

The two doctors Pellegrino then traveled to the great city of Philadelphia, where she completed a fellowship in medical genetics at The Children's Hospital of Philadelphia (CHOP) and he took a position as an attending physician at Children's Seashore House, a wonderful hospital for children with disabilities physically adjacent to CHOP and led by Mark L. Batshaw, M.D., editor of *When Your Child Has a Disability* (Paul H. Brookes Publishing Co., 2001). Under Dr. Batshaw's tutelage Dr. Pellegrino's career, then focused on working with children with cerebral palsy, expanded and thrived, and led to the creation of the book *Caring for Children with Cerebral Palsy: A Team Approach*, coedited with John P. Dormans, M.D. (Paul H. Brookes Publishing Co., 1998). While in Philadelphia the Pellegrinos were blessed with the birth of their beautiful daughter Elizabeth Marie.

The two-career path then led the Pellegrinos to central New Jersey, where their son Nicholas William was born. In New Jersey Dr. Pellegrino continued to teach medical students and see a broad range of children with wide range of developmental concerns, until the Pellegrinos felt a call to return home to Central New York.

Dr. Pellegrino is now Assistant Professor of Pediatrics and Director of the Child Development Program at the Center for Development, Behavior, and Genetics at the Upstate Golisano Children's Hospital, SUNY Upstate Medical University in Syracuse, New York. In addition to a very busy clinical practice, his scholarly activities have focused on the dissemination of information on developmental disabilities to medical and nonmedical professionals and, most especially, to the families of children with developmental concerns. He coedited (with Mark L. Batshaw, M.D., and Nancy J. Roizen, M.D.) the sixth edition of *Children with Disabilities* (Paul H. Brookes Publishing Co., 2007), a textbook for professionals who work with children with disabilities. With the publication of *The Common Sense Guide to Your Child's Special Needs: When to Worry, When to Wait, What to Do*, Dr. Pellegrino has distilled the experience of more than 20 years and the wisdom of his many wonderful teachers into a book that he hopes will be useful, enlightening, and encouraging to the parents of children with disabilities.

Foreword

As a developmental pediatrician, a frequent question I am asked by my families is, "Why my child?" Some families are consumed by the concern that they did something that caused their child to have a developmental disability. Certainly there are some things that a mother can do to protect her unborn child, like keeping healthy, avoiding using alcohol or illicit drugs, and seeing her doctor for regular appointments. But in most cases a mother does all these things and still her child has a disability. This is because in most cases developmental disabilities are highly influenced by our genes, the genetic code that defines us physically and cognitively. The good news is that we are beginning to unlock the secret of how genes affect us; the bad news is that it appears to be very complex, and it will likely be many years before what we know about genetics will influence clinical care or provide more substantive answers to parents to personalize treatment based on our genetic code.

So what are we to do until we know what causes most developmental disabilities or until we develop specific pharmacological therapies? We can focus on each child's needs and design an individualized program of supports and education to assist him or her to achieve all he or she can. For most children with disabilities this starts with a comprehensive examination that includes a health care team taking a history of the child's medical, behavioral, and developmental experience from birth; performing appropriate testing for diagnostic purposes; and developing a therapeutic program. This may be done in private practice, in a hospital setting, or in a school. Once a therapy and education program has been developed, there is the need for periodic checkups to evaluate the success of the program in improving function.

This all sounds quite straightforward, but, as a parent, you know how complicated and frustrating it actually can be. You may not understand all the medical terms being thrown at you and there may not be adequate time to have all your questions answered. The evaluation may not occur fast enough and the therapeutic interventions may not yield clear benefits and need to be adjusted. There may be inadequate social supports for you as you cope with unanticipated problems and unmet expectations.

These were the issues I sought to address when I wrote the precursor to this book, *When Your Child Has a Disability* (Paul H. Brookes Publishing Co., 2001). I wanted to provide answers to questions families had asked me, to provide them with up-to-date scientific information about what we are learning about specific developmental disabilities, and to offer some reassurance that parents often have the answers if they just take the time to observe what works with their child and what doesn't.

When it came time to write a follow-up book, I wanted to hand this important task over to someone I would entrust to provide well-reasoned information written in an accessible style. I found that person in Lou Pellegrino. Dr. Pellegrino is a sensitive and expert developmental pediatrician who has had many years of experience in caring for the full range of children with developmental disabilities. I have observed him as a clinician and teacher and he is simply exceptional. In addition, he is also a wonderful writer. When we coedited (with Nancy J. Roizen, M.D.) the sixth edition of *Children with Disabilities* (Paul H. Brookes Publishing Co., 2007), it became clear that he has a real talent with words and in conveying concepts. As you will see, he writes in an engaging manner, explains complex concepts clearly, and uses sidebars and illustrations to bring to life the information he is providing. You can use *The Common Sense Guide to Your Child's Special Needs* to better understand your child's specific disability and then follow approaches to diagnosis, treatment, and outcome. Resources are presented at the end of the book that allow you to dive more deeply into areas of particular concern. After reading this book I think you will come away feeling that you actually knew more than you thought about your child's problems and that your approach to treatment has been rational. It may help you know what to ask the members of your treatment and team and what to expect from them. And it may make you feel more comfortable knowing that there is light at the end of the tunnel.

Mark L. Batshaw, M.D.
Children's National Medical Center
Washington, D.C.

Acknowledgments

I very gratefully acknowledge Mark L. Batshaw, M.D., who has been a mentor and guide to a generation of neurodevelopmental pediatricians and whose inspiration and generosity made this book possible. Just as *When Your Child Has a Disability* (Paul H. Brookes Publishing Co., 2001) was Mark's baby, *The Common Sense Guide to Your Child's Special Needs* is mine, and it is my great hope that he will feel a grandfatherly pride in the result. I am particularly grateful to Mark and to the good people at Paul H. Brookes Publishing Co. for the creative freedom they allowed me in taking this book in a very different direction. It was Mark's vision of making ideas and information about child development and developmental disabilities widely available to families that inspired me to make this book as readable and accessible as possible. Nothing would make me happier than to know that my efforts have served to extend the reach of Mark's vision to a wider audience.

I also gratefully acknowledge my wife Joan, who has been my companion in life and in pediatrics (in the role of medical geneticist par excellence), and who kindly read the first draft of the manuscript (the entire first draft!) and offered sincere, if perhaps biased, encouragement that was most gratefully received.

Finally, I gratefully acknowledge my teachers, who have taught and continue to teach me through word and example, but most especially through the power of their special gifts and unique presence. Good teachers tell us what we need to know; great teachers show us who we need to be—we can never have too many great teachers.

For my dad, who taught me about gardens, and everything else

Introduction

How Your Garden Grows

I live and work in Syracuse, a medium-size city in Upstate New York best known for its basketball team (the Orange) and its dubious distinction as the snowiest city in the continental United States. We do have long, cold, snowy winters in our part of the world, so the first signs of spring are met with great enthusiasm. As the snow melts in my backyard, indistinct shapes of objects long submerged and half forgotten gradually reveal themselves. Among these are the raised garden beds I built several summers ago. Their reappearance every spring reawakens a primal yearning in me to plant and grow things. I do this every spring without fail, despite my less than distinguished career as a gardener. Every year I put in tomatoes, cucumbers, zucchini, spinach, and lettuce, and every year I try something new. And every year, something grows well: I may get a bonanza of delicious grape tomatoes, or a bumper crop of zucchini that I have trouble harvesting before they grow into green behemoths, or baskets brimming with crisp, sweet cucumbers.

And every year something I have planted with great expectation and optimism will turn out to be a complete bust. One year I bought a beautiful overpriced tomato plant that promised immense, dark red tomatoes of exceeding quality, excellent for slicing, the prime ingredient in the perfect summer sandwich. The plant grew with leafy vigor but produced only a few scrawny-looking, tasteless tomatoes. Another year all of my zucchini plants wilted. I have

1

long since given up on peppers, which refuse to grow for me. This year the cucumbers look surprisingly lackluster, though I have not given up on them yet. Despite my best efforts to amend the soil properly, choose plants carefully, and water and weed diligently, I must admit to a complete inability to predict the outcome of my efforts from one year to the next.

Raising a child is very much like gardening in its inherent unpredictability. First-time parents are often surprised by the striking individuality of their newest family member and how different their infant is from what they expected. Parents with several children are likewise surprised by how different their offspring are from one another—they often wonder how these siblings could possibly have the same parents! My oldest daughter, who has grown into a smart, talented, beautiful, vivacious teenager, was a colicky, high-maintenance infant who had to be held constantly, slept poorly, and demanded constant attention. My son, by contrast, was a docile, low-maintenance infant who has grown into an exceptionally creative, slightly disorganized, but always kind-hearted and thoughtful preteen. My wife and I like to think that our parenting skills have something to do with how great our kids are turning out, but I have a sneaking suspicion that we just got lucky.

Like the gardener who diligently attends to his crop, parents have an expectation that if they clothe, feed, and nurture their children well they will grow and develop in predictable ways with predictable and positive results. But things do not always turn out as expected. This is especially true if you discover that your child is developing in unexpected ways. Perhaps your child has been slow to acquire expected skills. You may have an 18-month-old who is not walking yet or a 24-month-old who has not started talking. Perhaps your preschooler is struggling to learn his colors and shapes or is having trouble with toilet training. Or perhaps your first grader is having unexpected difficulties learning to read. These are examples of delayed development. Mild delays may simply represent expected variations in development that naturally occur among children, but more significant delays may indicate a persistent difference in ability that has long-term functional implications.

Development can also go unexpectedly off track. Rather than experiencing a delay in acquiring an expected skill, your child may exhibit skills or behaviors that are qualitatively different from those of other children. For example, your child may randomly repeat bits of a favorite television show or movie, imitating precisely the words and intonation of the original, or he may be inclined to label objects compulsively but show little inclination to use words to communicate with others. Or your child may walk on her toes, or be unusually sensitive to noises, or exhibit unusual body movements, or have difficulty making eye contact. These are all examples of off-track or divergent development (divergent here referring to a tendency to diverge or deviate from an expected developmental path).

Your child may exhibit delays or divergence in multiple areas of development, including speech and language skills, motor skills (skills required for physical coordination), play skills, social skills, and skills that are required for daily living activities (e.g., eating, dressing, toileting). This pattern is called global developmental delay. Or your child may have an uneven pattern of skills, showing significantly delayed or divergent skills in some areas and being more usual or typical for her age in others. This is called dissociated development.

When a child shows persistent difficulties in one or several areas of development that clearly affect his or her ability to function in real-life situations, that child is said to have a developmental disability. Some developmental disabilities are common and relatively mild, such as language disorders, coordination problems, learning disabilities, and disorders of attention and impulse control. Other developmental disabilities are less common and more severe, including global learning problems, disorders associated with a lack of communication and social interaction skills, and disorders of movement and muscle control associated with abnormal reflexes and very tight or very loose muscles.

Knowing when your child has a developmental disability can be difficult. When your child first shows signs of developing in unexpected ways, it may take time to determine whether the problem is temporary or persistent and when consultation with a developmental specialist is warranted. The most important thing you can do to help your child when you suspect that there is a problem is to *trust your instincts*. Many parents, especially first-time parents, lack confidence in their ability to recognize developmental problems, but research has demonstrated time and again that parents are extraordinarily sensitive to their child's development and are almost always right when they suspect that there is a problem.

My goal in writing this book is to help with the next step: Once you have recognized that you have concerns about your child's development, you can use this book to learn more about the problem, fill in the gaps, and form a fuller picture about possible diagnoses and helpful interventions.

Section I is devoted to common areas of concern: speech, language, and communication skills; motor skills and coordination; activities of daily living; social skills; behavior; and learning skills. Specific developmental disabilities are considered within the context of these broader discussions: developmental language disorder (Chapter 1), developmental coordination disorder (Chapter 2), cerebral palsy (Chapters 2 and 9), social cognitive disability (Chapter 4), autism spectrum disorders (Chapter 4), attention-deficit/hyperactivity disorder (ADHD; Chapter 5), learning disability (Chapter 6), and intellectual disability (previously called mental retardation; Chapter 6).

Although particular developmental disabilities are highlighted in certain chapters, the elements of a diagnosis that relate to the main subject of another chapter are discussed in that chapter as well. For example, although ADHD is highlighted in Chapter 5, the coordination difficulties, writing problems, social difficulties, and learning problems associated with ADHD are discussed in Chapters 2, 4, and 6.

Ways to find and provide help for your child are discussed in each chapter, with a focus on interventions that relate specifically to the subject of that chapter. Chapter 7 ("When Your Child Needs Extra Help") offers a general discussion of interventions relevant to all areas of concern and all diagnoses, with a particular emphasis on early intervention and special education.

Section II takes up topics of general concern for children with various developmental disabilities. Hearing, vision, and sensory processing disorders are considered in Chapter 8. Special health care concerns relevant to all children with developmental disabilities are discussed in Chapter 9; particular attention is given to the unique health care concerns of children with Down syndrome, spina bifida, and cerebral palsy. Medication interventions for children with developmental disabilities are considered in Chapter

10, and the causes of developmental disabilities are discussed in Chapter 11.

It is my hope that as you read this book you will find information, insights, and suggestions relevant to the concerns you have about your child. I would be very glad to know that my book helped you to clear out some of the weeds of confusion from your garden, for it is my goal—as I know it is yours—to help your child grow and prosper and enjoy his or her time in the sun.

A word on some special elements used in this book: In addition to traditional illustrations and tables, I have made use of the following special devices to highlight or elaborate on elements of the main text:

 Every garden starts with seeds and the right sorts of seeds make for the best and most productive gardens. In this book, "Seeds" represent those pivotal concepts, important distinctions, and key recommendations for intervention that are developed and elaborated in the main text.

 Understanding your child's developmental problems necessarily involves grappling with a lot of professional jargon. I have made every attempt to stick to plain English wherever I can in this book, but it is impossible to completely avoid technical terminology. Jargon Busters are used to highlight and explain the definitions of key technical terms commonly used by professionals who work with children with disabilities.

 FYIs (For Your Information) are extra tidbits of information related to the main topic of discussion that offer additional detail, highlight related ideas and information, or explore a tangent that is (hopefully!) interesting and perhaps even entertaining.

I

··

Understanding
Your Child

1

When Your Child Has Trouble Talking
Understanding Problems with Speech and Language Development

*P*icture a family gathering. You are speaking with a grandparent about your concerns that your child's speech is delayed. "Zachary isn't talking yet," you begin, "and his second birthday is just around the corner. I'm wondering if I should talk with his pediatrician about this."

"Oh, you shouldn't worry," replies the well-meaning grandparent. "Zachary's Uncle Joe didn't talk until he was 3, and he did fine."

The problem with this all-too-common scenario is that very often, upon further inquiry, it is discovered that Uncle Joe actually did not do so well. He was frustrated and angry as a preschooler because people did not understand him, and he began to use his behavior as a means of communicating his frustration. Although his speech had improved significantly by kindergarten, he struggled with his ABCs and struggled even more with reading in first grade. After several years of heartache and frustration it was determined that Uncle Joe had a learning disability, and he finally received much-needed help—but not before he developed a profound dislike of school and a deep-seated suspicion about his own intelligence and competence.

The first and most important principle in addressing speech delay is to *take it seriously*. Although speech delay *may* be mild and temporary, it can often be persistent

9

The Uncle Joe Effect

seeds Do not dismiss concerns about your child's speech because other family members have had similar issues.

and troublesome, and it may also be an early indicator of other, broader developmental issues.

Speech comes naturally to most children, but it is very common for children to have speech delays. In fact, speech delay is the most common reason why parents become concerned about their child's development. After walking, talking is the first thing everyone asks about when inquiring about a child's development. Parents are often especially eager for their infant to look up at them lovingly and say "mama" or "dada," but many children are late to learn this, and many children break the rules and develop speech in unexpected ways.

HOW DO I KNOW IF MY CHILD HAS A SIGNIFICANT SPEECH DELAY?

The simplest and most important answer to this question is this: *If you think your child has a speech or communication problem, you are probably right!* Research bears this out: Parents are very good observers of their child's development and are usu-

Trust Yourself

seeds If you think your child has a speech, language, or communication problem, you are probably right.

ally right when they suspect that something is wrong. Parents, especially first-time parents, often doubt their ability to recognize a developmental problem, but *they should not!* Unfortunately, family members, friends, and even professionals are sometimes too quick to dismiss parental concerns. So it is worth emphasizing again: No one knows your child better than you do. If you are worried about your child's speech, stick up for yourself—and your child—and be persistent in expressing your concerns.

LANGUAGE 101

It is helpful at this point to review some terminology that professionals use and parents should know. So far this chapter mainly has talked about speech and speech delay, but speech is part of a broader phenomenon called *language*. Language has many aspects but is most often described in terms of expressive, receptive, and pragmatic language.

Expressive language refers to what a child says and how he says it. In common usage it is equivalent to what is usually meant by the term *speech*. Expressive language can be further described in terms of content and production. *Content* refers to the vocabulary, grammar, and syntax of speech (what a child says); *production* refers to the clarity and fluidity with which something is said (how a child speaks). How well a child produces (pronounces) sounds and words is called *articulation*. How fluidly and smoothly a child produces phrases and sentences is called *fluency*. How understandable a child's speech is to someone else is called *intelligibility*. How accurately a child adjusts her voice inflection to harmonize with the content and context of speech is called *prosody*. *Semantics* refers to the meaning of words.

Receptive language refers to what a child understands rather than what he says. If you ask your child to bring you his shoes and he does, he demonstrates comprehension of an instruction, which is an element of receptive language. If he points to his nose, to the dog, or to a picture in a book upon request, he is demonstrating another aspect of receptive language. It makes sense that a child must understand words (receptive language) before he can say them (expressive language), so intact receptive language function is usually a prerequisite for speech development.

Pragmatic language refers to the "how" of language and in particular how people use language to communicate in real-life situations. It is possible for a child to have an excellent vocabulary, create marvelous sentences, and have wonderful comprehension but still be very poor at communicating with others. Pragmatic language is closely connected with social communication skills and social interaction skills more generally. It includes the crucial nonverbal elements of communication, such as eye contact, facial expressions, gestures, body language, and the subtle explicit and implicit rules of conversation that govern human communication.

Just as expressive language is grounded in receptive language, both expressive and receptive language have a foundation in pragmatic language. Very early in their development infants engage in a process of wordless communication with their

jargon buster

Speech and Language Terminology

Expressive language: What a child says and how he or she says it

Receptive language: What a child understands

Pragmatic language: How a child uses language in real-life settings

Content and Structural Elements of Speech

Babbling: Repeated syllables ("bababa," "mamama," "dadada")

Jargon: Mixed syllables (gibberish)

Vocabulary: Words spoken and understood

Grammar: The rules for forming words into phrases and sentences

Syntax: The rules governing grammatical usage

Semantics: The meaning of speech

Process and Production Elements of Speech

Articulation: How sounds and words are pronounced

Intelligibility: How well others understand someone's speech

Fluency: The ability to produce continuous, unobstructed speech

Prosody: The "music" of speech; voice inflection

parents. They smile and vocalize responsively, imitate sounds and gestures, and become entrained with the rhythms of their parents' interactions with them. They become engaged in an elaborate conversational dance composed of complex visual and auditory cues, and it is this elaborate choreography that provides the basis for all human communication. Without this foundation language becomes hollow, technical, and devoid of emotional content.

Early Speech and Language Development

Infants progress rapidly in acquiring speech and language skills during the first year of life, starting with nonspecific vocalizations such as crying and advancing sequentially to cooing (using open vowel sounds), babbling (using repeated simple syllables, e.g., "babababa"), and jargon (using multisyllabic vocalizations with a variety of consonant and vowel sounds). The first recognizable words (*dada, mama*) often emerge from babbling (typically around 8–9 months), and single words other than *dada* and *mama* emerge from jargon (typically around 12 months). Research confirms that infants understand many words before they can say them. For example, infants can demonstrate an understanding of the word *no* as early as 6 months of age and should consistently respond to their names before 8 months of age. Infants can respond to one-step commands accompanied by a gesture by 9 months and to commands without a gesture by 12 months.

Languages, Phonemes, and Infants

Before they are 6 months of age infants can distinguish speech sounds (phonemes) for all world languages; by 12 months of age they can only easily distinguish sounds from their native language.

Although parents are understandably alert to the first use of the words *dada* or *mama*, it is notoriously difficult to determine when a particular infant switches from babbling to the use of these words to refer to her parents. From a clinical perspective it is much easier to identify when a child begins using single words other than *mama* or *dada*. So saying that children typically begin talking at a year of age means that they usually start using single words other than *mama* or *dada* at that time.

Why Dads Are Called "Dada"

Infants find certain sounds easier to produce than others in early infancy, so "dadada" often precedes "mamama." One theory suggests that in early societies, fathers in male-dominant cultures commandeered "dada" to refer to themselves.

Once talking starts, new words come at a steady trickle until about 18 months of age, and then the floodgates open. Between 18 and 24 months there is an enormous acceleration in the pace of word acquisition and language usage, such that by a child's second birthday she will typically be using between 50 and 250 words, with an average of about 125 words. Most children also begin to construct two- and three-word phrases at this time, show a dramatic increase in their ability to identify objects and pictures, show significant improvements in their ability to communicate wants and needs, and are able to respond to increasingly complex instructions.

This transformation in language skills is accompanied by an equally dramatic transformation of the child from a dependent infant to an independent, autonomous toddler. Brain research suggests that fairly dramatic changes in neurological organization occur at this time, and problems with making this transition may be associated with subsequent developmental disability. It is not too much of an exaggeration to compare this transformation to the metamorphosis of a caterpillar to a butterfly. The person who emerges from this process of language and social transformation is literally a new creature, endowed with uniquely human powers of symbol manipulation, communication, and social engagement.

Children continue to make dramatic gains in language skills through the toddler and preschool years. By 3 years of age a typically developing child is using complete grammatical sentences and has become much easier to understand. Whereas a 2-year-old may be intelligible to non–family members about 50% of the time at best, 3-year-olds are understandable to most people most of the time (greater than 75% intelligible). The typical 3-year-old uses pronouns (*I, me, you, he,* and *she*) appropriately and is usually fairly consistent with the use of prepositions (*in, on, for, with*) and plurals. By this age most children have a vocabulary of several hundred words (even the most diligent parents have usually lost count of their child's expressive vocabulary at this point). Although not fully conversational, 3-year-olds are able to engage in simple two- or three-step question-and-answer-style conversations, also known as *prompted conversations* (see Table 1.1).

Language Regression and Autism

About one third of children with autism undergo a period of language and social regression, which typically occurs between 18 and 24 months of age. This coincides with the period of accelerated language and social growth that occurs in typically developing children. Although research suggests that children with autism have differences in brain structure and function from birth, for some children the more notable symptoms of autism only become apparent during this unique period of neurologic reorganization.

The period from the second to the third birthdays represents an interesting time of transition from the perspective of language. Although not yet using complete sentences, a child at this stage is beginning to display the rudiments of grammar and typically speaks in partial or telegraphic sentences (by analogy to old-style telegraphs, which would typically omit nonessential words and grammatical elements to save money). Two-and-a-half-year-olds are more limited in their use of grammatical elements such as pronouns (most start by learning *me* and *you* and not uncommonly confuse the two) and cannot usually engage in extended

Table 1.1. Key early speech milestones

Milestone	Age
Cooing	2–3 months
Babbling	6 months
"Dada" and "mama"	8–9 months
Single words (other than "dada" and "mama")	12 months
Two-word phrases	22–24 months
Partial (telegraphic) sentences	28–30 months
Complete (grammatical) sentences	36 months

conversational interaction. The *Sesame Street* character Cookie Monster exemplifies the speech patterns of the typical two-and-a-half-year-old (his famous phrase "Me want cookie" being an especially apt example).

By 4 years of age sentence usage is well established and complex sentence forms are beginning to emerge. Many 4-year-olds are capable of extended reciprocal conversation that can be maintained without prompting by parents. Although many 4-year-olds still have trouble pronouncing certain sounds (e.g., /sh/, /th/), they are usually 100% intelligible. By 5 years of age conversation skills are well established, vocabulary and sentence complexity have increased, and the subtle nuances of social communication are better understood. Five-year-olds are often chatty and can tell stories about their interests and important events in their lives (knock-knock jokes are also very popular with this age group).

If language has a magical and mysterious quality, then it would be fair to say that the typical kindergartner is a veritable Houdini, conjuring words and phrases from thin air and using verbal sleight-of-hand with incredible facility. People tend to take for granted the commonplace yet miraculous emergence of language in early childhood, but the processes leading to this are sensitive, complex, and subject to many pitfalls. From this perspective perhaps it is not surprising that the most common developmental issues in early childhood almost always involve some degree of language delay or dysfunction.

Red Flags for Early Speech and Language Development

A number of specific red flags should raise concerns about a child's language development and alert you to the possible

Red Flags

If you notice any of these red flags, your child should be evaluated further to determine whether a problem with language development exists.

- You have a gut feeling that something is wrong with your child's language development.
- Your child shows little eye contact, responsive smiling, or vocalizations from infancy.
- Your child does not respond when you call him by name.
- Your child is not babbling by 9 months of age.
- Your child has limited vocalizations and is not saying any recognizable words by 15 months of age.
- Your child is not using at least a dozen words consistently by 18 months of age.
- Your child is not using at least 50 single words and some two-word phrases by 2 years of age.
- Your child is not using complete sentences or is still difficult to understand by 3 years of age.
- Your child is extremely frustrated because she cannot easily communicate wants or needs at any age.
- Your child shows little interest in communication at any age.
- Your child has stopped progressing or has had a regression in speech at any age.

presence of a language disorder. Before they are 1 year of age infants are very socially responsive; vocalize like crazy; and show that they understand words, especially their own names. Between 1 year and 1½ years infants should be saying their first words, and by 2 years of age they should be using at least 50 words, with some two-word combinations. They should show a consistent understanding of instructions (whether they carry them out or not is another question!); should be able to point out a few body parts on request; and should also be able to identify objects and pictures, at least to a limited degree. By 3 years of age children should be using complete, intelligible sentences. If your child is not showing skills consistent with these expectations, or if your child shows unusual frustration in attempting to communicate, you should seek further assessment and treatment to address the issue.

THE CAUSES OF SPEECH AND LANGUAGE DELAY

There are many potential causes of speech and language delay. Some are related to specific medical conditions, whereas others are part of a broader developmental disorder with speech and language delay as a component.

Hearing Loss

Although hearing loss is not the most common cause of speech and language delays, it is the most important cause to rule out initially when a delay is suspected. There are two main types of hearing loss: sensorineural hearing loss and conductive hearing loss (see Chapter 8). Sensorineural hearing loss, when severe, is sometimes called *nerve deafness.* It is caused by abnormalities of the cochlea or the auditory nerve. The cochlea is a snail-like structure that occupies the inner ear. It converts vibrations or sound energy to electrical impulses that are then transmitted to the brain by the auditory nerve. Different parts of the cochlea are sensitive to different frequencies of sound, so it is not uncommon for children with sensorineural hearing loss to exhibit variability in how well they can hear high-pitched (high-frequency) versus low-pitched (low-frequency) sounds. Children with moderate to severe sensorineural hearing loss may benefit from wearing a hearing aid; children with profound hearing loss may be eligible to receive a cochlear implant, a special high-tech device that is surgically threaded into the cochlea and replaces it as a sound-to-electrical-impulse converter. Although there are many different causes of sensorineural hearing loss (including infections during pregnancy, drug toxicity in sensitive premature infants, and brain injury), more than half of all cases of this type of hearing loss are due to genetic or hereditary conditions.

Conductive hearing loss is the result of problems in the middle ear, most often as a consequence of ear infections (see Chapter 8). The middle ear is drained by the eustachian tube. If your child has a cold it is easy for this tube to become blocked, and fluid can accumulate in the middle-ear space. If the fluid becomes infected, your child will develop an ear infection. Often fluid lingers in the middle-ear space for days or weeks after the infection clears, and many children run into problems with the fluid becoming reinfected. In some instances a special drainage tube can be placed through the eardrum to circumvent this vicious cycle of fluid accumulation and reinfection.

Although conductive hearing loss can certainly result in mild to moderate temporary hearing loss and may have transient effects on speech, it is not clear whether children with chronic middle-ear problems have long-term speech difficulties as a consequence of this. (Although research seems to suggest that it does not, many parents and professionals are still suspicious that it does.) By contrast, sensorineural hearing loss, which is often severe, is a definite cause of speech difficulties, and the newborn hearing screening now mandated in most states is primarily intended to identify children with this type of hearing problem.

Speech Delays and Hearing Loss

All children with speech and language delays should have their hearing tested, even if they passed newborn hearing screening tests.

If your child has a speech delay, or if you suspect that your child is not hearing well for other reasons, he should be tested be an audiologist, preferably someone who has significant experience testing children. Different techniques are used to test children at different ages and developmental levels. Although many pediatric and family practice offices and schools offer hearing screening, these screening tests and procedures are not adequate to evaluate a child who is already suspected of having a hearing loss; a formal assessment with an audiologist is a must.

Timing Is Everything for Deaf Children

Research suggests that children with severe or profound deafness have much better speech development if they receive hearing aids or cochlear implants early on, preferably during their first year of life and ideally before 6 months of age. Newborn hearing screening is critical for identifying these children.

Developmental Language Disorders

Developmental language disorders are the most common cause of speech and language problems in children. They are so common they are almost invisible, and they are often dismissed as insignificant (remember the Uncle Joe Effect). A child with a developmental language disorder may have some delays or difficulties in other nonlanguage areas, but the main concerns are with speech, language, and communication.

Delayed Speech: Expressive Language Disorder

You have a wonderful, happy, playful 2-year-old who is getting more and more frustrated because he cannot talk. He tries very hard to communicate by any means possible but mostly relies on pointing and grunting. If this does not work he looks at you with frustration and screams. If this does not work he throws himself on the floor and has a full-blown, no-holds-barred tantrum. His lack of speech is especially perplexing because he seems to understand everything that is said to him. He can follow complex commands, he can identify body parts ("Where's your nose?" "Where are your eyes?"), he can accurately identify pictures in books, and he runs to the door if you ask if he wants to go outside. He has picked up a bit of sign language, but this is not sufficient to allow him to express his thoughts and wishes adequately. His hearing has been tested and is normal. He is a little uncoordinated and was slightly delayed with walking, but otherwise he has demonstrated age-appropriate skills and social behavior.

This is a very typical story for a child with an expressive language disorder. Some children with expressive language disorders show evidence of significant difficulties with coordination and motor planning skills, especially as these relate to the use of the muscles involved in speech production. They are frequently very delayed in their ability to demonstrate various speech sounds—even at 2 years old they may not be able to produce more than a handful of consonant sounds, for example. Many have a history of difficulties tolerating certain food textures, and some drool excessively. Some have difficulties with other aspects of coordination, including delayed gross motor skills (e.g., walking) or delayed fine motor skills (e.g., using a spoon). This type of expressive language disorder is sometimes called *verbal apraxia* (or *verbal dyspraxia*; the terms *apraxia* and *dyspraxia* refer to problems with motor planning and control; see Chapter 2).

Other children with expressive language disorders have less severe speech delays and are able to produce an adequate variety of speech sounds but seem to have trouble using the right sound in the right place at the right time. They frequently drop parts of words, or condense two or three syllables into one, or substitute one sound for another. Instead of saying "twinkle, twinkle little star" they might say "dinka, dinka, lida

jargon buster

Developmental Language Disorders

Primarily expressive type: A disorder characterized by well-developed language comprehension and nonverbal communication skills (e.g., pointing to desired objects) but delayed speech

Receptive/expressive type: A disorder characterized by significant delays in both speech and comprehension

Pragmatic language disorder: A disorder characterized by difficulties in the social aspect of communication with or without expressive and receptive language delays

Lower order language skills: Skills related to the nuts and bolts of language, such as articulation, grammar, and vocabulary; the type of language skills most noticeably impaired in children with primary expressive and receptive/expressive language disorders

Higher order language skills: Skills related to the ability to process and produce complex language; the type of language skills most often impaired in children with certain forms of learning disability and pragmatic language disorders

Echolalia: The tendency to repeat random phrases from conversation or television without a clear intent to communicate

Scripted speech: Rote phrases or sentences (often borrowed from outside sources) used to substitute for spontaneously produced language

kar." In contrast to children with verbal apraxia, these children often use complete sentences by 3–3½ years of age but are still hard to understand. Most speak well by kindergarten, but some struggle with learning letters; are confused by rhyming; and find early reading, especially sounding out words (phonetic decoding), difficult. These children have a form of expressive language disorder known as *phonological disorder,* and a percentage will be diagnosed with a specific type of reading disability known as *dyslexia* (see Chapter 6).

Delays in Speech and Comprehension: Receptive-Expressive Language Disorder

Your daughter just celebrated her third birthday with a party that included several other 3-year-olds from her child care center. Although the party was a great success you were troubled by the contrast you noticed between your child and her peers. Although your daughter uses many words and some short phrases that are usually easy to understand, she does not yet use sentences. By contrast, some of her friends are quite talkative, use complete sentences, can answer questions, and can even hold short conversations. Among the birthday presents are several books, some with simple stories, and you know that your daughter has little interest in these and in fact cannot reliably identify pictures yet. And although she loves being around other children and is very friendly, her play skills are immature. She is also a little behind her friends with toilet training and seems to have a very short attention span even for a 3-year-old. As you think about it, your daughter seems in many ways more like a 2-year-old than a 3-year-old, although you recognize that she does have some age-appropriate skills. For instance, she can dress herself and ride a tricycle.

This child's story is typical of that of a child with a combined receptive-expressive language disorder. Although their most prominent and obvious developmental difficulty relates to speech and language delays, children with receptive-expressive language disorder tend to have milder difficulties in other aspects of development and often seem immature. The main issue with respect to their language disorder is a problem with language comprehension. Children with a fundamental problem with language assimilation and processing must by definition have speech delays as well (children cannot talk well until they understand the words they will be using). When viewed from a global perspective these children have a strikingly uneven pattern of skills. Some skills are age appropriate, others (particularly language skills) may be severely delayed, and other skills are more mildly delayed. As they grow and mature these children often catch up in some areas but tend to lag behind in others, and by the time they reach school age they may demonstrate gaps and inconsistencies in learning and attention skills. In other words, children with receptive-expressive language disorder are at increased risk for persistent problems with learning and attention, and some will ultimately be diagnosed with a learning disability or attention-deficit/hyperactivity disorder.

Difficulties with Social Communication: Pragmatic Language Disorder and the Autism Connection

Your 28-month-old has been a perplexing source of concern for some time, but you have been especially worried since his second birthday. In most respects he has always seemed precocious to you. He was an early walker. He is already independently using a spoon and fork, and he can almost get himself completely dressed without help. He is remarkably adept at puzzles and is quite expert at operating the television remote control and the computer. He loves books and already seems to recognize letters, numbers, and even some words. He has a large vocabulary, speaks with crystal clarity, and is already using some short sentences. Yet despite his apparently advanced abilities he is inexplicably uninterested in communication. Rather than using words to communicate he mainly uses words to label things. He has a marked tendency to repeat bits of conversation and snatches of television shows, often perfectly imitating the inflection of the speech, but without any apparent communicative intent. He is very independent and mostly does things for himself. On those rare occasions when he does need help he will usually grab you and pull you toward that which requires your attention rather than using his words to communicate. He makes inconsistent eye contact and makes poor use of pointing to clarify his intentions. Although his speech is not delayed, his lack of interest in communication has you worried.

Pointing, Eye Contact, and the Desire to Communicate

Most children start pointing to things they want by 14 months of age and shortly thereafter like to point to things to share experiences with others. Most children with language disorders use pointing accompanied by eye contact and vocalizations (grunting) to compensate for a lack of speech. Children with pragmatic language disorders, especially those on the autism spectrum, typically do not do this.

Despite this child's well-developed speech and language comprehension he demonstrates a marked problem with social communication, the hallmark of pragmatic language dysfunction. Pragmatic language dysfunction can occur in isolation but is most often seen in conjunction with broader difficulties with social interaction skills and may be an indicator of an autism spectrum disorder (see Chapter 4).

Although it is less common, children with various kinds of language processing difficulties may exhibit pragmatic language dysfunction in the absence of other signs of autism. In these children pragmatic language dysfunction may occur as part of a broader problem related to abstract language and may be a harbinger of a type of learning disability. Children with pragmatic language disorders often have noticeably quirky speech. They may repeat things from television shows, seemingly at random (this is called *echololia*). They may speak very loudly or very softly most of the time, or they may speak in a robotic, monotone, or singsong manner because of a lack of awareness of the nuances of voice inflection (this is called *impaired prosody*). They may use the same catchphrases over and over again when they do try to communicate (referred to as *rote* or *scripted speech*). School-age children with pragmatic language dysfunction are particularly noted for their poor conversation skills and for their lack of understanding of the social conventions of conversation.

Delayed Language and "Global Delays"

Your 4-year-old is having his annual checkup, and you tell your pediatrician that you are very concerned about your child's development. Although his hearing has tested normal, he can only speak in short phrases and still has trouble understanding even simple instructions. He cannot get dressed by himself, cannot pedal a bike or tricycle, and is not toilet trained. He does not know colors, shapes, letters, or numbers. Although he is very friendly, you feel that he acts much younger than his age; in fact, he reminds you very much of his 2-year-old cousin in terms of both his skills and his interests. The pediatrician tells you that she thinks your child has global developmental delays.

Most children with speech and language delays have skills in other areas that are better developed or closer to age level, but for some children speech and language delays are part of a generalized pattern of delayed development that affects skills in multiple areas, including language, social, problem-solving, self-care, play, and motor skills. Some children with global developmental delays will catch up in at least some areas, but some will not. In fact, some will tend to lag further and further behind their peers over time. Some children with milder delays will be diagnosed with a learning disability when they are older, but others with more profound delays will be diagnosed with intellectual disability (previously called mental retardation). The key issue in distinguishing between children with isolated language disorders and those with a significant general intellectual disability is understanding the big picture and recognizing when a child has delays in multiple areas as opposed to just a few (see Chapter 6).

Other Speech and Language Problems that Appear in Early Childhood

Other difficulties that affect the quality of speech often appear in early childhood. These may occur in isolation or may coexist with the various forms of developmental language disorder previously described.

The Child Who Stutters

Children who stutter have a dysfluency of speech: Although their vocabulary, grammar, and comprehension skills are often age appropriate, they have trouble producing words and sentences in an easy and fluid manner. They may get stuck on a sound ("l-l-l-l-like"), a syllable ("wa-wa-wa-water"), or a whole word ("my-my-my-my dog"). Brief episodes of dysfluency are common in early childhood and represent minor variations of typical development. Significant stuttering usually emerges between 1½ and 3 years of age. In many cases stuttering is mild and resolves spontaneously, but in some instances it persists and causes difficulties and distress. If stuttering continues beyond a few weeks or becomes a source of stress or embarrassment for a child, referral to a qualified speech-language pathologist (speech therapist) is warranted.

Helping the Child Who Stutters

- Be very patient with your child; give him time to speak and try not to rush him.
- Recognize that if your child feels anxious about speaking, this will aggravate the stuttering.
- Slow down the pace of the conversation.
- Institute the habit of turn taking in conversation among siblings.
- Be reassuring and sympathetic.
- Solicit the help of a speech-language pathologist if the problem is persistent or severe.

The Child with Dysarthria

Children with significant physical disabilities such as cerebral palsy may have severe problems with speech production based on an inability to coordinate the complex movements of the many muscle groups involved in speech (see Chapter 2). In some cases these children may need special communication devices to allow them to communicate.

The Child with Anatomical Abnormalities that Affect Speech

Some children may be born with congenital anomalies, such as a cleft palate (an opening in the roof of the mouth), that will affect speech. Special oral appliances and in some cases surgery can help these children, but they will often need the help of a speech-language pathologist as well.

COMMON MYTHS REGARDING CHILDREN WITH SPEECH DELAYS

Myth 1: Being tongue-tied is a common cause of speech delay.

Truth: Having a tight band of tissue between the bottom of the tongue and the floor of the mouth may have a minor impact on certain specific speech sounds but does not cause significant delays; surgery to clip the tongue does not usually result in the resolution of speech problems.

Myth 2: Having an older sibling speak for a younger sibling causes speech delay.

Truth: If anything, having an older sibling fosters speech development rather than inhibits it. Sensitive older siblings instinctively recognize when a younger sibling is having trouble speaking and often react by translating or speaking for the child, but their help is a consequence rather than a cause of the delay.

Myth 3: Living in a bilingual household causes speech delay.

Truth: Children with typical language skills are amazingly adept at learning language and usually have no trouble learning more than one language. Living in a bilingual home does not cause speech delay; in fact, research suggests that children brought up with two languages have better language skills overall than children raised in single-language homes (unless they have a language disorder that makes it difficult for them to learn *any* language).

Myth 4: Frequent ear infections are a major cause of speech delay.

Truth: This myth is controversial, but the best evidence suggests that although ear infections and middle-ear fluid can cause transient problems with hearing and speech, they cannot usually explain more significant, persistent problems.

Myth 5: Children usually outgrow speech delays.

Truth: Speech and language delays are often persistent and troublesome and may be an early sign of broader developmental problems.

HOW TO HELP YOUR CHILD WITH SPEECH AND LANGUAGE DELAYS

The fact that you are reading this book and thinking about the possibility that your child needs help means you have already taken the first step toward helping, which is to recognize the problem. The following points represent a review of some of the principles discussed earlier in this chapter and elaborate further on sources of help and support.

Talk to your child's primary doctor about your concerns. Remember to trust yourself and recognize that if you are concerned about your child's speech and language development, your child's doctor should be as well. Your child's doctor can play a critical role in referring you to local resources and in helping to determine whether any medical issues may have a bearing on your child's speech problem.

Have your child's hearing tested by a qualified audiologist. If your child's speech and language skills are delayed, he should have a formal hearing assessment, even if he passed a hearing screening test in the newborn period.

Obtain the assistance of a speech-language pathologist. If your child is younger than 3, the early intervention system (see Chapter 7) is the most important resource for speech therapy and educational support. If your child is older than 3, your local school district will typically provide this support. Parents often consider private speech therapy as well, but insurance coverage is inconsistent, and out-of-pocket expenses can be considerable. A speech-language pathologist can help in several ways. He or she will typically work directly with your child and may focus on articulation, comprehension, social communication, or all of these. He or she will also be a valuable resource for you as you look for ways to help your child at home.

Enroll your child in the right educational program. If your child has speech and language delays, it is advisable to start her in preschool as early as possible, typically at age 3. General education preschools are appropriate for many children with speech delays. These children benefit from exposure to the communication and socialization skills of their typically developing peers. If your child attends a general preschool he will usually receive speech therapy on an itinerant basis—the speech-language pathologist will go to the school or, in some cases, come to your home, and work with your child individually. For some children with speech and language delays a specialized preschool program is most appropriate. These are typically obtained through the local school district. Some districts provide their own programs, and some place children in local programs not specifically administered by the district. Specialized programs may enroll only children with special needs; others may be inclusive, with a mix of typically developing children and children with special needs (see Chapter 7).

Find ways to help at home. Your child learns most of his or her speech and language skills at home. In the course of the day your child will hear thousands of words in the form of greetings, instructions, commands, questions, descriptions, suggestions, identifications, promptings, and general conversation. There are a number of ways in which you can go beyond this to provide an enhanced language experience for your child at home. Very often the language used at home is oriented toward communicating what is needed to convey to keep the machinery of daily life operating smoothly. This can be adult-oriented language that relates more to what parents want their children to do and

Things to Do at Home

- Engage in child-oriented language and conversation.
- Encourage your child to initiate requests and to be as specific as possible in communicating her wants and needs.
- Schedule one-to-one time with your child away from distractions.
- Create opportunities for interaction with typically developing peers.
- Read to your child every day; make reading a part of the daily routine.
- With the advice of a speech-language pathologist, make judicious use of flashcards, computer programs, and special teaching materials to help your child.
- Limit television viewing.

less to what the child may be interested in or engaged with. Taking the time to engage your child in conversation and to make simple observations and comments about what the child is doing can be enormously beneficial.

You should also be wary of the tendency to read your child's mind. Parents often know what their children want before they ask, but it is important to let children work a little to express what they want in the clearest and fullest manner possible. If your child is nonverbal, prompting her to make eye contact with you and to point or in some other way indicate what she wants may be sufficient. If your child can speak, encouraging him to "use his words" helps him to develop better habits of communication. The general idea is to encourage, prompt, and if necessary cajole your child into becoming a more active participant in the communication process.

Of all the things you can do at home to help your child's speech and language development, reading is one of the most important. Books provide a special and focused means of engaging and immersing your child in vocabulary, grammar, and language concepts that rise above the more mundane language of everyday life. Younger children and those with short attention spans may not be able to sit through a whole story, but even spending a few minutes every day looking at pictures and talking with your child about what she can see can enrich her language experience manyfold. When it comes to reading, parents have a major advantage over professionals. Regular reading becomes an extension of your special relationship with your child and provides an especially powerful context for language learning that no one else can duplicate.

Many parents will use special materials and techniques, such as flashcards, vocabulary lists, and computer programs, to help their children improve their speech (tablet computers have become especially popular). These methods can be helpful for particular children but are often best used in consultation with a speech-language pathologist. There is a danger in trying to become a therapist for your child. Many children will rebel when a parent steps too far outside the boundaries of the parent–child relationship, and they many respond better to the rigors of therapy when an outsider administers it. The key is finding the right balance between helping your child and keeping it real in terms of your relationship with him or her.

Television has limited utility in promoting speech and language development. The passive nature of the medium limits the degree to which children can make use of the language to which they are exposed. Even educational programs cannot come close to duplicating the impact you have when you talk with and read to your child. Experts recommend limiting television viewing, especially among younger children, and this applies even more so to children with speech and language delays.

SUMMARY

What to Do if Your Child Has Trouble Talking

Here is a review of what you should do if your child has speech and language delays (see Figure 1.1):

Step 1: If you are concerned about your child's speech and language development, trust yourself and act on your concerns.

Step 2: Have your child's primary care doctor evaluate him or her, and request a referral from your child's doctor for a hearing evaluation.

Step 3: At the same time as Step 2, contact your local early intervention program (see Chapter 7) or school district to request an evaluation for your child.

Step 4: Obtain services for your child. These services may be home based, clinic based, or school based depending on your child's needs and the types of services available in your area.

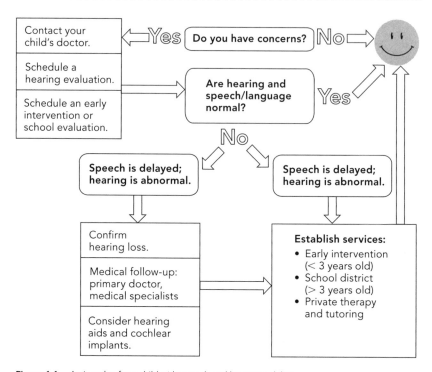

Figure 1.1. Action plan for a child with speech and language delays.

Speech-language therapy will almost always be included, but many children will also receive special education support and other therapy services.

2

When Your Child Has Trouble Walking

Understanding Problems with Motor Skills Development

*C*amcorders must have been invented so that parents would have a way to record their child's first steps. In the vast archives of family recordings there is undoubtedly a disproportionate percentage of footage devoted to documenting (in excruciating detail) that epic moment for posterity. Most parents know that children typically begin walking at about a year of age. They may not be clear about when their child should start talking, or using a spoon, or playing with toys, or learning to get dressed, but every parent knows that infants typically walk by their first birthday. So it is not surprising that a child's failure to achieve that milestone is a source of great distress to parents.

EMMA

Emma, a beautiful little girl born to first-time parents, was delivered prematurely at 29 weeks' gestation (a full-term pregnancy is 36 weeks or more). Emma's mother was admitted to the hospital in preterm labor, and Emma was delivered less than an hour later. Her birth weight was only 4 pounds. She was quite vigorous in the delivery room and had no special problems during her 3-week stay in the neonatal intensive care nursery. She was able to go home once she was eating well, and she was in every respect a healthy and happy infant.

jargon buster

Basic Terminology

Upper extremities: Arms

Lower extremities: Legs

Trunk: Torso

Muscle tone: How tight or how loose muscles feel when they are stretched or lengthened

Muscle strength: How much force a muscle generates when it contracts

Hypotonia: Low or decreased muscle tone

Hypertonia: High or increased muscle tone

Truncal hypotonia: Low muscle tone of the truck or torso, usually resulting in difficulties maintaining posture

seeds

Transient Dystonia of Prematurity

Transient dystonia of prematurity involves mild muscle tone abnormalities—especially mild "floppiness," or hypotonia of the trunk and mild hypertonia of the legs—in infants born prematurely that usually resolve by 18–24 months.

Emma's parents became concerned when their daughter did not seem to be able to hold her head up as well as they thought she should by 3 months of age. They became more concerned when she did not roll over by 5 months of age and then quite alarmed when she could not sit on her own by 6 months of age.

At her 6-month well-child checkup Emma's pediatrician noticed that she had low trunk tone and mild lower extremity hypertonia. Her parents were not reassured by these observations, but Emma's pediatrician told them that many infants born prematurely have similar difficulties. She told them that the technical term for this is *transient dystonia of prematurity* and that infants usually outgrow it.

Emma was referred for early intervention services, and a physical therapist began coming to her home twice weekly to work with Emma and her parents to facilitate her progress. By 8 months of age Emma's sitting balance was still inconsistent but she had made surprising progress with crawling on her belly and was also rolling well. By 9 months of age she was trying to pull up to a standing position while holding onto furniture. Her parents were bewildered by this—they had read that infants should sit well before they pull to stand, but Emma seemed to be doing things out of sequence. By her first birthday Emma's sitting balance was much better, and she could cruise (walk holding onto furniture). At first she was always up on her toes when she did this, and she would often topple over when she tried to get down to the floor (instead of catching herself with extended arms or making a soft landing on her bottom), but by 15 months she could safely get up and down from standing. By 18 months her feet stayed flat to the floor and she took her first glorious independent steps.

Emma's parents had done their best to anticipate the typical sequence of skills leading to walking, but as Emma's story illustrates children with delays in their motor skills may follow a different path with unexpected detours on the road to walking. Here I review the typical sequence of events leading to walking and talk about ways in which some children deviate from the expected path.

MOTOR SKILLS DEVELOPMENT 101

The term *motor skills* refers to the sequence of actions that involve muscle activation and movement that gives people the ability to move their bodies. *Gross (or large) motor skills* refers to those actions that promote postural control and mobility (e.g., sitting, walking). *Fine (or small) motor skills* refers to those actions that allows people to use their hands to manipulate objects. The sensorimotor system is composed of an input (sensory) component and an output (motor) component. On the input side, sensory information people receive from their eyes, skin, joints, muscles, and balance organs in the inner ear gives them real-time information about the position of their bodies in space as this relates to the flux of activities around them (see Chapter 8). On the output side, signals are sent from the brain to the spinal cord and then through special motor nerves to the muscles they control. In between the input and output sides of the sensorimotor equation is the brain, one's own private supercomputer. The brain continuously processes a complex stream of sensory data and executes instructions to tell people's arms and legs and the rest of their bodies what to do and how to move. For older children and adults, most of this happens subconsciously and automatically, but for infants and younger children, these skills are built from the ground up, starting with a foundation of sensory and motor responses with which everyone is born.

Primitive Reflexes: Setting the Stage

Newborn infants come into the world with a set of start-up skills known as *primitive reflexes* (see Figure 2.1). Anyone who has had contact with a newborn is probably familiar with some of these.

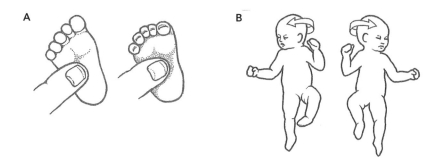

Figure 2.1.   Primitive reflexes. A) Plantar grasp reflex. Similar to the palmar grasp reflex, pressing on the bottom of a newborn's foot causes the toes to grasp (curl down). B) Asymmetric tonic neck reflex. Turning a newborn's head to one side causes the arm and leg on the same side to extend and the arm and leg on the opposite side to flex (bend). (From Dormans, J.P., & Pellegrino, L. [1998]. *Caring for children with cerebral palsy: A team approach* [pp. 37–38]. Baltimore, MD: Paul H. Brookes Publishing Co.; adapted by permission.)

If you press your index finger into the palm of a newborn's hand, he or she will automatically grab your finger (often quite firmly). This is known as the *palmar grasp reflex*. And as nursing mothers know, a light touch to the skin next to a newborn's mouth will cause him to turn his head and crinkle his mouth toward the stimulus in search of nourishment. This is called the *rooting reflex*. If he finds what he is looking for—a nipple—he will vigorously latch on with a tight seal and initiate a repetitive stripping action with his tongue to draw the nipple into and up against the roof of his mouth to extract milk. This is called the *suckling reflex*.

Other primitive reflexes control posture. For example, if a newborn infant turns her head to one side, her arm and leg on that side will extend and the arm and leg on the opposite side will bend or flex, assuming a fencer's posture. Turning the head the other way reverses the pattern. This is known as the *asymmetric tonic neck reflex (ATNR)*. Other primitive reflexes govern an infant's reaction to environmental stimuli. Make a loud noise or bump into a newborn's crib suddenly and you will elicit a startle reflex—when the arms extend out to the sides suddenly—followed by a slower return of the arms toward the body. This entire sequence is known as the *Moro reflex*.

Primitive Reflexes and Evolution

Some of the primitive reflexes in humans may reflect vestiges of functions important in other species. The palmar grasp, for example, is important in many primates because it provides a means for infants to hang onto their mothers as they search for food or flee from predators.

As the name implies, primitive reflexes are automatic and reflexive rather than voluntary. Each reflex is elicited by a particular stimulus (e.g., a touch to the skin; a turn of the head; a sudden, loud noise) and follows a specific, stereotypical pattern with little variation. Some of these reflexes (e.g., the rooting and suckling reflexes) have an obvious purpose, but others do not. Collectively the primitive reflexes are thought to provide a kind of neurological scaffolding upon which more complex and voluntary motor responses are built. And just as scaffolding serves its purpose and is then removed, primitive reflexes must gradually give way to voluntary motor skills. Rooting and suckling give way to a more effective voluntary sucking response (see Chapter 3). The palmar grasp reflex gives way as an infant develops the ability to grasp objects voluntarily. The ATNR gives way as an infant learns to roll over and sit (if you are trying to learn to roll over or sit, automatically sticking your arm out every time you turn your head is not very helpful!). In typically developing infants, the gradual integration of the primitive reflexes dovetails neatly with the emergence of voluntary motor skills, but in children with motor skills difficulties, such as cerebral palsy (CP), it may not.

Protective Reactions: The Supporting Cast

If one compares the primitive reflexes to the backstage and technical crew involved with staging a play, then the protective reactions (also known as *automatic movement reactions*) would be the supporting cast (see Figure 2.2). Whereas the primitive reflexes are meant to step out of the spotlight when the main actors—rolling over, sitting, crawling, standing, and walking—come on stage, the protective reactions have to be available in their supporting roles to help the stars of the show look their best.

Many of the protective reactions serve an antigravity function. For example, newborn infants have little in the way of head and trunk control, but within the first few months they develop head and trunk righting responses, which allow them to adjust the position of the head and trunk to compensate for body tilt. Prop reactions develop between 4 and 7 months to allow infants to sit safely: If an infant tips over while sitting, she will automatically extend an arm—or prop—to catch herself. A similar response, the parachute reaction, emerges by about 9 months to assist in the development of standing and walking skills. If an infant is prac-

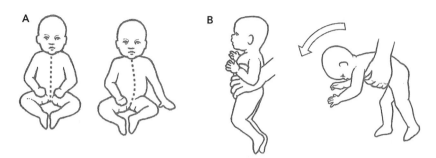

Figure 2.2. Protective responses. A) Lateral prop response (by 6 months). Tipping a sitting baby to the side causes the arm on the same side to extend so that the baby catches himself. B) Parachute response (by 9 months). Tilting a baby forward (or a baby falling forward on his own from a standing position) causes the arms and legs to extend forward and out so that the baby catches himself. (From Dormans, J.P., & Pellegrino, L. [1998]. *Caring for children with cerebral palsy: A team approach* [p. 39]. Baltimore, MD: Paul H. Brookes Publishing Co.; reprinted by permission.)

ticing these skills and happens to fall forward, she will automatically reach out with her arms and legs to catch herself.

The primitive reflexes and the protective responses are often confused with each other, but they are really very different. The primitive reflexes are neurologically hardwired in the primitive areas of the brain and spinal cord, are present at birth, and are gradually superseded by voluntary motor responses controlled by higher brain centers. The protective reactions emerge in parallel with the motor skills they support, and although they are automatic, they are subject to some degree of voluntary control.

Learning to Move in a Three-Dimensional World

Human beings have evolved to move in a three-dimensional world governed by gravity, and as a species we have mastered the particularly difficult balancing act known as *walking.* Most infants manage to do this, with little help, within the first 12 months of life! It is such a commonplace occurrence that people tend to take it for granted. They expect the motor milestones to develop in a logical, predictable sequence—rolling over, sitting, crawling, standing, and finally walking—and in most cases they do. But as Emma's story illustrates, this sequence is not entirely set in stone, and many things can slow it down or alter its course. In this three-dimensional world human beings have to deal with the vertical (working with and against gravity) and the horizontal (moving in parallel with the ground in a roughly flat landscape). The various milestones on the road to walking are affected by the vertical and horizontal aspects of the environment in different ways. In particular, the events leading to sitting and the events leading to standing and walking follow parallel paths that eventually converge if all goes well (see Table 2.1).

Dealing with a Vertical World: The Sitting Sequence

Newborn infants are trapped in a horizontal world. They can only get to vertical if someone holds them up. Within a few short months, this situation changes dramatically. By 6 months of age most infants can sit independently, and by 7 months of age most can push and twist themselves up into a sitting position. This represents the first major step toward conquering the vertical world. On their way to sitting, infants must first develop head control (heads are much less wobbly by 3 months of age) and trunk control (which is notably better by 4 months of age). The antigravity head and trunk righting responses already mentioned emerge in parallel with these skills. By 5 months of age, most infants have enough head and trunk control to maintain a slumped-over sitting posture and usually exhibit a forward prop reaction—that is, they catch themselves if they tip forward. By 6 months of age infants will prop to the sides as well. Having forward and side prop responses plus adequate postural control is usually sufficient to allow for unsupported sitting. By 7 months of age infants will learn to twist and rotate their bodies and to prop backward, which allows them to move up and down between lying down and sitting, making them fully independent sitters.

A number of factors can interfere with the development of sitting skills. Simply being big, or having a relatively large head, can make it difficult for some infants to sit. Infants with low mus-

Table 2.1. Key early gross motor milestones

Milestone	Age
Rolling	3–5 months
Belly crawling	4–6 months
Sitting independently	6 months
Getting to sitting	7–8 months
Hand–knee crawling (creeping)	7–9 months
Pulling to stand	8–10 months
Cruising	9–11 months
Taking one's first independent steps	10–14 months

Sleep Position, Infant Apnea, and Sudden Infant Death Syndrome

The American Academy of Pediatrics recommends that newborn infants be placed on their backs for sleeping to decrease the occurrence of sudden infant death syndrome. Sudden infant death syndrome is thought to be related to compromised breathing (apnea) during sleep and is more likely to occur when infants are sleeping on their bellies. Parents sometimes misunderstand this recommendation to mean that infants should always be placed on their backs, even while awake. When infants are awake and properly supervised by a parent, they should be allowed belly time, which is crucial to developing floor mobility skills and is a prerequisite to learning to stand and walk.

cle tone of the trunk, such as Emma, may have relatively poor head and trunk control, and this may delay the acquisition of sitting skills. Other infants may have other challenges, such as persistent primitive reflexes (e.g., persistent ATNR) that may interfere with sitting balance or the delayed emergence of protective responses (e.g., the prop reactions) that provide for safe sitting.

Dealing with a Horizontal World: The Crawling Sequence

Standing and walking seem, at first glance, to be all about working against gravity and getting vertical, but the foundation for these skills begins on the ground. Conquering the horizontal world first involves finding ways of moving on the floor. If you place a newborn infant on her back (or belly or side) she will stay pretty much where you put her, but that changes quickly. An infant placed on her back will learn early on how to roll to one side or the other, and an infant on her belly will do the same, and through trial and error she will eventually find herself rolling all the way over. Most infants find it easier to roll first from belly to back and then from back to belly. For most infants, rolling over becomes easy by about 5 months of age.

Moving on the floor also involves a lot of squirming, pivoting, kicking, and pushing with the arms and especially the legs. Many parents are surprised the first time they find their infant in a different part of the crib, head pointed in a different direction, than where they placed the infant at bed time. Some infants "back surf" by pushing themselves along with their feet while on their backs. Infants learn to combine these movements to achieve limited mobility on the floor but really get going when they learn to belly crawl (also known as the *combat crawl*). The first prerequisite to developing this skill is having some head control. A newborn infant on his belly will keep his head to one side or the other but within a few weeks will learn to turn his head from side to side, eventually clearing his nose. When he is able to get his head up to about a 45-degree angle he will learn to pull his arms under his shoulders so that he can prop himself up on his elbows. Once an infant can do this he can combine leg, arm, and trunk movements to belly crawl. Many infants have an amusing tendency to crawl backward at first but quickly learn to aim themselves forward.

The next stage in the process of conquering the horizontal world does involve some vertical elements. Infants have to learn how to do pushups! Crawling on their elbows is fine for a while, but if they can push themselves all the way up on fully extended arms, they can really start to see the world.

But why stop there? If they can manage to pull their knees under them they can begin to combine lifting their front end with lifting their

Crawling Is Optional

Hand–knee crawling and learning to stand usually occur about the same time for most infants, but they are separate skills. Some children skip crawling and go straight to standing and walking, whereas other children rely on crawling for some time before learning to walk. Although typically developing children may skip crawling, lack of crawling is seen more often in children with delayed motor skills.

bottom, and they have the basis for hand–knee crawling, which is sometimes called *creeping*. Crawling on one's hands and knees is a much better way to get around than belly crawling. Although essentially still a horizontal mode of locomotion, creeping gives an infant a much better view of the vertical world, setting the stage for the final act in this drama.

Moving in a Three-Dimensional World: The Standing and Walking Sequence

Infant pushups set the stage for crawling on hands and knees, but they are also the prerequisite for learning to stand. Once an infant can get her head up and push herself up with fully extended arms, she can then pull up on a convenient person or piece of furniture, at first propping on her knees and then eventually pulling up to a full stand while still holding on. The key point here is that although pulling to stand involves vertical antigravity movement, it starts with an infant on the floor, pushing up from her belly. Physical therapists who work with children with delayed motor skills emphasize the importance of prone skills—moving on your belly skills—as providing the foundation for standing and walking. Infants have to learn to push up, and then to pull up to stand, before they can walk. Once an infant can pull to stand, she can advance to walking while holding onto something. This is called *cruising*. And once she has developed enough confidence and skill to get up and down from the floor to a standing position and back again—and if she has developed a parachute reaction—she will be able to take her first tentative steps toward independent walking.

Infant Walkers Do Not Help Infants Learn to Walk

seeds

Infants need to learn how to work against gravity by pushing up on their arms and pulling up on furniture to stand. Infant walkers circumvent this normal process and can also be dangerous (infants who are not developmentally ready to walk can move very quickly in a walker and fall down stairs before a parent is aware of what has happened).

Beyond Walking: Taking the World by Storm

Walking is one of the earliest and most dramatic events in a child's motor development, but it is by no means the last, or even the most important (see Table 2.2). Once a child learns to walk he advances

Table 2.2.   Later gross motor milestones

Milestone	Age
Walking backward	12–18 months
Running	18–21 months
Climbing on furniture	15–21 months
Jumping in place	22–26 months
Kicking a ball	24 months
Throwing a ball	36 months
Climbing steps (two feet per step)	21–30 months
Climbing steps (alternating feet)	30–36 months
Pedaling a tricycle	3–3 ½ years
Standing on one foot	3–5 years
Hopping forward with two feet	3–4 years
Skipping	5–5 ½ years
Riding a bicycle without training wheels	5–8 years

rapidly to running, walking backward, climbing furniture and stairs, jumping, hopping, and skipping and gradually branches out into the myriad physical activities associated with playing outside and participating in sports. Most children who do well attaining the early motor milestones also do well acquiring more advanced motor skills, but there are significant variations in ability, ranging from athletically gifted to awkward or clumsy. In some instances, however, problems with early motor development may be a sign of more significant developmental or neurological problems.

Red Flags for Early Motor Development

Most children attain the various milestones of motor development by the expected ages in the expected sequence. Other children, such as Emma, may have mild early difficulties in one or more aspects of motor development and may follow a slightly unusual path to walking, but they do eventually attain their goal. Other children have more significant delays in attaining motor milestones or have more notable difficulties with muscle tone, strength, or the sequencing and planning of movement that may be indicative of a more significant problem. In general, a child is considered delayed for a specific skill if he or she has reached an age at which 90% or more of children would have typically achieved that skill. For example, although the majority of children—75% or more—begin walking by about 12 months of age, 90% of children are walking by 15 months of age. A child is therefore considered delayed for walking if he has not taken his first steps by 15 months of age.

THE CAUSES OF DELAYED MOTOR DEVELOPMENT

Delayed motor skills can occur in isolation or as part of a broader developmental problem. Motor delays can be mild or severe and may be associated with specific neurological abnormalities that can provide a clue to the diagnosis of the problem.

Developmental Coordination Disorder

Irene is a 5-year-old girl whose parents have been concerned for some time about her lack of coordination. As an infant she was not able to

Red Flags

If you notice any of these red flags, you should consider having your child evaluated further for possible problems with motor skills development.

- You have a gut feeling that something is wrong with your child's motor development.
- Your child's muscles seem very stiff or very loose.
- Prior to 12 months, your child seems stronger on one side of the body and weaker on the other (e.g., he or she shows a hand preference before 12 months).
- Your child cannot hold his or her head up by 4 months.
- Your child cannot roll over by 5 months.
- Your child cannot maintain a sitting position by 7 months.
- Your child cannot pull to stand by 11 months.
- Your child is not starting to walk without holding on by 15 months.
- After your child starts walking, he or she seems excessively clumsy.
- After your child starts walking, he or she walks on his or her toes persistently.

sit until 10 months of age and could not pull to stand until 18 months of age. Instead of crawling she preferred to move about in the sitting position, scooting on her bottom by reaching out with her feet and using her legs to pull herself forward. She began physical therapy at 15 months of age, and her therapist found her to be rather passive and seemingly reluctant to try new activities. The therapist noted that Irene had low muscle tone: Her leg and arm muscles seemed loose and overly flexible, and she had a slight tendency to slide through the therapist's hands when the therapist held her under the arms. She noticed that Irene did not have a fully developed parachute reaction until about 17 months of age. After Irene became comfortable standing she slowly learned to cruise, and by 22 months of age she finally took her first independent steps, although she did not walk consistently until almost 27 months of age. As a preschooler Irene exhibited excellent language, social, and play skills but had trouble learning to dress and undress, and she had trouble keeping up with her peers on the playground. She is now in kindergarten, and her teachers have noticed that Irene has trouble using scissors, seems reluctant to draw or write her name, and does not seem to have a clear hand preference. Although she knows how to pedal a tricycle, she does not like riding her bike with training wheels and is clearly not ready to have the training wheels removed. Her parents want her to try soccer, but they are not sure whether she will be able to keep up with her peers, and they wonder whether she may have a neurological reason for her coordination difficulties.

Irene's story is typical for a child with a developmental coordination disorder (DCD). Children with DCD do not usually show evidence of a serious neurological abnormality (e.g., brain scans such as magnetic resonance imaging [MRI] are almost always normal), but they often have mild hypotonia, or low muscle tone. Usually their reflexes and other elements of their neurological examination are normal. Although they have normal muscle strength, they have trouble organizing their movements to use their strength effectively. Their most noticeable difficulties at first are with basic gross motor skills, such as sitting, standing, and walking, but they often have trouble with fine motor skills as well. Self-care skills, such as using utensils, dressing, and toileting, may also be delayed. These problems usually become evident during the toddler and preschool years. School-age children with DCD typically walk, run, and climb well enough to get by with most activities but often struggle with more challenging playground games and sports. In the classroom they may have trouble with fine motor skills that affect pencil-and-paper tasks and may also have trouble with arts and crafts (using scissors is notoriously difficult for many).

As they get older children with DCD often find activities with which they are more comfortable and skilled. For example, a child may have trouble running quickly and kicking a ball accurately on the soccer field but may do very well at swimming. Team sports that emphasize competition may be frustrating, but activities that are more individually oriented may be better suited to many children with DCD. Popular choices include swimming, dance, martial arts (e.g., karate, tae kwon do), bowling, tennis, horseback riding, and golf. Many children show significant improvements in motor skills as they mature, and improved strength, speed, and endurance can be seen as children enter adolescence.

Developmental Disabilities Associated with Developmental Coordination Disorder

Although DCD may be seen in isolation, it is often observed in association with other development issues and diagnoses. In fact, early delays in motor skills are often harbingers or red flags for other developmental problems.

Developmental Coordination Disorder and Sensory Processing Disorders

Many children with DCD have exaggerated reactions to sensory stimuli. Some children are overly sensitive to tactile stimuli (e.g., many children are bothered by tags in clothing or tight-fitting clothes). Some may be overly reactive to differences in hot and cold; others may hate being barefoot or may become upset if their hands get messy. Other children seem to be underresponsive to certain sensations. For example, these children may not respond to pain as expected. Other children may be "sensory seekers": They seem to crave certain sensations and seem to have a need for constant stimulation. Although a particular child may be mainly overresponsive, or underresponsive, or sensory seeking, it is not uncommon for a child to exhibit some combination of all three.

Children with exaggerated responses to sensory stimuli are described as having sensory integration dysfunction and may be diagnosed with a sensory processing disorder (see Chapter 8). The term *dyspraxia* is sometimes used to describe motor planning problems that are closely connected with sensory integration dysfunction. In fact, the term *developmental dyspraxia* is often used interchangeably with the term *developmental coordination disorder.*

Developmental Coordination Disorder and Developmental Language Disorders

Many children who walk late also talk late. A child may first enter early intervention services because of motor delays, but with time the emphasis often shifts from worries about motor skills to worries about speech and language development (see Chapter 7). DCD is often associated with verbal apraxia, a form of expressive language delay thought to be caused by motor planning problems that impair speech production (see Chapter 1).

Developmental Coordination Disorder, Learning Disability, and Intellectual Disability

Many children with learning disabilities and many more children with intellectual disability (formerly called mental retardation) have early and persistent delays with motor skills, although this certainly is not the case for every child with these diagnoses. For example, many children with learning disabilities take solace in the fact that they are good at sports or that they are good at working with their hands. But as a group, children with learning or cognitive difficulties are more likely than typically developing children to have DCD (see Chapter 6).

Developmental Coordination Disorder and Attention-Deficit/Hyperactivity Disorder

Children with attention-deficit/hyperactivity disorder (ADHD) are known for their love of activity and movement, but their motor skills are more variable. Some children have excellent coordination; others could be described as clumsy. It may be difficult to determine whether a child with ADHD is uncoordinated because of a primary problem with motor skills or because of problems he may experience as a consequence of impulsivity and distractibility (i.e., not paying attention to where he is going). School-age children with ADHD are particularly known for having difficulties with writing, or dysgraphia (see Chapter 5).

Developmental Coordination Disorder in Autism Spectrum Disorders

As with children with learning disabilities, intellectual disability, or ADHD, children with autism spectrum disorders are more prone than typically developing children to having delays and difficulties with motor skills. Children with Asperger syndrome in particular frequently have prominent DCD, often in association with prominent sensory processing dysfunction. In fact, some experts argue that prominent DCD is one of the distinguishing characteristics of Asperger syndrome (see Chapter 4).

Cerebral Palsy

Charlie is a 3-year-old boy who was born 15 weeks early, at 25 weeks' gestation. His birth weight was only 2 pounds, 7 ounces. Charlie's lungs were very immature, and he required the support of a ventilator (a machine to help him breathe) for the first 2 weeks of life. He weaned off of the ventilator quickly after this but still needed supplemental

jargon buster

Cerebral Palsy Terminology

Cerebral palsy: A disorder of movement, muscle tone, and posture that is caused by injury to or abnormal development of the immature brain

Spasticity: High muscle tone associated with exaggerated reflexes, a hallmark of spastic cerebral palsy

Dyskinesia: Involuntary jerky or writhing movements associated with some nonspastic forms of cerebral palsy

Ataxia: Problems with balance and tremors associated with some forms of cerebral palsy

Spastic cerebral palsy: Cerebral palsy characterized by spasticity that may involve some parts of the body more than others

Extrapyramidal cerebral palsy: Nonspastic forms of cerebral palsy characterized by fluctuating muscle tone and sometimes associated with involuntary movements; also called dyskinetic cerebral palsy

Ataxic cerebral palsy: Cerebral palsy associated with ataxia, often with low muscle tone

oxygen until his discharge from the neonatal intensive care unit at 2 months of age. An ultrasound examination of his brain revealed enlarged fluid spaces, or ventricles, at the center of his brain and evidence of injury to adjacent areas of brain white matter. His parents were told that these findings were consistent with a condition called *periventricular leukomalacia*, which could be associated with later developmental problems.

Charlie's body seemed floppy in the newborn period, but by the time he was 3 months of age his parents noticed that the muscles in his legs seemed a bit tight. They also noticed that Charlie had a tendency to arch his back stiffly when he got irritated with a diaper change. At his 6-month well-child visit he was not sitting or rolling over yet, and his doctor noticed that he still had a prominent ATNR, or fencer's posture reflex. By 1 year of age he was able to sit but he tended to slouch over noticeably, and his therapists said he had poor trunk support. By 15 months of age he could crawl and pull to stand, but his legs were very stiff and he always stood up on his toes. At 18 months of age his pediatrician noticed that Charlie's leg muscles were still very tight and that he had overreactive tendon reflexes; she told Charlie's parents that she suspected that Charlie was showing signs of CP.

If your child has significant delays in the development of motor skills, especially if these delays are associated with signs of neurological dysfunction such as muscle tightness or overactive reflexes, he may have CP. Like DCD, the hallmark of CP is trouble with coordinating movement. Unlike with DCD, the delays in the motor milestones for a child with CP are usually more significant, and some milestones, such as walking, may never be achieved by children with severe forms of CP.

What Are the Characteristics and Types of Cerebral Palsy?

In contrast to DCD, CP is associated with more obvious signs that the brain's ability to control movement has been disrupted. The body's motor control system can be roughly divided into an upper motor neuron system and a lower motor neuron system (see Figure 2.3). The upper motor neuron system includes the motor control centers in the brain and the motor nerve pathways (called *corticospinal pathways*) that carry signals from the motor cortex of the brain to different levels of the spinal cord. The lower motor neuron system starts where the upper motor neuron system leaves off. Like a baton pass in a relay race, nerve impulses starting in the brain and traveling down the spinal cord are "passed" to lower motor neurons, which then carry the signals to target muscles, which respond by contracting, creating movement. Microscopic sensors called *muscle spindles* react to the stretch and contraction in muscles and send signals back to the spinal cord, creating a feedback loop called the *stretch reflex arc*. This reflex arc is the basis for regulating muscle tone (how tight or how loose muscles feel), and it also mediates reflexes, such as the familiar knee-jerk response.

In CP, the upper motor neuron system is disrupted in some way. In the spastic forms of CP, the corticospinal pathways themselves are damaged. The transmission of upper motor neuron signals is disrupted, with two main consequences: The control of muscle contraction is compromised, and the inhibitory influence of these signals on the stretch reflex arc is lost. When the control of muscle contraction is compromised, motor planning, sequencing, and coordination are impaired. When stretch reflex inhibition is lost, reflexes are exaggerated—children with spastic CP typically have overactive or jumpy reflexes—and increased muscle tone (hypertonia) is observed in some parts of the body. The combination of exaggerated reflexes, increased muscle tone, and loss of coordination is called *spasticity*, from which the term *spastic cerebral palsy* is derived.

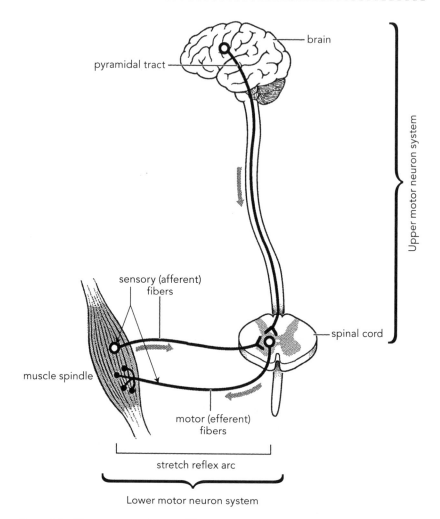

Figure 2.3. The motor control system. The upper motor neuron system carries signals from the motor cortex through the spinal cord via the pyramidal tract in the brain and spinal cord. The lower motor neuron system relays the signal to muscles via motor neurons (fibers), causing muscle contraction. Muscle spindles sense muscle contraction and stretch, sending signals back to the spinal cord via sensory fibers and forming the stretch reflex arc that regulates reflexes and muscle tone. (From Dormans, J.P., & Pellegrino, L. [1998]. *Caring for children with cerebral palsy: A team approach* [p. 46]. Baltimore, MD: Paul H. Brookes Publishing Co.; adapted by permission.)

In nonspastic CP, or extrapyramidal CP, the corticospinal pathways are intact but other elements of the brain's motor control system are compromised. Deep brain structures called the *basal ganglia* and a cauliflower-like projection on the undersurface of the brain, the cerebellum, are particularly important elements in this system. They help to refine and regulate movement in time and space and are important for muscle memory, or the ability to make movement patterns automatic and habitual. Damage to or dysfunction of the extrapyramidal system may result in loss of movement control associated with fluctuating muscle tone patterns and may occasionally be associated with involuntary jerking movements (chorea) or involuntary writhing movements (athetosis). Rigid posturing of the body, called *dystonia*, may also be seen. This type of CP is also called *dyskinetic cerebral palsy* (from the term *dyskinesia*, which refers to atypical, involuntary movements). Ataxic cerebral palsy, another uncommon, nonspastic type of CP, is especially associated with ataxia, or problems with balance, tremors, and the finely graded control of movement. Children with ataxic CP often have low muscle tone, or hypotonia.

If your child has spastic CP (the most common type of CP) some parts of his body may be more affected than others. In spastic diplegia (the type of CP that Charlie has) the legs are most affected. This type of CP is especially common among infants born prematurely. If your child has spastic hemiplegia, one side of his body will be more affected than the other. If your child has spastic quadriplegia, the whole body, including all four limbs, will be affected. The dyskinetic and ataxic forms of CP are much less common than the spastic forms and vary considerably in their degree of severity, but they always involve the entire body to a certain extent.

What Causes Cerebral Palsy?

In contrast to DCD, which often runs in families, CP frequently appears out of the blue; a child with CP is often the first and only family member with the condition. And unlike DCD, CP is associated by definition with evidence of neurological dysfunction, such as spasticity. Brain imaging studies such as MRI often provide clues about the cause of CP in particular children.

The prevalence of CP is about 2 per 1,000 people in the general population. Even though premature births account for a minority (about 13%) of all births, about 50% of children with CP are born premature. This is because premature infants are particularly vulnerable to injury to the white matter of the brain, an area located near the central fluid spaces, or ventricles, of the brain. The white matter contains the "wiring" of the brain, including motor nerve fibers that control the muscles of the body; damage to these nerve fibers can cause CP.

The white matter next to the ventricles can be damaged in two ways. The first way relates to the fact that the blood supply to the white matter in the premature brain is still a work in progress. Intermittent episodes of oxygen deprivation—the result of stresses before, during, and after birth—can cause damage to the area; this is called *periventricular leukomalacia.* This type of damage is most often associated with spastic diplegia, the type of CP in which the legs are most affected. Charlie's story and his physical findings are consistent with this pattern (see Figure 2.4).

The second way that white matter in the premature brain is damaged has to do with the immaturity of blood vessels surrounding the ventricles in an area called the *subependymal zone.* These delicate blood vessels are prone to rupturing if there are significant fluctuations in blood flow to the brain due to changes in blood pressure in the infant's body. These changes in blood pressure occur most often during the stressful first week after birth, especially in sick premature infants. When bleeding does occur, the result is called *intraventricular hemorrhage.* A grading

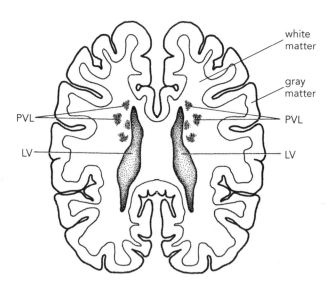

Figure 2.4. Periventricular leukomalacia (PVL). Insufficient blood supply to the brain white matter near the fluid-filled lateral ventricles (LV) in premature infants makes this area vulnerable to damage (i.e., PVL). PVL disrupts motor control fibers that pass through this region, causing spastic cerebral palsy. (From Batshaw, M.L., Pellegrino, L., & Roizen, N. [Eds.]. [2007]. *Children with disabilities* [6th ed., p. 114]. Baltimore, MD: Paul H. Brookes Publishing Co.; adapted by permission.)

system characterizes the extent of the bleeding. For Grade I intraventricular hemorrhage, the bleeding remains confined to the subependymal zone. For Grade II, blood escapes into the ventricles. For Grade III, the ventricles become dilated, and for Grade IV, blood extends into the adjacent white matter. Grades III and IV are associated with an increased risk of CP (most often spastic hemiplegia or an asymmetric form of spastic quadriplegia, which affects the entire body). Grades I and II usually resolve without neurological or functional consequences.

Full-term infants may develop CP for many different reasons. Some are born with abnormalities in brain development (which may be due to genetic mutations) that cause CP. Some can have an intrauterine stroke (bleeding from a major brain blood vessel during pregnancy) that may result in CP (especially spastic hemiplegia) and is sometimes associated with blood clotting abnormalities. (An intrauterine stroke is different from intraventricular hemorrhage, which is the result of bleeding from small subependymal vessels after birth.) Some infants may suffer from an infection during pregnancy or during the early weeks of life that causes brain damage and CP (see Chapter 11).

In less than 10% of cases CP may be caused by major problems at the time of birth that lead to neurological injury due to lack of blood flow and oxygen delivery to the brain. This is sometimes referred to inaccurately as *birth asphyxia*. Its proper term is *hypoxic-ischemic encephalopathy* (*hypoxia* refers to a lack of oxygen, *ischemia* refers to a lack of blood flow, and *encephalopathy* refers to brain damage or dysfunction).

Many children and their mothers experience difficulties in labor and delivery, but problems at birth rarely cause CP. Exceptions may include placental abruption (when the placenta pulls away from the wall of the uterus during labor, resulting in maternal bleeding and loss of blood flow to the infant and the infant's brain) and umbilical cord prolapse (when the umbilical cord is delivered ahead of the infant and gets compressed, resulting in a disruption of blood flow and oxygen delivery to the infant). Children with true hypoxic-ischemic encephalopathy are very sick in the newborn period, requiring intensive care support and often exhibiting signs of neurological compromise, especially seizures. Problems such as the umbilical cord wrapping around the neck, or mild respiratory difficulties at birth, almost never cause CP.

Although it is less common, neurological damage that occurs in early childhood while the brain is still developing rapidly can cause CP. Traumatic brain injury (due to accident or abuse), hypoxia (a lack of oxygen, as may occur in an episode of near-drowning), or serious infection (e.g., meningitis [an infection of the membranes surrounding the brain], encephalitis [an infection of the brain itself]) may cause CP.

There are also conditions that mimic CP. CP is considered a nonprogressive, or static, neurological condition. This means that the causes of CP happen once and only once early in life and do not change or progress. Regression over time suggests the presence of a degenerative neurological condition that may have similar characteristics to CP (e.g., spasticity) but is otherwise very different from CP.

How Is Cerebral Palsy Diagnosed?

Pictures of the Brain

There are several different ways to obtain images of the brain. Brain ultrasound studies are used with premature infants to screen for periventricular leukomalacia and intraventricular hemorrhage. Although ultrasound waves cannot penetrate the bones of the skull, the still-open soft spot, or fontanel, at the top of a newborn's head can be used as a window through which ultrasound waves can pass. Computed tomography uses x rays to take a picture of the brain and can capture images quickly, making it especially useful in an emergency room. Magnetic resonance imaging uses powerful magnets to create very detailed images—but obtaining such an image of the brain typically requires a person to remain perfectly still for 45–60 minutes, so most children (and many adults) need to be sedated for the procedure.

The process of diagnosing CP usually begins with the suspicion of risk in early infancy and ends when a child has reached a stage in his or her development that allows for the recognition of the developmental and neurological characteristics of CP. Charlie's story offers a good example of this. He was recognized to be at risk for CP because of his prematurity and, especially, because of the identification of periventricular leukomalacia on an ultrasound of the brain. At birth he showed nonspecific neurological abnormalities ("floppiness"), but within a few months his parents noticed that he had developed tight leg muscles and his primitive reflexes, especially the ATNR, persisted longer than usual. By 1 year of age he was showing clear delays in motor development, and by 18 months of age he was demonstrating clear evidence of spasticity, especially in the legs. At that point his doctor was able to diagnosis CP and to characterize the type as spastic diplegia.

In a way, the signs of CP take time to fully mature. The features of CP emerge as an infant's nervous system develops and matures. It should also be noted that the diagnosis does not always require special medical tests, such as a brain MRI. Although these tests are usually done once CP is diagnosed (to determine, if possible, the cause of the condition), CP itself is a clinical diagnosis: Its diagnosis is based solely on a history of motor delays and the presence of specific findings on neurological examination.

What Are the Outcomes for Children with Cerebral Palsy?

If your child has CP, his prognosis relates to the severity of his physical disability and the presence or absence of associated cognitive, sensory, and health problems (special health and medical treatment issues for CP are discussed in Chapter 9). A child with mild spastic hemiplegia, typical intelligence, and good health will usually have a better long-term outlook than a child with severe spastic quadriplegia who requires special tube feedings and has severe intellectual disability and seizures. It is perhaps surprising that children with more severe physical disabilities but typical intelligence tend to have a better prognosis than children with the opposite pattern (severe intellectual disability with milder motor impairments). Although parents often—and understandably— focus on physical disability issues, such as maximizing the use of physical therapy to help their child to walk, it is a child's learning and social skills that best predict his or her long-term independence and integration into society.

The prognosis for walking is of course still a very important issue. Children with spastic diplegia and hemiplegia are more likely to learn to walk than children with CP involving the whole body; in fact, almost all children with simple spastic hemiplegia will eventually walk. By contrast, the majority of children with spastic quadriplegia and the more severe, nonspastic forms of CP will have challenges learning to walk, and most come to rely on the use of a wheelchair for getting around the home and community. Observations of early motor development can be used to predict, in a very rough and approximate way, the likelihood that a child will walk. For example, most children who can sit independently by 2 years of age will eventually learn to walk, whereas those who still cannot sit independently by 4 years of age will usually not.

In order to maximize the probability of a favorable outcome, children with CP often require the help of many different developmental, rehabilitation, education, and medical specialists; your child's primary physician is a key person in helping you to determine who should be involved in your child's care. It is especially important that a child see a pediatric orthopedic specialist as soon as a diagnosis of CP is suspected. Early problems with hip dislocation may be prevented if recognized and monitored by an orthopedic physician. Potential problems with hearing and vision should also be assessed as early as possible. The involvement of other professionals and specialists, such as neurologists, developmental pediatricians, gastroenterologists, pulmonologists, and other medical specialists, is determined on a case-by-case basis. These and other special health and medical treatment issues for CP are discussed in Chapter 9.

Congenital Conditions
Associated with Impaired Motor Skills

A number of congenital disorders and diseases—conditions that are present at birth—are associated with significant motor impairments and physical disability (see Table 2.3). As mentioned earlier, in some rare cases CP is caused by a congenital anomaly of brain development. By contrast, other congenital conditions that cause motor impairments and physical disability are due

Table 2.3. Congenital conditions with associated physical disability

Spinal cord malformations (spina bifida)
Spinal motor neuron disease
Peripheral nerve disease
Diseases of the neuromuscular junction
Primary muscle disease
Skeletal disease
Connective tissue disease
Congenital joint deformities

to problems that are in the lower end of the motor control system: problems with spinal cord development; disturbances of the lower motor neuron system; primary muscle disorders; and problems with bones, joints, and the body's connective tissues.

Spina bifida is a particularly important congenital condition associated with motor impairment, physical disability, and a range of learning difficulties and medical complications (see Chapter 9 for a detailed discussion). Spina bifida occurs when the precursor to the spinal cord, called the *neural tube*, fails to form properly early in fetal development. A very mild form of this called *spina bifida occulta* occurs in about 10% of the population and affects only the vertebrae (segments of the backbone) that surround the spinal cord. There are no physical symptoms or signs of spina bifida occulta; it is only seen on an x ray, which reveals a small "split" in the bones that cover a small segment of the spinal cord. In more severe forms of spina bifida a segment of the spinal cord and the nerves that are connected to it are also involved. A sac containing spinal and nerve tissue, called a *meningomyelocele,* bulges out of the back where the split occurs. The sac must be surgically closed shortly after birth to prevent serious infection and to forestall further damage to adjacent healthy areas of the spinal cord.

The degree of motor impairment and physical disability associated with spina bifida is directly related to the level of the spinal abnormality. Muscle paralysis and loss of sensation occur below the level of the lesion, so the higher on the spine the lesion occurs, the more severe the effect will be. A child with a sacral-level lesion (involving the lowest spine segment near the tailbone) can walk without crutches but may occasionally need a foot or ankle brace for support. A child with a lower lumbar lesion (involving the lower part of the lumbar curve of the spine at the base of the back) may need braces and may also need crutches for support. A child with a lumbar lesion (involving spinal segments in the middle and upper parts of the lower back curve) usually needs braces and crutches to walk and often prefers to use a wheelchair for getting around the community when older. A child with a thoracic lesion (involving spinal segments in the middle or upper levels of the back) requires extensive bracing with crutches and almost always relies mainly on the use of a wheelchair for mobility.

A number of rare diseases can cause motor impairment by disrupting the lower motor neuron system (see Figure 2.3). The lower motor neuron system consists of the motor neurons in the spinal cord (called *anterior horn cells* because of their anatomical location); the peripheral nerves that enclose motor nerve fibers going to muscles and sensory nerve fibers heading back to the spinal cord; the neuromuscular junction, or the point of contact between the end of the peripheral nerve and its target muscle; and the muscle itself. Diseases of the lower motor neuron system generally involve muscle weakness or paralysis, which is sometimes present at birth and sometimes emerges as a progressive process during childhood. For example, several congenital myopathies (inborn muscle disorders) are present at birth and are associated with low muscle tone and weakness. The muscle disease associated with these myopathies is static (it does not progress or worsen with time). By contrast, children with muscular dystrophies (the best known example being Duchenne muscular dystrophy, a hereditary condition that affects boys) or spinal muscular atrophy (a disease of the anterior horn cell) may have normal motor development initially but will go on to exhibit progressive muscle weakness or paralysis, which in some instances is associated with a shortened life span.

A number of disorders of the bones, joints, and connective tissues (the tissues that bind together and provide shape to tendons, ligaments, organs, and skin) may be associated with motor impairments. These impairments are usually the result of problems with the bones, ligaments, tendons, and joints themselves rather than problems with the motor control system, although there are some exceptions. For example, arthrogryposis, a congenital condition characterized by limb deformities and stiff, restricted muscles and joints, is thought to be related to lack of fetal movement in the uterus due to an underlying neurological or muscle disorder. Some skeletal dysplasias (genetic conditions that cause abnormalities of spine and limb development, often resulting in short stature) and some connective tissue disorders (e.g., osteogenesis imperfecta, a condition associated with brittle bones and hyperextensible joints and skin) may be associated with spinal cord problems.

HOW TO HELP YOUR CHILD WITH MOTOR DELAYS

Talk to your child's primary doctor. The first step in helping your child with motor delays is to recognize that you have concerns and to bring those concerns to the attention of your child's primary care doctor. Your child's doctor should also be alert to these concerns and should let you know if your child's motor skills are delayed or dysfunctional. The early involvement of your child's doctor is especially important because he or she is in the best position to determine whether these delays are associated with atypical neurological signs that may be suggestive of CP or some other neurological condition that may require further medical evaluation.

Obtain the help of physical and occupational therapists. Children younger than 3 years of age usually obtain therapy through early intervention programs (see Chapter 7). Physical therapists typically focus on gross motor skills and occupational therapists on fine motor skills, but there is considerable overlap between what these therapists do, especially with very young children. Preschool- and school-age children typically receive services through their school districts, although there is an enormous amount of variability in the amount of support for motor-oriented therapies in schools (e.g., physical therapy may not be provided because it is deemed not directly relevant to educational goals). In these instances, supplemental therapy supported through private insurance may be pursued.

Enroll your child in the right educational program. Many children with delayed motor skills have other developmental delays and concerns and will often benefit from specialized educational support throughout the preschool and school years. The type and degree of support will vary based on each child's specific needs. For children with delayed motor skills and coordination difficulties, adaptations to the physical education program (often referred to as *adaptive physical education*) are incorporated into the child's individualized education program.

Get down on the floor with your infant. If your infant has delayed motor skills, she needs floor time and especially belly time, preferably several times every day, to practice the basic skills and movements required to advance these skills. Getting down on the floor with your child (or having a sibling do the same— older siblings are often the best therapists!) and playing with her can be enormously helpful, especially if she does not enjoy being on her belly and needs the distraction and motivation of your company.

Provide recreational activities for older children. Simply providing your child with opportunities for physically oriented play can be enormously helpful in promoting his or her motor skills; no amount of therapy can replace the real-life trial-and-error learning that happens naturally in the backyard or on the playground. More structured activities such as team sports may be appropriate, but many parents find that children with coordination challenges prefer activities that are less focused on winning and losing focused and more oriented toward achieving individual goals. Swimming, gymnastics, martial arts (karate, tae kwon do), horseback riding, track and field, tennis, bowling, and golf are examples. Many children with coordination challenges resist becoming involved in these activities, so a careful balance must be struck between encouraging your child in activities that can help him develop his motor skills but at the same time recognizing when an activity is not a good fit for your child. Recreation programs for children with more significant physical disabilities can provide access to a range of activities that might otherwise be unavailable through typical school- and community-based programs.

SUMMARY

What to Do if Your Child Has Trouble Walking

Here is a review of what you should do if your child has motor skills delays:

Step 1: If you are concerned about your child's motor skills development, trust yourself and act on your concerns.

Step 2: Have your child's primary care doctor evaluate him or her to determine the nature of his or her motor difficulties and to obtain referrals for further medical assessments if these are warranted.

Step 3: At the same time as Step 2, contact your local early intervention program or school district to request an evaluation for your child (see Chapter 7).

Step 4: Obtain services for your child. These services may be home based, clinic based, or school based depending on your child's needs and the types of services available in your area. Physical and occupational therapy will almost always be included, but many children will also receive special education support and other therapy services.

Step 5: Determine in consultation with your child's doctor and therapist whether additional therapy or special equipment is needed to help advance your child's motor skills.

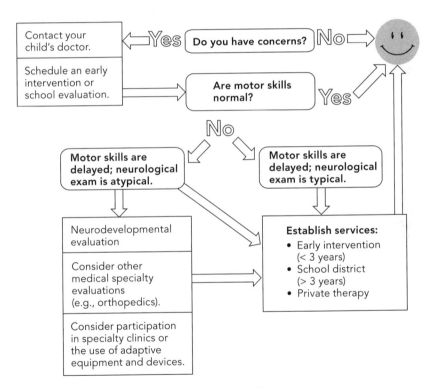

Figure 2.5. Action plan for a child with delayed motor skills.

3

When Your Child Has Trouble with Activities of Daily Living

Understanding Problems with Developing Functional Independence

....

"Before everything else, getting *ready* is the secret of success."
—Henry Ford

"Talent alone won't make you a success. Neither will being in the right place at the right time, unless you are *ready*. The most important question is 'Are you *ready*?'"
—Johnny Carson

"*Ready*, set, go!"
—Anonymous

....

*P*eople spend much of their time growing up getting ready for life. Very young children learn to walk and talk, and socialize and play, so that they can navigate their environment and engage the people in their world. Older children learn to read and write and do math so that they can be prepared for higher education. And along the way, everyone has to learn how to take care of themselves, to become independent with basic life activities, and eventually to become independent with more complex skills that make it possible to have a family and a job, manage a home, and take care of others. These readiness skills are called *activities of daily living* (ADLs) or simply *daily living skills,* and along with communication, socialization, and mobility skills they constitute one of the major categories of skills for living independently called *adaptive skills.*

Basic ADLs are those activities that most children have made significant progress with, if not mastered, by the time they enter kindergarten. These include feeding, sleeping (sleep hygiene and sleep regulation), toileting, personal hygiene, and grooming. More advanced ADLs, those that are typically required for independent living with little or no supervision, are sometimes called *instrumental ADLs.* These include meal preparation, housework, shopping, basic money management, taking medications, and using telephones and other basic forms of technology. Children begin to acquire skills in these areas (often as chores) as early as the preschool years and will typically master most of these activities by the time they are ready to graduate from high school (although truthfully, many otherwise functional adults continue to struggle with some of these skills!). Advanced ADLs, those required to function independently in the adult world and wider community, driving or making use of public transportation, using a computer and navigating the Internet, developing skills for work and acquiring and holding a job, managing a household, planning finances, and caring for other people. (In fact, one of the most challenging of all of the advanced ADLs is parenting, but ironically parenting skills are rarely taught in any formal way—parents are somehow just expected to know how to raise children!)

One of the most notable characteristics of ADLs is that they require the effective integration of multiple abilities and must be learned through experience and practice. People are not born knowing how to dress or feed themselves, and they are certainly not born knowing how (or even why!) they should use a toilet. Even a basic function such as sleeping requires acclimation to a defined schedule, with expectations about where, when, how, and with whom sleep should occur. In order to learn these skills a child must have 1) the basic motor skills necessary to accomplish the task, 2) sufficient language and communication skills to be able to follow instructions and provide necessary responses, 3) an understanding of the social expectations for the activity, 4) sufficient impulse control and attention span to initiate and complete the activity, and 5) sufficient learning skills to comprehend the nature of the task. It should not be surprising that children with developmental disabilities often have trouble acquiring at least some basic ADLs.

THE KEY ROLE OF FINE MOTOR SKILLS IN THE ACQUISITION OF ACTIVITIES OF DAILY LIVING

The skilled use of the hands, often referred to as *fine motor skills,* is required to perform most ADLs. Fine motor skills, in contrast to gross motor skills (which primarily involve the use of large muscles in the legs and trunk), mainly involve the coordinated action of smaller muscles in the arms and hands. Fine motor skills can be further divided into grasping/manipulation skills, eye–hand coordination skills, and fine motor/adaptive skills. *Grasping/manipulation skills* (also called *prehensile* or *in-hand skills*) refers to the ability to plan and sequence hand movements and manipulate objects (think of the things that you can do with your hands with your eyes closed). *Eye–hand coordination skills* (also called *visual-motor integration skills*) refers to fine motor activities that involve the integration of visual input and eye movements with arm and hand movements and object manipulation. *Fine motor/adaptive skills* refers to fine motor activities that are goal oriented and that draw on problem-solving and cognitive processes for their

jargon buster

Fine Motor Function and Adaptive Skills

Upper extremities: Arms and hands

Fine motor skills: Skills that involve the use of the hands

Prehensile skills: The ability to plan and sequence hand movements and manipulate objects; also called in-hand skills

Visual-motor integration: The ability to coordinate visual skills with hand movement; also called eye–hand coordination

Fine motor/adaptive skills: The goal-directed use of fine motor skills that involve higher cognitive processes and problem-solving skills initiation and completion. For example, holding a pencil properly involves specific grasping and manipulation skills, making marks or scribbling on paper requires eye–hand coordination, and drawing shapes or writing a sentence involves the activation of higher level cognitive processes and problem-solving skills. People's hands are in fact amazingly versatile, acting as vassals in the service of their brains and allowing them to manipulate and adapt their environment to their needs and purposes.

THE DEVELOPMENT OF FINE MOTOR SKILLS

Key milestones in the development of early fine motor skills at different ages are summarized in Table 3.1. It is also helpful to consider how the different elements of fine motor control (grasping/manipulating, eye–hand coordination, and fine motor/adaptive skills) emerge during early childhood.

The Development of Grasping/Manipulation Skills

First-time parents are often delighted to discover that their newborn will grasp onto their finger when it comes into contact with their infant's palm. This is called the *palmar grasp reflex*. As the name implies, the response is an involuntary reaction to the sensation of an object (e.g., a parent's finger) coming into contact with the skin of the palm of the hand rather than a deliberately controlled movement. The palmar grasp reflex belongs to a group of reflex responses called *primitive reflexes* with which all infants are born (see Chapter 2 for other examples). The primitive reflexes all follow a similar pattern: They are present at birth and gradually fade during the first year of life, usually in time to be replaced by more advanced forms of movement under voluntary control.

The palmar grasp reflex typically fades by 3–4 months of age and is replaced by the ability to grasp objects deliberately. At first this grasp is rather tentative (especially in comparison to the rather robust newborn grasp reflex), and infants tend to use the pinkie finger side of the hand to loosely grab onto objects. By 6 months this evolves into a confident grasping of objects using the whole hand with all of the fingers curling together in unison around the object. This is called the *palmar grasp pattern* (not to

Table 3.1. Milestones in the development of fine motor skills: Birth to age 5

At birth
- Hands are mostly fisted
- Objects that come into contact with the palms are grasped reflexively
- Arms move randomly at the sides

By 3 months
- Eyes move together to track objects and faces
- Watches movement of hands and brings hand to mouth
- Brings hands together at the midline of the body
- Swings at a target using the entire arm
- Begins to grasp objects deliberately

By 6 months
- Uses palmar (whole-hand) grasp
- Transfers objects from one hand to another
- Looks at objects a few feet away
- Reaches and grasps objects actively
- Holds one object at a time

By 9 months
- Makes the transition from radial grasp, to thumb–finger grasp, to pincer grasp
- Holds one object in each hand simultaneously
- Bangs and mouths objects

By 12 months
- Can release objects onto the floor or into a container
- Turns book pages a few at a time
- Pokes and points at things using the index finger
- Makes marks with a crayon
- Begins to use a spoon

By 18 months
- Builds a tower of two or three blocks
- Scribbles with a crayon
- Stacks two or three cubes
- May begin to show a hand preference
- Can hold an object with one hand and manipulate it with the other hand

By 24 months
- Copies a crayon stroke (line)
- Turns pages of a book one at a time
- Strings 1- to 3-inch beads
- Cuts paper using scissors
- Builds a tower with three to five blocks; lines up three or four blocks

By 3 years
- Cuts across paper with a small scissors
- Draws or copies a complete circle
- Makes a bridge with three cubes

(continued)

Table 3.1. *(continued)*

By 4 years
- Prints first name
- Draws a square
- Draws a person with at least three parts: head, eyes, nose, and so forth

By 5 years
- Draws a triangle
- Draws recognizable pictures
- Prints some or all of the last name as well as some other letters and numbers

be confused with the palmar grasp reflex). Because of the way the fingers move together as a unit, the palmar grasp pattern has been likened to how people tend to use their hand when they are wearing a mitten (which forces their fingers to move together). Between 6 and 12 months of age infants gradually develop the ability to move the fingers independently, and the grasp pattern evolves accordingly. By 7 months infants tend to mainly use the radial side, or thumb side, of the hand to grasp objects (this is called the *radial grasp*). By 8 months infants begin to grab objects using the ends of the thumb and the first two fingers (tripod grasp) or just the end of the thumb and the index finger (thumb–finger grasp). This makes it possible to grasp and hold smaller objects. By 9 months infants can pick up very small objects with greater control using just the tips of the thumb and index finger—this is famously known as the *pincer grasp.*

The ability to move the fingers and thumb independently is continually developed and refined over the next several months. By 10 months of age infants can isolate the index finger and promptly begin to experiment by poking and prodding the nooks and crannies of objects. They soon learn to use this skill to point to things, at first just for fun and then as a way to communicate, pointing to desired objects to get their parents' attention. By 12 months infants also develop the crucial ability to release objects on purpose, called the *voluntary release response* (younger infants may seem to do this, but close observation reveals that they inadvertently let go of things when their attention is diverted away from the object they are holding). Whereas the hand of a 6-month-old operates like a mitten, the hand of a 12-month-old works like a glove, with independent finger and thumb control and infinite possibilities for object manipulation.

The Development of Eye–Hand Coordination

The eyes and the hands work together from a very early age. At birth infants can see light and distinguish objects, but their ability to recognize fine detail and to distinguish colors is still limited. Initially the eyes have trouble moving together in tandem, making it difficult to focus on objects and track movements. By 3 months of age all of these skills have improved considerably. From an early age infants show a strong preference for striking visual contrasts and for faces. Oddly enough, at first they particularly like to look at the forehead and hairline when viewing a face, but by 6 months infants show a preference for looking at the eyes.

At birth infants move their arms mostly at their sides and are mainly aware of their hands through touch and movement, but they gradually become aware of their hands as visual objects as they move in and out of their visual field. This is an early example of sensorimotor integration. Even at this very early age infants begin to correlate the movement and sensations of their arms and hands with the experience of seeing their arms and hands. This provides the foundation for all later eye–hand coordination skills. By 3 months of age infants can bring their hands deliberately to their mouths and can touch their hands together at the midline of their bodies. This provides yet another layer of sensorimotor experience, including the particularly important discovery that the movements and sensations of one hand can be associated with the movements and sensations of the other, which forms the basis for all later two-handed or bimanual activities.

Several aspects of eye–hand coordination begin to gel at 3 months of age. The eyes can move together to focus and track movement, the hands have switched from grasping reflexively to grasping deliberately, and vision is used to monitor the hands and provide continuous feedback about the results of hand movement. One important consequence of this integration of skills is the ability of infants, beginning at about 3 months of age, to target, reach, and grasp onto objects. By 6 months this skill has advanced considerably, and infants add to this the ability to transfer objects from one hand to the other. By 9 months infants can hold one object in each hand simultaneously (prior to this they seem only able to focus on holding one thing at a time). It is at this age that infants typically discover that two objects, one held in each hand, make a delightful noise when banged together forcefully (or banged against a tabletop or highchair tray). This game is made even better by bringing the objects to the mouth for biting, licking, and lubrication. Banging and mouthing is a preferred activity for the next several months. By 12 months eye–hand coordination has been further refined to allow the infant to pick up small objects, point at close objects, and deliberately release objects. In fact, a favorite game of 12-month-olds, called *casting,* involves the impish release of an object from a height (typically that of a highchair); followed by a clang, bang, or crash of the object on the floor; followed by the retrieval of the object by a parent or pet. This is then repeated as often as possible.

By 18 months of age infants can hold an object in one hand while manipulating it in the other and may start to show a preference for using one hand over the other. Although it may not be apparent for several months or even years after this that a child is right or left handed, a child should not show an obvious hand preference much earlier than this. Showing an obvious hand preference before 12 months of age is particularly concerning and raises questions about possible weakness or dysfunction on the side of the body opposite the preferred hand.

Handedness Should Not Be Obvious Prior to 12 Months of Age

Most children do not show a hand preference until after 18 months of age, and some do so much later than this. Showing an obvious hand preference before 12 months of age raises concerns about weakness on the nonpreferred side and may be an early indication of a neurologically based problem such as cerebral palsy.

Beyond 12 months the focus of eye–hand coordination development shifts from the acquisition of basic skills to the refinement of those skills to support the functional and purposeful use of objects. Together with grasping/manipulating skills, eye–hand coordination skills form the foundation for the acquisition and development of fine motor/adaptive skills.

The Development of Fine Motor/Adaptive Skills

A radical shift in the focus of fine motor development occurs beginning at about 12 months of age. Prior to this children relate to objects mainly as generic things to be grabbed, banged, poked, prodded, mouthed, or dropped. After this children relate to objects as tools, as things that have a purpose or function to be discovered and used. The spoon is one of the very first things that children begin to use as a tool with a purpose. Hand a typical 9-month-old a spoon and she will likely mouth it or bang it but will not think to use it. A 12-month-old may do the same but may also turn the spoon this way and that to observe it more closely, and if given the opportunity may try to insert the spoon into a conveniently proximate bowl of rice cereal or strained sweet potatoes. She will notice the food sticking to the spoon, and through happy trial and error will eventually discover that the sequence of inserting the spoon into the bowl followed by bringing the spoon to the mouth results in a delightful reward. A sequence of fine motor actions has been used to adapt an object to a specific purpose—a thing has been transformed by the child's actions into a tool. This is the essence of fine motor/adaptive skills.

Fine Motor Control, Tool Use, and Human Evolution

The uniquely human ability to use tools to change the environment (which allows us to adapt the world to our needs) is thought to be a key development in human evolution. It is interesting to note that three key abilities critical to the success of the human species—the ability to talk, the ability to walk, and the ability to use tools—all emerge at about 1 year of age in typically developing infants.

What constitutes a tool for a toddler? Anything he can get his hands on, including the contents of the kitchen cupboards, a parent's pocketbook, or the DVD player he is not supposed to be able to reach. Experimentation and problem solving characterize the play of children at this stage, and anything is fair game. Household objects are frequently more interesting than the many and varied toys found in the toddler and preschool aisles at the store. It has often been said that play is the work of childhood, and it may be added that toys are the tools that children use to accomplish this work. In fact, play really is critical to the development of daily living skills and the tools involved in their implementation. Play is a child's way of figuring out how the world works, and it is through play that the foundation for functional independence is laid.

When therapists, psychologists, teachers, and other child development specialists evaluate fine motor/adaptive skills, they usually use a few select objects and activities to determine whether a child is on track or delayed for these skills. Among the myriad potential objects and activities that could be used, those few that prove testworthy are selected not for their intrinsic importance but because they are easy to use and produce reliable, reproducible results when testing children. Typical objects and activities include blocks (for stacking, releasing and removing from containers, and constructing), crayons (for scribbling, drawing shapes, creating pictures, and writing words), puzzles, pegboards, formboards, and various and sundry other objects found in a typical preschool classroom. It is important to recognize that when testing fine motor/adaptive skills experts are really assessing multiple aspects of motor, sensorimotor integration, and cognitive function that relate to the successful acquisition these skills.

THE DEVELOPMENT OF BASIC ACTIVITIES OF DAILY LIVING SKILLS

"Intelligence is the ability to adapt to change."
—Stephen Hawking

The development of daily living skills is a key element of humans' ability to adapt to their environment. Some basic daily living skills, such as feeding, sleeping, and toileting, are biological necessities that are shaped by social and cultural expectations. Others, such as grooming, hygiene, and dressing skills, though important to health and well-being, are based more on social than biological imperatives. These skills, like so many other skills discussed in this book, have a developmental progression that must be understood before one can really understand why some children have difficulties acquiring independence with these basic ADLs.

Feeding

Feeding is a complex behavior that we tend to take for granted when it is working well, but which is a source of enormous anxiety for parents when it is not. Many factors contribute to the feeding problems that frequently develop in early childhood.

Developmental Aspects of Feeding

Feeding is fundamental to survival. During pregnancy infants receive all of their nutrition from their mother through the umbilical cord and placenta; after they are born they must quickly switch to acquiring nutrients through feeding. Infants are born with feeding reflexes that ensure that this switch begins immediately, within hours after birth. The rooting reflex helps the infant find his mother's nipple. When something (especially skin) comes into contact with the area around an infant's mouth, his head automatically turns toward the sensation and his lips and tongue stretch and shape themselves to reach toward it. When the newborn's mouth comes into contact with a nipple, the suckling reflex is triggered. The tongue moves in and out in tandem with opening and closing movements of the jaws, and the stripping action of this movement creates a vacuum that draws milk into the infant's mouth.

The rooting and suckling reflexes, like the palmar grasp reflex discussed earlier, are primitive reflexes that infants are born with and that gradually fade to be replaced by more sophisticated patterns of movement that are under greater voluntary control. Between 3 and 6 months of age infants switch from reflexive suckling to deliberate and controlled sucking. Sucking involves up-and-down movements of the tongue that occur independently of jaw movements, both of which are under the infant's control. This arrangement allows for greater flexibility in handling food substances; it is at this stage that it becomes possible to introduce pureed solids and soft cereals (e.g., rice cereal) into the diet (in a sense, infants can suck these foods off a spoon).

Between 6 and 9 months of age infants develop the ability to eat soft solids. At first they do this by using a primitive form of chewing called *munching*. Finely graded up-and-down movements of the jaw replace earlier and cruder jaw movements, and side-to-side movements of the tongue are recruited to gather food that collects in the cheeks. Between 9 and 12 months infants advance to true chewing. This differs from munching in that a rotary movement of the jaws is engaged to grind food, making it possible to include more varied food textures. Chewing and tongue movements are increasingly coordinated and refined until about 36 months, when an adult chewing pattern is achieved.

Infants take an active role in the feeding process from an early age. The development of fine motor skills has a direct bearing on this process. When infants develop the ability to bring their hands together and hold objects between 3 and 6 months of age, they learn to use these skills to hold onto a bottle. The ability to reach for and grasp onto small objects emerges at the same time that munching emerges (between 6 and 9 months). This is handy (both literally and figuratively!) because it allows the infant to finger-feed himself small bits of soft food. When a child develops the ability to manipulate objects purposefully after 12 months it becomes possible to introduce the use of utensils. Most infants learn how to scoop purees and semi-solid foods with a spoon between 12 and 18 months and acquire the ability to stab and pick up bits of solid food with a fork between 18 and 24 months. Use of the knife is introduced cautiously, for obvious reasons. Kid-friendly butter knives are widely available, although supervision is still required. Many children learn to spread a bit of peanut butter on a piece of bread during the preschool years. The use of a real knife for cutting food is usually postponed until school age, when a child has sufficient fine motor control to accomplish the task and sufficient maturity and safety awareness to do so safely.

Learning Chopsticks (the Utensil, Not the Song)

In China children begin to learn to use chopsticks after age 12 months (the same age that children in Western countries begin to use a spoon). Special training chopsticks for children (and adults!) are widely available; it may take several years for a young child to fully master the use of this ubiquitous utensil.

Cup-drinking skills develop in parallel with utensil use. The timing of this transition varies, but infants typically begin to switch from breast or bottle feeding to sipping from straws and sippy cups by 12 months of age, and they learn to drink from an open cup between 12 and 24 months.

Social, Cultural, and Communication Aspects of Feeding

Expectations for what constitutes typical eating behavior vary widely from family to family and from culture to culture. In the United States there is generally an expectation that most eating will occur at one of three meals (breakfast, lunch, and dinner) and that certain types and quantities of food will be consumed at these meals. Family members traditionally gather around a table for meals, and there is an expectation that family members will start and finish meals at approximately the same time. The challenges of modern life and the busy schedules of children and adults often preclude rigid adherence to this scheme—snacking, grazing, and eating meals on the fly or in front of a television or computer is the norm for many families. Nevertheless, the ideal remains, and there is an expectation that children will not simply learn to feed themselves but will also learn to eat in ways that are socially acceptable.

In other words, eating is a powerful, culturally determined social activity. Although children are to some degree born with a basic ability to feed and nourish themselves, they must be taught how to eat in this broader social sense. Parents teach their children to eat through example, through practice, and through words. Feeding and eating skills must be communicated through language, and any child who has significant problems with language use or comprehension will therefore be at a significant disadvantage when it comes to learning how to eat.

Feeding Problems in Children with Disabilities

Feeding and eating problems are very common (few parents have been spared the experience of the picky eater). If your child has developmental delays or an identified developmental disability, he or she is considerably more vulnerable to developing feeding problems for a wide variety of reasons (see Table 3.2).

Feeding problems also change and evolve over time. Very often a feeding problem starts out as a developmental or medical issue and evolves into a behavioral and social one. For example, if your child has trouble coordinating the movements of swallowing, she may tend to choke on food or drink of certain types or textures and may even be prone to aspiration (the inadvertent inhalation of liquid or solid foods into the lungs). She could then understandably develop an aversion to eating the foods that cause her to choke; if you continue to press her to eat these foods, a pattern of food refusal may develop. You may interpret her refusal as a challenging behavior and resort to rewards, threats, or

Table 3.2. Feeding and eating problems in children with disabilities

Area of difficulty	Problems or concerns	Consequences
Oral motor skills	Problems with drinking, chewing, and swallowing	Gagging, choking, aspiration (inhaling food into the lungs), variable tolerance of textures and food types, nutritional insufficiency
Fine motor skills	Problems with using utensils	Delayed development of independent self-feeding
Sensory sensitivities	Sensitivity or aversion to the texture, taste, smell, or appearance of food	Mild, moderate, or severe restrictions on food preference; possible insufficiency of specific nutrients
Communication and learning skills	Problems learning to use utensils and understanding the social expectations for eating behavior	Delayed development of independent self-feeding, problems with adapting to the social aspects of eating, mealtime conflicts
Medical problems	Dental problems, anatomical abnormalities, gastrointestinal problems	The association of discomfort and pain with eating, refusal to eat food, mealtime conflicts, nutritional insufficiency

other behavioral strategies and tactics to try to get her to eat. If she continues to refuse, a pattern of escalation may ensue until a battle of wills develops that becomes a sometimes bigger problem than the one that caused the feeding issue in the first place. Oddly enough, all of the extra attention (albeit negative attention) your child receives during meals may inadvertently reinforce or encourage continued resistance.

Food refusal can also develop for other reasons. For example, if your child has significant sensitivities to specific sensations such as food texture, smell, taste, or appearance (these types of sensitivities are particularly common in children with autism spectrum disorders), he will most likely try to avoid foods with the offending characteristics. In this situation, your child may develop a significant problem with food selectivity (eating a restricted variety of foods).

Or your child may have specific medical problems that make eating unpleasant. For example, if your child has a dental problem (e.g., a cavity), or is constipated, or has a problem with regurgitating the acidic contents of the stomach into the esophagus after a meal (called *gastroesophageal reflux;* see Chapter 9), eating may be uncomfortable or even painful. Food refusal is an understandable consequence of these medical problems and is unlikely to improve until the underlying issue is recognized and addressed.

Food refusal may result in the insufficient intake of specific nutrients, such as protein, vitamins, and minerals, and may or may not result in poor growth due to insufficient caloric intake (in fact, many children who significantly restrict the variety of foods they will eat consume too much of their preferred foods and become obese). Children who are chronically undernourished will typically have trouble gaining weight initially, but if the issue is severe and prolonged, problems with height and head growth may develop as well.

Your child may also develop feeding and eating difficulties due to problems with coordination, communication, socialization, or learning. These developmental problems may cause delays in the acquisition of specific feeding-related skills, such as utensil use, or may make it hard for your child to understand the social expectations associated with eating.

If your child has a feeding problem, the root causes and contributing factors that created the problem in the first place must be identified before effective interventions can be implemented. Medical, developmental, social, and behavioral factors must all be considered, and a collaborative effort between parents and professionals is often needed to address the complexities of these problems. In some communities feeding therapists (professionals with particular expertise in feeding difficulties and who often have a background in speech-language pathology or occupational therapy) can be particularly helpful in designing feeding interventions. Feeding problems can also be addressed in the context of an education or therapy program, and addressing them may be a specific goal in a child's early intervention or special education plan (see Chapter 7).

Sleeping

Sleeping, like feeding, is necessary to survival. People are born with an inherent drive to sleep—one might even say that they are biologically programmed for sleep. This is true in the sense that people cannot escape the need for sleep but is not true in the sense that sleep is not entirely governed by internal processes.

Environmental cues have a decisive impact on sleep. Most notably, people's sleep–wake cycles are governed by the rhythms of day and night, and in the absence of these external signals the internal sleep clock, or Circadian rhythm, falls out of sync with the rhythms of daily life. Sleep patterns are also influenced by human activity and artifice. Artificial lighting and alarm clocks make it possible to stay up past the setting of the sun and to wake early or sleep in as the occasion warrants. In fact, the demands of modern life have created a culture that precludes natural sleep patterns and a society of the chronically sleep deprived.

Sleep is also decisively influenced by learned patterns of behavior that are taught and reinforced by parents and by aspects of the home environment. In this sense sleep can be thought of as an adaptive skill. Although sleep happens no matter what they do, how children get to sleep, how they stay asleep, and whether their sleep patterns harmonize with the routines of family life are strongly determined by the habits of sleep they learn in early childhood. Many common sleep problems in children result from difficulties with establishing appropriate sleep routines and habits.

The Biology of Sleep

The need for sleep is inversely correlated with age. Infants and young children need much more sleep than older children and adults. Infants typically need about 13–15 hours of sleep each day, toddlers and preschoolers need 11–12 hours, school-age children need 10–11 hours, adolescents need 9–10 hours, and adults need 7–8 hours. During the first few months of life infants sleep at irregular intervals, although nighttime sleep predominates, and many infants are able to sleep through the night by 6 months of age. Toddlers typically take a morning and an afternoon nap, preschoolers usually take one afternoon nap, and kindergartners nap inconsistently or not at all.

Sleep has a structure or architecture that changes with age as well. There are two main types of sleep: rapid eye movement sleep and non–rapid eye movement sleep. Non–rapid eye movement sleep is also called *deep sleep* and is associated with a reduction in brain activity; rapid eye movement sleep is associated with dreaming and with high levels of brain activity. Sleep tends to occur in

90-minute cycles throughout the night (infants' sleep cycles are shorter, typically about 60 minutes). Early in the night sleep cycles are dominated by non–rapid eye movement sleep. In between periods of deep sleep, short periods of light sleep, rapid eye movement sleep, and occasional episodes of nighttime awakening occur. Later in the night sleep cycles are increasingly dominated by light sleep and rapid eye movement sleep. Rapid eye movement sleep predominates in infants and young children; non–rapid eye movement sleep predominates in older children and adults.

Night Terrors and Nightmares

Night terrors and recurrent nightmares are relatively common in childhood. Night terrors, most common in 4- to 12-year-olds, usually occur early in the night. The child appears to rouse but is actually asleep and exhibits fear and agitation. The episode is not usually remembered in the morning. Nightmares occur later in the night, are often remembered, and may be associated with significant anxiety. Special interventions are not usually required; a low-key, reassuring approach to night terrors and nightmares is most helpful.

Understanding that sleep occurs in cycles is key to understanding one of the common sleep problems that occur in young children. It is normal and common for children to occasionally awaken during the night between sleep cycles. Most children fall back to sleep on their own, but when this does not happen, parents find themselves faced with the often daunting task of reestablishing a more favorable pattern of sleep.

Sleep Habits, Bedtime Routines, and Sleep Hygiene

The key to helping your child develop good sleep habits is establishing a bedtime routine that is predictable, consistent, and not overly complex. The first goal of the bedtime routine is to encourage a calm, settled state of mind that will allow your child to fall asleep. *Sleep hygiene* refers to the elements of the bedtime routine and bedroom environment that tend to encourage this. The bedroom should be cool, dark, and quiet. Television, music, and video games are too engaging and stimulating for most children and tend to discourage sleep. The second goal of the bedtime routine is to help your child learn to fall asleep on his own. If your child needs to have you present at the bedside to fall asleep at the beginning of the night, there is a good chance that he will need to have you there when he awakens at 2 a.m. Your job is to encourage your child to quiet and soothe himself so that he can get back to sleep on his own. Likewise, if your child needs to have music playing, or a television on, or a snack or a drink to get to sleep, he will probably need these to get back to sleep if he awakens in the middle of the night.

The two most common types of sleep disturbance (insomnia) in children are problems with sleep onset (getting to sleep) and sleep maintenance (staying asleep). Children with sleep-onset difficulties frequently have trouble settling themselves at bedtime or may have difficulties complying with a bedtime routine. The main intervention is to establish and reinforce a reasonable bedtime routine and practice good sleep hygiene (especially by avoiding bedtime activities that are too stimulating). Helping your child learn to quiet himself and fall asleep on his own at the beginning of the night helps him to do the same if he awakens during the night. If he has become dependent on you to get to sleep (or to get back to sleep), the goal of intervention is to gradually wean him away from his need for your help to settle himself. This is often easier said than done, but many helpful books are available for parents on how this can be accomplished (e.g., *Solving Your Child's Sleep Problems* by Richard Ferber).

Sleep Problems in Children with Disabilities

If your child has developmental delays or an identified developmental disability, she may be more prone to developing sleep problems than other children. For example, if your child has communication or learning difficulties, it may be difficult for her to understand what you expect for the bedtime routine. If your child has high amounts of energy or tends to be anxious, it may be hard for her to settle down at night to get to sleep and harder still to get back to sleep if she wakes up during the night.

Children with disabilities are also more prone to developing medical problems that contribute to sleep difficulties. Obstructive sleep apnea is a major concern for children who sleep poorly, awaken frequently, and show evidence of obstructed breathing during sleep (especially snoring). Obstructive sleep apnea in typically developing children is often associated with enlarged tonsils and adenoids in younger children and obesity in older children.

Children with disabilities have additional risk factors for obstructive sleep apnea. For example, children with Down syndrome tend to have low muscle tone in the muscles of the throat that may be associated with a "floppy airway" (see Chapter 9). Their breathing passages tend to collapse when they are lying down, and this can contribute to obstruction during sleep. Likewise, children with cerebral palsy may have muscle tone and movement control problems that increase the risk of obstructive sleep apnea (see Chapters 2 and 9). Obstructive sleep apnea is best diagnosed as the result of a formal sleep study, during which a child's sleep, breathing patterns, and vital signs are monitored in a controlled environment.

A variety of other medical problems that occur more commonly in children with disabilities can negatively affect sleep (see Chapter 9). For example, gastroesophageal reflux (heartburn due to the backing up of acidic stomach contents into the esophagus) is often worse at night when a child is lying down and causes pain and discomfort that disturb sleep.

Sleep–wake cycles may also be disrupted in some children with developmental disabilities. Children with severe visual impairment in particular may have trouble aligning their sleep patterns to day–night cycles (see Chapter 8). In some instances children with intellectual disability (Chapter 6) or autism (Chapter 4) may also exhibit disturbances in their sleep–wake cycles. Melatonin, a naturally occurring brain hormone, is available as a supplement and has been used with some success to address sleep problems of this type.

Toileting

Although going to the bathroom (i.e., peeing and pooping) is arguably the most natural of the ADLs, becoming toilet trained is anything but! Helping your child to understand how, where, when, and especially why he should do his business in a cold, hard chair with a strategic but uncomfortable hole hovering above a watery abyss in a sequestered room away from anywhere fun requires time, patience, and creativity. If your child has a disability, the challenges of toilet training are often multiplied several fold. In fact, it is almost the rule rather than the exception that children with disabilities will have difficulties with toilet training.

The Process

In order for a child to begin the process of toilet training, he or she must be ready. Toilet training readiness has several components. A child first needs to show an awareness of or interest in the toilet. Most children have a chance to observe other family members doing their business, and curiosity coupled with a desire to imitate creates an opportunity to begin the process of training. Parents can also create an interest in sitting on the potty by associating it with something enjoyable (e.g., looking at a book). A child must also have an awareness of the need to go. A child who hides under a table or retreats to a special corner to have a poop in private is demonstrating an awareness of the need to go. A child who tugs on her diaper to indicate that she needs a diaper change is also demonstrating an awareness of the processes of elimination. Other prerequisites include the attainment of sufficient comprehension and communication skills to be able to understand toileting instructions and sufficient physical coordination to pull one's pants down, balance on a toilet seat, and carry out the act of elimination itself. Most children acquire this combination of toileting readiness skills between 2 and 2½ years of age; toilet training is usually difficult or impossible for children who are chronologically or developmentally much younger than this.

For children who demonstrate sufficient readiness, the actual process of training varies greatly—every child seems to take his own slightly different path to the final goal. Some children are very motivated to learn and almost train themselves. Others are very reluctant, or even fearful of the toilet, and need to be accommodated through the process one step at a time. Others seem to know what to do but resist using the toilet until one day they just decide they are ready. Amid these differences there are some commonalities in the training process. It is usually very helpful to observe a child's pattern of elimination. Most children will need to go to the bathroom at fairly predictable times. For example, many children feel the urge to poop about a half-hour or so after a meal. Once a pattern is recognized, a toileting schedule can be created so that the child will (hopefully) be sitting on the potty at the opportune moment.

A common pitfall in the process of toilet training is that a child may come to associate the potty with unpleasantness. He may be afraid of the bathroom, or the watery whirlpool to oblivion at the bottom of the toilet bowl, or the unpleasant sound of flushing. He may be annoyed that he is interrupted while playing, only to be consigned to the potty equivalent of a time-out. He may also sense the tension in the air from his parents, who are eager to be done with the hassles and expense of diapers and want their child toilet trained in time for admission to the preferred local preschool. It is therefore very helpful for parents to take a very low-key, business-like approach to potty training and to try to find creative ways to make the process more pleasant. Rewards and praise, sticker charts, and games are common ways to do this.

Toilet Training Children with Disabilities

If your child has developmental delays or an identified disability, he or she may have special difficulties with the process of toilet training. In some cases medical problems can complicate the process of toilet training. Constipation is a particularly common problem and can make the process of going to the bathroom considerably more complicated, if not painful (see Chapter 9). It is easy for a child to fall into a cycle of stool retention, toileting refusal, and fecal soiling due to overflow incontinence. Treating the constipation problem with dietary and medical interventions early and effectively, with a goal of establishing daily bowel movements, can prevent or remediate many toileting problems. Many medications have constipation as a side effect, so adjustments to these may be necessary.

In addition to the general approaches to toilet training already discussed it is also important to recognize your child's developmental strengths and weaknesses and adjust the toilet-training regimen accordingly. For example, if your child has communication difficulties, she may have trouble understanding verbal instructions, and it can be very helpful to create visual prompts and picture schedules that can provide a concrete reference to help anchor these skills. A variation on this idea is the use of Social Stories. Social Stories come in many forms but are typically a group of pictures arranged in a logical sequence that depict an activity or social interaction that may be difficult for a child to understand (they are called *Social Stories* because they are often used to teach basic social skills, but they are equally useful in teaching ADLs). If your child has difficulties with balance and coordination, a toilet seat insert with hand holds and a footstool may give her a sense of stability and security. If your child has a very short attention span, giving her a special potty activity to do while sitting on the toilet may help engage her attention.

It is also helpful to break the toilet-training process down into steps (see Table 3.3) and focus initially on teaching those steps that are most accessible and acceptable. Parents are naturally focused on the goal, which is sitting on the toilet and actually going to the bathroom, but it may be better to focus on the preliminary steps (getting to the bathroom, pulling down the pants) or the final steps (pulling up the pants, washing the hands) to give your child a taste of success and to reinforce the toileting process and schedule.

Most of all, keep it light, keep it fun, and encourage but do not force the process; it will happen when it happens.

Dressing, Grooming, and Hygiene Skills

By age 3, most typically developing children have mastered most of the basic dressing, grooming, and hygiene skills (see Table 3.4). For example, a typical 3-year-old can brush his teeth, wash and dry his hands and face, brush his hair, blow his nose, and wash up in the bath, although he often needs some help and supervision with specific activities. He can usually dress and undress and can often manage some fasteners, although he may need help with snaps and zippers (especially starting zippers in jackets). By contrast, a typical 2-year-old is often intensely interested in these activities but usually needs quite a bit of help to complete them. She can help with brushing her teeth and washing up, can undress (but not dress), and tries to blow her nose, often with comi-

Table 3.3. Toilet training: Steps to success

Recognize the urge to go.
Communicate the need to go.
Get to the toilet.
Pull down pants, pull-ups, or underwear.
Sit on the toilet.
Stay on the toilet.
Go on the toilet.
Pull up pants, pull-ups, or underwear.
Flush.
Wash up.

Table 3.4. Dressing, grooming, and hygiene skills

Brushing teeth
Washing and drying hands
Bathing
Combing or brushing hair
Blowing or wiping the nose
Undressing
Dressing
Managing buttons, zippers, and snaps
Picking out clothes

cal results. A 1-year-old will cooperate with these activities but is mostly dependent on his parents to carry them out.

Children become increasingly independent with these skills throughout the preschool and school years. For school-age children, preteens, and teenagers, the main focus is usually on taking responsibility and initiative in carrying out these tasks (e.g., choosing and laying out clothes for school). Planning and organizational skills are critical to becoming successful with these and more advanced adaptive skills. Chores are a useful way to introduce older children to these advanced adaptive skills.

For children with developmental disabilities, delays in fine motor/adaptive skills, difficulties with communication, learning problems, trouble reading social cues, and difficulties with attention span and impulse control can all affect the acquisition of dressing, grooming, and hygiene skills. Patience, practice, and professional assistance (especially in the form of therapy provided through the mechanisms of early intervention and special education) can facilitate the process of helping your child attain these skills.

SUMMARY

What to Do if Your Child Has Trouble with Activities of Daily Living

There is considerable variability in how children develop independence with daily living skills. Many typically developing children will have a little trouble with toilet training, or will go through periods of getting up during the night, or will have trouble learning to use a spoon, or may be picky eaters. If your child has substantial difficulties in one or more of the basic ADLs, however, this may be a sign of persistent problems with developing independence and may also signal the presence of an underlying developmental disability.

Step 1: Trust your instincts if you believe there is a problem.

Step 2: Discuss your concerns with your child's doctor to determine whether your child's difficulties with ADLs may be associated with other developmental or medical issues.

Step 3: Have your child evaluated though early intervention (if younger than age 3) or by your home school district special education team (if older than age 3) to assess his or her ADLs and overall development; establish early intervention or special education services as needed.

Step 4: Consider specialized evaluations and medical tests when indicated.

Step 5: Continue to provide your child with opportunities to practice ADLs at home.

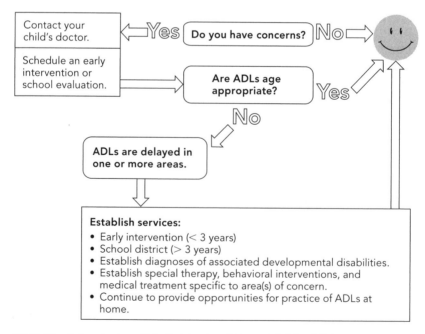

Figure 3.1.   Action plan for a child with delays in activities of daily living (ADLs).

4

When Your Child Has Trouble with Social Skills

Understanding Problems with Social Interaction

*H*uman beings live in two different worlds. With our fellow nonhuman creatures we share the physical world, the world of light and sound, earth and sky, the world of cause and effect—the world of things. But human beings also inhabit another, entirely different world—a kind of parallel universe, a separate dimension of reality that is ruled by invisible laws and held together by bonds of thought and emotion that link us to one another in a web of relationships that connect one mind and heart to the next. Within and beyond the world of things we live in a world of people. And as human beings we are born with an innate ability to connect to that world. From infancy we form bonds of attachment with our parents and learn to communicate our wants and needs. From an early age we begin to distinguish the difference between self and others, friend and stranger. Most of us gradually come to recognize that the social dimension of our lives is populated by beings who, like us, have their own ideas, perceptions, and experiences. We take for granted the existence of this world, and most of us are so immersed in the web of social relationships that surround, penetrate, and define us that we can hardly imagine that it could be otherwise. But for many children and adults, the ability to connect and relate to the world of people, to be a part of society, is difficult at best and excruciatingly painful at worst. And for some children and adults, the world of things is so dominant in their lives that they only dimly perceive the existence of this parallel universe as a specter hovering at the periphery of their awareness.

DONNY

Donny was always a precocious child. His parents proudly describe how he started talking well before his first birthday and using complete sentences by 2 years of age. By his second birthday Donny had also already learned the alphabet, and by 3 years of age he could read simple books. He was the delight of his preschool teachers, who loved to showcase Donny's precocious reading and math skills and who found Donny's adult-like conversational style charming and noteworthy. Donny's parents were proud of their "little scientist," who had a nearly unquenchable appetite for anything related to space and space travel: By 4 years of age he had become a veritable expert on the history of space travel, and his bookshelves were overflowing with encyclopedic tomes on his favorite subject.

As delighted as they were, though, Donny's parents did have concerns about his quirkiness. Although he always seemed friendly and outgoing Donny related much better to adults than children and found his peers to be bewildering and somewhat bothersome. In preschool other children seemed to enjoy his enthusiasm for outer space and would willingly indulge his desire to dominate playground activities with space-related games interspersed with lectures on the same topic. But by first grade Donny's classmates had become impatient with his bossiness, and his parents noted with some concern that he was not being asked to play dates or birthday parties anymore. By second grade Donny had come home from school on several occasions crying because children at school were making fun of him, and one boy called him "weird." Donny's parents had to meet with the school principal because of several episodes of bullying that had occurred on the school bus, with Donny as the target.

Donny became anxious and moody, and his schoolwork began to suffer. His parents tried to help him by coaching him on how to play cooperatively with other children, but Donny struggled with even the most basic rules of the playground. They signed him up for soccer, but Donny's lack of coordination and distractibility on the soccer field did not endear him to his teammates. By 9 years of age, Donny had become more and more withdrawn from social interaction of any kind and immersed himself in his books and video games. Donny's parents were at a loss, not knowing how they could reclaim their formerly happy, precocious little boy.

Donny's story is a surprisingly common one. All of us can remember children we grew up with who were just a little odd, who seemed to be on the fringes of childhood society. In truth, all of us know adults (or perhaps suspect that we ourselves are those adults) who struggled socially through childhood and adolescence, and who still struggle. The loners, the outcasts, the socially awkward have always been with us, and sometimes are us. Historically speaking, those who are lacking in the social graces have been seen as undesirable or, at the more extreme end, as morally defective. In recent years people with serious social difficulties have come to be seen as having, at least in some instances, a type of disability. At the same time people recognize the unique value that many individuals with social disabilities contribute to society because of their ability to see the world differently, to think outside the box. We are just beginning to understand the ways in which our lives as social beings are inextricably linked with our existence as human beings and how those linkages can become tangled and, in some instances, unraveled.

NATURE, NURTURE, AND THE TIES THAT BIND

Infants are not blank slates, and they are not born into a vacuum. Infants are born with definite traits that are eventually described with terms such as *temperament* and *personality*, and as every parent knows no child is like any other. It is said that the apple doesn't fall far from the tree, which means that children tend to take after their parents, and siblings tend to take after each other. However, parents are often astonished at how different their children are from themselves and from each other from the moment they come home from the hospital. Studies of identical twins separated at birth and raised in very different home environments have demonstrated surprising similarities in interests, personality characteristics, career choices, and even style preferences as adults. Thus, people's attributes as social beings are determined by their genes.

But the home environment is crucial to a person's development. Studies of children raised in orphanages in the early 20th century demonstrated poignantly that severe social deprivation in the early months of life can have devastating and permanent consequences on social development. Children raised in orphanages that used an assembly line approach to care had no opportunity to develop bonds with specific caregivers and as a consequence their ability to communicate, form relationships, and learn was severely impaired. By contrast, children raised in institutions that provided primary caregivers for each child were able to develop critical social bonds early on and as a consequence had much more typical development. These observations led to theories of attachment that emphasize the importance of forming healthy attachments with consistent caregivers, especially during the first year of life. Thus, people are a product of their environment.

In the field of developmental psychology the pendulum has swung alternately between theories that emphasize nature and those that emphasize nurture in the genesis of the human personality. More recently, theories have emerged that integrate the two perspectives by looking at human development from the perspective of the broader social context. These ecological theories of human development emphasize the notion that human beings have evolved the capacity to adapt to a variety of social settings and circumstances, and just as they are born with the capacity to see and breathe and walk, they are born with the capacity to perceive and move in and draw sustenance from their social environment.

THE DEVELOPMENT OF
SOCIAL RESPONSES IN INFANCY

Human infants are born in an extremely immature state; in a sense, all infants are born prematurely. Compared to other primates, human infants are much more dependent and vulnerable as newborns, having little more than a few basic, instinctual mechanisms that allow them to feed and respond in rudimentary ways to the environment. But even at this early, primitive stage of development, infants begin to recognize and respond to their specific caregivers, and they are born with the innate ability to elicit attentive responses from these doting adults. Studies suggest that even before birth an infant comes to recognize her mother's voice, breathing, and heartbeat, and this recognition is demonstrable through the subtle differences in behavior that newborns exhibit in the presence of their mothers. And mothers, for their part, are exquisitely sensitive to their infant's specific cry and smell and the subtle nuances of their infant's behavior. It is often said that the infant and his or her mother form a dyad and that the newborn as a social being exists only within the context of this intimate relationship.

The Fetal Newborn and the Human Brain

Human infants are born in an immature or fetal state to accommodate their large brains. Humans have very large brains—and therefore heads—relative to their overall body size. Yet 75% of brain and head growth occurs after birth. If the percentage of brain growth prior to birth were similar for humans as it is for other nonhuman primates, the human birth canal (which is narrow in human females because of the upright posture of the species) would not be large enough to accommodate the proportionately larger head.

By 3 months of age infants look at their parents and smile for the first time. Every parent remembers when this happens, and it always feels like a miracle, because it is at this moment that the infant begins to seem like a person with individual characteristics and an individual personality. Even before responsive smiling (smiling in reaction to another person's smile) begins infants are closely attuned to their parents and move and react in synchrony and rhythm with their parents' movements and actions. But after learning to smile, the infant's part in this intricate social dance becomes much more apparent.

From 3 to 6 months of age infants build on their new-found ability to smile, engaging their parents in a complex choreography of facial expressions, shifts of attention and eye gaze, gestures, body language, and elaborate vocalizations. Baby talk is especially important. Parents instinctively find themselves engaging in crazy, exaggerated, slightly embarrassing conversations of singsong, repetitive, silly speech accompanied by an equally comical

Table 4.1.   Key early social milestones

Milestone	Age
Social smile	2–3 months
Differential response to strangers	4–6 months
Person permanence and stranger anxiety	6–8 months
Imitative play, gesture games play	8–12 months
Gestural communication	12 months
Initiating shared experiences (pointing out or showing things)	14–16 months
Limit-testing behavior	16–18 months
Copying parental activities	18–21 months
Attention-seeking behavior or tantrums	18–24 months
Perceiving self in mirror	30 months
Self-identifying name, age, and sex	36 months
Naming two friends	4 years

vaudeville of expressions and gestures that bring about delighted responses from their little ones. This silliness has a very serious purpose: The complex parent–child interactions that occur in early infancy create a matrix and foundation for the subsequent development of communication and social responses.

By 6 months of age infants can recognize and respond differently to caregivers than to strangers, although infants are not typically fearful of strangers at this stage. The situation changes dramatically by 8 months of age. This is when grandparents are often bewildered that their darling grandchild, who previously loved to be picked up and held, protests vigorously at the intrusion and reaches out pleadingly to be rescued by a parent. This reaction, often referred to as *stranger anxiety*, is based on a fundamental cognitive change that occurs in infants after 6 months of age. At this stage infants develop the capacity to remember things that are not a part of their immediate perceptual environment; this understanding is called *object permanence* (or *person permanence*, as it relates to people). For a typical 6-month-old, when a parent walks

A Little Stranger Anxiety Is a Good Thing

By the end of their first year of life infants typically demonstrate some degree of wariness around strangers (stranger anxiety) that varies in intensity depending on the age and temperament of the child. A complete lack of stranger anxiety raises concerns about a child's social development. For example, children with autism spectrum disorders often do not demonstrate stranger anxiety.

out of the room, it is as if the parent has literally disappeared or ceased to exist—for infants younger than 6 months of age, the expression "out of sight, out of mind" aptly describes their view of the world.

By 8 months of age if the mother leaves the room the infant will typically look to see where she went, and if the child needs her mother she will call out or cry until the mother reappears. An 8-month-old has the ability to form a mental image of a parent that allows her to remember that the parent exists when he or she is not immediately present. This seemingly trivial behavior change actually represents a seismic shift in the infant's perception of the world. The child becomes able to place people and objects into their proper relation in time and space and as a consequence has a dawning recognition of his or her own position in that broader landscape. Parents often comment that their child's personality really starts to come out at this time.

The period from 8 to 18 months is often a happy time of discovery for parents and children alike. Children are learning to walk and talk, they are learning to play, they develop the important capacity to imitate others (starting with simple gesture games such as Peekaboo and Pat-a-cake), and their social development is characterized by a cautious but enthusiastic interest in the people around them. They become aware of the ways in which people react to their behavior, and most important they develop the capacity to share experiences. A typical 15-month-old will point to a dog across the street, or a truck going by, and look at his parents inquiringly to see whether they have seen these remarkable sights themselves. He will pick up all manner of sundry objects, handing them to his parents for their consideration and attention. In doing this the child demonstrates that he intuitively understands that other people see things from their own unique perspective (after all, he would not have to show his parents the worm he just found if they experienced the same things he did). In technical terms the child is said to have developed a theory of mind. He has come to understand at an intuitive level that other people exist as he exists, with their own minds and their own unique perspectives and perceptions. This understanding is critical to subsequent social development: Children who lack this theory of mind are prone to severe disturbances in their ability to relate to their social environment.

TODDLERS AND THEIR TURF

The terrible twos, as they are popularly known, actually start for most children at about 18 months of age. Between 18 and 24 months children experience another critical shift in cognition and personality development. First-time parents may be taken aback by the dramatic change in behavior that accompanies this shift—their previously happy, cooperative, engaging "yes" child has become a limit-testing, cranky, tantrum-prone "no" child. This apparently negative change is actually an extremely positive development. As a child approaches his second birthday he becomes more aware of his individuality, and his negative behavior is really a healthy and appropriate attempt to stake out his territory. The challenges of this period derive from the tension between the child's continued dependence on his parents and his need to exert his new-found autonomy.

The Toddler Brain

Radical changes in brain architecture and organization that begin at about 18 months of age correlate with a burgeoning capacity for using and understanding language and parallel changes in social and behavioral development. This is a neurologically and developmentally sensitive time during which many children with autism spectrum disorders are first recognized.

PRESCHOOLERS AND THEIR PLAY

During the preschool years the desire for independence and autonomy that characterized the toddler stage is tempered by a more nuanced desire to reengage the world in a more positive and proactive way. This change is reflected in the dramatic expansion of play activities and interests that characterize the preschool years. Whereas toddlers tend to engage in simple imitative play—copying their parents and siblings, pretending to talk on the telephone, or engaging in simple games with dolls and stuffed animals—preschoolers show an interest in more elaborate pretend play that often has a strong social component. In contrast to toddlers, who engaged in parallel play (playing next to, but not with, others), preschoolers are able to cooperate in shared or asso-

Table 4.2. Milestones in the development of social play

Milestone	Age
Baby talk games	3–6 months
Gesture games (Peekaboo, Pat-a-cake)	8–10 months
Simple imitative pretend play (e.g., pretend cleanup, talking on the telephone)	12–18 months
Social imitative play (dolls, stuffed animals)	18–24 months
Parallel play	18–36 months
Cooperative or associative play	3–4 years
Turn taking	4–5 years
Board games	4–6 years

ciative play (which is not to say that preschoolers are always good at sharing—that can be a challenge for lots of different reasons). It is often said that play is the work of childhood, and this is especially true for preschoolers. Play pervades every aspect of the preschooler's life and is one of the primary ways in which children at this stage learn to engage and interact with the people around them. Their newly acquired language and motor skills are put to the test in the games that they play, and their newly acquired understanding of their existence as individuals is exercised and expanded through the myriad social interactions that occur in the context of cooperative play. Children who lack the ability to engage others well in their play during the preschool years are at a significant disadvantage in their social development; it is often at this stage that parents first become concerned about their child's social skills.

SCHOOL-AGE CHILDREN: THE DRIVE TO BE COMPETENT

School-age children are driven to learn; they want to understand the world around them, and they want especially to understand the rules that govern adult expectations of life and behavior. Children at this stage thirst for adult approval and attention, and they are equally driven by the desire to be smart, to be strong, to be fast, to be funny, to be winners—to be good at something. More than anything else, school-age children need to feel competent, and they tend to judge one another based on a sometimes brutal analysis of how good somebody is at something.

Popularity, Rejection, and Everything in Between

Researchers have identified five main popularity subgroups in school-age children:

- Popular children are well liked and respected by most.
- Controversial children are well liked by some but disliked by others.
- Amiable children are accepted but not well known.
- Neglected children are un-noticed and loners.
- Rejected children are disliked and actively excluded by others.

At this stage adult standards and expectations are still generally respected as the ultimate source of authority, so judgments of goodness and competence are still made with reference to these standards. But judgments about who fits in and who does not are also influenced by factors unique to the life of the school-age child. The society of school-age children is surprisingly complex and has been rightly characterized as a kind of subculture with its own rules and expectations. School-age children have their own ideas about what is cool and what is not, and what is interesting and what is not, and they tend to have very definite ideas about what makes someone a winner or a loser both on the playground and in the contest to find friends and become popular. Children who do well in school, who are good at sports, who look nice, and who have stable home lives and reasonably good social skills have a big advantage in the school-age subculture and are likely to develop a general sense of confidence and competence that will carry them forward. Children with learning difficulties, social immaturity, poor coordination, or unstable home lives are at a major disadvantage socially and are at risk of developing a sense of doubt about their own competence and worthiness.

ADOLESCENTS: IDENTITY AND BEYOND

Erik Erikson, a psychologist and disciple of the psychoanalyst Sigmund Freud, coined the term *identity crisis* to characterize the central drama of the adolescent phase of development. Adult authority comes into question, peer group expectations become a dominant concern, and horizons expand as these young people become aware of the wider world of society, ideas, opinions, and work. Echoes of the toddler drive for autonomy are reawakened at this stage as the adolescent seeks to achieve greater independence and differentiation from his or her parents. Establishing an independent, healthy sense of personal identity at this juncture provides the foundation for a successful and fruitful work and family life as an adult, but it is a difficult achievement. In the complex culture of the United States, the work of adolescence typically extends well beyond the teenage years, as many young adults still struggle to establish themselves as individuals and as members of society.

THE SOCIAL NARRATIVE: BECOMING A "REAL PERSON"

From infancy to adulthood the seeds of social development that are present at birth grow and develop in response to the social context. The innate competencies of the infant first find expression in the intimacy of the mother–child relationship and then expand to include the broader context of home, school, community, and culture. At its most basic level social competence begins with the simple yet profound ability of an infant to recognize people as people and to learn to share life experiences with them. These life experiences unfold and connect with the experiences of others in the myriad settings of life as the child grows and matures and gradually take the shape of a narrative that becomes the story of that child's life.

Remember the story of Pinocchio. The woodcarver Geppetto creates a wooden puppet and wishes it to be a real boy. He gets his wish, up to a point. Pinocchio comes to life, but he does not become a real boy until he has a series of life experiences that culminate in his being swallowed by a whale as he attempts to rescue Geppetto. His courage is rewarded, and Pinocchio is transformed into a real boy. If Pinocchio had stayed in Geppetto's shop, there would be no story. The narrative takes shape, and the puppet becomes real, through Pinocchio's contact with other people. Likewise people become real as their lives take shape and their stories unfold through the interactions and relationships they form with others. For some people the process unfolds naturally; for others it is a harrowing process that is complicated by significant difficulties with understanding and relating to the social environment.

SOCIAL DISABILITIES IN CONTEXT

Many children, and many adults for that matter, struggle with social skills. Some children have a fundamental inability to connect and relate to the people around them; others are clearly tuned in socially but are lacking in social skills for one reason or another. Understanding the developmental context of social difficulty is the first step toward addressing the issue effectively.

Social-Cognitive Disability

Becca is a fifth grader who is often described as a model student, although her teachers have commented that she tends to be quiet at school. She is a generally happy child, has typical play interests, and acts her age. But lately Becca has seemed sad and out of sorts when she comes home from school. Her parents are worried that she might be having a problem with bullying, but they have found no evidence of that. In fact, Becca seems to be fairly well accepted by her peers, although they do not actively seek her out on the playground, and Becca has recently realized that she has no friends, or at least no good friends. When a child approaches her Becca seems stymied; she is not sure what to say, or how to react, and by the time she decides how she will respond the other child has typically moved on. Her parents have noticed that when a group of the neighborhood girls are clustered together in conversation while waiting for the school bus Becca stands at the fringes of the group and has no idea how to join the conversation. Although not a generally anxious child, Becca has become more and more anxious in dealing with social situations and has taken to spending hours in her bedroom reading alone. Her parents are baffled that a child who seems so likeable and "normal" should have so much difficulty making friends.

People tend to think of social skills as a given—like height or eye color, they are something people just have or acquire automatically. Dr. Mel Levine, a developmental-behavioral pediatrician and expert on learning disabilities and differences, has promoted the idea that social skills are learned, just as language and motor skills are learned, and have a foundation in how the brain works and processes information. Just as some people have cognitive strengths that make them good at math or writing or fix-

Table 4.3. Elements of social cognition

Perception
- Reading facial expressions and body language
- Perceiving and processing language
- Recognizing the nuances of voice intonation
- Recognizing the emotional tone of an interaction
- Perceiving body space
- Perceiving self-image

Cognition
- Understanding the social context
- Understanding social expectations based on context
- Understanding the rules of conversation
- Understanding another person's point of view
- Recognizing humor, sarcasm, and implied meanings

Action
- Knowing how and when to speak
- Using eye contact, gestures, and body language effectively
- Respecting personal boundaries
- Initiating and maintaining interaction and conversation
- Using appropriate topics of conversation
- Modulating voice inflection appropriately
- Matching one's mood to the mood of others in interactions
- Using humor appropriately

ing things, some people have cognitive abilities that make them good at perceiving social interactions and responding effectively and appropriately. Conversely, just as some people have trouble reading or drawing or paying attention, many people have weak social-cognitive skills and are slow or inefficient at recognizing, processing, and responding to social cues. In most instances, social-cognitive dysfunction occurs in the context of other developmental problems, but some children, such as Becca, with isolated social difficulties would be accurately characterized as having a social-cognitive disability. Social cognition is in fact an enormously complicated process involving an almost instantaneous analysis of myriad social signals (perceptions), followed by a rapid analysis of the signals as they relate to the social context (cognition) and leading to the execution of a series of complex social responses (actions) that are socially appropriate. Children with inefficient social-cognitive processing are at a major disadvantage in making friends and often become socially rejected or neglected.

Social Disability in
Attention-Deficit/Hyperactivity Disorder

Sadie is a rambunctious third grader who loves attention and has an unfortunate habit of doing nearly anything to get it. She has a teacher who, fortunately, loves and appreciates her enthusiasm and energy, but the teacher has had a number of telephone and e-mail conversations with Sadie's parents about her tendency to overdo things. She is a bright, intelligent child, and she does have a few good friends, but many of her classmates find her annoying, and she has been the occasional target of bullying. Sadie often makes impulsive comments or intrudes on games, and she is not very good at noticing when other children react negatively to her behavior. Some of her classmates, whom she characterizes as "the popular kids," make fun of her and ostracize her on the playground. Sadie has lately become very irritable and moody as a consequence and has begun to make comments about hating school. Her parents took her to see her pediatrician, who suspects she has attention-deficit/hyperactivity disorder (ADHD).

Children with ADHD have as their primary difficulty problems with impulse control and attention skills (see Chapter 5). These difficulties have a well-known impact on academic performance but can also have an enormous effect on social interactions. Although some children with ADHD have associated weaknesses in social cognition, many experience social difficulties mainly because of their inattentiveness and impulsivity. Sadie's lack of focus makes it difficult for her to recognize social cues, so she misses the key signals that would let her know that someone is reacting negatively to her. Her impulsivity leads her to do or say things that are aggravating, annoying, or insulting. She often recognizes after the fact that she has made a mistake, but in the heat of the moment she finds it difficult to consider the consequences of her actions. Children with ADHD are often characterized as being socially immature and often seem to relate more easily to children who are younger than they are. Children with ADHD often do better playing in small groups or one-to-one with compatible friends, and over time they can learn to temper their impulsivity and listen more carefully. In some instances the use of medications that help these children to focus and regulate their behavior can increase the likelihood that efforts to teach social skills will be more effective.

Social Disability and Learning Disabilities

Gavin is a fourth grader who receives special education services for a language-based learning disability (he has trouble with reading comprehension, spelling, and writing). He received speech therapy beginning in preschool, but it was discontinued in first grade. Although he speaks in clear, complete sentences he has trouble keeping up with long conversations and often has trouble expressing himself. Lately he has developed a problem with stuttering that is aggravated when he is nervous. Although he often talks about wanting to have friends, he has struggled with this and has become socially neglected. His parents suspect that his speech difficulties may be a part of the problem; Gavin seems to have become very self-conscious about his stuttering in particular. Fortunately, Gavin is very good at sports, and his success on the soccer field has provided a way for him to successfully interact with his peers without making great demands on his weak conversation skills.

Children with learning disabilities frequently have social difficulties for a variety of reasons. Many of the social-cognitive processes discussed previously actually overlap significantly with cognitive processes involved in learning (see Chapter 6). Gavin's speech and language difficulties have had an impact both on academics and on social interactions. Learning disabilities, by virtue of their name, are frequently misunderstood to affect learning and academic activities only; in fact, difficulties with information processing, cognition, and learning affect multiple aspects of daily life, including social interactions. Children with more severe disorders of cognition, such as intellectual disability (formerly called *mental retardation*) are at even greater risk for social difficulties for these same reasons.

The Autism Spectrum Disorders: The Prototypical Social Disability

Austin is a 4-year-old boy with autism. When he was diagnosed at age 2, he did not talk; did not respond to his name; showed little or no interest in other people; and engaged in a great deal of repetitive behavior, such as spinning the wheels of toys obsessively, turning light switches on and off repeatedly, and spinning in circles while flapping his hands. By 3 years of age he had begun to talk, and by 4 years of age he had shown remarkable improvements. He can now use complete sentences, although much of his speech involves repeating things that he hears in conversation and on television. He shows a definite interest in people but has poor eye contact and tends to interact on his own terms. He plays with toys appropriately now but seems more interested in the mechanical aspects of how his toys work than in their typical use as playthings, and he has no interest in pretend or imaginative play. He is in a specialized preschool program and is well received by the other children, but he tends to prefer to play on his own and will only interact with other children if prompted by an adult. He has been a bit precocious with learning his letters and numbers: He recognizes about two dozen words and loves to look at books. His teachers indicate that academically speaking he is ready for kindergarten, but there are significant concerns about his lack of social skills and his ability to function in a general classroom.

Recognizing the Signs of Autism

In years past autism was thought to be rare, but since the turn of the millennium experts have come to recognize that it is fairly common (affecting about 1 in 88 children, according to the Centers for Disease Control and Prevention). Likewise, a fairly narrow concept of autism prevailed years ago; for many people the main character in the movie *Rain Man,* in which Dustin Hoffman plays an adult with severe autism, reflected the view most people had of autism. Experts have since come to recognize that the manifestations of autism are quite varied, and the term *autism spectrum disorders* (ASDs) has emerged to capture this more nuanced understanding of the complexities of autism.

What all individuals on the autism spectrum share in common is a fundamental problem with connecting and relating to people individually and to the social environment more generally. In contrast to people with other forms of social disability, people on the autism spectrum exhibit a more profound social disconnect. A child with ADHD or a learning disability may have trouble navigating the social environment but is usually interested in learning and motivated to learn and can manage if given a "map" to guide him; a child on the autism spectrum is unable even to read the map and moreover may have little or no inter-

Table 4.4.   Red flags for autism

Social interaction
- Poor or absent eye contact
- Lack of interest in people or extreme social awkwardness
- Lack of spontaneous sharing of experiences
- Lack of social-emotional empathy
- Lack of interactive play
- Poor differentiation between familiar people and strangers
- Poor understanding of social boundaries and personal space

Language and communication
- Lack of interest in communication, with or without language delay
- Failure to respond consistently to one's name
- Poor use of pointing, gestures, and nonverbal cues such as eye gaze and body language to aid communication
- Atypical or idiosyncratic use of language (e.g., noncommunicative parroting of phrases from television shows, excessive interest in labeling objects)
- If the child is verbal, an inability to initiate or sustain conversation
- Difficulty modulating voice inflection (e.g., robotic or sing-song speech)

Atypical behaviors and interests
- Restricted or obsessive play interests
- Lack of imitative or pretend play
- Rigid adherence to nonfunctional routines
- Repetitive or stereotyped movements (e.g., hand flapping, excessive rocking or spinning)
- Preoccupation with parts of objects (e.g., spinning wheels, mechanical aspects of toys)
- Obsessive interest in a particular activity or topic
- Obsessive interest in letters or numbers
- Excessive interest in collecting objects or collating data
- Excessive sensitivity to sensations (e.g., tags on clothes, loud noises, food textures)

est in being guided. The social difficulties associated with ASDs range from being socially aloof and in one's own world to being superficially friendly but quirky and having a poor notion of how to read and respond to social cues.

Children on the autism spectrum are thought to be lacking in theory of mind (see "The Development of Social Responses in Infancy"). This is the idea that most people are born with an instinctive, intuitive understanding that other people have minds like their own and that each person experiences the world from his or her own unique perspective. Individuals with ASDs have trouble grasping this; they cannot easily put themselves in another person's shoes, and in extreme instances they act as if their view of the world is the only view. The social environment consists of individuals who recognize each person's unique perspective and experience and who can bridge these differences by creating opportunities for shared experiences and activities. A child who picks up an interesting rock and hands it to her father to show him her discovery is demonstrating this ability to share an experience. A child who looks out the window when he notices his sister gazing at something in the backyard (perhaps a squirrel) is showing that he understands that his sister sees something that he may want to experience as well. If people are like islands of individual experience, then society consists of the bridges they create among these islands through their many shared experiences and activities; a child with an ASD who is unable to partake of these shared experiences is literally an island unto himself.

Children on the autism spectrum also exhibit a variety of difficulties with language and communication skills. As noted in Chapter 1, children with language disorders may exhibit difficulties with expressive language (speech), receptive language (comprehension), or pragmatic language (social communication). Children with ASDs often have trouble with expressive and receptive language skills, but their most basic difficulty is with pragmatic language. Some children are nonverbal, and rather than looking at their parents and pointing to show them what they want, they may grab a parent's hand and pull him or her to the desired object; parents often feel that they are being used like a tool or an object when this happens.

Other children with ASDs may use a great deal of nonpurposeful or noncommunicative speech. The random repeating of words or phrases extracted from overheard conversation or from television shows or video games (called *echolalia*) may predominate over functional language. Some children much prefer to use language to label or categorize things than to communicate wants and needs.

Still other children may have a large vocabulary and be able to use complete sentences but have a poor understanding of the rules of conversation. They may have trouble adjusting the volume and tone, or inflection, of their speech (speech-language pathologists refer to this as impaired prosody). Some children seem like little adults in their manner of speech and may come across as lecturing or pedantic; parents of a child with this style of communication often feel that their child talks at rather than with people.

These children often have a marked tendency to dwell on topics with which they are obsessed and often do not recognize when others are tiring of their prolonged dissertations.

Children on the autism spectrum are often lacking in nonverbal communication skills as well as verbal communication skills. Lack of eye contact and directed eye gaze, poor use of pointing and other communicative gestures, and poor use of facial expressions and body language are all common problems for children with ASDs.

Unusual, atypical, idiosyncratic, quirky, or repetitive behaviors and interests are often noted in children with ASDs. A common source of confusion for parents and professionals alike relates to the fact that these unusual or atypical behaviors are often seen in children with other developmental disorders and even in typically developing children. For example, many children find it comforting to rock back and forth repetitively, especially before they go to sleep; many children like to do the same activity over and over again; many children are picky eaters; many children are sensitive to loud noises; many children have a strong need for routine—if a child exhibits any one or even several of these behaviors, it does not mean that she has an ASD. An ASD is present if and only if such behaviors are associated with significant impairments in social relatedness and communication.

A common thread among children with ASDs is an overarching need for predictability and sameness in their lives. Because social interactions and human behavior are by definition unpredictable, most children with ASDs feel much more comfortable dealing with the world of objects and things. There are several ways in which children can achieve predictability in this domain. Some children engage in primitive forms of repetition, such as opening and closing doors repetitively, turning light switches on and off again and again, lining up or arranging objects in predictable and repetitive patterns, or focusing on objects that exhibit repetitive motion (e.g., spinning wheels or fans). Other children are drawn to more complex forms of repetition, such as collecting and classifying objects or creating catalogs of detailed information and statistics about a preferred topic—this often takes the form of an obsessive interest in vehicles, animals, science, or history.

Most children on the autism spectrum have a strong preference for predicable routines in daily activities. Although all children tend to respond well to routine and structure in their lives, children with ASDs have an excessive need for this and often impose arbitrary requirements in their activities and schedules that must not be violated. Likewise, many children with ASDs have trouble with transitions and cannot easily cope with the change in routine or expectations that occurs when they must shift from one activity to another. Poor adaptability and behavioral rigidity are often considered hallmarks of ASDs, although these traits are frequently observed in children who are not on the autism spectrum.

Atypical or unusual reactions to sensory stimuli are also frequently observed in children with ASDs (see Chapter 8). Many of these children are excessively sensitive to loud noises. Common tactile sensitivities include poor tolerance for tags on clothes, tight-fitting clothes, dirty or messy things that come into contact with a child's hands, certain food textures, and temperature differences. Some children with ASDs may also be excessively sensitive to light, smell, or taste. Some may be underreactive to pain. Others exhibit sensory-seeking behavior and seem to crave tight hugs or crashing into things, or they will seek out repetitive stimuli through their own activities (e.g., self-stimulatory behaviors such as hand flapping, finger flicking, or repetitive spinning).

The Varieties of Autism

Most professionals who diagnose ASDs use a standard reference known as the *Diagnostic and Statistical Manual of Mental Disorders, Fourth Edition (DSM-IV),* published by the American Psychiatric Association, as their gold standard for establishing diagnostic criteria and for defining the subtypes of autism. The *DSM-IV* actually uses the confusing term *pervasive developmental disorders* rather than the more commonly used term *autism spectrum disorders* to characterize this group of conditions.

Five separate types of pervasive developmental disorder, sometimes called PDD, are recognized. Autistic disorder is diagnosed in children who show significant qualitative impairments in communication and socialization along with evidence for restricted repetitive and stereotyped patterns of behavior, interests, and activities. Asperger syndrome is defined by the same criteria except that there is no clinically significant delay in language or cognitive development. Pervasive developmental disorder not otherwise specified is used when a child shows characteristics of an autistic disorder but does not meet the technical criteria for autistic disorder or Asperger syndrome.

Two other diagnoses, Rett's disorder and childhood disintegrative disorder, are also included among the pervasive developmental disorders. Rett's disorder, more commonly referred to as *Rett syndrome,* is a relatively rare genetic condition that affects girls and that includes autism-like symptoms along with other specific physical and behavior changes (e.g., abnormal head growth and the presence of midline hand wringing, characteristics not typically seen in other pervasive developmental disorders). Children with childhood disintegrative disorder have symptoms associated with autistic disorder. They appear to develop typically for at least the first 2 years of life and then experience a significant deterioration in skills that is associated with autism-like symptoms (about one third of children with autistic disorder experience regression, but this usually occurs before age 2 and involves primarily language and social skills; individuals with childhood disintegrative disorder experience regression in other areas as well).

The term *autism spectrum disorders,* as it is generally used, coincides with the *DSM-IV* diagnoses of autistic disorder, Asperger syndrome, and pervasive developmental disorder not otherwise specified. Rett's disorder and childhood disintegrative disorder are thought of as special cases that are often associated with concerns about specific genetic (Rett's disorder) or suspected neurodegenerative (childhood disintegrative disorder) conditions.

The Diagnosis of Autism

Autism is a clinical diagnosis, which means it is based on a recognition of the behavior and developmental characteristics associated with autism and consideration of the features associated with the specific types of ASD. Diagnosing autism, similar to diagnosing other developmental disabilities, is a process that typically begins when a parent or professional becomes concerned that a child is exhibiting atypical development. These concerns often arise spontaneously in the natural course of observing a child at home, at school, or at the doctor's office, but autism may be identified through the use of formal screening tests as well.

The American Academy of Pediatrics mandates that primary care doctors administer a specific screening test for autism at 18 and 24 months of age (see Chapter 7). A commonly used screening tool is the Modified Checklist for Autism in Toddlers. Parents complete a questionnaire that is reviewed by the child's doctor; if the screening test indicates cause for concern, the child is referred for further evaluation and diagnosis (see Table 4.5).

Table 4.5. The Modified Checklist for Autism in Toddlers (M-CHAT)

The Modified Checklist for Autism in Toddlers is a test commonly used by primary care physicians to screen children for signs of autism. Parents answer "yes" or "no" to the questions, and the doctor reviews the answers. If the initial results indicate cause for concern about autism, the doctor interviews the parents and determines whether further assessment is warranted. The answers shown in italics are those expected for typically developing children.

1. Does your child enjoy being swung, bounced on your knee, etc.? *(Yes)*
2. Does your child take an interest in other children? *(Yes)*
3. Does your child like climbing on things, such as up stairs? *(Yes)*
4. Does your child enjoy playing Peekaboo/Hide and Seek? *(Yes)*
5. Does your child ever pretend, for example, to talk on the telephone or take care of a doll or pretend other things? *(Yes)*
6. Does your child ever use his or her index finger to point, to ask for something? *(Yes)*
7. Does your child ever use his or her index finger to point, to indicate interest in something? *(Yes)*
8. Can your child play properly with small toys (e.g., cars, blocks) without just mouthing, fiddling, or dropping them? *(Yes)*
9. Does your child ever bring objects over to you (parent) to show you something? *(Yes)*
10. Does your child look you in the eye for more than a second or two? *(Yes)*
11. Does your child ever seem oversensitive to noise (e.g., plugging ears)? *(No)*
12. Does your child smile in response to your face or your smile? *(Yes)*
13. Does your child imitate you (e.g., you make a face—will your child imitate it)? *(Yes)*
14. Does your child respond to his or her name when you call? *(Yes)*
15. If you point at a toy across the room, does your child look at it? *(Yes)*
16. Does your child walk? *(Yes)*
17. Does your child look at things you are looking at? *(Yes)*
18. Does your child make unusual finger movements near his or her face? *(No)*
19. Does your child try to attract your attention to his or her own activity? *(Yes)*
20. Have you ever wondered if your child is deaf? *(No)*
21. Does your child understand what people say? *(Yes)*
22. Does your child sometimes stare at nothing or wander with no purpose? *(No)*
23. Does your child look at your face to check your reaction when faced with something unfamiliar? *(Yes)*

The diagnosis of autism is usually confirmed by a physician or a psychologist with a doctorate and specific training and expertise in diagnosing developmental disabilities. Although the diagnosis is based primarily on the recognition that a child meets standardized criteria (e.g., those offered in the *DSM-IV*), some specialists also complete standardized tests to aid in making the diagnosis. A number of questionnaire-based assessment tools are use. Some, such as the Child Autism Rating Scale–2 and the Gilliam Autism Rating Scale–2, are designed to aid in the diagnosis of ASD in general. Others, such as the Krug Asperger's Disorder Index, target specific subtypes of ASD.

Some standardized assessments, such as the Autism Diagnostic Observation Schedule, require clinicians to undergo special training in order to learn how to administer and interpret the test. Administering the Autism Diagnostic Observation Schedule involves engaging a child in a series of carefully orchestrated play and social interactive activities designed to elicit the core features of ASDs. Although administering tests such as the Autism Diagnostic Observation Schedule is not required to make a diagnosis, such tests offer valuable insights into a child's communication and social interaction skills. The Autism Diagnostic Observation Schedule in particular is considered the gold standard among tests for autism and is frequently used in autism research.

The Future of Autism

Many professionals and parents alike are dissatisfied with the way experts diagnose and classify ASDs. Many feel that the distinctions made among autistic disorder, Asperger syndrome, and pervasive developmental disorder not otherwise specified are artificial, and there seems to be significant variation in how different professionals apply diagnostic criteria. Some have suggested using the terms *low-functioning* and *high-functioning autism* to distinguish children with significant cognitive delays who are socially aloof from those with typical cognitive ability who are socially engaged but awkward. Beginning with the fifth edition of the *DSM* (due to be published in 2013), the subcategories of pervasive developmental disorder may be eliminated altogether, recognizing the general term *autism spectrum disorder* as capturing

Is Asperger Syndrome Unique?

Many parents and professionals feel that children with Asperger syndrome are very different from children with autism, including those with high-functioning autism. They point out that children with Asperger syndrome have excellent language abilities (although their conversation skills are weak and they have trouble adjusting the loudness and inflection of their voices), are very intelligent, and are often precocious readers. Moreover, their repetitive interests are often related to sophisticated, complex topics rather than the simple repetitive activities and interests associated with autistic disorder. Children with Asperger syndrome also seem to be particularly prone to difficulties with coordination, they have symptoms that mirror those of attention-deficit/hyperactivity disorder, and they have frequent difficulties with anxiety. Autism researchers have disagreed on this point, but most of the evidence suggests that despite these perceptions, there is no consistent way to distinguish Asperger syndrome from other high-functioning forms of autism. Asperger syndrome may be more of a culturally defined condition than a scientifically distinguishable form of autism.

the broad variations known to occur among the individuals on the autism spectrum. In this scheme, individual differences would be characterized by describing a person's unique and specific profile of skills rather than on the basis of artificial distinctions and overly general diagnoses.

HOW TO HELP YOUR CHILD WITH A SOCIAL DISABILITY

If your child has a social disability, finding ways to help him can be particularly challenging. Speech therapists work with children with speech delays, occupational and physical therapists work with children with delayed motor skills, special educators work with children with learning disorders, but there is no specific social skills professional to whom a child with a social disability can be referred. Many mental health professionals, including psychologists and social workers who are trained to provide therapy and counseling, do offer support for social skills development as a part of their counseling, but this is often done in the context of providing interventions for emotional problems and challenging behavior. In practice finding ways to help a child with a social disability is a collaborative process among family members and professionals of many stripes.

The process begins by identifying the nature of the social disability. A child with social immaturity related to ADHD needs a very different kind of help than a socially disengaged child with an ASD. Several special teaching and therapy techniques have been developed specifically for use with children with autism. A child's age and level of insight must also be considered. Many younger children with social difficulties are unaware that they have social difficulties, so parents, teachers, and therapists often need to find ways to motivate and reward appropriate social behavior that may seem arbitrary to the young child. By contrast, an older child who has become aware of his social difficulties and has expressed frustration with his inability to make friends would benefit from insight-oriented counseling and interventions.

The Setting: Home, School, and Beyond

In the 1996 film *The Truman Show* Jim Carrey plays a man who is the unwitting participant in the ultimate reality show. An entire

---

Table 4.6. Special therapy and teaching approaches for autism

Applied behavior analysis (ABA): A teaching technique based on the application of basic principles of behavioral psychology that uses positive reinforcement (rewards) to encourage the development of specific skills or behavior. Several forms of ABA exist:

Discrete trial instruction: An ABA therapist provides clear instructions requesting a desired behavior (e.g., "Hand me the crayon"). If the child complies, a reward is given; if not, the therapist provides additional prompts to encourage the behavior.

Pivotal Response Training: ABA techniques are used to encourage the development of key behavioral responses that are thought to generalize to other behaviors.

Incidental teaching: ABA strategies are applied in the context of the child's daily experiences and activities.

Fluency building: Each element of a complex behavior is reinforced through ABA techniques until it is automatic (fluent).

Developmental, Individual Differences, Relationship-based approach (DIR/Floortime): Therapists and parents approach the child at his developmental level, building on the child's existing skills to create new skills.

Relationship development intervention: This approach emphasizes expanding beyond the development of specific skills toward encouraging a child's ability to establish a genuine emotional connection.

Treatment and Education of Autistic and Related Communication-Handicapped Children: A classroom-based intervention that emphasizes accommodating children with autism in a highly structured environment, focusing on well-defined individual and group activities with a heavy emphasis of schedules, pictures, and other visual teaching techniques.

world is created to simulate real life, and Carrey's character is unaware, until the end of the movie, that his whole life and everything he has ever known has been artificial and fabricated.

In a sense, every child is similarly born into a specific, arbitrary social environment that becomes his social reality. Parents, siblings, extended family members, neighbors, and friends are the actors, and the varied roles they play and the activities they engage in provide the stage and script for the child's early social development. It is the ultimate immersion experience. Most children manage to sort out their part in the drama without a great deal of external help. Children with social disabilities do not manage this as well. If they are unaware of social practices and conventions, they must be taught explicitly what they should do and how they should act. They may feel that the demands of the social environment are arbitrary and incomprehensible, and they need help coping with the feelings of anxiety and disconnection that occur as a consequence.

Early Intervention and the Home Environment

Early intervention therapists often provide support to parents of infants and toddlers as these parents try to help their children develop basic communication and social interaction skills (see Chapter 7). These interventions often center on imitative and interactive play activities. Through play children discover who they are, what they can do, and how they can and should interact with others. For young children, therapy might be described as play with a purpose. If your child has trouble with a physical skill, such as climbing stairs, a therapist will often engage her in a game that will encourage her to practice motor skills that build toward the goal of climbing stairs.

Similarly, if your child has trouble interacting with others, teachers and therapists will create play scenarios that encourage interaction. One popular technique for encouraging social interaction in children with ASDs, sometimes called *floortime,* is based on this concept. The parent, teacher, or therapist observes the child's play and then attempts to engage the child by incorporating himself or herself into the child's play and subtly redirecting it. For example, if your child is obsessed with a particular puzzle, a therapist might engage her by offering her puzzle pieces and then applauding enthusiastically when she puts a piece in place, thereby garnering her attention. The therapist might then pretend that a puzzle piece is a hat or a cookie and encourage the child to do the same, thus redirecting the play toward an activity that is imitative and social rather than repetitive and self-directed.

Social Skills Development at School

School is by definition a social experience. For most children school is second only to home as a key life setting for social skills development. Preschool-level educational options vary from community to community. General preschools and child care centers offer all children opportunities for learning and social interaction, but they are sometimes not sufficiently well suited to the needs of children with social challenges. Specialized preschool programs exist, from those designed to cater specifically to children with special needs to those that are inclusive, blending typically developing children together with those with special needs.

Inclusive programs help children with social difficulties by providing a balance between structured support for social skills development and opportunities for meaningful social interaction. Similar classroom options exist for school-age children but tend to vary dramatically from state to state and school district to school district. In some schools social skills development activities may be offered. Lunch groups—small gatherings of children under the guidance of a counselor, psychologist, or social worker—come together to practice social skills and discuss social scenarios, such as dealing with a bully on the school bus.

Beyond Home and School: Opportunities for Community Integration

Many important opportunities for social development occur outside of your child's home and school. These include a variety of recreational activities, sports, clubs, and scouting. A significant amount of trial and error may be required to identify which activities are best suited to your child's needs and interests. Many parents report that some of the more typical team sports, such as soccer, basketball, and baseball, can be overwhelming for their socially challenged children. Activities that are less driven by competition and more focused on individual achievement and advancement are often more suitable. Swimming, gymnastics, the martial arts, and scouting are frequently cited examples. Participating in these activities provides your child with opportunities for social interaction through the mechanism of a shared activity or interest without putting the spotlight on explicitly practicing social skills. Your child may find it easier to interact with others in the context of a structured activity, such as a karate class, that provides a ready-made script of expected social behavior as opposed to a less structured, free-wheeling activity that requires social flexibility and improvisation, such as a birthday party or a play date.

Special Interventions: Social Stories

Many younger children with social difficulties are unaware that they have social difficulties. It can be very challenging to convey instructions regarding appropriate social responses to these children, especially through verbal means. Parental reminders to greet people, to not pick your nose in public, to be nice, or to not run off at the grocery store often seem to go in one ear and out the other. Providing concrete, visual cues and reminders of these basic skills can be very helpful. One way to do this is through the use of Social Stories. Popularized by Carol Gray, Social Stories are simply reminders of how to do simple tasks and activities put into story form. Social Stories are often used to help children learn daily living skills—toilet training is a popular example—but they are equally useful in making simple social responses clear and memorable to a young child. Social Stories can be created for almost any social situation imaginable, including meeting and greeting people, knowing how to act at a restaurant, knowing what to do on a play date, or knowing how to respond if another child hits you or takes your toy. Ready-made Social Stories exist for purchase, but parents, teachers, and therapists are often quite resourceful in creating their own customized Social Stories. Some consist of just pictures (simple drawings, clip art, magazine cutouts, or photographs are often used), some consist of words and narrative, and some combine pictures and words in a cartoon or comic book style. In some instances, visual schedules, charts, and lists can serve a similar function as Social Stories.

Special Interventions: Social Skills Groups

Older children, especially those who have become aware of their social difficulties, may benefit from programs specifically designed to teach social skills. Children are brought together in small groups to discuss and practice social skills in a nonjudgmental environment under the guidance of an adult with experience in social skills training. Social skills programs often have a parental component designed to instruct parents in how to implement social skills strategies at home. Though not available everywhere, these programs are becoming more prevalent as public awareness of the need for social skills training options increases.

SUMMARY

What to Do if Your Child Has Trouble with Social Skills

Here is a review of what you should do if your child has trouble with social skills:

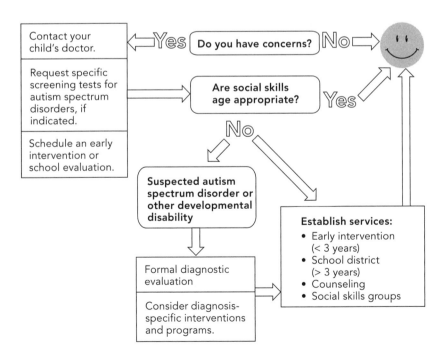

Figure 4.1. Action plan for a child with social skills difficulties.

Step 1: Trust your instincts if you believe there is a problem.

Step 2: Discuss your concerns with your child's doctor and request that your doctor complete specific screening tests for ASDs, if warranted.

Step 3: Have your child evaluated though early intervention (if younger than age 3) or by your home school district special education team (if older than age 3) to assess his or her social skills and overall development. Establish early intervention or special education services as needed.

Step 4: Consider obtaining specialized therapy (e.g., applied behavior analysis discrete trial instruction for autism), counseling, or special social skills training activities (e.g., social skills groups).

Step 5: Continue to provide your child with opportunities for social skills development at home and through involvement in community and extracurricular activities.

5

When Your Child Has Trouble Behaving

Understanding Problems with Behavioral Control and Attention Skills

▪▪

"I wish he would behave!"

"How could they allow their child to behave like that?"

"You need to be on your best behavior."

"If you don't behave, you won't get a toy."

"That child's behavior is out of control."

"Behave!"

▪▪

The words *behavior* and *behave* are supercharged in U.S. culture, especially as they are used in conversations about children! The word *behavior* is actually relatively neutral and can refer to any action, good, bad, or neutral, that a person can exhibit in response to his or her surroundings. In this sense behavior is all about adapting, about coping with circumstances and dealing with the world. The word *behave* is more about expectations of behavior: When a child behaves, he is doing what he is supposed to be doing. In the grocery store behaving

jargon buster

Definitions of Behavior and Behave

Behavior (noun)
1. Anything that anyone does that anyone else can observe.
2. How something works, acts, or functions.
3. A manner of conduct.

Synonyms: action; bearing; conduct; demeanor; deportment; function; manner

Behave (verb)
1. To act or respond in a particular or specific way.
2. To act or respond in a proper or expected manner; to conform.

Synonyms: act; acquit; deport; conform; execute; exert; function; perform; respond

means not grabbing things off the shelves or running off; in school it means sitting in your seat and paying attention to the teacher; on the soccer field it means kicking the ball and not members of the opposing team. So behaving is about being good, doing what is expected, and staying within certain boundaries. But these boundaries are fluid and are defined by the immediate circumstances, the social setting, and the culture at large. It is not okay to yell in the classroom, but it is okay to yell at a football game. It is not usually okay to hit or kick someone, but it is okay if it occurs as part of a boxing or martial arts competition. It is not okay to say mean things about people, but it might be okay if you are a talk show host and you say it as part of a late-night monologue.

Behavioral expectations can also vary greatly from family to family. Some parents are happy to let their infants make a mess as they experiment with feeding themselves; others will not let their children feed themselves until they have learned not to be messy. Some parents encourage their children to be assertive and even aggressive; others emphasize self-control and deference to authority. Behavioral expectations also vary greatly from one culture to another. In most Western cultures it is generally considered rude to burp, but in some Middle Eastern and Asian cultures it is considered a compliment to the cook to burp after a meal. Even within a particular culture expectations of what is considered proper behavior can change dramatically over time (the culture changes of the 1960s and 1970s come to mind). As they grow and develop children must learn, mainly through a process of trial and error, what constitutes acceptable and unacceptable behavior. Most children manage to do this successfully, but many have trouble understanding and responding to these wildly variable and seemingly arbitrary expectations.

WHAT CONSTITUTES BAD BEHAVIOR?

If we as parents are honest, we should admit that we tend to define bad behavior in our children as those actions that disturb, aggravate, annoy, or otherwise bother us. A behavior may be immediately bothersome to us (e.g., our child is yelling while we are trying to watch the news), or it may embarrass us (e.g., our child has a tantrum in the middle of the store). We may also be bothered for what we consider to be our child's best interest. If a child is very impulsive and often says or does things that annoy other children, we may be bothered that our child is making a

Table 5.1.   Behaviors that frequently concern parents

Aggression
Agitation
Anxiousness
Argumentativeness
Cheating
Compulsiveness
Controlling
Defiance
Hyperactivity
Impulsivity
Lying
Manipulativeness
Meanness
Negativity or nastiness
Noncompliance
Obsessiveness
Oversensitivity or being touchy
Perseveration
Rigidity
Self-injury
Self-stimulation
Swearing
Tantrums, outbursts, or meltdowns
Trouble with transition
Willfulness

bad impression socially—and we may worry that his behavior will reflect badly on us as parents. We should also be honest and admit that those behaviors we tend to find most troublesome in our children may be a reflection of things that were troublesome for us themselves at some stage in our lives. We also know that as parents, we vary greatly from one another with regard to how well we are able to tolerate different aspects of our child's behavior. One parent may find a child's talkativeness endearing; another may find it annoying. One parent may encourage assertiveness; another may experience this as pushiness or rudeness. A major challenge for parents is to recognize when a child's behavior is a problem for the parent rather than for the child; this distinction is critical as a foundation for defining an appropriate response to a behavioral concern.

GOOD AND BAD VERSUS ADAPTIVE AND DYSFUNCTIONAL BEHAVIOR

When people say that a child's behavior is good or bad, they are really describing their own reaction to the behavior—how the behavior makes them feel. A "bad" behavior may not necessarily be problematic for the child and may or may not have functional consequences. For example, tantrums are common among

Table 5.2. Adaptive versus dysfunctional behavior

Attributes of adaptive behavior
- Promotes social interaction and relationships
- Promotes communication
- Engages others
- Engenders positive reactions
- Encourages learning
- Increases a person's capacity to respond appropriately in the future

Attributes of dysfunctional behavior
- Is antisocial
- Shuts down communication
- Isolates individuals
- Elicits negative responses
- Short-circuits the learning process
- Allows negative patterns of response (bad habits) to become entrenched

toddlers and are generally considered a normal aspect of their development, but most parents would not describe a tantrum as a good behavior. By contrast, defining behaviors as being adaptive or dysfunctional puts the focus on the impact behaviors may have on a child's ability to function in the real world.

TROUBLE IN FIRST GRADE

Jacob is a 6-year-old boy in first grade who has been having trouble in school. His parents have been called in for a parent–teacher conference because of concerns about his disruptive behavior.

"Jacob is one of my brightest students," the teacher begins,

But he is also one of my most challenging. I've noticed that he tends to be very restless, and I find that I must redirect him frequently to keep him on task. He also likes to be the center of attention, and I am afraid he will do almost anything to get the other children to laugh, and this frequently disrupts our lessons. He seems to get frustrated very easily, and I have had some trouble with him being openly defiant when I ask him to do something that he feels is too hard to do. He also has trouble with transitions from one activity to another. The other day he was busy drawing a picture, and he continued to work on this after I had instructed the class that it was time to move on to math. I approached his desk as unobtrusively as I could, put my hand on his shoulder, and quietly reminded him that it was time to put his drawing away and open his math book. At first he ignored me, then he refused, and then he threw his pencil across the room, started yelling loudly, and hid under his desk. I had to call another teacher in to help me with the class, and it took about 15 minutes for me to calm Jacob and get him to come back out from under his desk. I'm afraid that as a consequence we weren't able to complete the lesson plan for math for the day.

Jacob's parents are upset, embarrassed, and concerned to hear this, but they are not entirely surprised. He had had similar difficulties in kindergarten and is prone to similar outbursts at home.

The teacher continues:

The other concern I have is the trouble he is having getting along with his classmates. Jacob is actually fairly popular. He is very creative and comes up with amazing, complicated games that his classmates find fascinating. Unfortunately he also needs to be in complete control of these games, and when the other children don't follow along, he often gets quite angry. Yesterday there was an incident on the playground. One of the other children tried to change the rules of one of Jacob's games, and he became very agitated, started screaming at the other child, and pushed her down. She had to go to the school nurse for a scrape on her elbow, and Jacob spent the rest of recess in the principal's office. He did say he was sorry afterward, and I think he was sincere. He promised not to do it again, and I believe he meant it, but in the heat of the moment he forgets himself, and I am afraid these incidents are becoming more frequent. I have asked the school psychologist to come and observe Jacob in the classroom, and she and I are working on a behavior plan for Jacob, but I did want to make you aware of our concerns.

Because of Jacob's "bad" behaviors he is at risk of being labeled (either implicitly or explicitly) as a *behavior problem* or even as a *bad child*. These unfortunate labels reflect the negative responses that Jacob's behavior tends to elicit in others. But more important, Jacob's behaviors can be described as maladaptive or dysfunctional, reflecting the effect that Jacob's behavioral responses have on his ability to cope with and react to his surroundings. In practical terms this means that we should carefully consider how challenging behaviors affect a child's ability to get along with others and function in real-life settings—especially at home and in school.

BEHAVIOR PROBLEMS VERSUS SOCIAL SKILLS DEFICITS

Jacob's dilemma illustrates two different ways in which a behavioral concern can be approached. One can think of Jacob as having bad or problematic behaviors. This way of thinking tends to lead to responses aimed at reducing or eliminating the "bad" behaviors. Putting a child in time-out, for example, or taking away privileges (e.g., restricting video games or television time) are examples of this approach. Alternatively, one can think of Jacob's difficulties as representing a deficit in coping mechanisms and social skills. Thinking this way leads to response strategies aimed at teaching and encouraging the child to use more successful ways of coping with the world and dealing with others. To quote a popular tune from the 1940s, when dealing with a behavioral concern one can either "accentuate the positive" or try to "eliminate the negative." In general, helping a child to build positive social skills and effective coping strategies works better in the long run than trying to stamp out unwanted behavior.

In fact, one of the most effective ways to reduce or eliminate a problematic behavior is to teach and reward a child for using a more appropriate, more socially acceptable alternative behavior. For example, your children may constantly fight over which television show they want to watch. Yelling at them will probably not help and may make matters worse. Punishing them may stop the fighting temporarily, but hostilities will likely resume the next time the television goes on. Or you can sit down with the children and draw up a schedule of times and days to clarify who watches what, when. Rewarding and reinforcing their efforts to adhere to the schedule directly competes with their former tendency to argue, and with time this will hopefully eliminate the problem.

DEALING WITH STRESS
AND THE CAPACITY TO COPE

Life is full of stress, and people differ in their ability to cope with it. Although the capacity to cope with stress varies, there is a point beyond which a situation becomes so stressful that anyone's ability to cope would be compromised. Children are amazingly resilient, and yet those who live in extreme poverty; those whose home lives are filled with stress and uncertainty; those who are neglected; and especially those who are subjected to physical, sexual, or emotional abuse are likely to exhibit significant behavior disturbances as a consequence of their circumstances. Transient stressors may also appear periodically in a child's life. If a child who is usually behaviorally and emotionally stable shows a sudden, unexpected regression, a change in the child's home or school situation should be considered as a possible factor in the change. For example, if a child who normally enjoys school comes home in a terrible mood, she may have had an unfortunate encounter with a bully on the playground at recess or on the school bus. Adults who know a child well will have a sense of whether a behavior problem is chronic or whether it has emerged recently, and patient inquiry will help determine the source of the change. There are many instances, however, of a child with a stable, nurturing home environment and no unusual stressors in his life exhibiting pronounced behavior difficulties. In these instances one has to look carefully at the child's individual characteristics to sort things out.

DEVELOPMENTAL PROBLEMS THAT LEAD TO BEHAVIORAL CONCERNS

Shari is a 4-year-old girl who, everyone agrees, is as smart as a whip. She has excellent pretend play skills, knows her letters and numbers, writes her name, and can run circles around her 7-year-old brother. But Shari has trouble talking. She did not start talking until she was almost 3, and although she is able to use sentences now, strangers can only understand her about 30% of the time. Shari's parents say that she is not a terribly patient child and that she gets frustrated very easily. She has a short fuse when she wants to tell someone something but has to repeat herself because they do not understand her. Lately she has been acting up in preschool, and her teachers believe that the problem stems from her frustration with communicating. They have recommended that Shari be evaluated for speech-language therapy.

Because Shari's behavior difficulties are clearly related to her frustration with her speech problem, the most appropriate intervention is not a behavioral intervention but therapy directed toward the underlying developmental issue. For many children with speech and language difficulties behavior becomes a form of communication and a means of controlling the reactions of the people around them when they are unable to use words for the same purpose.

Developmental Problems and Behavior

Any child with a significant behavioral concern should have a thorough assessment to determine whether an underlying developmental or learning problem may be associated with or contributing to the behavior.

Other developmental problems may also manifest as behavioral concerns. A child who has trouble with fine motor control may act up when he is asked to use a spoon or draw a picture. A child with reading difficulties may become defiant when she is asked to read aloud. Children with learning disabilities often become frustrated with school, may react with withdrawal and depression, or may push back and become defiant and even aggressive. In general, any child with significant behavioral challenges should be assessed carefully to determine whether a previously unrecognized developmental or learning problem may be at the heart of the issue.

TEMPERAMENT, RESILIENCE, AND BEHAVIOR

Temperament is defined as the innate tendencies with which all people are born that inform how they typically respond to the world around them. Temperament is a foundational element of personality and social development but is an equally important element of how people deal with the stresses of daily existence. How well a particular parent is able to relate to a particular child's temperamental style is called *goodness of fit*. Theories of temperament and development identify three types of children:

The easy child: These children are very regular in their eating, sleeping, and elimination patterns; adapt quickly to new situations; and are in a good mood most of the time. They pay attention well, demonstrate a moderate level of activity, and tolerate frustration well.

The difficult child: These children have irregular eating, sleeping, and elimination patterns; adapt poorly to change; and tend to have a low frustration tolerance. They are overreactive to environmental stimuli, have trouble with attention and task persistence, and tend to react with defiance or aggression if they become overwhelmed. Mood tends to be negative.

The slow-to-warm-up child: These children tend to be underreactive to environmental stimuli, and though slow to adapt to new situations, they can usually adjust if given sufficient time. When faced with an overwhelming situation these children tend to withdraw rather than react defiantly or aggressively. Mood is variable.

About 60% of children fall into one of these three groups, and about 40% show mixed characteristics. Children who fall in the easy child group tend to be the most resilient and, in particular, tend to be the most adaptable when things do not go as expected. In a more general sense, these children have an easier time regulating their behavioral responses. A key aspect of this is the ability to exhibit behavioral inhibition. *Behavioral inhibition* refers to the ability to delay reacting to a stimulus or situation long enough to formulate and implement the most effective response; stated differently, behavioral inhibition is all about impulse control!

Children in the difficult child group tend to have trouble regulating their reaction to the environment and, as a consequence, tend to be more easily frustrated and less adaptable to unexpected change. In many instances children with this temperamental style tend to be impulsive in their reactions. Children in the slow-to-warm-up child group tend to fall between the other two groups in terms of their adaptability and resilience.

Jacob, the child who was having troubles in first grade, falls into the difficult child group with regard to his temperamental style. But whereas other difficult children nevertheless manage to function reasonably well at home and at school, Jacob's situation has become dysfunctional. When a child's behavior difficulties begin to affect his ability to function in real-life settings on a consistent basis, one must consider the possibility that this challenging behavior has become a disability for that child.

CHILDHOOD BEHAVIOR DISORDERS

Child behavior disorders are specific conditions that are commonly associated with challenging behavior in children. These include attention-deficit/hyperactivity disorder (ADHD), oppositional defiant disorder (ODD), and conduct disorder (CD).

Attention-Deficit/Hyperactivity Disorder

Jill is a bright but restless 12-year-old who was a fidgety 8-year-old, a hyperactive 4-year-old, and a busy 2-year-old. Jill has always done well academically, but sometimes her grades suffer because she makes careless mistakes, has sloppy handwriting, forgets to hand in her homework, and in general has a lot of trouble staying organized. She tends to daydream and often needs to be reminded by her teachers to stay on task. She is friendly and has always had a few good friends, but lately her peers have ostracized her for being weird and immature. She is not generally considered to be a behavior problem, but she often makes odd, random noises in the classroom and sometimes blurts out answers without being called on. Her parents have lately become concerned that their normally cheerful child has become sullen and irritable, and they are not sure how to help her.

Jill demonstrates characteristics of ADHD, including inattentiveness, distractibility, impulsiveness, and hyperactivity. The term *attention-deficit/hyperactivity disorder* emphasizes the inattentiveness, but research suggests that the fundamental problem with which children with ADHD must contend is a lack of impulse control or behavioral inhibition. Russell Barkley, an acclaimed expert on ADHD, described three major and several associated characteristics of ADHD.

Major Characteristics

1. *Impaired response inhibition (impulsivity):* Children who are impulsive have a fundamental problem delaying a reaction or response to a situation or stimulus. Children with ADHD cannot easily stop and think before they do something. They tend to interrupt and intrude on others, cannot wait their turn, and tend to be motivated by immediate gratification as opposed to long-term rewards (i.e., they have trouble with delayed gratification).

Behavioral Inhibition, Impulse Control, and Executive Function

Executive function refers to the cognitive ability to inhibit immediate, impulse responses in order to organize and implement more adaptive reactions to events. Executive functions are thought to be based in the most highly evolved frontal areas of the human brain. Goal-directed behavior, which requires the ability to look backward and forward in time in order to plan a sequence of actions, is based on executive function and is thought to be lacking in disorders of impulse control such as attention-deficit/hyperactivity disorder.

2. *Excessive task-irrelevant activity (restlessness or hyperactivity):* Children with ADHD have trouble regulating their activity to suit the situation. Younger children with ADHD tend to be more notably hyperactive, but older children, teens, and adults with ADHD are often challenged with overt or subjective fidgetiness

jargon buster

Attention-Deficit/ Hyperactivity Disorder

The diagnostic scheme for **Attention-Deficit/Hyperactivity Disorder** from the *Diagnostic and Statistical Manual of Mental Disorders, Fourth Edition, Text Revision (DSM-IV-TR)*, is shown below. Three subtypes are recognized.

Diagnostic Criteria for Attention Deficit/ Hyperactivity Disorder:

A. Either (1) or (2):

1) six (or more) of the following symptoms of **inattention** have persisted for at least 6 months to a degree that is maladaptive and inconsistent with developmental level:

Inattention

a) often fails to give close attention to details or makes careless mistakes in schoolwork, work, or other activities

b) often has difficulty sustaining attention in tasks or play activities

c) often does not seem to listen when spoken to directly

d) often does not follow through on instructions and fails to finish schoolwork, chores, or duties in the workplace (not due to oppositional behavior or failure to understand instructions)

e) often has difficulty organizing tasks and activities

f) often avoids, dislikes, or is reluctant to engage in tasks that require sustained mental effort (such as schoolwork or homework)

g) often loses things necessary for tasks or activities (e.g., toys, school assignments, pencils, books, or tools)

h) is often easily distracted by extraneous stimuli

i) is often forgetful in daily activities

2) six (or more) of the following symptoms of **hyperactivity-impulsivity** have persisted for at least 6 months to a degree that is maladaptive and inconsistent with developmental level:

Hyperactivity

a) often fidgets with hands or feet or squirms in seat

b) often leaves seat in classroom or in other situations in which remaining seated is expected

c) often runs about or climbs excessively in situations in which it is inappropriate (in adolescents or adults, may be limited to subjective feelings of restlessness)

(continued)

and restlessness and have trouble calibrating their level of activity to the demands of the situation at hand.

3. *Poor sustained attention and lack of task persistence:* Barkley's formulation suggests that for individuals with typical ADHD (ADHD combined type), attention skills are not deficient so much as they are inconsistent in their application. Many children with ADHD actually have a tendency to "get stuck" on tasks that are intrinsically interesting or motivating—video games and television shows immediately come to mind. However, they have considerably less ability to ward off distractions when engaged in tasks that are less motivating (e.g., homework!). Thus, the lack of attention is really about the difficulty of regulating one's reactions to distractions when the activity at hand is not sufficiently interesting.

Associated Characteristics

1. *Problems with working memory:* People with ADHD often have trouble keeping important information handy in what psychologists call *working memory,* or the area of memory where bits of data are stored for im-

mediate or later use (this is in contrast to long-term memory, where information and facts are archived more or less permanently). In order to organize their activities people have to keep several things in mind as they look forward and backward in time and plan their next step. An inefficient working memory leads to forgetfulness, disorganization, tardiness, missed deadlines, forgotten homework, lost wallets and keys, and an array of other assorted misadventures that everyone experiences from time to time but that people with ADHD are constantly plagued by.

2. *Delayed development of internal speech (the mind's voice):* Psychologists describe a kind of inner speech that people use to help organize their thoughts, formulate their plans, and reflect on their experiences. This internal speech appears to be essential to the development of self-awareness, and its development is delayed in children with ADHD.

3. *Difficulties regulating emotions:* Children, teens, and adults with ADHD often have a short fuse, are quick to

jargon buster

(continued)

d) often has difficulty playing or engaging in leisure activities quietly

e) is often "on the go" or often acts as if "driven by a motor"

f) often talks excessively

Impulsivity

g) often blurts out answers before questions have been completed

h) often has difficulty awaiting turn

i) often interrupts or intrudes on others (e.g., butts into conversations or games)

B. Some hyperactive-impulsive or inattentive symptoms that caused impairment were present before age 7 years.

C. Some impairment from the symptoms is present in two or more settings (e.g., at school [or work] and at home).

D. There must be clear evidence of clinically significant impairment in social, academic, or occupational functioning.

E. The symptoms do not occur exclusively during the course of a Pervasive Developmental Disorder, Schizophrenia, or other Psychotic Disorder and are not better accounted for by another Mental Disorder (e.g., Mood Disorder, Anxiety Disorder, Dissociative Disorder, or a Personality Disorder).

Code based on type:

314.01 Attention-Deficit/Hyperactivity Disorder, Combined Type: if both Criteria A1 and A2 are met for the past 6 months

314.00 Attention-Deficit/Hyperactivity Disorder, Predominantly Inattentive Type: if Criterion A1 is met but Criterion A2 is not met for the past 6 months

314.01 Attention-Deficit/Hyperactivity Disorder, Predominantly Hyperactive-Impulsive Type: if Criterion A2 is met but Criterion A1 is not met for the past 6 months

Coding note: For individuals (especially adolescents and adults) who currently have symptoms that no longer meet full criteria, "In Partial Remission" should be specified.

Reprinted with permission from the *Diagnostic and Statistical Manual of Mental Disorders, Fourth Edition, Text Revision,* (Copyright © 2000). American Psychiatric Association.

fly off the handle, and are prone to tantrums and other behavioral outbursts because of an inability to regulate emotional responses. This is again based on a core difficulty with behavioral inhibition:

Everyone gets angry or frustrated or upset at times, but people learn to inhibit or suppress their initial reactions and take the time to consider the most appropriate and adaptive response. People with ADHD have much more trouble doing this.

4. *Difficulties planning and pursuing long-term goals:* People with ADHD tend to live in the moment and often have trouble projecting activities and plans into the future. An essential aspect of being organized is being mindful of goals and prioritizing long-term objectives over short-term rewards. This is especially difficult for young children with ADHD.

5. *Variability in work or school performance:* Children with ADHD are particularly known for the "I" word: *inconsistency.* A child may fail a spelling test one week and ace it the next. The ability of a person with ADHD to respond well from one situation to the next is critically dependent on his motivation to complete the task, and most children with ADHD find many necessary tasks, such as homework, not sufficiently motivating in and of themselves (parent and teacher prodding, or the use of some external method of motivation or reward, is often required to get them to complete the task).

Although the clinical classification scheme in the *Diagnostic and Statistical Manual of Mental Disorders, Fourth Edition,* includes three variants of ADHD, Barkley suggested that younger children who experience mainly hyperactivity and impulsivity will usually demonstrate associated problems with attention, distractibility, memory, and organizational skills when they are older, whereas children with attention problems but not impulsivity may have problems primarily with information processing, similar to children with learning disabilities (see Chapter 6).

Other Conditions Associated with Attention-Deficit/Hyperactivity Disorder

ADHD is frequently seen in association with other developmental delays and disabilities. Clinicians who are evaluating children with ADHD must not only know how to diagnose ADHD itself but also be alert to the presence of these associated conditions, which may be of equal or greater importance than the child's ADHD.

Learning Disabilities   Learning disabilities are more common in children with ADHD than without ADHD. A common problem for children with ADHD (especially the ones who tend to be disruptive) is a tendency to attribute all of their academic difficulties to their ADHD when specific special education interventions are needed for their associated learning disabilities. For example, a child with ADHD who is having notable problems with reading should be evaluated for a possible reading disorder such as dyslexia. Because learning disabilities can mimic ADHD, figuring out what is the chicken and what is the egg can be tricky. A good rule of thumb is that all children diagnosed with or suspected of having ADHD should be assessed for a possible primary or associated learning disability.

Mood Disorders   Children with ADHD often have trouble regulating their mood. Some children are generally happy and upbeat but may be prone to moodiness or more significant fluctuations in mood. Parents often describe their children with ADHD as being like Jekyll and Hyde, seemingly happy and content one moment and irritable and out of control the next. Other children tend to be negative and sullen much of the time and may develop sadness, irritability, loss of interest in activities, or changes in eating and sleeping behavior that mirror the changes seen in adults with depression. Still others seem to rapidly cycle between exuberantly happy states and extremely angry, sad, irritable states that are reminiscent of those seen in adults with bipolar disorder. In fact, many children with extremes of mood and behavior have been diagnosed with bipolar disorder, although there is great concern among experts that this diagnosis has been overused and misapplied in many children.

Bipolar Disorder versus Temper Dysregulation Disorder

A new diagnosis, temper dysregulation disorder with dysphoria, has been proposed for the *Diagnostic and Statistical Manual of Mental Disorders, Fifth Edition.* This diagnosis is meant to more accurately characterize children with significant problems with mood regulation and temper outbursts that are associated with a chronically negative mood (dysphoria), irritability, or sadness and serves as an alternative to a diagnosis of bipolar disorder.

Anxiety Disorders and Obsessive-Compulsive Disorder
Everyone experiences anxiety, which is a normal response to the

stresses of life, and many people obsess about things they are interested in or worried about. Likewise, many people are compulsive in the sense that they like things to be ordered and predictable. This is different from the excessive, irrational, and debilitating anxieties, fears, obsessions and compulsions associated with anxiety disorders, phobias, and obsessive-compulsive disorder. People with ADHD seem to be subject to a strong tendency to both experience excessive anxiety and obsess or dwell on things they are worried about. Moreover, they are more prone than people without ADHD to developing full-fledged obsessions and compulsions.

jargon buster

Anxiety, Obsessions, and Compulsions

Anxiety disorders: Excessive, irrational worry about everyday things that is out of proportion to the source of the worry

Phobias: Excessive, irrational fears (anxiety) about specific people, places, things, animals, or situations

Obsessions: Recurrent, persistent, and intrusive ideas, thoughts, impulses, or images that cause distress and anxiety and that a person has difficulty suppressing

Compulsions: Irrational, repetitive behaviors (e.g., ordering or checking behaviors) or repetitive mental acts (e.g., counting, word or phrase repetition) that are performed in response to obsessions to reduce the anxiety associated with the obsessions

Tic Disorders and Tourette Syndrome Tics are very common in early childhood, and more so in children with ADHD than without ADHD (see Chapter 9). Simple motor tics, such as eye twitches or facial grimaces, are especially common. Complex motor tics (which involve sudden jerky movements of several body parts; e.g., a shoulder shrug associated with a head twist) and vocal or phonic tics (i.e., sudden repetitive sounds; e.g., grunts, sniffs, coughs) are less common. Transient tics (tics that occur for a few days or weeks and then disappear) are common and are generally benign. Chronic or recurrent tics (i.e., those that last for weeks or months) may be more concerning. A child with a combination of chronic motor and vocal or phonic tics may have Tourette syndrome.

Tics that are mild and do not disrupt a child's life often do not require any special intervention, but tics that become intrusive, embarrassing, or debilitating should be addressed. Children with tic disorders and ADHD often have more trouble with their ADHD than with their tics. Some of the medications used to treat ADHD may aggravate tics in some individuals, so particular caution is warranted when one is considering medication interventions in these children (see Chapter 10).

Autism Spectrum Disorders   Children with autism spectrum disorders (ASDs) often have associated difficulties with attention skills and impulse control, and experts disagree about whether it is appropriate to assign diagnoses of both ADHD and ASD to the same child. In practice the signs and symptoms of ADHD are similar in children with and without ASD, as are the interventions, although some distinctions apply. For example, children with symptoms of ASD and ADHD are less predictable in their response to stimulant medications and more prone to emotional and behavioral side effects (e.g., increased anxiety or irritability) than children with ADHD without ASD. To complicate matters further, many children have autism-like traits (e.g., social awkwardness or obsessive interests) but do not actually meet criteria for ASD.

Developmental Coordination Disorder and Sensory Processing Disorder   Many children with ADHD have difficulties with coordination, especially with fine motor control. More specifically, they often struggle with drawing and writing (this is referred to as dysgraphia; see Chapter 6). Writing problems in children with ADHD are often blamed on laziness when in fact these children should be receiving help in the form of classroom accommodations and occupational therapy directed toward improving writing skills and providing practice with alternative methods of writing (e.g., keyboarding, so that the children can compensate for their writing difficulties by doing some assignments on a computer).

Likewise, many children with ADHD have sensory sensitivities or exhibit sensory-seeking behavior (see Chapter 8). Sensitivities to loud noises and overstimulating environments are among the most common sensory sensitivities. Sensory-seeking behavior includes an insatiable need to bite or chew on things, a need to bang or crash into things, or just a need to engage in constant repetitive motion (e.g., jumping up and down, spinning).

Common Questions and Concerns
About Attention-Deficit/Hyperactivity Disorder

There is a fair amount of confusion, skepticism, and misinformation surrounding the ADHD diagnosis. Here are some common questions and concerns that many parents express.

How common is ADHD?

The fact that almost everyone who reads this book has probably already heard of ADHD suggests something about how common it is. About 5% of children are thought to meet criteria for ADHD; a somewhat smaller percentage of adults show clinical characteristics of ADHD, although research suggests that most people do not outgrow their ADHD (the more obvious manifestations, e.g., hyperactivity, become less apparent, but the core impairments remain).

Is ADHD overdiagnosed?

Probably not. Research strongly suggests that the core difficulties associated with ADHD are consistent across time and culture, although differences exist in how different people in different places categorize and respond to these issues. For example, physicians in the United States prescribe medications for ADHD at higher rates than their counterparts in Europe, although estimates of the prevalence of ADHD in the United States and Europe are similar.

Is ADHD misdiagnosed in children who are "immature," or in boys who are just "being boys"?

Two issues frequently arise in discussions about the validity of the ADHD diagnosis. It is widely and rightly recognized that many, especially younger, children exhibit impulsivity and distractibility to a greater or lesser degree and that many of these children outgrow these tendencies. It is also widely recognized that boys are more prone to this pattern of behavior and development than girls. The key phrase here is *to a greater or lesser degree*. Just as verbal skills, musical acumen, and athletic ability vary from individual to individual, so too do skills connected with behavioral regulation, impulse control, and the ability to maintain focus. Many children are a little disorganized, a little unfocused, or a bit restless at times, but if they are fairly typical for their age, and if the issue does not interfere with daily activities or social interactions, then it would not be appropriate to diagnose them with ADHD. However, if a child has notably greater difficulties with these issues than his peers, and if these tendencies have created functional problems at home or school, then a line has been crossed and an area of weakness has rightly been recognized as disabling for that child.

Likewise the issue of boys will be boys: It is true that younger boys tend to be more impulsive and distractible than girls of a similar age, but it is also true that as a group boys are more likely to have sufficient difficulties with behavioral inhibition to cause them difficulties in real-life settings. So it actually makes sense that more boys than girls are recognized as having symptoms of ADHD (research indicates that the ratio of boys to girls with ADHD is about 3:1).

Is ADHD caused by sugar or additives in the diet?

No. Research does not support the idea that diet causes ADHD, although some food additives may have subtle, transient, negative behavioral effects that are not specific to children with ADHD. However, there are many reasons to avoid sugars, highly processed foods, and artificial additives; what is healthy for typical children is certainly healthy for children with ADHD as well.

Can other developmental problems mimic ADHD?

Yes. For example, children with reading difficulties may be very inattentive, distracted, and restless when faced with a difficult reading assignment. The key is to recognize that children with ADHD have consistent difficulties with impulse control and attention across multiple settings and varied circumstances.

Can medical problems mimic ADHD?

Yes. For example, children who get inadequate sleep because of obstructed breathing during sleep (obstructive sleep apnea) often appear unfocused, impulsive, and irritable (see Chapter 3).

Other children may rarely have seizures—episodes of abnormal brain electrical discharge—that may be mistaken for the loss of focus associated with ADHD. Most seizures are associated with abnormal, involuntary movements and loss of consciousness, and would not be mistaken for ADHD, but a rare seizure type known as absence (petit mal) seizures may manifest only as very brief (3–5 seconds) episodes of interrupted consciousness, and may mimic ADHD (see Chapter 9). Absence seizures occur at random, so preferred activities are interrupted as much as nonpreferred activities. By contrast, children with ADHD often daydream, especially when they are bored, but can be very focused for preferred activities. Your child's doctor should be able to help you determine whether undiagnosed medical issues have a bearing on your child's behavior or ability to focus.

If my child is diagnosed with ADHD, does that mean he has to take medications?

No. Although medications used to improve impulse control and attention skills can be very helpful for some children with ADHD (see Chapter 9), they do not work for every child, and some children may experience side effects. As a parent of a child with ADHD, it is always ultimately up to you to decide whether medications are in your child's best interest.

If my child takes a medication for ADHD and does not respond, does that mean the diagnosis was incorrect?

No. Although many children with ADHD respond positively to medications, not all do. The diagnosis is in no way influenced or determined by the presence or absence of a treatment response to medications.

Oppositional Defiant Disorder

Danny is an 8-year-old who seems to refuse to do anything that his parents or teachers ask him to do. He seems irritable and moody much of the time and tends to see things in a negative light. He is touchy and easily annoyed, blames others for his mistakes, and seeks revenge if he thinks someone has wronged him. He was diagnosed with ADHD at 6 years of age and at that time was notably impulsive and often inadvertently annoyed others. His impulsivity is better now that he takes medication, but he seems to have developed a concerning tendency to annoy others deliberately to see their reaction. He seems to enjoy the negative attention his behavior elicits and is even proud of the fact that people see him as a bad kid. He was recently suspended from school for hitting another student, and his parents and teachers agree that more intensive behavioral interventions and counseling are needed.

Although Danny has been diagnosed with ADHD, this vignette describes a range of behavioral concerns that go well beyond the behavioral regulation difficulties associated with ADHD. Danny has developed a pattern of oppositional and defiant behavior that is associated with a tendency toward moodiness and irritably that is affecting his ability to relate well to peers and adults at school and at home. Although most children exhibit these behaviors from time to time, a child with persistent, severe difficulties meets criteria for ODD. A child with ODD exhibits the following characteristics:

- Often loses his or her temper
- Often argues with adults
- Often actively defies or refuses to comply with adults' requests or rules
- Often deliberately annoys people
- Often blames others for his or her mistakes or misbehavior
- Often is touchy or easily annoyed by others
- Often is angry and resentful
- Often is spiteful or vindictive

Although children with ADHD are more prone to developing ODD, not all children with ADHD have ODD (and likewise not all children with ODD have ADHD). Many factors are thought to contribute to the development of ODD. Children with difficulties with self-regulation, children with difficult temperaments, children with developmental delays, and children from difficult family circumstances are more prone to develop ODD. Whereas ADHD is thought to represent a specific neurologically based problem with behavioral inhibition and impulse control with which a child is born, ODD represents a pattern of behavior that develops over several years as a consequence of a child's individual characteristics and life circumstances. Thus, it may be possible to prevent the development of ODD if a child receives proper care and behavioral support early on.

Conduct Disorder

Steven is a 12-year-old with serious behavior problems. He lives with his mother, who suffers from depression and has a history of alcoholism, and his 4-year-old sister, who has autism. His father is under a restraining order and is not allowed contact with the family because of alleged physical abuse directed toward the mother. From early childhood Steven has been impulsive, defiant, moody, and aggressive, but over the past 3 years he has developed behavior that is antisocial at best and dangerous at worst. He has been suspended from school multiple times for starting fights, and on one occasion he threatened to hit someone with a rock. He was caught shoplifting, although the shopkeeper did not press charges. He has missed school on multiple occasions and run away from home three times. He has been accused of vandalism (creating graffiti on a wall at a nearby park) and adamantly maintains his innocence despite several witnesses. Steven's mother recently received complaints that he attempted to blackmail a 10-year-old neighbor, demanding money in exchange for not getting beat up. Steven's mother is desperately concerned that he will soon be in trouble with the law and worries that he may appear on the evening news as the perpetrator of a terrible crime.

Steven demonstrates characteristics of CD, the most severe and concerning childhood behavior disorder. A child or adolescent with CD demonstrates aggression toward people or animals (e.g., bullying, starting fights, exhibiting cruelty toward people or animals, mugging or pick-pocketing, forcing someone into sexual activity), deliberate destruction of property (e.g., setting fires or engaging in other forms of vandalism), deceitfulness and theft (e.g., conning others, breaking and entering, shoplifting), and serious violations of rules (e.g., staying out late, missing school, running away from home). For some children the characteristics of CD emerge in early childhood, for others during adolescence.

Children with ODD are at increased risk for developing CD. In fact, some experts consider CD to be a more severe form of ODD, although research suggests that the roots of ODD and CD are distinguishable. Children with CD often come from challenging home environments, and parents of these children frequently suffer from financial and personal stress, mental illness, or drug and alcohol problems. CD is thought to be a precursor to antisocial personality disorder (APD) in adults. Adults with APD have a persistent disregard for rules and for the safety and well-being of others, engage in deceitful behavior, demonstrate irritability and aggression, and show a lack remorse for the harm they inflict on others. They have a notable disregard for the law and for societal norms in general and engage repeatedly in criminal behavior.

Whereas the behaviors associated with ADHD and ODD tend to be disruptive mainly to the child and to the people in the child's immediate environment, the behaviors associated with CD and adult APD have an impact in the wider circles of the community and society. Although the exact causes of these conditions and their connections with one another are still uncertain, there is a general recognition that intervening at a young age when behavioral concerns first emerge is key to achieving successful outcomes.

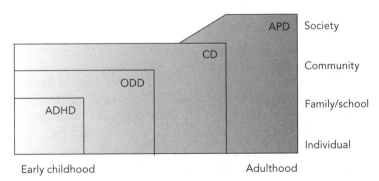

Figure 5.1. Behavior disorders of childhood and APD of adulthood. ADHD and ODD tend to emerge in early childhood and are associated with problems regulating individual behavior and relating to people in the immediate environment. CD tends to emerge in later childhood and adolescence and is associated with a more severe disregard of rules and the rights of others. APD, which occurs among adults, is associated with previous CD and characterized by a pervasive disregard of cultural and societal norms. (*Key:* ADHD, attention-deficit/hyperactivity disorder; ODD, oppositional defiant disorder; CD, conduct disorder; APD, antisocial personality disorder.)

HOW TO HELP YOUR CHILD
WITH BEHAVIORAL CONCERNS:
TAKING A DEVELOPMENTAL PERSPECTIVE

Dealing with behavioral concerns in a 2-year-old is entirely different from dealing with behavioral concerns in a 4-year-old, or a 10-year-old, or a teenager. The behavior young children exhibit from moment to moment is largely the result of their effort to seek out interesting, stimulating, and pleasurable experiences, and this behavior changes largely based on the rewards and consequences that it engenders. Rewards and consequences are still important to older children, but these children are also driven by the desire to become more independent and competent, and teenagers are additionally driven by the desire to establish a sense of their own identity and personal worth. Using simple rewards and time-outs can work well for toddlers and preschoolers but often backfires with older children and teens. As children grow and mature, there should be a gradual shift from using behavioral strategies that focus on how adults respond to the child's behavior to using strategies that focus on teaching a child more appropriate and effective methods for coping with difficulties and relating to others. The old adage "Give a man a fish, feed him for a day; teach a man to fish, feed him for life" applies here. The ultimate goal is to help a child grow into an adult who is able to control his own behavior such that he is able to realize his full potential in life.

Helping at Home

The most important thing that we as parents can do at home to help our children with behavior difficulties is to make a commitment to be the best and most effective parents we can be. There is a temptation to look at a behavioral concern as a problem that needs to be fixed, which tends to place the focus on what is wrong with the child. If instead we focus on becoming skilled and effective parents, the emphasis shifts from fixing the child to finding ways of becoming excellent teachers, coaches, cheerleaders, mentors, and even heroes for our children.

We grown-ups start the process of becoming excellent parents by recognizing where we are starting. As adults who were once children, we are both blessed and cursed by the lessons of our own upbringing. As we raise our own children, we naturally fall back on the experiences of our own childhoods, sometimes consciously but often unconsciously reacting to our children based on those experiences. If we grew up in homes that offered patience, encouragement, and firm but appropriate expectations for our behavior, we are more likely to provide the same for our own children. If we grew up in homes

There Are No Quick Fixes

Learning to be an effective parent is one of the toughest jobs you will ever have, but nothing can substitute for effective parenting. If your child's behavior is concerning, the best way to help him is to make becoming an effective parent your top priority rather than focusing on finding a way to fix the behavior.

seeds

that were insecure, and especially if we experienced harshness or, even worse, abuse as children, we may inadvertently recapitulate those experiences as we react and relate to our own children. The first step in helping your child with challenging behaviors is to honestly and charitably appraise your own upbringing and learn when to draw on the positives of that experience and when to take the negatives of that experience and redirect your efforts in a positive direction.

The next step is to take concrete steps toward making parenting (and becoming effective parents) your top priority. We parents often pay lip service to the idea that being a good parent is our most important goal, but if we honestly appraise the amount of time and effort we put into parenting, we may find that we fall short. A good way to begin the process of evaluating your own parenting skills is by creating a parenting diary in which you simply make a commitment to write down on a daily basis your parenting successes and shortcomings. In his book *The Compound Effect*, Darren Hardy talks about "tracking" as a powerful technique for changing behavior to become successful at any goal one might choose to pursue. For example, if a person wants to lose weight, tracking exactly what he eats every day for a few weeks makes that person much more aware of his dietary habits and gives him the basis for changing those. Likewise, taking the time to track how you respond to your children when they misbehave helps you become more aware of your own parenting strategies and provides the foundation for improving those strategies.

As mentioned in "Behavior Problems versus Social Skills Deficits," a good place to start in your efforts to improve your parenting strategies is to find ways to accentuate the positive—notice what your child is doing well, and draw attention to that. Make an effort to catch your child being good rather than reacting only to her "bad" behavior. Even better, create opportunities for your child to be good so that the child has the experience of pleasing you (e.g., give her a small job helping you with something—whether you need the help does not matter—and then praise her for her efforts). Let her see which behaviors elicit your praise and attention and which tend to reduce these. Discipline in the sense of using time-outs or removing privileges should be administered with consistency but should be reserved mainly for the most problematic or egregious behaviors. Ideally, as a child grows and matures, she will internalize these behavioral expectations such that you will hardly ever need to discipline her at all (the goal, after all, is to help your child grow into an adult who has self-discipline).

Many parents seek out advice from other parents in dealing with behavior difficulties, and a great deal of valuable information can be found in books and web sites (several excellent resources are included in the Resources section at the end of this book). Most communities offer parenting classes that can be very valuable in helping a person become a better parent. It does take a certain amount of humility to accept the idea that you might need help with your parenting skills, but you should be proud rather than embarrassed that you are willing to seek out this advice. After all, most of us have not been explicitly taught how to raise children. Imagine if we were expected to learn how to read without any formal instruction. It would be impossible for most of us—and yet when faced with the task of raising children, one of the most complicated and taxing jobs in the world, we parents are pretty much expected to figure it out on our own! And the amazing thing is, most people do somehow manage to learn to be effective parents, but it is certainly a sign of wisdom rather than weakness if a parent recognizes that from time to time he or she may need a little help.

Helping at School

Child care, nursery school, preschool, and kindergarten are generally the first settings outside of the home that challenge a child's adaptability, and behavioral concerns may become more noticeable under the stress of that challenge. Child care and classroom settings also provide a tremendous opportunity for the development of social skills and improved coping responses. Many parents find that their children are much happier once they have settled into the routine of school. The structure and stimulation provided by a quality school provides a rhythm to a child's day and week that has benefits that often carry over to the child's home.

Children with behavior difficulties are often as challenging to their teachers as they are to their parents. Your child's teacher can therefore be a valuable resource and ally when it comes to dealing with the challenges of parenting. A major aspect of a teacher's job, after all, is knowing how to manage a classroom, so teachers are quite familiar with the varied behavioral challenges that children may exhibit. Keeping the lines of communication open with your child's teacher is key to taking full advantage of this alliance.

For children with behavior difficulties associated with other developmental disabilities such as developmental language disorder, learning disability, and ASDs, early intervention prior to the age of 3 and special education after age 3 offers a way to further support a child (see Chapter 7). Although people tend to think of special education as being mainly about teaching academic skills and providing therapy to support educational goals, teachers and therapists must also work to foster a child's behavior control so that she is able to fully benefit from her educational program and achieve her academic goals. Indeed, a child's individualized education program can and should contain special goals for the development of adequate social interactions and adaptive and appropriate behavioral responses.

Counseling and Social Skills Training

Many schools offer individual counseling, social skills groups, and various activities designed to promote prosocial behavior, although the availability of such activities varies widely from one community to the next. Most communities have options for private counseling, which is usually offered by psychologists and social workers who have specific training to provide counseling. Counseling resources also vary greatly from one community to the next. State and local mental health agencies offer them, as do nonprofit charitable organizations (e.g., Catholic Charities offers behavioral resources in many locations). Behavioral resources may also be found at colleges, universities, and medical schools that provide training to counseling providers. Finally, private, for-profit professional offices in many communities offer behavioral counseling. For younger children, counseling tends to be focused on helping parents develop and implement strategies to address their child's behavioral challenges. As children get older, counseling and social skills training tends to be directed more to the child with the goal of fostering internal mechanisms of behavior control.

Medication Interventions

The decision to consider medication interventions for children with behavior difficulties is a complex one (see Chapter 10 for a detailed discussion). It must take into account a child's diagnoses, family and life circumstances, and medical history. Most important, it must include a clear description and accurate characterization of the behavioral concerns themselves. Parents' personal philosophies about the use of medications that have effects on behavior also vary greatly. Some parents are strictly opposed to the use of medications on principle. Others are quick to consider medications, hoping for a dramatic response or a quick fix to their child's behavior. Most parents are in the middle: They worry about the possible side effects of medications and are generally reluctant to put their child on a drug but also feel that they should consider the option of medication if their child could derive a significant benefit from it. In general, it should be recognized that medications are not a quick fix for behavior problems and should not replace efforts to provide effective educational, social, and behavioral interventions. However, there are circumstances when many parents and professionals find that medications can be used safety and effectively to help specific children in specific circumstances; keeping an open mind and considering accurate information and good clinical research is the key to making good decisions about the use of medications in children.

SUMMARY

What to Do if Your Child Has Trouble Behaving

Here is a review of what you should do if your child has behavioral challenges:

Step 1: Honestly assess whether your child's behaviors are a problem for your child or a problem for you.

Step 2: Make a commitment to finding ways to improve your parenting skills.

Step 3: Focus on encouraging and rewarding positive and prosocial behavior in your child while having consistent and appropriate expectations for his or her behavior.

Step 4: Apply specific discipline strategies selectively and judiciously; avoid yelling and nagging, keep explanations to a minimum (especially for younger children), and never hit or spank your child.

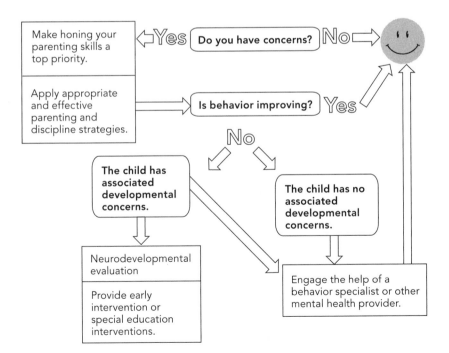

Figure 5.2. Action plan for a child with behavior difficulties.

Step 5: Talk with your child's doctor about whether a formal assessment by a specialist in your child's developmental and behavioral challenges is warranted.

Step 6: Seek out support and help from books, parent training courses, and professionals (including counselors, psychologists, social workers, child psychiatrists and developmental-behavioral pediatricians).

6

When Your Child Has Trouble Learning

Understanding Problems with Learning and Cognitive Development

Many a parent would love to be able to be the proverbial fly on the wall and have a chance to, well, spy on their child's classroom to see how things are really going at school. This is especially true if you are the parent of a child who has been having trouble learning. You know your child is smart (and after all, aren't all children, like the children of Garrison Keillor's mythical town of Lake Wobegon, Minnesota, at least above average?), and you are constantly amazed by your child's curiosity and creativity, but you are equally dumbfounded by his apparent inability to do well at school. Is it laziness, is it the teacher, is he distracted, or is it something else?

So imagine you are the fly. Your son Matt's second-grade teacher has recently sent you an e-mail expressing concern that he has been very distracted at school lately and wondering whether problems at home could be affecting him at school. You reply that things have been fine at home and that you are surprised to hear that Matt has been having difficulties. You decide to investigate. You have found a cozy spot on the side wall of Matt's second-grade classroom opposite the windows and just above a map of the world. The sun is streaming in; it is a beautiful October morning, the leaves on the maple tree just outside the window are already an intense golden orange, and with each gust of wind a few lose hold of their branches and skitter across the schoolyard.

The children themselves look a bit wind-tousled, having just been delivered by their school buses and having unburdened themselves of their coats in their cubbies. You see your son Matt: He is all smiles, happily settling into his chair, and quickly finishing a conversation with his best friend Nick about their plans to compare Pokémon cards on the way home from school. Mrs. Donahue calls the class to order and, after the students finish reciting the Pledge of Allegiance, she instructs the class to pull out their binders. She hands out a sheet of three-hole-punched paper that lists the assignments and activities for the day. She draws up to the front of the classroom, where an exact copy of the assignment sheet hovers luminously on the SMART Board (you marvel at the technology as the teacher makes virtual notations on this modern blackboard). As Mrs. Donahue reviews the plan for the day you look down at your son: So far so good—binder out, Matt is focused on the teacher, and he seems engaged.

Their first activity is to complete a math sheet (you know the teacher has the children do this first thing every morning when they are most focused). Matt's pencil is moving busily. He seems to be making nice progress as he works his way down the sheet and then sets his pencil down as he waits for the rest of the class to finish the assignment. When the teacher asks for a volunteer to demonstrate the solution to the first problem, Matt's hand shoots up, and he is all smiles as he confidently accepts the virtual marker from the teacher and both writes and describes how he got the correct answer. You can tell he is pleased with himself as he saunters back to his desk with his teacher's "Good work, Matthew" still ringing in his ears.

His fellow classmates file up to the SMART Board one after another until all of the problems are completed. Then Mrs. Donahue introduces the class to the next type of math problem they will be working on and reviews what they will be doing for their math homework. Some of the children in the classroom get a bit fidgety and distracted (but, you note, Matt is not one of them), and you are impressed with how deftly the teacher redirects them without missing a beat as she proceeds through her lesson plan.

Everything goes swimmingly until Mrs. Donahue hands out what you have come to think of as the Dreaded Reading Sheet. Matt has told you that he hates the reading sheet, and you have been surprised by this because Matt has always loved books, loves to be read to, and seems to have a good understanding of the things he reads to himself. The teacher asks for volunteers to begin reading aloud to the rest of the class, and you notice that Matt is squirming nervously, looking out the window, and sinking lower and lower into his seat. You have the distinct impression that he is trying to disappear. (You want to go to him and ask him what's wrong, but you can't—you are a fly.) Mrs. Donahue notices the squirming and asks Matt to sit up. Three minutes later he asks to get a drink ("After we complete the reading sheet," she replies). More squirming. More looking out the window. Finally the reading sheet is done, and Matt seems visibly relieved—you suspect this is because he was not called on. He gets his drink, but for the rest of the morning he seems a bit distracted and out of sorts. Your brain is buzzing as you try to sort out what has just happened, but you are pretty sure that the reading sheet is the key to the puzzle of Matt's distractibility. Parent–teacher conferences are coming up in November, but you know that your concerns cannot wait until then. You decide to give the teacher a buzz later to schedule a meeting as soon as possible.

LEARNING PROBLEMS VERSUS LEARNING DIFFERENCES

Everyone learns in different ways. Some people are visual learners. They love diagrams and illustrations, and they like to picture things in their minds and use their imaginations to visualize how things work and relate to each other. Some people are auditory learners. They much prefer listening to someone describe and explain a topic, and they find that they can understand and remember things best if they can think out loud and describe their thoughts and ideas to someone else. Some people are hands-on learners. They learn best by doing, by getting into the thick of things, trying things out, experimenting, and getting their hands dirty. These different ways of learning are reflected in the ways in which people prefer to express themselves. Some people are very articulate and gifted at expressing themselves verbally. Others find that they are best able to express themselves in writing. Others feel more comfortable with artistic forms of expression; still others express themselves most effectively through their work or

Intelligence versus Multiple Intelligences

In the 1980s Howard Gardner argued that the idea of general intelligence (as measured by IQ tests) is flawed and proposed a theory of multiple intelligences. This theory suggests that there are multiple domains of intellectual ability (e.g., spatial, linguistic, logical-mathematical, musical, interpersonal) that vary from person to person and that are not equally well measured by traditional cognitive tests. Although the theory is not universally accepted by psychologists, it did lay the foundation for subsequent theories and concepts, such as the idea of emotional intelligence (the ability to perceive, use, understand, and manage emotion).

through physical and athletic endeavors. People recognize in themselves a complex profile of skills, abilities, interests, aptitudes, and experiences that make up much of who they are, what they like to do, and what they aspire to be. Likewise, children are an equally complex mix of attributes, and parents do the best they can to help them discover their strengths and build on them while recognizing areas of weakness and finding ways to remediate them.

Deciding when a learning difference becomes a learning problem is a tricky thing. Admittedly it involves some arbitrary distinctions, and certainly it has something to do with cultural and societal expectations. A 9-year-old child who is unable to read would undoubtedly be described as having a significant learning problem if he happens to have been born in a developed country in the 21st century. If, however, he had been born into a preliterate hunter–gatherer culture—the dominant form of human society for many thousands of years before the advent of civilization—an inability to read would be irrelevant to his ability to function in society.

Likewise, an inability to do something only becomes a disability when it results in a functional disadvantage to an individual relative to his or her peers in a particular setting. From a practical standpoint, children who live in developed countries in the 21st century are expected to go to school; to attain a certain minimal level of competence in reading, math, writing, and spelling; and to become knowledgeable in several academic areas (science, social studies, literature, etc.). If they are unable to do this, they truly are at a significant disadvantage and their learning difference is indeed a problem for both their current functioning and future livelihood: They most likely have a form of learning disability.

LEARNING DISABILITY
VERSUS PROCESSING DISORDER

Learning disabilities are most often classified based on the academic areas that are affected, especially reading, math, and writing. By contrast, experts in the psychological and cognitive sciences characterize learning ability and disability as a complex amalgam of neurological processes involving perception, information processing, integration and storage, and organization of output responses.

Think of a third grader who has been given an assignment to read a story and write a brief summary of that story. As her eyes scan from left to right across the lines of written material, her brain's visual system (occipital lobes) processes that information and makes it available to the parts of the brain related to reading (at the juncture of the occipital, temporal, and parietal lobes). Specific areas of the brain that are primed to decode the component

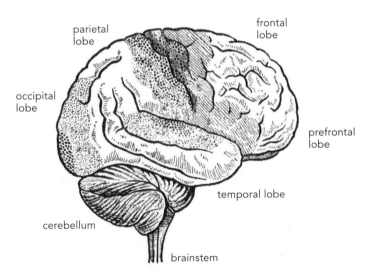

Figure 6.1. The brain. The parietal, occipital, and temporal lobes are the main input areas of the brain, processing tactile, visual, and auditory information, respectively. The frontal lobe is the main output area of the brain and is involved in generating speech and motor responses. The prefrontal area is the seat of higher reasoning and the "boss" of the brain, responsible for orchestrating and organizing output (executive function). The brainstem, cerebellum, and other lower brain areas (not shown) regulate basic body functions and provide automated support for the higher brain areas.

sounds (phonemes) of written words are engaged, as are areas of the brain that have become primed for nearly instantaneous word recognition. The decoded or recognized words are correlated with memory archives of previously learned words, and strings of words are further processed in brain association areas (multiple areas of the brain) to determine the meaning of the words and to integrate that information with previous knowledge related to the subject and context of the story—in other words, she comprehends what she has read!

Now she is ready to write a summary of the story. She engages the parts of her brain involved with motor output and writing (frontal lobes) and the areas of the brain involved in organizing and executing responses (prefrontal lobes). Using continuous feedback from the tactile, position sense (parietal lobes), and visual areas of the brain to fine-tune her motor control, she successfully negotiates the incredibly complex movement patterns of her fingers and hands required for writing—*don't forget to breathe!*—all the while drawing on streams of data provided by the reading and association areas of the brain.

As complicated as this sounds, any neuroscientist will tell you that this description is actually a gross over-simplification of the mind-boggling (pun intended) processes involved in even the simplest academic tasks. The important thing to recognize is that learning involves information process-

Central Auditory Processing Disorder

Many children have difficulties listening, and even though their hearing is normal, some of these children are thought to have specific difficulties processing and perceiving auditory information. This type of disorder is known as central auditory processing disorder (CAPD). Some audiologists offer specialized testing for CAPD that involves measuring a person's ability to filter out background noise and making recommendations for classroom accommodations and modifications. Personal FM amplification systems (called "auditory trainers") are sometimes recommended: The teacher wears a microphone and the child with CAPD wears headphones that enhance her ability to filter out distractions and process the teacher's instructions. There is controversy over whether CAPD exists as a distinguishable entity or whether it is part of various forms of learning disability, and there is uncertainty regarding the efficacy and value of specific interventions for CAPD.

ing, and at their most basic level the two are really just the same thing. The information processing involved in learning can be divided into four components:

Input: Information from the senses is processed (perceived) and made available for higher order processing.

Integration: Perceived information is sequenced, categorized, and associated with other current and previously learned information, providing the basis for understanding and comprehension.

Storage: Information is stored in short-term memory, making it available for further processing for both the input and output stages and for the formation of long-term memories.

Output: Speech and motor responses are organized and executed, drawing on information made available though the perception, integration, and memory functions.

Most learning disabilities are associated with problems at some or all of these stages. For example, many children with language-based learning disabilities (see "Language-Based Learning Disabilities") have problems with reading decoding skills (input), reading comprehension (integration), writing (output), and retaining information they have previously learned (storage or memory).

SPECIFIC LEARNING DISABILITIES

Learning disabilities are often referred to as *specific learning disabilities* by professionals who diagnose these conditions to emphasize the specific nature of the information-processing problem involved and the particular academic area most affected by that problem. Specific reading disorder, or *dyslexia,* is the most commonly diagnosed learning disability, affecting 5%–10% of children. Other specific learning disabilities include math disability (also known as *dyscalculia*) and writing disability (also known as *disorder of written expression* or *dysgraphia*). In practice the boundaries between these different forms of learning disability can be fuzzy, and many children exhibit complex patterns of learning ability and disability that affect multiple academic areas.

Reading Disability and Dyslexia

Consider two children, Marla and Jeff, whose respective parents are concerned about their reading and their tendency to reverse their letters.

Marla is a bright, enthusiastic 5-year-old in kindergarten who learned to recognize her letters and numbers when she was 3; learned to write her name at 4; and now can recognize a number of words, knows the sounds of the letters, and is clever with rhyming games. She is starting to write some words in her great enthusiasm to demonstrate her skills. Her parents are delighted with her progress, but they are concerned because they notice that she often writes letters and words backward, and they wonder whether she is showing early signs of dyslexia. The kindergarten teacher reassures Marla's parents that many children reverse their letters when they first learn to write, and Marla in fact seems to be precocious with her prereading skills. The teacher does not suspect she has dyslexia.

Jeff is a bright, enthusiastic, but increasingly frustrated 7-year-old who, at the end of first grade, is still struggling with basic reading skills. His parents decided to hold him back in kindergarten because he seemed to need some extra time to learn basic prereading skills. He struggled to learn his letters in preschool and continued to struggle with this through his first year of kindergarten. Although he had mastered the alphabet by the time he started first grade, he still had trouble reproducing the sounds of individual letters and had only memorized a few sight words (frequently used words, e.g., *and, a,* and *the*). His parents noticed that he often wrote his words and letters backward, but his teacher reassured them that this was common at the beginning of first grade and that many children with early reading delays tend to catch up with their classmates by the end of the year. By the end of first grade, Jeff has managed to memorize a few words, but he has no idea how to sound out new words and has fallen further behind his classmates. The teacher has suggested that Jeff might need to repeat first grade to give him a chance to mature and consolidate his reading skills.

Marla's teacher is probably right: Marla seems to be making excellent progress with her early reading, and, as her teacher says, many children reverse letters, words, and numbers when they are first learning to read and write.

However, there is cause for concern about Jeff's teacher's assessment. Jeff has already repeated kindergarten, and despite the extra year of work he is still struggling with the basics of reading. It is very unlikely that Jeff's reading problems are the result of immaturity and much more likely that he has a specific problem with reading that requires further assessment and remediation. In fact, Jeff's story strongly hints at the possibility that he has a specific reading disability.

Reading Decoding versus Reading Comprehension

Some children with reading problems mainly have trouble sounding out or decoding words. Like Matt, the second grader in Mrs. Donahue's class, these children seem to understand well what is read to them and manage to extract the meaning of written passages despite the difficulties they have recognizing specific words in those passages. Frequently these children rely heavily on context and meaning to infer the identity of specific words. By contrast, other children seem to do fairly well with early reading skills but run into problems as the material becomes more complex. They learn the alphabet easily, can identify the sounds of the letters without difficulty, and acquire the ability to sound out (decode) words with the usual amount of effort, but they begin to struggle when expectations for the comprehension of written materials increase.

Children like Matt and Jeff who mainly have trouble with decoding skills are thought to have a fundamental problem with phonological processing, or the ability of the brain to accurately and efficiently process the individual sounds or phonemes that make up a given language. They may have early speech delays, especially a form of expressive language dysfunction known as *phonological disorder* (see Chapter 1), and by kindergarten they may begin to struggle with basic prereading skills. Some children have trouble learning the alphabet; others do well memorizing their letters by sight but have trouble learning the sounds of the letters. Recognizing and reproducing rhymes may be difficult, and recognizing alliteration (the repetition of a consonant sound at the beginning of multiple words) may also be challenging. These difficulties are all signs of problems with phonemic awareness, which is the basic ability to recognize that spoken and

jargon buster

The "*Ph*'s" of Reading: Phonemes, Phonetics, and Phonics

Phoneme: The smallest unit of speech that distinguishes one word from another; the sounds that make up a language. A total of 44 phonemes are used in various combinations to create thousands of words in the English language. For example, the word *sat* is made up of three phonemes: /s/, /a/, and /t/.

Phonemic awareness: The ability to recognize and use phonemes in spoken language, or to notice that the words one hears are composed of separate sounds or phonemes

Phonological: Referring to those aspects of language and brain function involved with perceiving, processing, and using phonemes

Alphabetic principle (letter–sound association): The idea that letters represent phonemes and that letter combinations represent the merging of phonemes to create words

Phonics: The knowledge and practice of analyzing and reconstructing written words through the application of the alphabetic principle

Phonetic decoding: Sounding out words, a basic element of phonics

Phonologic model: The theory that dyslexia is caused by inefficiencies in the brain's ability to recognize phonemes (weak phonemic awareness), which results in difficulties analyzing the phonetic composition of written words

written words are composed of individual sounds or phonemes. Children with weak phonemic awareness often have trouble learning how to decode or sound out words, a major focus in first grade. Although they may do better memorizing sight words, their decoding disadvantage compounds over time and they tend to fall further and further behind their peers.

By contrast, a child with well-developed phonemic awareness tends to learn reading decoding skills easily or at least without great difficulty, and with practice she will improve her decoding skills and increase her repertoire of automatically recognized words, gradually becoming an independent, accurate reader by third or fourth grade. With further practice and experience, reading becomes a mostly unconscious, automatic process such that the child's reading mastery allows her to focus on the content of what she reads rather than on the process itself—at this stage she is said to be a fluent reader. A child with a decoding disadvantage is hobbled right from the start of this process. A vicious cycle ensues such that the child's reading dif-

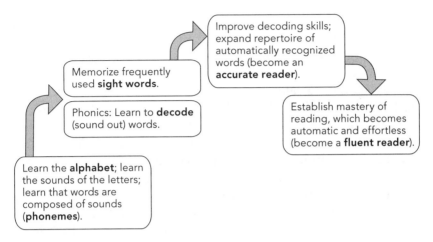

Figure 6.2. The reading process: Progressing to fluency.

ficulties result in less reading practice and experience, which results in delayed attainment of reading accuracy, which delays or prevents the child from attaining the ultimate goal, reading mastery and fluency.

Dyslexia (also called *developmental dyslexia*) is the diagnostic term used to define the specific reading disability that is a consequence of weaknesses in phonological processing, phonemic awareness, and phonetic decoding. In popular discourse dyslexia has unfortunately become associated with letter and word reversals—which, as noted earlier, is a common developmental phenomenon—and this has led to the erroneous impression that dyslexia is somehow caused by a disturbance in visual perception. A large body of scientific research has firmly established that dyslexia is not the result of a visual processing problem; it is the result of a phonological processing problem. Sally Shaywitz, a noted clinician and researcher at Yale University, has written extensively on the subject of dyslexia. In her highly

Letter Reversals ≠ Dyslexia!

seeds

Children with dyslexia do not see letters and numbers backward. All children typically reverse letters and words in the early elementary grades; children with dyslexia tend to persist longer in reversing letters and words, but this represents a developmental lag and is not the primary cause of their reading problem.

recommended book *Overcoming Dyslexia* she offers an excellent and fascinating summary of the clinical and brain research that has begun to pinpoint the exact nature of the neurological impairments involved in the genesis of dyslexia.

Research indicates that recognizing reading problems very early and providing comprehensive, intensive intervention is critical to helping a child overcome dyslexia. Interventions should ideally begin as early as preschool and kindergarten. They should initially focus on helping the child with dyslexia recognize phonemes (enhancing phonemic awareness) and then progress to intensive instruction and practice in the fundamentals of reading, with a strong emphasis on phonics and decoding skills. Brain imaging studies that have compared children with dyslexia who receive this type of instruction to those who do not suggest that it may even be possible to re-wire the dyslexic brain to process written language as a nondyslexic brain would. There is actually scientific evidence that it is possible to change the brain of a child with dyslexia through appropriate, high-quality education!

Overcoming Dyslexia: The (Not So Secret) Secret to Success

Early recognition and intensive, high-quality instruction provided by experienced, creative, and well-trained teachers is the key to successfully overcoming dyslexia or any other learning disability.

Many excellent reading curricula incorporate the key elements of a successful reading program (information about evidence-based reading programs and interventions for dyslexia is available at http://www.nationalreadingpanel.org). More important than the program itself is the involvement of an experienced teacher with specific training in providing high-quality reading instruction.

Language-Based Learning Disabilities

Children with dyslexia generally have good reading comprehension when they can get past their decoding problems. They typically have well-developed verbal skills and can easily understand complex, abstract language. By contrast, many children who struggle academically have problems with reading comprehension, verbal expression, and abstract or complex language. These children often have trouble with what is referred to in academic circles as the *English language arts* (reading, spelling, writing, and literature). Many of these children have a history of speech and language delays, and typically they have had difficulties with both expressive (speech) and receptive (comprehension) aspects of language (see Chapter 1). Although these children often have better developed abilities in areas not related to language (e.g., visuospatial skills, eye–hand coordination, math), their language difficulties tend to have an impact on their ability to function in most academic areas. This pattern of disability is described by the term *language-based learning disability*. Language-based learning disabilities as a group are probably the most common type of learning disability and are among the most complex to characterize and to design interventions for. Every child with a language-based learning disability has a unique pattern of learning strengths and weaknesses that must be dealt with on its own terms. As with dyslexia, early recognition and the involvement of experienced, creative, and well-trained teachers is the key to helping these children.

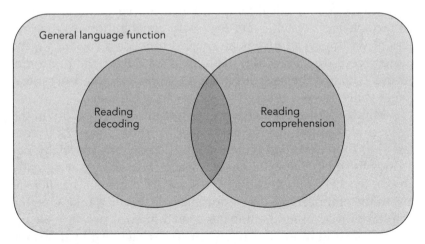

Figure 6.3. Language-based learning disabilities. Children with dyslexia have problems decoding what they read but have good reading comprehension and good general language skills. Children with reading comprehension difficulties mainly have problems inferring meaning from written material and have variable degrees of decoding and general language dysfunction. Children with broad-based language-based learning disabilities have difficulties with most forms of reading, writing, and verbal expression and comprehension.

Disabilities of Writing and Written Expression

Damian is a third grader whose handwriting is "atrocious," as his mother describes it. He is an excellent student, although a little distractible at times, and his teacher and parents notice that he has an unfortunate tendency to rush through things and that he is prone to careless mistakes. His teacher says that when he applies himself he is quite capable of printing neatly, but he generally needs prompting to do this, and the word *lazy* has come up in descriptions of his approach to writing. Damian is actually very creative and excels at telling stories; on a few occasions he has used a computer to type out a story successfully. His parents are a little surprised that his writing has improved a bit since he was introduced to cursive, but they wonder whether this positive development will last.

Writing is a complex activity involving the concerted and coordinated application of multiple skills involving eye–hand coordination, fine motor control, language processing and output, word analysis and production, and planning and sequencing. How people write is very much like how a symphony orchestra performs a piece of music. Just as the strings, woodwinds, brass, and percussion sections all make their unique contributions to the performance of a musical composition, multiple areas of the brain all provide their specific and necessary contributions to the process of writing. And just as an orchestra needs a conductor, the writer needs direction from the brain's conductor, the prefrontal cortex, which is the seat of planning, sequencing, and organizational skills (known collectively as *executive functions*).

Minor writing problems are very common, especially in the early grades, and a surprising number of adults are quick to confess that they have bad handwriting (doctors are especially notorious for this!). Expectations for neat handwriting vary greatly among teachers, and the advent of the word processor has helped lessen the emphasis on the importance of legibility. Likewise, the emphasis on accurate spelling has been diluted as people have become more and more dependent on spell-check. And yet despite the ubiquitous presence of computers in people's lives, writing (with pen or pencil) is still an essential work and life skill. There is also good evidence in education research that accuracy in spelling is correlated to competence in reading and writing generally and that reading, spelling, and writing tend to reinforce one another. In other words, poor spellers are often poor readers and writers, and vice versa.

For some children writing is an excessively difficult and laborious process. Children with writing difficulties tend to fall into one of three groups. For the first group of children, the main difficulty relates to the mechanics of writing. These children may have an odd or inefficient pencil grasp and may find it exceedingly difficult to write legibly. Some of these children may have trouble drawing and coloring as well, and some may have more general difficulties with fine motor skills (e.g., they may struggle with using scissors or utensils and may find it awkward to use buttons and zippers). Children with this type of writing problem are said to have weak graphomotor skills or dysgraphia (some experts use the term *dysgraphia* to describe all types of writing disability, however).

For the second group of children, the main difficulty is with expressing themselves in writing or getting their thoughts down on paper. Many of these children are quite good at expressing themselves verbally but seem to have a glitch or disconnect when it comes to getting their thoughts from their brain to the paper. Many other children, especially those with language-based learning disabilities, have more general difficulties with language expression, and writing problems are just one manifestation of this. Children with these types of writing difficulties are said to have a disorder of written expression.

For the third group of children a combination of graphomotor and expressive deficits is evident. The relative contribution of mechanical and expressive difficulties varies greatly, and interventions to address the struggles that these children have with writing must be customized to their specific pattern of ability and disability.

Given how common these problems are, it can be difficult to determine when it is appropriate to describe a writing problem as a disability. Damian's story is a case in point. He is generally doing well in school, but writing has been his downfall. He seems to be able to express himself well verbally and shows evidence of being able to express himself in writing under the right conditions (e.g., being able to use a word processor seems to allow him to bypass the issue he has with pencil-and-paper writing). He does have weak graphomotor skills, but under some circumstances he can write neatly, as when he uses cursive. (Although cursive is very difficult for some children, a surprising number prefer it.) His primary difficulty seems to be with organization and implementation, issues that frequently come to a head in third grade. Although many children such as Damian seem to be able to work through these issues with practice and proper instruction, some have persistent difficulties that affect multiple aspects of their schoolwork and thus are properly described as having a writing disability.

Children with significant writing disabilities can become very frustrated and discouraged about school. Every day their difficulties are on full display for their teachers, parents, and classmates to see. They are greeted daily with reminders of their problem in the form of red-ink corrections on homework and class assignments; comments about sloppiness, messiness, and the need to apply themselves; and the not infrequent implication of laziness. Indeed, these children often do try to avoid or rush through writing assignments, but this is an understandable reaction to their disability rather than the cause of it. There almost seems to be a form of discrimination at work here: Children with other types of learning disability are recognized more readily as needing help, whereas children with writing disabilities are more often blamed for their problem! Writing is hard work for most children, and many need some gentle nudging to keep them on track with their writing assignments. But it is important for parents and teachers to balance reasonable expectations against an awareness that some children have serious writing challenges that require recognition and remediation.

Math Disability

Children have trouble with math for many different reasons. Children with language-based learning disabilities may have trouble with math because of their reading difficulties (especially when they have to deal with word problems). Children who are easily distracted as a consequence of attention-deficit/hyperactivity disorder (ADHD) may find it difficult to focus enough to work through problems that have several steps (see Chapter 5). Children with writing difficulties may get lost in the tangle of calculations and erasures that multiply as they grapple with pencil and paper. Other children seem to have specific difficulties with different aspects of math itself. These children are said to have a specific math disability (also referred to as *dyscalculia*), analogous to specific reading disability. In practice it is very difficult to distinguish children with a pure math learning disability from those with math learning problems secondary to other issues. This is because math is actually not a single subject or process but an amalgam of several related learning activities that focus on the manipulation of numbers, symbols, and geometric objects. A particular child may have trouble with some aspects of math more than other depending on the nature of his learning disability. Several mathematical domains offer challenges for particular children.

Math Facts

Some children have trouble learning basic number and math facts. They may be delayed in learning to count and recognize numbers and may have difficulties remembering basic facts of addition, subtraction, multiplication, and division. They are overly reliant on finger counting and the use of other tangible items to help them through these activities. Calculators are a godsend for these children! (But of course the good teacher and conscientious parent will want to work with the child, giving him or her extra practice to master these facts.)

Math Computation

Many children who struggle with basic math facts, and some who do not, have difficulties with the intricacies of arithmetic computation. Complex sequential operations involving carrying, borrowing, place holding, and sign recognition (e.g., adding versus subtracting) befuddle many novice mathematicians. Children with trouble organizing activities and staying focused through several steps in a sequential calculation may have trouble with this aspect of math (this is often a problem area for children with ADHD). What is surprising is that children who struggle with math computation may do well with higher forms of math that are more oriented toward concepts; trouble with math computation does not necessarily translate into poor general math ability.

Math Language

Math involves the use of both symbols and language. Children with difficulties dealing with abstract language, such as children with language-based learning disability, often have trouble with this aspect of math. These children may do fairly well with basic math facts and computation, but they struggle with word problems and often have difficulty with concept-oriented, higher order math. These children are often visual learners and benefit from the use of visual prompts, diagrams, and concrete materials to help them see the problem and its potential solution.

Visuospatial Math

A small percentage of children with math difficulties exhibit a learning profile that is almost the mirror-image opposite of the pattern seen in children with language-based learning disability. These children often have well-developed language and verbal skills but have trouble with eye–hand coordination, body awareness, and the perception of spatial relations. These children are auditory learners: They learn best through verbal instruction and struggle mightily with visual materials, diagrams, geometric representations, and pencil-and-paper tasks. Some of these children seem to have poor number sense (analogous to poor phonemic awareness in children with dyslexia), which can be characterized as a basic lack of awareness of the meaning of numbers and the quantities and comparisons they represent. This type of learning difficulty, though making up only a fraction of math learning disabilities, probably comes closest to representing a specific math learning disability in the sense that dyslexia represents a specific reading disability.

Nonverbal Learning Disabilities

Children with visuospatial math problems overlap with a group of children with a broader array of learning, cognitive, and social difficulties referred to as *nonverbal learning disabilities.* Like children with visuospatial math disability, these children tend to have well-developed verbal skills but often have trouble with the social aspects of communication, especially conversation skills (see the discussion of pragmatic language skills in Chapter 1). They often have difficulties with spatial relationships, eye–hand coordination, and visual-motor tasks (e.g., puzzles), and many in fact show evidence of a visuospatial math disability. Most notably, children with nonverbal learning disabilities have a particular cognitive style that characterizes their approach to learning. They are very good at rote memorization and often remember facts and figures with extraordinary accuracy, but they may have trouble working with concepts and understanding things in context. They tend to be black and white in their thinking, do not do well with ambiguities or gray areas, and tend to take things very literally (e.g., the expression "he was hot under the collar" might be taken to mean that someone had a sweaty neck). Sometimes this cognitive rigidity extends to other areas of these children's lives and can complicate social interactions. It has often been observed that children with Asperger syndrome (see Chapter 4) have a similar cognitive profile to that seen in children with nonverbal learning disabilities, and children with nonverbal learning disabilities often have traits, such as social difficulties, weaknesses with pragmatic language, and obsessive tendencies, reminiscent of those seen in children with Asperger syndrome.

Intellectual Disability

Rose is a 6-year-old girl who has always been late in acquiring developmental milestones. She started walking at 20 months of age and is still uncoordinated (she struggles with pedaling a tricycle and stops with both feet on each step when she is climbing or descending stairs). She did not start to talk until after 2 years of age and did not use sentences until just recently. Her grammar is still inconsistent, she is hard to understand, and she cannot hold a sustained conversation, although she does fairly well complying with simple commands when she is paying attention. She depends on help from her parents for many self-care activities. She still needs to be reminded to use a spoon and a fork (both of which are awkward for her), and she cannot use a knife for buttering or cutting. She is able to get undressed by herself but still has trouble getting dressed and cannot manage buttons or zippers. She was toilet trained at age 5.

Rose has just started kindergarten and receives therapy and special education support in an inclusive classroom. (In this type of classroom, typical children and children with special needs are together in the same classroom.) She knows basic colors and shapes, she can count to 7, and she can recognize some of the letters in her name, but she does not recognize most letters and numbers despite adequate instruction and exposure. Her parents describe her as happy and playful, but they see her as being immature in her interests and abilities; in fact, they say that she acts more like her 3-year-old cousin than her 6-year-old peers.

The school psychologist recently completed a psychoeducational evaluation that included an IQ or intelligence test that yielded a full-scale score of 58. Rose's mother completed a questionnaire about Rose's daily living skills, and the standard scores derived from this questionnaire were in the 50s and low 60s. The psychologist explained that average scores on these tests are usually in the 90s or low 100s and that Rose's scores are in the clinically significant or deficient range and are indicative of a mild cognitive or mental deficiency. When Rose's parents brought this information to their pediatrician they were shocked to learn that these results are consistent with a mild form of intellectual disability (formerly *mental retardation*). They felt that the tests must be wrong: They told the doctor that although they recognized that Rose is a slow learner, she is clearly making progress and, although immature, she seems perfectly happy and normal.

Mental retardation is a widely disliked and misunderstood term. It was originally intended to characterize significantly below average intellectual functioning (prominent learning problems in multiple areas) associated with significant deficits in adaptive behavior (impairments in daily living skills, including self-care, communication, social skills, and academic or work skills). The term has unfortunately developed a bad reputation; it is often (inappropriately) used in a pejorative manner and is misunderstood to automatically imply atypical physical and behavioral traits. For these reasons, *intellectual disability* has been promoted to replace *mental retardation* as the preferred diagnosis for people with generalized, significant impairments of cognition and adaptive function. Although *intellectual disability* has gained traction among professionals who work with people with disabilities, it is not widely known to the general public, and *mental retardation* is still fairly well entrenched in the language of the law and public education. It is hoped that with time the newer term will replace the older one as a much more appropriate, much less stigmatizing description of this form of disability.

RECOGNIZING INTELLECTUAL DISABILITY AND LEARNING DISABILITY

Although it is important to recognize intellectual disability and learning disability as early as possible, it often takes several years before a definitive diagnosis can be made. While it should be possible to diagnose (or at least suspect) intellectual disability by the preschool years, subtle learning disabilities are often not diagnosed until well into a child's elementary school years.

Global Developmental Delay and Intellectual Disability in Young Children

The thing that most distinguishes Rose from Matt, Marla, Jeff, and Damian is the fact that whereas these other children have fairly specific problems in relatively discrete areas of learning, Rose has generalized or global learning problems that affect both her academic functioning and daily living skills. In fact, many children who are initially described or diagnosed as having global developmental delay are later recognized as having intellectual disability. It can be very difficult or impossible to diagnose intellectual disability in very young children for several reasons. IQ testing is not a fully reliable indicator of learning potential in very young children, and IQ does not stabilize until a child is school age, so a low IQ in a toddler or preschooler may change when the child is retested in grade school.

It is also very easy to underestimate a very young child's learning potential because of confounding factors. For example, many children born prematurely have prominent delays in motor skills, especially during the first 2 years of life. These delays affect the development of adaptive skills and may negatively affect the performance of problem-solving tasks (e.g., puzzles) that are often included in tests of intelligence. Likewise, children with autism spectrum disorders often perform poorly on standardized tests because of an inability to imitate or to understand that an examiner intends them to respond to a test item in a particular way.

Intellectual disability, although often suspected in globally delayed toddlers and preschoolers, is often not officially diagnosed until the child is school age. In place of an intelligence quotient (IQ), a developmental quotient is often used to characterize younger children with global developmental delay. The developmental quotient is defined as follows:

Developmental Quotient = Developmental Age/Chronological Age

For example, if Rose's overall abilities are estimated as being equivalent to those of a typical 3-year-old, then her developmental quotient would be 3 years divided by 6 years, or 0.50 (50%). In other words, based on this estimate, Rose is developing at about 50% of the expected rate. Another way of characterizing global developmental delay is to indicate the difference between the developmental and chronological ages. For example, Rose could be described as being 3 years behind her peers (6 years minus 3 years). Although this is a more intuitive way to characterize delay, it can be misleading as a way of tracking delay over time. For example, a 3-year-old with a developmental age of 1 year and a 7-year-old with a developmental age of 5 years are both 2 years behind, but the 3-year-old (with a developmental quotient of 0.33) is developing at a much slower rate than the 7-year-old (with a developmental quotient of 0.71). In general, the lower the developmental quotient during the toddler, preschool, and early school years (especially if it is consistently below 0.50 or 50%), the more likely it is that a child will eventually qualify as having an intellectual disability.

Characterizing Learning and Intellectual Disabilities in Older Children and Adults

When children reach school age, developmental quotients become less useful as a way of tracking developmental delays and learning problems, and it becomes preferable to characterize ability and progress with the use of standardized tests. The most important and widely used are tests of intelligence, achievement, and adaptive behavior. IQ tests measure learning ability or potential, achievement tests measure academic performance (reading, math, spelling, and writing), and tests of adaptive behavior measure functional independence with daily living skills. Results are most often reported as standard scores (see Figure 6.4).

Children with specific, well-circumscribed learning disabilities such as dyslexia typically have average (or better) results on tests of IQ and adaptive function but score poorly on those portions of achievement tests related to their specific learning disability. Children with intellectual disability demonstrate significantly below average scores in all three areas (with standard scores below 70). Children with complex learning disabilities (e.g., language-based learning disability) demonstrate below average or significantly below average scores in their weakest areas but usually demonstrate average or below average scores in other areas, with significant variability across tests and among subtests. Children with intellectual disability demonstrate significantly below average scores in all three areas (with standard scores below

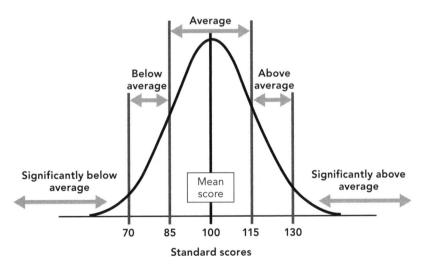

Figure 6.4. Standardized tests and the bell-shaped curve. Standardized tests (e.g., IQ or intelligence tests) compare a child's scores with the scores of other children the same age. Most children fall in the average range (on most psychoeducational tests, 100 is the mean or average score, and the average range is 85–115). Some children are above average (115–130) or below average (70–85). About 2%–3% of children are significantly above average (above 130), and a similar percentage are significantly below average (below 70). On IQ tests, > 130 is referred to as the *superior range* and < 70 is referred to as the *deficient range*.

70). Occasionally children straddle the divide between learning disability and intellectual disability, with some scores above 70 and some below 70; these children are sometimes described as having a borderline intellectual disability.

Among children with intellectual disability, the degree of disability is often classified relative to IQ and adaptive behavior scores, as follows:

Mild intellectual disability: IQ and adaptive levels 55–70

Moderate intellectual disability: IQ and adaptive levels 40–55

Severe intellectual disability: IQ and adaptive levels 25–40

Profound intellectual disability: IQ and adaptive levels below 25

These levels correlate roughly—but only roughly—with long-term prognosis. People with mild intellectual disability can often learn to read, write, and perform basic math operations; can learn to live independently; and are capable of holding down a job and, in some instances, raising a family. People with moderate intellectual disability may be able to learn very basic academic skills, but their education is generally focused on developing maximum independence with daily living skills, and they usually need a moderate level of assistance and supervision at home and in work activities as adults. People with severe intellectual disability need more intense support and supervision, although they can learn basic communication and self-care skills, and people with profound intellectual disability are generally nonverbal and totally dependent for all aspects of their care.

The Numbers Game: The Educational Classification of Learning and Intellectual Disabilities

Jasmine is a friendly, eager-to-please 9-year-old girl in third grade who has consistently struggled in school. Her parents help her get through her homework, and she has been lucky to have excellent, caring teachers who have tried to give her extra consideration in the classroom. But despite everyone's best efforts, Jasmine continues to fall further and further behind her classmates in all of her subjects. She was referred to her school district special education team and underwent standardized testing. She was found to have a full-scale IQ of 81, and achievement testing (which assessed reading, math, and spelling) yielded scores in the 70s. The special education team indicated that although Jasmine's academic skills are significantly below average, they are consistent with her below average IQ results and thus she does not qualify for special education services. Her parents were bewildered by the reasoning behind this statement and were more bewildered still when they learned that if she had had a higher IQ, she might have qualified for services as a child with a learning disability. They could not understand how a child with a lower IQ could be considered to have less of a learning disability than a child with similar academic skills but a higher IQ.

Most children with global delays and profound to moderate levels of intellectual disability are recognized during the preschool years, and certainly by the time they reach kindergarten, as having a significant disability that merits special education support. Some children with mild to borderline intellectual disability, and many children with learning disabilities, such as Jasmine, run into difficulties qualifying for special education services. This occurs because learning disabilities have traditionally

Table 6.1. Learning disability, intellectual disability, and standardized testing

Diagnosis	Intelligence test result	Adaptive skills	Achievement test result
Dyslexia, dyscalculia, dysgraphia	Average (slight discrepancies in subtests may be evident)	Average (slight discrepancies may be evident in specific areas)	Below average or significantly below average for areas of academic difficulty; average in other areas
Language-based learning disability; nonverbal learning disability	Average to below average full-scale IQ; discrepancies may be evident, with lower verbal IQ (for language-based learning disability) or lower performance IQ (for nonverbal learning disability)	Average to below average	Below average to significantly below average for areas of academic difficulty; average to below average in other areas
Borderline intellectual disability	Below average to significantly below average	Below average to significantly below average	Below average to significantly below average
Intellectual disability	Significantly below average	Significantly below average	Significantly below average

Note: The results of standardized tests mirror a child's pattern of functional ability.

been diagnosed based on discrepancy criteria. The idea is that children with learning disabilities should have typical or average ability (IQ) associated with unexpectedly poor performance (academic achievement), whereas children with intellectual disability should have significantly below average ability and comparably low performance.

In practice the line between a learning disability and milder forms of intellectual disability is fuzzy, and a large gray area exists between children with classic discrepancy-evident learning disability and classic intellectual disability. Despite the fact that learning disability experts universally dispute the validity of the discrepancy concept and argue convincingly that children such as Jasmine have an even greater need for special education support than children with learning disability with average IQ, the discrepancy formula has become entrenched in the special education code in many states and continues to be rigidly applied, sometimes without regard to obvious difficulties that a child such as Jasmine is having in the classroom.

One possible way to address concerns about the discrepancy model is to move away from defining learning disability using standardized testing and to redefine it as an inadequate response to instruction. The response to intervention model focuses on identifying children who are at risk and providing them with gradually increasing levels of intensive instruction in small groups within the structure of the general education curriculum. Children who do not respond to this intensified instruction are then referred for testing and presumably for special education intervention. The positives of this approach are its proactive stance and focus on educational outcomes rather than test scores. The potential negatives are the variably that exists in how well the response to intervention approach is implemented and the delays inherent in a process that requires that a child must fail before he can be identified for special education services.

SPECIAL EDUCATION FOR CHILDREN WITH LEARNING OR INTELLECTUAL DISABILITY

Children with learning or intellectual disabilities usually require special education support (a detailed discussion of special education can be found in Chapter 7). Typically a child in need of special education services is evaluated by his or her home school district (or other regional or local entities charged with this responsibility under state law), and through this process it is determined whether he or she qualifies for services based on state-specific criteria. An individualized education program is written—ideally as a collaborative process between family members and school personnel—that details the classroom environment and services suitable to the child's needs as well as specific goals for education and therapy.

There is a strong emphasis on providing these services in the least restrictive educational environment. This means that all other things being equal, a child should be in the most typical classroom possible that is still able to accommodate his special needs. Most children with mild to moderate learning disabilities are based in a general classroom and either they are "pulled out" to work with a special education teacher or therapist or the teachers and therapists "push in" to the classroom to work with them individually or in a group. Students with more severe learning disabilities or mild intellectual disability may require more intensive support. They may receive most of their academic instruction in a self-contained special education classroom but still have opportunities to be mainstreamed with other students, especially for nonacademic subjects (e.g., music, art, physical education; often referred to as *specials*). In some instances, children with more severe forms of intellectual disability may not be able to benefit from a typical classroom environment and may receive services in a classroom devoted entirely to children with special needs.

504 Plans

Children who do not qualify for special education services under an individualized education program may qualify for a 504 plan, which is based on broader definitions of disability and has more liberal inclusion criteria (see Chapter 7 for a detailed discussion). Although 504 plans formalize special accommodations, modifications, and adaptations of the educational program and classroom environment, they do not typically provide special education or related services such as therapy. A 504 plan, though easier to obtain than an individualized education program, may not meet the needs of children with significant learning disabilities.

Many schools increasingly offer inclusive classrooms that are structured to seamlessly integrate general education and special education services. Though difficult to implement, these programs offer many advantages to both typical students and those with special needs by balancing the provision of services with the advantages of a more typical social classroom environment.

HOW TO HELP YOUR CHILD WITH A LEARNING DISABILITY

As the parent of a child with learning difficulties, you are in a unique position to help your child to grow and prosper despite his special challenges. You do this both through your interactions with teachers, therapists, and the education system and even more so through the help and encouragement you provide to your child daily.

Being an Advocate for Your Child

If you are the parent of a child with a learning or intellectual disability, you will frequently find yourself in the position of having to advocate for your child's best interests. Teachers, school systems, and special education programs would ideally always be geared toward providing for the needs of your child, but in reality teachers vary in their skills and experience, school systems are constantly struggling with budgets and resources, and special education programs vary in their philosophies and effectiveness. There may be times when your child's best interests and the interests of the educational system clash and your role as an advocate will be put to the test. The following are keys to being a good advocate for your child:

- Do your homework. Know what your child needs and know the services available in your school system and community to meet those needs.
- Communicate effectively with teachers, psychologists, and other key players in the educational system who are involved in assessing your child's needs and designing and implementing interventions.

- In all of your dealings, treat others respectfully and convey your confidence that they have your child's best interests at heart. People have a natural inclination to want to live up to such positive expectations—your belief in their good intentions increases the probability that they will have good intentions. (This is human nature: If we are viewed positively by someone, we do not want to let them down.)

- Trust your own judgment. If you feel that the classroom placement or services being offered are not well suited for your child—or if you believe a needed service is not being offered—believe in your judgment and stick to your guns. This can be very hard to do, especially when you are faced with experts at dealing with learning problems in children. The thing to remember is that although these people have their professional expertise, *no one has more expertise on the characteristics and needs of your child than you!*

Helping at Home

Helping your child establish a consistent homework routine and becoming an effective homework coach are very important ways you can help your child at home. Every child works differently; some need a break after they get home from school before starting on homework, whereas others do best when they jump into their homework as soon as they get off the bus. Most children do best in a quiet, nondistracting environment; others do best sitting at the kitchen table in the middle of all the action. The key is to establish a routine and stick to it. As a homework coach it is important to remember that helping with your child's homework and doing your child's homework are two different things: If your child is unable to do his homework fairly independently and in a reason-

Learning Centers versus Individual Tutoring

Learning centers are private enterprises that offer supplemental educational services. These services are often marketed to parents of children with learning disabilities with claims (unsupported by research) of dramatically improving academic performance. The quality of these programs varies considerably; parents tend to report greater satisfaction with individual tutoring.

able amount of time, you should contact his teacher to discuss whether modifications to the homework may be warranted.

Some parents will consider supplementing their child's educational services outside of school hours by hiring a tutor. Private tutors are usually teachers who are paid on a fee-for-service basis, and most often they are identified by word of mouth (they are often special education teachers who have previously worked with a child). Tutoring can be especially helpful if you find that you and your child are getting frustrated with each other as you attempt to help her with her schoolwork. The advantages of tutoring must be balanced against your child's need for downtime and the expense of hiring the tutor (which may be substantial).

The Power of Believing

It is hard to be the parent of a child with a learning problem, and harder still be a child who struggles to learn. As a parent you will likely spend countless hours helping your child through homework, meeting with teachers, and consulting experts, and there will be times when you become frustrated: frustrated with the school, frustrated with your child, frustrated with yourself. You will sometimes get confused about your role—should you be your child's tutor, counselor, coach, friend, taskmaster, or something else? Your child will likewise experience intense frustration and confusion. He will face constant reminders of his deficits and deficiencies, and he will not understand why he cannot learn when his peers find it so easy to succeed. He may think that he is stupid and may experience the emotional and behavioral consequences of that negative self-perception. Children are remarkably resilient, but in the face of so many challenges and the constant experience of negativity, even the most exuberant attitude will eventually erode. All children, but most of all children with learning disabilities, need to feel that they are capable and competent human beings. And yet in so many ways, the cards are stacked against children with learning disabilities.

The only answer to all of this frustration, confusion, and negativity is the power of belief. As a parent you must learn to believe in yourself, and you must learn to believe in your child, so that he can come to believe in himself. No one else can do this for your child as well as you can. Many children are blessed with excellent, caring teachers who believe in them and help them to believe in themselves. But teachers come and go, and classrooms and schools change. You are the constant in your child's life. You know your child, you know what makes him special, and you are in the best position to help him discover his special abilities so that he can eventually find his niche in life. Believing in your child may seem obvious, something that is assumed, automatic, given—"Of course I believe in my child," you say to yourself. "I'm his mother. I'm his father. How else should I feel?"

But it is not always so easy and automatic. Some parents of children with learning disabilities find it difficult to see the positive in their children. They focus entirely on fixing the problem: remediating the reading deficit, practicing math, drilling spelling lists, getting a tutor, advocating for more services, encouraging their child, pushing their child, getting frustrated with their child—and sometimes feeling like they want to give up on their child. If you are taking this approach, you may inadvertently be reinforcing your child's sense that he is a substandard human being. The only remedy to this is your belief. You must look hard and deep, find what about your child you believe in, and tell him what you believe again and again until he believes it too. If you do not do this for your child, who will? What you discover may not be what you originally wished or imagined for your child when he was born; it may be something better! Help your child discover what he is good at and what he loves to do, encourage him to work hard and believe that he is capable of great things, and he will prove you right!

SUMMARY

What to Do if Your Child Has Trouble Learning

Here is a reminder of some of the basic steps to consider taking if you suspect that your child has a learning problem (see Figure 6.5):

Step 1: Provide early intervention support if your child is showing developmental delays before age 3 (see Chapter 7). Developmental delays in infants and toddlers may be an early sign of learning or intellectual disability.

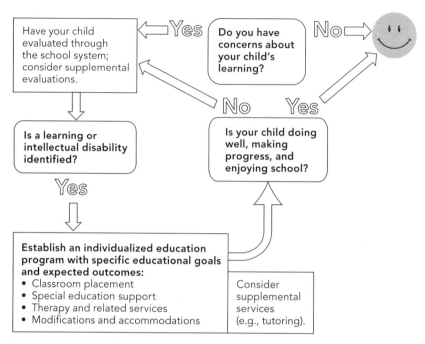

Figure 6.5. Action plan for a child with learning difficulties.

Step 2: Become a strong advocate for your child within the educational system, and have him or her evaluated by the regional entity (typically your child's home school district) responsible for determining eligibility for special education support.

Step 3: Collaborate with the special education team to establish a special education plan (e.g., an individualized education program).

Step 4: Maintain close contact and regular communication with teachers and therapists about your child's progress.

Step 5: Seek out additional evaluations and services outside of the educational system based on your child's specific needs and your particular concerns (e.g., behavioral or medical concerns that may be associated with your child's learning difficulties).

Step 6: In some cases, consider supplemental tutoring for your child.

7

When Your Child Needs Extra Help

Understanding How to Help When Your Child Has a Disability

- -

"He's just a boy; boys always develop more slowly."

"Uncle Joe didn't talk until he
was 3 years old, and he turned out fine."

"You're not being strict enough.
That's why your child doesn't behave."

"Everyone learns at a different pace.
Just give it time and she'll catch up."

- -

When your child has developmental delays, or has behavior difficulties, or is struggling in school, or does not interact with other children well, or is physically uncoordinated, you may find it difficult to get helpful advice about how best to help your child. Well-meaning friends and relatives may be helpful, but just as often parents receive suggestions and advice—often unsolicited—that is sometimes less than helpful. This chapter offers some (I hope helpful!) suggestions and advice for identifying supportive services, resources, and interventions that will truly help you and your child.

SOURCES OF HELP

You are an essential resource for your child, but rely on friends and family, as well as your child's doctor, for advice about your child.

You

As a loving and involved parent, *you* are the most important resource available to help your child. No one on the planet knows and understands your child better than you. No one else has listened to your child, observed your child's behavior, watched your child's interactions, played with your child, taught your child, or encouraged your child to try new things as often or as well as you have. And no one is better qualified to raise concerns if something seems wrong in the way your child is developing. Do not allow others to dismiss your concerns. Seek out help and support from those who listen to your concerns and take them seriously. Trust the unassailable truth that you are the ultimate expert on your child.

Family and Friends

When you suspect, or have confirmed, that your child has a disability, it is important to seek out the support of family and friends, but do so carefully. Most parents find that people who are supportive and nonjudgmental are most helpful. Relatives and friends who listen to your concerns, offer suggestions and advice when you ask for it, and offer practical help and support (e.g., babysitting to give you a break, or going with you to medical appointments for your child) are your natural allies in your efforts to help your child. Relatives and friends who try to take control, tell you what you should do, or deny that there is a problem are usually less helpful. A family expert, someone who may have some personal or professional experience with developmental disabilities, can be very helpful, but there can be a downside to relying on this person for support. A relative or friend who takes on the role of expert may have a tendency to be overly directive or paternalistic, or even pushy, in his or her advice. Recognize also that the family expert may be ambivalent about giving advice. As a doctor, I know that giving family members and friends medical advice is very different than giving advice to my patients and their families. I often worry that my advice will be taken the wrong way or may have a negative impact on my relationship with that person. It is often best to keep professional roles and family and friendship roles separate.

Your Child's Doctor

Your child's primary care doctor can be an invaluable resource in helping you to confirm developmental problems, diagnose specific developmental disabilities, and identify resources to help your child. Pediatricians and family practitioners are usually very attuned to developmental concerns and incorporate questions and observations of your child's development into each routine (well-child) visit. The American Academy of Pediatrics has specific guidelines about how primary care physicians should monitor young children for developmental concerns. Developmental surveillance, or the routine practice of asking questions about and making observations of a child's developmental progress, is recommended for every well-child visit. The administration of specific developmental screening tests is also recommended. These tests are typically questionnaires administered to parents or formal observations of developmental skills made by a child's doctor. The American Academy of Pediatrics recommends that a screening test for general developmental problems be administered to all children at 9, 18, and 30 months (or 24 months if a child is not seen for a routine visit at 30 months). A screening test should also be administered at any age if the surveillance process raises any concerns. The American

jargon buster

Developmental Surveillance and Screening

Developmental surveillance: The ongoing process of assessing a child's developmental progress though questions and observations that are typically incorporated into the structure of each well-child visit

Developmental screening: The administration of a specific developmental screening instrument (e.g., a parent questionnaire or a structured observation of developmental skills), which yields a pass or fail grade (a failed test triggers rescreening or further assessment)

Developmental assessment: The process of formally evaluating a child with a suspected developmental disability

Academy of Pediatrics also recommends administering a specific screening test for autism spectrum disorders at 18 and 24 months (see Chapter 4). If a child fails a screening test, he or she should be referred for formal assessment, which is often carried out by professionals who specialize in developmental assessment and diagnosis. Even if a child passes a screening test, the child's doctor always has the option of pursuing further testing and assessment based on his or her clinical judgment that a problem exists.

Primary care doctors typically see thousands of children in the course of their careers and become keenly aware of the enormous variability in typical child development. Not all children develop in the same way, and mild, transient lags in specific areas of development are common. Likewise, all children have strengths and weaknesses, and it is overly optimistic to expect that all children will be good at everything they do. A doctor's experience with and perspective on this variability can be very helpful when you are trying to see your child's developmental differences in a larger context. But there is a pitfall in this for doctors and families. When a child has more significant developmental concerns there may be a temptation to wait and see in the hopes that the delay will prove to be transient and the child will outgrow the problem. The wait-and-see approach is a gamble, a throw of the dice, and it is often a mistake. Especially given the evidence of the importance of early intervention (EI), it is better to err on the side of caution and formally assess a concern and intervene in a timely fashion.

Wait and See:
A Throw of the Dice

seeds

Developmental concerns should be taken seriously, assessed appropriately, and addressed promptly. Taking a wait-and-see approach to a developmental concern is a throw of the dice, a gamble that the problem will go away on its own. It may represent a lost opportunity for early intervention with the potential for long-term adverse consequences.

GETTING A
DIAGNOSIS

Diagnosing a developmental disability is not as straightforward as diagnosing an ear infection or a rash. Very often parents notice subtle problems very early, but a definitive diagnosis is not made for several months or even years. A 6-month-old may not roll over yet but is able to maintain a sitting posture. An 8-month-old may not make eye contact or smile consistently but seems interested in people and is appropriately anxious around strangers. A 12-month-old may not babble or try to say "mama" or "dada" but seems to understand most of what is said to him. An 18-month-old may not play with toys but says a number of words and likes to look at pictures in books. In very young children especially it may take some time to determine whether subtle inconsistencies in early development will work themselves out or turn out to be the first signs of a developmental disability. Figure 7.1 shows the fairly wide range of ages when particular diagnoses tend to become apparent. In general, children with more severe developmental problems are diagnosed at a younger age; this is especially true of the more severe forms of cerebral palsy, intellectual disability, and autism. Some conditions, such as learning disability, are not recognized until a child is in school, although suspicions may arise as early as preschool. Other conditions, such as attention-deficit/hyperactivity disorder (ADHD), may be strongly suspected at an early age (witness the extraordinarily hyperactive, impulsive preschooler who gets kicked out of multiple nursery schools because of out-of-control behavior) but cannot be confirmed until a child is 5 or 6 years of age, by which time maturation should have corrected any typical variations in the development of behavior control.

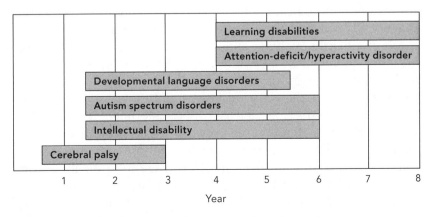

Figure 7.1. Ages when developmental disabilities are typically diagnosed.

In still other cases a diagnosis of something is suspected at an early age but only through a long process of observation and assessment involving multiple individuals, including family members, parents of children with similar disabilities, and a variety of professionals, does the nature of that diagnosis emerge. For example, a preschooler with unusual, obsessive interests and precocious reading skills may seem fairly social and communicative, but as the demands and expectations for social skills and conversation increase with age (typically by the early elementary grades), the features of the child's Asperger syndrome finally surface.

The professionals involved with diagnosing developmental disabilities are many and varied. Most often medical professionals are involved with making or confirming the diagnosis of a developmental disability. Primary care doctors vary in their level of comfort with diagnosing specific disabilities and may refer a child to a specialist to establish or confirm a diagnosis. These specialists are most often pediatricians who have had additional training in developmental and behavior disorders in children (known variously as *developmental, developmental-behavioral, behavioral,* or *neurodevelopment disabilities pediatricians*), neurologists with special training in pediatric neurological disorders (child neurologists), or psychiatrists with specific training and expertise in psychiatric disorders in children (child psychiatrists). A major problem in many regions of the country is a lack of these specialists, who tend to congregate in metropolitan areas and at academic medical centers.

Many nonmedical professionals are closely involved in the diagnostic process as well. School psychologists and special educators frequently evaluate children for learning disabilities and are often involved in assessing other disorders such as ADHD and autism spectrum disorders. Clinical psychologists and neuropsychologists have doctoral-level training and are especially well qualified to diagnose a variety of developmental disabilities, particularly those that involve learning, cognition, and social disability. Speech-language pathologists diagnose and characterize the various disorders of speech and language and contribute critical information about the language components of many other developmental disabilities. Physical and occupational therapists assess children for a variety of motor and sensory disorders and provide invaluable information about a child's motor-planning skills, mobility, and adaptive functioning. Indeed, some localities are fortunate to have interdisciplinary teams of professionals who pool their talents and expertise, offering multifaceted assessments and diagnostic evaluations. These programs are few and far between and have become less common because few insurance companies cover their comprehensive but expensive assessments.

GETTING HELP: EARLY INTERVENTION

When you suspect that your child has a developmental delay or disability, the first question you may ask—"What's wrong?"—is usually followed closely by "What do I do to help?" If your child is very young (birth to age 3), the answer to this second question will usually involve referral to EI services.

EI refers to a system of services mandated by law to provide education, therapy, and related services and support for children from birth to age 3 who have confirmed developmental disabilities or substantial delays in one or more areas (including physical, cognitive, communication, social-emotional, and adaptive skills). Children who, by virtue of specific diagnoses and medical conditions (e.g., prematurity or prenatal drug exposure), are known to be at risk for developmental problems also qualify for EI services. Although EI is federally mandated, its implementation varies from state to state, and even within states there is some variability in the availability and delivery of EI services. In New York, for example, EI is administered at the county level, and services are predominantly home based rather than center based (in center-based programs, services are offered in an environment similar to a classroom or child care center). Federal regulations mandate that children who receive EI should have an individualized family service plan (IFSP), which summarizes the services and goals of the intervention. Most commonly these services include one or several types of therapy (speech, occupational, or physical therapy) but may also include special instruction (provided by a special educator), family support (often provided by a social worker), or a variety of other services (see Table 7.1). Elements of

The Individuals with Disabilities Education Act

The Individuals with Disabilities Education Act of 1990 (Public Law, or PL, 101-476) (reenacted and updated as the Individuals with Disabilities Education Improvement Act of 2004 [PL 108-446]) is a federal law that mandates and governs the provision of early intervention, special education, and related services by states to people with disabilities from birth to age 21. Part C of this law mandates early intervention services for infants and toddlers from birth to age 3; Part B mandates special education from ages 3 to 21. Related services include speech-language, occupational, and physical therapies as well an array of other activities and interventions that support the goals of special education, such as transportation; counseling; and audiology, psychological, and medical services.

EI, including Child Find (an initiative to identify children who need EI), evaluation and assessment, IFSP development, and service coordination, are free to families by law. Actual interventions such as therapy are paid for differently in different states. In New York, for example, private insurance and Medicaid can be billed for services, but there is never a direct cost to families.

EI is provided in a child's natural environments, which usually means a child's home or child care center but could also include other settings in which the child's typically developing peers would be found. Specialized facilities and classrooms, parent–child groups, family support groups, and groups devoted to providing interventions to several children at once are all potential venues for the provision of EI.

Table 7.1. Services offered through early intervention

Family education and counseling, home visits, and parent support groups
Special instruction
Speech pathology and audiology
Occupational therapy
Physical therapy
Psychological services
Service coordination
Nursing services
Nutrition services
Social work services
Vision services
Assistive technology devices and services

There are six steps to the EI process, beginning with entry into EI and ending with the transition to preschool services.

Step 1: Referring Your Child to Early Intervention

Anyone can refer a child to EI, although most often this is done by parents or primary care providers such as pediatricians or family practitioners. You will typically need to contact the local division of EI in your state (e.g., in New York EI is administered through the Department of Health at the county level, so referrals go to the county Department of Health or EI office). Information about obtaining EI in your state is now easily accessible on the Internet. All it takes is a telephone call to start the process.

Step 2: Meeting Your Service Coordinator

After your child is referred to EI you will meet with an EI representative known as a *service coordinator*. The service coordinator's job is to inform you about EI and about your legal rights to obtain (or decline) services for your child, to establish a plan to have your child evaluated for EI, to explain the IFSP, and to explain how services are paid for. The service coordinator can help with establishing an interim (temporary) IFSP if services are urgently needed and your child cannot wait to complete the formal assessment process.

Step 3: Evaluating Your Child

Your service coordinator will help to determine which members of the EI team should evaluate your child based on your expressed concerns. For example, a child with speech delays will typically be evaluated by a speech-language pathologist. Usually at least two professionals will be involved with your child's assessment, which will focus on establishing a profile of your child's physical, cognitive, communication, social-emotional, and adaptive skills. Vision and hearing screening are also performed, and pertinent health information is reviewed. Your questions and concerns are reviewed, and needs specific to your family (e.g., transportation issues) are discussed. The final outcome of the evaluation process is a written summary of the evaluation that includes a detailed review of findings and a statement about your child's eligibility for EI services. Eligibility requirements vary from state to state but typically involve a documented developmental delay of a certain magnitude in one or more areas or the presence of a diagnosis or condition known to be associated with the risk of developmental disability.

Step 4: Writing the Individualized Family Service Plan

If it is determined that your child is eligible for EI, you, your service coordinator, and members of the evaluation team will meet to draw up a detailed plan for services (the IFSP). The heart of the IFSP is the summary of goals and expected outcomes determined based on your child's and your family's needs and the specific services that will be provided to advance those goals and meet those needs. The IFSP must include descriptions of the following:

- Your child's current levels of development
- Your family's strengths, priorities, and concerns
- The services that will be provided and the duration of the services
- The natural environments in which the services will be provided
- Other services that your child needs but that are not provided by the EI (e.g., medical services)
- The outcomes expected from the services and how the outcomes will be monitored
- Respite services (e.g., temporary child care)
- A permanent service coordinator

Parents choose the permanent service coordinator, who is typically a professional whose background and experience is most relevant to their child's needs and concerns.

Step 5: Implementing and Reviewing the Individualized Family Service Plan

After services are started, the IFSP is reviewed regularly by the EI team (typically every 6 months), and adjustments to the program are made based on your child's response to the intervention and her changing needs. You are considered a key member of the EI team, and your input and consent are needed and required to ensure that your child's and family's needs are being met.

Step 6: Establishing a Transition Plan

Your child will age out of EI services when she reaches her third birthday. Some children no longer require special services or therapy after this, but many need continued intervention and support. The IFSP must include a plan for transition so that the progress made through EI will be maintained and advanced through the preschool years.

GETTING HELP: SPECIAL EDUCATION AND THE PRESCHOOL-AGE CHILD

The Individuals with Disabilities Education Improvement Act of 2004 (Public Law [PL] 108-446) the law that mandates that states provide EI services for children from birth to age 3, also mandates the provision of special education services for children after age 3. In particular, it guarantees free appropriate public education for all children with disabilities ages 3–21. State departments of education are charged with administering special education, which is implemented locally by school districts.

If your child has developmental concerns or an identified developmental disability, you can begin the process of establishing special education support for him by writing a letter to your school district requesting that he be evaluated and considered for special education services. A group of professionals within the district, typically headed by a school psychologist, is charged with evaluating children for developmental, behavioral, and learning concerns; determining eligibility for special education services; and creating an individualized education program (IEP), which is analogous to an IFSP. By law you as the child's parent are considered a key member of the team charged with developing the IEP. If your child previously received EI services, the EI team has a responsibility to help with the transition from EI to special education services.

jargon buster

Special Education

Individualized education program (IEP): A written summary of special services and accommodations for a child with special education needs based on his or her individualized goals

Free appropriate public education (FAPE): Part of the mandate of the Individuals with Disabilities Education Improvement Act of 2004 that guarantees that all children, regardless of disability, are to be educated within the public school system

Least restrictive environment (LRE): The educational setting (e.g., classroom) that is best able to provide for a child's special education needs while still affording maximum access to typical classrooms and peers

Related services: Services beyond special education that advance individualized education program goals and improve access to interventions (including therapy, classroom aides, transportation, special equipment)

Mainstreaming, integration, and inclusion: Ways of ensuring that children gain access to typical classrooms, curricula, and peers. *Mainstreaming* refers to participation in general education curricula with little or no modifications. *Integration* refers to active participation in a general education classroom, particularly to promote social interaction with typically developing peers. *Inclusion* refers to a balanced provision of services in a typical classroom environment that incorporates elements of general and special education and that

(continued)

At the preschool level, the goals and provisions of an IEP are implemented differently in different states and in different locales within states. The types of services will also vary depending on the needs of the individual child. In some school districts specialized preschool classrooms exist within the public school system to provide services. In the past these were most often geared to the exclusive provision of special education services, but a more recent trend has been to implement special education within inclusive classroom environments that incorporate typically developing children together with children with disabilities. This better serves the goal (and the specific provision of the Individuals with Disabilities Education Improvement Act of 2004 [PL 108-446]) to provide special education within the least restrictive environment appropriate to a child's educational needs. The least restrictive environment concept is intended to remedy the past error of segregating individuals with disabilities from the rest of society and resonates with the main intention of other important disability legislation, such as the Americans with Disabilities Act of 1990 (PL 101-336).

In some school districts public preschool programs are lacking and services are provided at child care centers, private preschools, or special classrooms in community centers. In some locales independent agencies provide specialized and inclusive (integrated) preschool services.

Some preschoolers who have an IEP are able to function well in general preschool settings but are in need of targeted special education or therapy services. These children may receive itinerant services, similar to the kinds of home- and center-based interventions provided through EI.

jargon buster

(continued)

includes a mix of typically developing children and children with disabilities and special needs.

Resource model: Special education instruction provided either within a general classroom (push-in services) or as one-to-one or small-group sessions outside of the general classroom (pull-out services)

Self-contained classrooms: Classrooms devoted entirely to special education instruction, characterized by their small size, increased individualized attention, and lack of typically developing children

Individualized transition plan (ITP): A specific plan for making the transition from school to the wider community that is required by law for students age 14 and older

GETTING HELP: SPECIAL EDUCATION AND THE SCHOOL-AGE CHILD

Beginning when they are in kindergarten, children with disabilities generally receive all of their educational services within programs provided by the school district, with some exceptions. Even if they have an IEP for preschool services, children are typically reassessed for special education eligibility upon entry into kindergarten. The criteria for special education support may change markedly at this point. For example, in New York a single educational designation, "preschooler with a disability," applies to all preschool-age children, even though they may qualify for this designation for a variety of reasons. For children kindergarten age and older, 13 different educational labels or designa-

Elements of the Individualized Education Program

The Individuals with Disabilities Education Improvement Act of 2004 requires that every individualized education program state the following:

- The child's current level of academic achievement and functional performance
- Measurable annual academic and functional goals
- Plans for measuring progress toward goals
- Special education services, related services and aids, and modifications the child is to receive
- The extent to which the child will participate with typically developing children in the general education classroom
- Required modifications to participation in state- or district-wide assessments of academic achievement
- The start date, duration, frequency, and location of services

tions are used, and a child must meet criteria for one of these in order to qualify for services. Some of these, such as learning disability, are defined by strict criteria related to the results of standardized cognitive and academic (achievement) tests; children who do not meet these criteria do not qualify for an IEP. Other designations, such autism, are based on diagnoses.

What is surprising is that having a diagnosis such as autism or ADHD does not automatically qualify a child to receive an IEP. School districts also look for evidence that the child's diagnosis or medical condition has had a negative impact on his educational performance—in other words, an educational disability must be evident. If a child is doing well academically he may not qualify for an IEP, even if he is having significant difficulties functioning in the classroom environment and may be at risk for developing learning problems.

If your school-age child does qualify for special education services, an IEP will be formulated that is specific to her needs. The IEP will include several components, including a description of the educational (classroom) setting, the types and frequencies of services to be provided (both special education and related services), the goals for intervention and plans for monitoring progress toward those goals, and any specific program modifications that may be required.

The Setting

As mentioned earlier, a primary goal of special education is to provide services in the least restrictive environment appropriate to a child's educational needs. In fact, most children who receive special education services under an IEP are not in a special education classroom. For example, many children are based in a general education classroom and receive push-in support. In these cases, a special education teacher may come into the classroom to work with a child individually or may have a coteaching arrangement with the general education teacher, or she may provide consultative support, working collaboratively with the classroom teacher to make adjustments to the presentation of the curriculum without making substantial changes to the curriculum itself.

The next level of support, modified general education, involves pull-out services. In this instance the child still follows the general classroom curriculum but is taken out of the classroom to work individually with a special education teacher or therapist. For example, many children receive speech therapy under this model.

If a child needs more intensive special education support, and especially if specific modifications to the academic curriculum are warranted, the child can receive resource services. The child will typically spend a designated amount of time each day in a resource room with a resource, or special education, teacher and a small group of other students who need a similar degree of support. The rest of the school day is spent in the general education classroom. This model offers a great deal of flexibility; by adjusting the amount of time in the resource room and the range of academic material covered, it is possible to meet a wide variety of special education needs while keeping the goal of serving the child in the least restrictive environment in mind.

In some instances the resource model does not provide sufficient support. For example, if it becomes apparent that a child needs to spend much more time in the resource classroom to make academic progress, seems lost or disconnected from the activities in the general classroom, or needs constant one-to-one support from an adult to participate meaningfully in educational activities or social interactions, then it may be appropriate to consider a specialized or self-contained special education classroom. The advantages of a self-contained classroom—which provides intensive, individualized educational support with fewer students and a higher teacher-to-student ratio—must be weighed against the academic and social disadvantages of being away from general education settings and activities. One way to address this is to include self-contained special education students with general education students in nonacademic activities such as music, art, and physical education (these are commonly referred to as *specials*). It is often possible to mainstream students for specific academic subjects when they have made sufficient progress. In some instances, children will have a blended program, spending part of the day in a self-contained classroom and part of the day in the general classroom, usually in the company of a one-to-one aide or teaching assistant who facilitates the process of engagement with activities in the general classroom.

In some cases children with challenging behavior are considered for placement in a self-contained classroom because of their behavior. For example, a child with ADHD who is very impulsive, who is prone to getting out of his seat or blurting out answers, and who needs frequent redirection to stay on track with classroom activities may represent a major challenge for many teachers and may be disruptive to other students. Even if he is doing well academically, there may be a temptation to place him in a more controlled, self-contained classroom. This is usually a mistake! This is counter to the philosophy of the least restrictive environment and ultimately will not be in the best interest of the child. A better solution would be to find ways to accommodate the child's difficulties so that he can function more effectively in the general education classroom. This will often involve having additional adults (typically teacher's assistants or aides) in the classroom to provide prompts, reminders, and redirection when needed. This is often a conten-

Educational Needs Should Determine Classroom Placement

The ideal classroom setting for a child should be determined primarily by his or her educational needs and goals, with the goal of offering the least restrictive or most typical classroom that is appropriate. Children should not be placed in more restrictive classrooms based on behavioral concerns alone.

tious issue because budgetary constraints make it difficult for school districts to find money to hire additional personnel.

In rare instances children will be considered for placement in highly specialized schools outside of typical public schools (either special day schools or residential programs) that offer intensive special education programs and related therapies. These programs often specialize in helping a specific population of students (e.g., teaching children with autism) and are typically considered when a child has a severe developmental disability and has not made adequate progress in public school settings. The major disadvantage of these programs is the lack of opportunities to mainstream the child or to enable him or her to integrate socially with more typically developing children. These programs are also very expensive, and school districts may be unwilling to pay for a student's tuition.

A major trend in public education has been the creation of inclusion classrooms. These are intended to be a flexible alternative to traditional models of special education. Inclusion classrooms typically blend elements of special education and general education in one setting. Classroom size is usually smaller, with a higher teacher-to-student ratio than in a typical general education classroom. Special education students (typically less the one quarter of the total number of children in the classroom) are included with a majority of typically developing students. General education and special education teachers work together as a team to create a seamless curriculum that incorporates a foundation of general education academics along with customizations based on the specific goals and modifications included in each child's IEP. Activities during the course of the day flow easily from whole-class to small-group to individual activities to accommodate varying levels of customization. Therapists frequently "push in" to the classroom to provide interventions to individuals and small groups; pull-out services are kept to a minimum.

Although it can be difficult to implement, a well-conceived, well-executed inclusion program offers many advantages for all students. Special education students receive needed support without the disruption and potential social stigma of being segregated from the general classroom; general education students benefit from the increased support and individualized attention provided by inclusion. The implementation of inclusion programs has varied greatly among states and even among school districts within the same state. In many locales, few if any inclusion classrooms exist, and those that do tend to focus on kindergarten and the early elementary grades. Fortunately, the inclusion model has been spreading steadily to higher grades and broader geographic regions, a trend that will likely continue.

The Services

The primary service offered to a child with an IEP is special education instruction provided by a special education teacher. Many children also receive related services, most commonly speech therapy, occupational therapy, or physical therapy. The duration, frequency, and location of each therapy are specified in the IEP. A number of other related services are also available, including individual counseling, consultative behavioral services, and small-group activities. Many children benefit from access to a shared classroom aide or teaching assistant; some children require a one-on-one relationship with an aide both to ensure classroom participation and to provide for their safety and, in some instances, the safety of others. Group activities are often led by a school psychologist, social worker, or guidance counselor and frequently focus on social skills, classroom independence, or organizational skills (an IEP is not necessarily required for participation in some of these activities). Other related services include the provision of special transportation, medical and nursing services, audiology services, orientation and mobility services (for children with visual impairment), recreational services, and a variety of psychological and social work services.

The Goals

The heart and soul of the IEP are annual goals and benchmarks to help monitor progress toward specific goals. In addition to academic goals, many children have specific goals for communication skills, daily living skills, mobility, social skills development, behavior control, and functional independence. Although letter grades may be used to monitor academic progress, very often progress toward goals is reported using performance criteria with gradations from "no progress" to "progress" to "goal met." Narrative descriptions provide additional detail regarding the nature of the progress and the areas that continue to be challenging. Progress is recorded at the same intervals as report cards are distributed (usually quarterly).

Accommodations, Modifications, and Adaptations

IEP goals usually represent areas of significant departure from or addition to the general education curriculum. In many instances, however, children with special education needs are able to follow the general education curriculum with modest adjustments. Accommodations are changes that improve a child's ability to obtain and engage with academic materials without substantially changing the content or instructional level of learning. For example, if the class is given an assignment to complete a list of 20 double-digit addition problems, a child may be allowed to complete 10 problems instead. Modifications involve a more significant adjustment to the curriculum (e.g., allowing a child to work on single-digit addition when the class has moved on to double-digit addition). Adaptations involve environmental and functional adjustments, such as providing preferential seating, giving extra time for tests, allowing access to a less distracting environment for selected activities, allowing the use of a laptop computer as an alternative to writing by hand, or providing specialized instructional materials for children with vision or hearing impairments. In practice the terms *accommodation, modification,* and *adaptation* tend to be used interchangeably to convey the idea of making adjustments for a particular child's needs.

ALTERNATIVES TO SPECIAL EDUCATION

Alternatives to a formal special education plan are often considered for children who are struggling in school. These interventions, which have their advantages and disadvantages, are often implemented in place of special education but may also serve as transitional strategies toward providing a child with a full special education program.

Section 504 Plans

Children who either do not need or do not qualify for an IEP may receive accommodations under what is known as a *Section 504 plan* (or simply a *504 plan*). Section 504 refers to a component of a federal civil rights law, the Rehabilitation Act of 1973 (PL 93-112), which prohibits discrimination based on disability and requires that public schools meet the needs of students with disabilities. An individual with a disability is defined broadly as a person with a mental or physical impairment that significantly limits one or more major life activities. Major life activities are also defined broadly and include activities of daily living, walking and mobility, communication, learning and academics, and a wide variety of typical basic life activities. Because Section 504 defines disability in such a general and liberal way it tends to encompass a wider variety of children than the Individuals with Disabilities Education Improvement Act of 2004 (PL 108-446), and thus it is generally easier for a child to qualify for a 504 plan than for an IEP.

The process for obtaining a 504 plan varies but generally involves contacting a school administrator, guidance counselor, or school psychologist. A team of individuals (not necessarily the same team that evaluates children for an IEP) meets, determines whether the child qualifies for a 504 plan, and begins the process of constructing the actual plan. The plan is typically a listing of accommodations that will be made for the child, similar to the accommodations, modifications, and adaptations that can be included in an IEP. Unlike the procedure for an IEP, schools are not required to respond to a parent's request for a 504 plan (although they do have a legal obligation to inform parents of their rights under the law), nor are they required to involve parents directly in creating a 504 plan, although most schools do. There is also no requirement to evaluate or formally test the child prior to drawing up a 504 plan. This makes it easier to obtain a 504 plan than an IEP, but it also means that the interventions the child will receive are much less formalized, more modest in scope, and less closely monitored with regard to outcomes. Most important, the 504 plan does not provide for special education or related services, so any child who needs these interventions will not be adequately served by a 504 plan.

Response to Intervention

Strictly speaking, response to intervention is not considered an alternative to special education but an approach to general education that recognizes variability in academic progress and learning skills among students. The approach focuses on providing students with increasingly intense support based on measured academic progress within the structure of the general education classroom. A three-tiered system is often used. Tier 1 involves providing instruction in the general education curriculum, with close monitoring of student progress with a goal of identifying students who are at risk for ongoing learning difficulties. Tier 2 involves providing at-risk students with supplemental, targeted instruction, usually individually or in small groups. Tier 2 students who continue to struggle advance to Tier 3, which involves providing more intensive, specialized instruction, typically under the auspices of an IEP.

A potential advantage of the response to intervention approach for children with learning disabilities is that it is data driven and outcome oriented. Moreover, it does not rely on arbitrary and often controversial definitions of learning disabilities but is based solely on a child's demonstrated need for extra help. A significant concern about response to intervention is that it may delay the implementation of special education services for students who need more intensive educational support. It also places a heavy burden on general education teachers to provide stratified instruction and complex monitoring of outcomes. Another significant concern is that response to intervention may not be responsive to the needs of students with developmental disabilities other than learning disabilities. Given the significant cost of special education, critics of response to intervention have raised concerns that some school districts might use this approach to delay or restrict student access to appropriate and necessary special education services.

BEYOND EARLY
INTERVENTION AND SPECIAL EDUCATION:
COMMUNITY SERVICES AND RESOURCES

For most children with developmental disabilities, the EI and special education systems serve as their primary source of education, therapy, and support for disability-related needs. Many service options exist in the wider community, but these tend to vary greatly from state to state and from region to region. Like medical services, disability-related services tend to be clustered in metropolitan areas, and even within these areas access to services may be limited by societal, economic, and cultural barriers.

Supplemental and Alternative Educational Services

Many parents consider tutoring for their children as a way to supplement school-based instruction, often targeting areas of particular academic concern or reinforcing material learned at school. Tutoring may occur during the school year or during school vacations and breaks (especially over summer vacation) to maintain progress and prevent the child from regressing. For-profit learning centers also provide supplemental educational support. However, the quality of these programs varies considerably, and it is often difficult for them to provide the customized and individualized attention that a tutor can offer.

Many communities have private or parochial school options, and in some cases parents will opt to send their children with developmental disabilities to these schools. Private schools offer a number of advantages over public schools. Many have smaller classrooms and offer increased individual attention. Many families feel that the philosophy and cultural environment of a particular school better reflect their values and beliefs, to the benefit of their children with special needs. A significant disadvantage of private schools relative to public schools is decreased access to special education and related services. Although a child attending a private school may have an IEP (typically obtained through the child's home school district) and can qualify for the same services as children who attend public schools, there are often logistical difficulties with delivering those services. Integrating special and general education services is challenging if not impossible. The significant expense of a private school must also be considered.

Some families also consider home schooling their children with disabilities. Parents may be dissatisfied with the social environment or services offered through public schools, or for philosophical, religious, or cultural reasons they may opt for home schooling. Home schooling has some of the same advantages and disadvantages as private schools. Children can receive highly in-dividualized attention and instruction, but it falls to parents to provide financially for their entire education. This can be quite challenging for any parent.

Supplemental Therapy

Speech, occupational, and physical therapies are provided to chil-dren as related services through EI and special education. This level of support is often adequate, but parents may consider supple-menting these therapy services. Because therapy that is included as part of an IFSP or IEP tends to be provided mainly in the service of educational goals, there may be greater flexibility for therapists working independently of the EI and special education systems. There also may be limited time in the school day to provide the level of therapy that a particular child needs. For example, a child with significant articulation difficulties or problems with stuttering may benefit from working one on one with a speech-language pa-thologist several times a week but can only receive this level of sup-port once a week at school. Another child may be having significant difficulties with dressing skills, but improving these skills is not a goal in the child's IEP, and working with an occupational therapist outside of school would help address this need. Or a child with cere-bral palsy who has recently undergone tendon-release surgery may need intensive short-term physical therapy to recover her walking skills but cannot receive this type of therapy through school.

Certain specialized therapy services may not be available through EI or the schools. For example, applied behavior analysis therapy for children on the autism spectrum tends to be offered mainly through programs that specialize in autism interventions (see Chapter 4). Many parents, aware of the research supporting the efficacy of applied behavior analysis, will seek out indepen-dent therapists certified in this type of therapy. Other specialized therapies, such as music therapy, are not typically offered through EI or the schools.

Assistive Technology

Many forms of assistive technology exist to assist children with disabilities. Although people tend to think of technology in terms of high-tech, computerized devices, low-tech assistive technologies are widely available and in many instances are more practical and functional than their high-tech counterparts. Assistive technology may augment and advance a child's skills in any of several functional areas, including communication, mobility, daily living, learning, and sensory processing (see Table 7.2). Many specialized forms of assistive technology are also available to address special medical needs (e.g., feeding tubes for children with oral feeding difficulties or ventilators for children who cannot breathe sufficiently on their own because of severe physical disability). *Adaptive equipment*, a form of assistive technology, refers to devices that aid in mobility or activities of daily living, such as crutches and walkers to help with walking or bath chairs to aid in bathing. Orthoses and prosthetics are special types of assistive technology that augment or replace the function of specific body parts (braces and prosthetic limbs are familiar examples). Although special education law mandates the provision of needed assistive technology to advance IEP goals, in practice it may be difficult to obtain many types of assistive technology through schools, and parents will need to turn to specialty clinics and disability agencies to obtain highly specialized equipment and devices.

Counseling

Counseling comes in many forms. Counseling for younger children is often focused on parents and the family. Behavior management counseling targets behavioral concerns and supports parents in developing more effective strategies for responding to challenging behavioral issues. This type of counseling is often offered by psychologists in private practice settings. Parenting

Table 7.2.   Examples of assistive technology

Functional area	Low-tech device	High-tech device
Mobility	Crutches	Power wheelchair
Daily living skills	Pencil grip	Laptop computer with word processor
Communication	Picture board	Computerized augmentative and alternative communication device
Learning	Flashcards	Learning software
Sensory processing	Magnifying glass	Digital hearing aid

classes, which are available in many communities, offer groups of parents similar training focused on behavior management. Individual counseling for older children focuses more specifically on the child and involves direct child–counselor interaction. Many children meet with private counselors to discuss emotional concerns (especially those related to anxiety and depression), and counselors help children to develop better coping mechanisms and social skills for dealing with situations that arise at home and at school.

There are specific forms of individual counseling. For example, cognitive-behavioral therapy, as its name implies, uses a combination of cognitive and behavioral strategies to empower individuals to control a number of emotional and behavior difficulties, including anxiety and obsessive-compulsive patterns of thought and behavior. A child must have sufficient maturity and insight into the nature of his or her disability in order to benefit from this type of therapy.

Family counseling is also widely available and is often provided by psychologists and social workers with training and experience in counseling. Whereas other forms of counseling focus on the child with the disability, family counseling is directed toward helping families cope with the challenges and stresses associated with having a child with a disability.

Recreational Activities for Children with Developmental Disabilities

Recreational activities (including sports, music, art, dance, and scouting) offer enormous satisfaction to children with disabilities and their families as well as afford them invaluable opportunities for social integration. In addition to the traditional activities available to all children, specialized programs for children with disabilities and special needs (e.g., the Special Olympics program) are available in many communities. A certain amount of trial and error is needed to ascertain which types of activities are best suited to a particular child. Many parents of children with disabilities find that group competitive sports are less congenial to their children's temperament and needs than activities that are oriented more toward the individual—in other words, activities that are directed toward attaining personal goals usually work better for children with disabilities than activities that focus on winning games. Popular activities that meet this criterion include swimming, dance, gymnastics, bowling, tennis, and martial arts. Talking with other parents of children with disabilities can be very helpful in determining the philosophy and attitudes of certain coaches and instructors.

Many families are quite creative in their efforts to identify activities that are a good fit for their child; one should not be limited to traditional choices. It is particularly empowering if a recreational activity can become an interest or project for the entire family.

Assessing Community Resources

Finding services for children with developmental disabilities in any community can be challenging, and finding ways to pay for these services can be more daunting still. The advent of the Internet has been a boon to parents looking for such services, although caution is advised when one is considering the list of options generated by a Google search. Although much valuable information exists online, it is important to consider the reputability of the source, and guard against those with inaccurate information, personal agendas, or ulterior financial motives. Developmental disability agencies exist within most state governments (usually in the state Department of Health), and their web sites can be an excellent starting point for identifying the types of services available in the state and in particular communities. Your child's primary care doctor, his EI coordinator, or members of his special education team can also be valuable resources in beginning the process of identifying services. Local medical specialty clinics (especially those specifically devoted to developmental disabilities) and not-for-profit agencies for individuals with disabilities can be particularly helpful. Social workers associated with these programs are experts at working with families to identify relevant community resources and can often provide guidance in finding ways to pay for these services.

Whereas EI and special education services are mandated by law to be available to all children with developmental disabilities free of charge, community-based and private resources and services are not. Private insurance tends to be woefully inadequate when it comes to covering services such as therapy and counseling and does not cover other services (e.g., tutoring) at all. Although some families are fortunate enough to be able to afford to pay for these services out of pocket, most are not. Some states have developed specific statutes that require private insurance companies to pay for specific types of services (e.g., New York passed a law in 2011 that requires private insurers to cover services for children on the autism spectrum); these legal mandates are, however, few and far between.

Supplemental Security Income (SSI) and Medicaid are major sources of financial support and health insurance for families of children with disabilities. Supplemental Security Income provides financial support to families who can demonstrate that their child's disability is associated with significant functional limitations and who qualify based on strict income and asset standards. In practice it is very difficult to qualify for Supplemental Security Income. Those who do qualify receive a steady supplemental income that can be used at the family's discretion; families who qualify for Supplemental Security Income are also automatically eligible for Medicaid.

Medicaid is a need-based program jointly funded by states and the federal government to ensure the provision of health care for low-income families who do not have access to private health insurance. Families who qualify for Medicaid benefits can receive a variety of services referred to collectively as early and periodic screening, diagnosis, and treatment services. Developmental and medical assessments, immunizations, laboratory tests, hearing and vision screening, therapy and rehabilitative services, and transportation for medical appointments are some examples of the types of services included under early and periodic screening, diagnosis, and treatment. Service coordination is a particularly important service. The Medicaid service coordinator works with families to ensure that they are aware of their rights under the law and helps families identify and obtain these services.

Medicaid waivers are an important option for families of children with developmental disabilities who would not otherwise qualify for Medicaid. In particular, waiver programs offer a means of obtaining home- and community-based services not covered by private insurance. These programs, which vary from state to state, target specific at-risk populations, such as children with developmental disabilities. Eligibility is determined by the existence of a developmental disability, not by family income. In an era of increasing budgetary constraints there are strict criteria for determining what may qualify as an eligible developmental disability, but waiver programs remain a vital source of support for many families seeking care and interventions beyond those offered through EI and special education.

II

....

Special Children,
Special Needs

8

Hearing, Vision, and Sensory Processing Problems

*P*roblems with hearing, vision, and the processing of sensory information are very common in children with disabilities. Understanding the general characteristics of sensory processing and the particular problems of the hearing and vision systems is the focus of this chapter.

WHAT IS UMAMI?

Can you name the five senses? Most people remember learning about them in grade school, and because they frequently find reason to make use of them, most can still name them. They are hearing, sight, touch, taste, and smell. And most people can probably remember specific things that they learned about the senses. For example, four basic tastes (sweet, salty, sour, and bitter) can be sensed with different parts of the tongue, right?

Well, as it turns out, there are actually five basic tastes, the fifth being umami. Umami is closely allied to savoriness; it is the taste that makes homemade chicken soup taste so much better than canned soup and gives meats, dairy products, and ripe tomatoes their culinary allure. Umami is the secret weapon of many a successful chef. No one taught about umami in grade school.

And no one taught that there are in fact seven senses. This is perhaps only a little less disturbing than finding out that Pluto is not considered a full-fledged planet anymore (sorry folks, it's a dwarf planet). Added to the familiar five (hearing, sight, touch, taste, and smell) are the vestibular sense (or the sense of balance), which tells the brain where the body is with respect to gravity, and proprioception, which helps keep track of body posture and limb position from moment to moment. Both of these senses are important for one's ability to sense the position and orientation of his or her body in space.

But at least we know that people see with their eyes, and hear with their ears, and taste with their tongues, and so on—right? Well, not really. Although the eyes and ears and tongue are obviously critical to one's ability to see, hear, and taste, the brain is the ultimate organ of sensation and perception. The eyes, ears, and other sensory organs mainly work by turning external or internal stimuli (e.g., light and sound waves) into electrical impulses (signals) that are transmitted to the brain by way of sensory nerves—this conversion process is called *signal transduction*. Signals are then processed by lower brain centers on the way to higher levels of the brain, where processing is completed and perception occurs. This chain of events can be summarized as shown in Figure 8.1.

The ways in which people perceive the world around them (and within them) are certainly much more complicated than their grade school teachers led them to believe, and the ways in which things may go awry with one's ability to sense and perceive the world are equally confusing and complicated. Problems can occur at any point in the chain of events leading to perception. People's understanding of these problems, especially those related to processing and perception, is limited. Nevertheless, problems with hearing, vision, and sensory processing are com-

Figure 8.1. The chain of events leading to perception.

mon in children with developmental disabilities, and it is important to consider what is known about these issues in order to better understand how these problems may be recognized early and treated appropriately.

DO YOU HEAR WHAT I HEAR? HEARING PROBLEMS IN CHILDREN WITH DEVELOPMENTAL DISABILITIES

Juliette is a charming 3-year-old with significant speech delays. Although she can say a large number of words, and she tries to put words together to make phrases and sentences, she is very difficult to understand. Yet she seems to understand everything that is said to her, and her parents say the she can hear a pin drop; they are convinced that her hearing is normal. Juliette passed her newborn hearing screen and has never had an ear infection, but her pediatrician recommended a formal hearing evaluation with an audiologist just in case. Her parents were shocked to learn that Juliette has moderate to severe sensorineural hearing loss in both ears and that she may need hearing aids.

Although most children with speech delays have normal hearing, there are exceptions. Moreover, it can be very difficult to identify hearing loss based on observations of a child's responses to environmental sounds. Many children with hearing loss can hear some sounds, and they are often very good at using visual cues to compensate for their hearing loss. Prior to the institution of universal newborn hearing screening, children with milder degrees of hearing loss were often not identified until 5 or 6 years of age, and children with profound deafness were not identified until after 2 years of age! Newborn hearing screening is not perfect, though, and as Juliette's story illustrates, in rare instances a child with significant hearing may fall through the cracks. This may occur because the result of the initial screening test was a false negative (i.e., the

Speech Delays and Hearing Loss

All children with speech and language delays should have their hearing tested, even if they passed newborn hearing screening tests.

seeds

test failed to demonstrate an abnormality), or it may occur because a child's ability to hear changed after the newborn period. For example, some genetic forms of hearing loss are progressive, meaning that they worsen or progress with time. The only way to identify hearing problems in these instances is to recognize when a child has a risk factor for hearing loss (see Table 8.1).

What People Hear

Sounds are vibrations that are transmitted by waves through a medium such as air. The denser the medium, the faster (and farther) a sound wave is transmitted, so sound moves faster underwater than through the air and faster still through solids (remember how characters in Westerns listened for the distant approach of hooves by putting their ears to the ground?). If there is no medium, there is no possibility of sound transmission (sorry Star Wars fans, all those space battle sound effects are fake—no sound is transmitted in the void of space).

Sound waves have two main characteristics: *frequency* or *pitch*, which refers to how high or low a sound is (think soprano versus bass), and *amplitude* or *intensity*, which refers to the loudness or softness of a sound (think rock concert versus whisper). Imagine waves on the surface of a lake as representing sound waves. Picture yourself clinging to a buoy in the middle of the lake as a rowboat slowly passes by. The crests and troughs of the

Table 8.1.　Risk factors for hearing loss

Children with these risk factors should have their hearing evaluated by a qualified audiologist, even if the newborn hearing screen was normal.

- Speech delay
- Parental concern about hearing
- Prematurity
- Infections during pregnancy
- Down syndrome or other specific genetic conditions
- Recurrent ear infections
- Family history of childhood-onset hearing loss
- Exposure to medications with known toxic effects to hearing
- Severe jaundice in the newborn period
- Meningitis and infections of the nervous system
- Head injury
- Hydrocephalus (excessive accumulation of cerebrospinal fluid in the brain)

waves it makes are far apart, and you bounce up and down slowly as the boat passes. If you counted how many times per second you bounce up (or down), you would have a measure of the frequency of the rowboat waves in cycles per second, also known as *Hertz* (the rowboat waves would be analogous to a low-pitched or low-frequency sound). Now imagine a speedboat roars by. The waves it produces are packed closely together, and the crests and troughs it makes bounce you up and down violently. You count many more cycles per second in comparison to the rowboat (the speedboat is analogous to a high-pitched or high-frequency sound).

Now imagine that a canoe passes by. You bounce up and down gently, and if you measured how high (or low) you bounce (perhaps in inches) you would have a measure of the amplitude of the wave. Amplitude is analogous to the intensity or loudness of a sound, which is measured in decibels (dB); the canoe represents a low-decibel or soft sound. Now imagine that a stately yacht follows in the wake of the humble canoe. Although the waves from the yacht arrive at the same frequency as those from the canoe (i.e., they are traveling at the same speed), the crests and troughs produced by the yacht are much higher and deeper, and the amplitude of the waves is much larger (representing a high-decibel or loud sound).

So the sounds people hear can come in any combination of pitch (frequency) and loudness (amplitude). Figure 8.2 shows the relative pitch and loudness of various sounds. Speech sounds vary from high to low pitched (250–5000 Hertz) and from very soft to moderately loud (5–50 dB). By contrast, 18-wheelers, jets, and motorcycles are very loud (90–120 dB) over a wide range of frequencies.

How People Hear

Figure 8.3 shows the anatomy of the ear. The external ear includes the auricle (the part of the ear that is visible) and the ear canal (the part that produces ear wax or cerumen). The external ear serves mainly as a mechanism for funneling sound to the eardrum, or tympanic membrane, which is the first part of the middle ear. Vibrations of the eardrum are then transmitted along a chain of three tiny oddly shaped bones called the *ossicles*, which have the

Frequency/pitch (cycles per second)

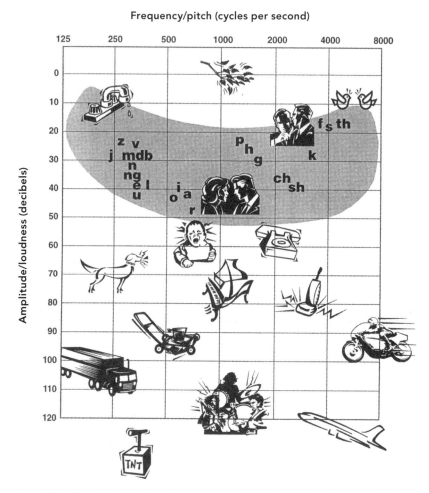

Figure 8.2. The pitch and loudness of common sounds. High-pitched sounds are toward the right of the diagram, and low-pitched sounds are toward the left; soft sounds are toward the top, and loud sounds are toward the bottom. Speech sounds are represented in the shaded area. (From Northern, J.L., and Downs, M.P. [1992]. *Hearing in children* [5th ed., p. 18]. Philadelphia, PA: Lippincott Williams & Wilkins. Copyright © Lippincott Williams & Wilkins; adapted by permission.)

fanciful names *malleus* ("hammer"), *incus* ("anvil"), and *stapes* ("stirrup") based on the objects they are thought to resemble. The ossicles serve to amplify sound vibrations and transmit these vibrations to the oval window, a membrane on the surface of the cochlea, which is one of two main components of the inner ear (the vestibular apparatus, which is the primary organ of balance, is the other). The cochlea is essentially a fluid-filled tube coiled

A) External ear B) Middle ear C) Inner ear

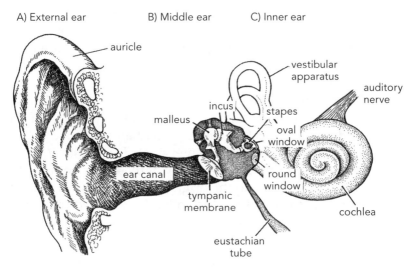

Figure 8.3. The anatomy of the ear. A) The external ear funnels sound to the eardrum (tympanic membrane). B) Tiny bones (ossicles) in the middle ear transmit vibrations to the cochlea of the inner ear. C) The cochlea converts sound to electrical impulses that are transmitted to the brain by the auditory nerve. (From Batshaw, M.L., Pellegrino, L., & Roizen, N. [Eds.]. [2007]. *Children with disabilities* [6th ed., p. 161]. Baltimore, MD: Paul H. Brookes Publishing Co.; reprinted by permission.)

into a snail-like shape. Vibrations transmitted by the ossicles to the oval window are transformed into fluid waves within the cochlea, and tiny hair-like structures lining a membrane that bisects the interior of the cochlea sense these waves and translate them into a barrage of electrical impulses that are transmitted to the brain by the auditory nerve.

The process of hearing can be likened to a passenger getting on a train headed for a metaphorical town, Centerville. Imagine that you are the passenger (sound wave). You enter the train station foyer (the external ear) and walk up to the ticket window (the eardrum). After purchasing your ticket you push through a series of turnstiles (the ossicles) until you arrive at the train platform (the oval window). The conductor collects and punches your ticket and admits you onto the train (cochlea), and you take your seat. As the train begins to accelerate, you muse philosophically that your ticket has, in essence, been converted into the motion of the train (electrical impulse) that is now carrying you along the train tracks (auditory nerve) to your destination (the brain).

In the case of the auditory system the train is not an express but a local—it makes several stops on the way to its final destination. These stops (or transfer points) occur in the medulla and midbrain, which are parts of the lower brain area called the *brainstem* (the rural outskirts and suburbs of Centerville). The final destination is the auditory cortex on either side of the brain (this is not really the final destination, though; after you get off the train you do not stay at the station—you hail a cab and take it to various points of interest in Centerville). The auditory signal can be influenced (or processed) at any of these stops or transfer points; the modifications to the original auditory signal that occur along this path are referred to collectively as *central auditory processing*.

How Is Hearing Tested?

Everyone remembers having their hearing screened by the school nurse in elementary school. In this type of screening, people don a pair of headphones (more properly referred to as *earphones*), and the nurse instructs them to raise their hand on the side that they hear the tone. Tones of higher and lower pitch are used, starting off louder and getting gradually softer until they can no longer be heard. This type of hearing test, which audiologists (hearing specialists) also use with older children and adults, is called *pure tone audiometry*. At each pitch tested (measured in Hertz), the lowest level of loudness (measured in decibels) at which a sound can be heard is noted; this is called the *hearing threshold*. A profile of pitch versus hearing threshold is generated for each ear; this is called an *audiogram*. For a person with normal hearing, the hearing threshold across all tested frequencies is typically below 15 dB; thresholds that measure above this are indicative of hearing loss. The ranges of hearing loss are slight (15–25 dB), mild (25–30 dB), moderate (30–50 dB), severe (50–70 dB), and profound (above 70 dB).

Younger children (typically those younger than 2½ or 3 years of age) are usually not developmentally able to participate in hearing tests with earphones. Audiologists test these children using an array of techniques referred to collectively as *behavioral audiometry*. The children are typically tested in a soundproof booth that is outfitted with a stereo sound system. A child's behavioral response, such as turning toward a sound, is used as a gauge of hearing; a visual reinforcer (e.g., a puppet appearing in conjunction with a sound) can increase the reliability of this behavioral response (this particular technique is called *visual reinforcement audiometry*). Some preschool- and early school-age children who are able to wear earphones but who are inconsistent with raising their hand in response to a tone can be taught to exhibit a play behavior (e.g., putting a block in a cup) in response to a tone (this is called *conditioned play audiometry*).

Very young children and some children with developmental disabilities are unable to participate in any form of behavioral audiometry. Their hearing can be assessed using techniques that rely on the physiological responses of the auditory and nervous systems to auditory stimuli; the child's cooperation is not required. For the auditory brainstem response technique, electrodes that are sensitive to the brain's electrical responses are taped to the scalp. Clicks of varying frequencies are presented to each ear, and the electrodes register the brain's response to the clicks. (The test will not work if the child is moving, so typically mild sedation is needed, which is a disadvantage of this technique.) A depressed or absent brain electrical response to the sound stimuli indicates hearing loss.

Another technique, known as *evoked otoacoustic emissions,* also does not require a child's cooperation and can usually be performed without sedation. Clicks or tones are presented to each ear, and if the cochlea receives the sound, it emits an echo that can be detected by a tiny microphone in a probe. In most instances the presence of this echo can be assumed to indicate normal hearing.

Evoked otoacoustic emissions and a modification of the auditory brainstem response technique are also used to screen for hearing loss in newborns because the tests are easy to administer and because newborns are obviously unable to cooperate with other forms of hearing testing. Despite the advantages of these techniques, tests that require some type of behavioral or communicative response to sound are still preferred, and pure tone audiometry in particular is considered the gold standard of hearing tests.

Tests of central auditory processing require a high level of cooperation from the person being testing and so are typically done in children older than 7. A child who has normal hearing (based on the results of a traditional hearing test) is subjected to a battery of tests aimed at evaluating the efficiency and consistency of auditory perception under a variety of listening conditions (e.g., identifying meaningful speech in the presence of competing background noise). A pattern of difficulties with processing and perceiving auditory information despite having normal hearing is thought to be indicative of a central auditory processing disorder.

Hearing Loss

There are two main types of hearing loss: conductive hearing loss and sensorineural hearing loss. Conductive hearing loss is the result of problems in the middle ear, most often as a consequence of ear infections. The middle ear is drained by the eustachian tube. When a child has a cold it is easy for this tube to become blocked, and fluid can accumulate in the middle-ear space as a consequence. If the fluid becomes infected, the child has an ear infection. Often the fluid lingers in the middle-ear space for days or weeks after the infection clears, and many children run into problems with the fluid becoming reinfected. In some instances a special drainage tube can be placed through the eardrum to circumvent this vicious cycle of fluid accumulation and reinfection (see Figure 8.4).

Although conductive hearing loss can certainly result in mild to moderate temporary hearing loss and may have transient effects on speech, it is not clear whether children with chronic middle-ear problems have long-term speech

jargon buster

Earaches and Beyond

Acute otitis media: The common ear infection, usually associated with ear pain and fever, caused by both viruses and bacteria and sometimes treated with antibiotics

Serous otitis media: Persistent middle-ear fluid without infection

Chronic otitis media: Long-term or recurrent ear infections

Myringotomy: A medical procedure in which a small hole is created in the eardrum to drain the middle ear

Pressure equalization tube: A tube placed in the hole created by myringotomy to allow for continuous drainage of the middle ear

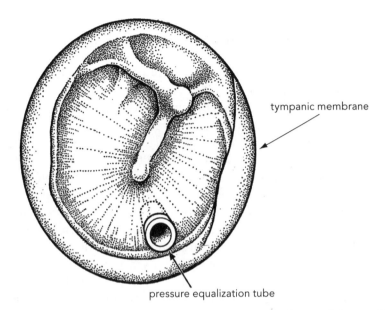

Figure 8.4.   A pressure equalization (PE) tube. PE tubes augment the function of the eustachian tube by providing an alternative path for fluid to drain from the middle ear through the tympanic membrane (eardrum) to the external ear canal. (From Batshaw, M.L., Pellegrino, L., & Roizen, N. [Eds.]. [2007]. *Children with disabilities* [6th ed., p. 165]. Baltimore, MD: Paul H. Brookes Publishing Co.; adapted by permission.)

difficulties as a consequence. (Although research seems to suggest that it does not, many parents and professionals are still suspicious that it does.)

Sensorineural hearing loss, by contrast, is a definite cause of speech difficulties. Newborn hearing screening, which is now mandated in most states, is primarily intended to identify children with this type of hearing problem. Sensorineural hearing loss is the result of dysfunction of the cochlea or the auditory nerve. When severe, it is sometimes called *nerve deafness.* Different parts of the cochlea are sensitive to different frequencies of sound, so it is not uncommon for children with sensorineural hearing loss to exhibit variability in how well they can hear high-pitched (high-frequency) versus low-pitched (low-frequency) sounds—high-frequency hearing loss is especially common. Although there are many different causes of sensorineural hearing loss (including infections during pregnancy, drug toxicity in sensitive premature infants, and brain injury), more than half of all cases of this type of hearing loss are due to genetic or hereditary conditions.

What Should You Do If You
Suspect that Your Child Has Hearing Loss?

As Juliette's story illustrates, it is fairly easy to miss hearing loss in a young child, especially if it is a mild or partial loss. So the first and most important step in helping a child with hearing loss is to know when to suspect that it may be present.

The second step is to have your child tested by an audiologist, preferably someone who has significant experience testing children. Your child's doctor will typically provide a referral for this assessment and will very likely know which audiologists in your community are the most appropriate and experienced to test your child. Although many pediatric and family practice offices and schools offer hearing screening, these screening tests and procedures are meant to identify children who were not previously suspected of having hearing loss. These screening tests are not adequate for evaluating a child who is already suspected of having a hearing loss—a formal assessment with an audiologist is a must.

The goal of a formal audiological evaluation is to determine the degree of hearing loss; to determine whether it involves one ear or both; and to assess whether the hearing loss is conductive, sensorineural, or mixed. Once the nature of your child's hearing loss has been characterized, your child's primary doctor should review the test results and assist you in determining the most appropriate course of action. If your child has a slight or mild hearing loss that is due to persistent middle-ear fluid, his doctor may elect to monitor him with close follow-up. Many children will have spontaneous resolution of middle-ear fluid without special treatment. If the fluid persists beyond a certain length of time, and if your child is having frequent, recurrent ear infections, his doctor may elect to treat him with antibiotics for a period of time until the fluid clears. If these more conservative strategies are ineffective, your child's doctor may refer you to an ear, nose, and throat specialist (informally referred to as an *ENT*, but formally known as an *otolaryngologist*), a doctor who specializes in such problems and who can offer surgical interventions (most often the placement of pressure equalization tubes) if these are needed.

An otolaryngologist should also be involved if your child has conductive hearing loss that is more severe or that is due to anatomical abnormalities rather than to simple otitis. An otolaryngologist should also be involved if there is evidence of sensorineural hearing loss. In addition to offering options for intervention, the specialist should advise you regarding the need for further evaluations. For example, some children are born with anatomical abnormalities that cause hearing loss but that also predispose them to worsening hearing loss if they experience any type of head trauma, sometimes even just a bump on the head. The specialist will typically recommend imaging studies (computed tomography scans or magnetic resonance imaging) to identify these anatomical changes.

As mentioned previously, many children with sensorineural hearing loss have a genetic basis for their condition. Your child's primary doctor or otolaryngologist may recommend specific genetic testing (typically blood tests) that could identify some of the more common genetic causes. You may also be referred to a genetic counselor or medical geneticist (a physician who specializes in genetic problems) to obtain a more detailed assessment and advice regarding recurrence risk (whether the hearing problem may run in your family) and the need for other medical tests.

How Can You Help Your Child with Hearing Loss?

In an ideal world, significant hearing loss, especially significant sensorineural hearing loss, will be identified in early infancy and treated immediately and aggressively. Recent research provides convincing evidence that the early recognition and treatment of hearing loss (ideally during the first year of life) results in dramatically improved developmental outcomes, especially with regard to speech and language development. Children with moderate to severe hearing loss may benefit from wearing a hearing aid, a device that amplifies sound. The most common type of hearing aid, a behind-the-ear hearing aid (shown in Figure 8.5 part A) has a tiny microphone that picks up sound, which is then amplified and presented to the ear via a speaker embedded in a special plastic tip that fits snugly into the entrance of the ear canal. Children with severe to profound hearing loss may be eligible for a cochlear implant (shown in Figure 8.5 part B), a special high-tech device that is surgically threaded into the cochlea and replaces it as a converter of sound to electrical impulses.

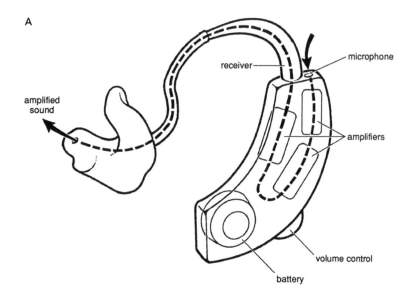

A

amplified
sound

receiver —

microphone

amplifiers

volume control

battery

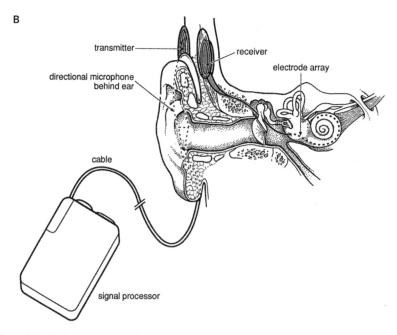

B

transmitter —

receiver

electrode array

directional microphone
behind ear

cable

signal processor

Figure 8.5. High-tech hearing help. A) Hearing aids amplify sound. B) Cochlear implants convert sound to electrical signals that are presented directly to the cochlea and auditory nerve. (From Batshaw, M.L., Pellegrino, L., & Roizen, N. [Eds.]. [2007]. *Children with disabilities* [6th ed., pp. 176–177]. Baltimore, MD: Paul H. Brookes Publishing Co.; adapted by permission.)

Whether your child has isolated hearing loss or her hearing loss is associated with other physical or developmental problems, she will likely benefit from early intervention, therapy, and special education support. Some teachers and therapists have special training and experience working with children with hearing impairments, and in some locations special programs exist that are tailored to the developmental and educational needs of children with hearing impairment.

Different teachers, therapists, and educational programs emphasize different approaches to teaching communication skills. One approach, referred to as the *auditory-oral method* or *oralism*, emphasizes speech as the primary means of communication. This method focuses on improving listening skills and developing speechreading (lipreading) with the goal of maximizing a child's ability to recognize and use speech in a world in which it is the default mode of communication.

An alternative approach emphasizes the use of gestures, or sign language, as the primary means of communication. Many different forms of sign language exist. In the United States the most prevalent form is American Sign Language. Although American Sign Language corresponds with spoken English, it has its own unique vocabulary and grammar, which makes it a truly distinct language in its own right. Other forms of sign language correspond more exactly with spoken English and are often used in conjunction with spoken language.

You may encounter parents, teachers, therapists, and other professionals with very strong opinions about what constitutes the most appropriate method of teaching communication skills to a child with hearing impairment. It is important to consider these options carefully but also to trust your own judgment as you assess what will work best for your child given his or her unique characteristics and concerns.

DO YOU SEE WHAT I SEE? VISUAL PROBLEMS IN CHILDREN WITH DEVELOPMENTAL DISABILITIES

Tony is a 4-year-old with a lazy eye. Although his eyes seem to move together most of the time, his parents frequently notice that his left eye drifts in toward his nose, especially when Tony is tired. Tony was evaluated by an eye doctor, who recommended patching. His parents were instructed to have Tony wear a patch over his good eye for a few hours every day, but they are having a hard time getting Tony to keep the patch on and wonder whether it is worth the effort.

Eye and vision problems are fairly common in children generally and are particularly common in children with developmental disabilities. In order to understand the nature of these problems it is helpful to review some basic information about the visual system.

What People See

In essence, what people see is light, or its absence. Light is a form of energy, in particular a part of the electromagnetic spectrum that the eye is designed to detect (which is by definition the visible portion of the electromagnetic spectrum). Visible light sits between higher energy forms of electromagnetic radiation (ultraviolet rays, x rays, and gamma rays) and lower energy forms of electromagnetic radiation (infrared, microwave, and radio waves).

Like sound, light can be described in terms of frequency and intensity. *Intensity* refers to how bright or dim a source of light is (think sun versus moon), and *frequency* refers to the amount of energy associated with the light, which people perceive as color (violet is high-energy light, red is low-energy light, and the other colors of the rainbow fall somewhere in between). The main and most important source of natural light is of course the sun (remember that moonlight is reflected sunlight). Humans augment sunlight with the use of fire (e.g., candles, fireplaces) and artificial light (e.g., lightbulbs). Most of what people see of the world is actually reflected light (staring directly at sources of light is generally inadvisable!). Objects in the physical world interact with light energy in different ways. "Light" objects tend to reflect light and "dark" objects tend to absorb light (that is why it is usually better to wear a light-colored T-shirt on a sunny summer day). Objects are different colors depending on the frequencies of light reflected or absorbed by the materials with which they are composed. For example, objects that are predominantly red reflect red light and absorb other colors. Black objects absorb most colors; white objects reflect most colors. The kaleidoscope of colors and shades of dark and light reflected to the eye by objects provide the raw material for vision. What people actually see, however, is very much determined by how they see, which is a function of the design of the eyes and visual system.

How People See

Just as the ears change sound waves into electrical impulses that the brain interprets as sound, they eyes turn patterns of light into electrical activity that the brain can "see." Figure 8.6 shows the anatomy of the eye, which is often likened to a camera. Light en-

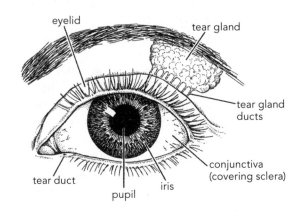

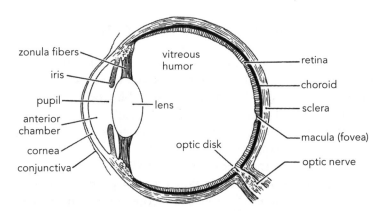

Figure 8.6.   The anatomy of the eye. The pupil is like a window that admits light into the interior of the eye. The amount of light that enters is controlled by the iris (the colored part of the eye), which expands and contracts to change the size of the pupil. The clear cornea and lens work together to focus light on the retina (and particularly on the fovea, the center of vision) at the back of the eye, which turns patterns of light into electrical impulses that are sent to the brain via the optic nerve. (From Batshaw, M.L., Pellegrino, L., & Roizen, N. [Eds.]. [2007]. *Children with disabilities* [6th ed., p. 138]. Baltimore, MD: Paul H. Brookes Publishing Co.; reprinted by permission.)

ters through the pupil and is focused on the back of the eye (the retina) by the lens and cornea. Patterns of light are projected onto the retina, which is like a movie screen at the back of the eye. Tiny cells in the retina called *cones* are specialized to sense color and are mainly used for day vision; cells called *rods* are sensitive to small differences in light and dark and are mainly used for night vision. The shifting patterns of light received by the retina are transformed into electrical signals that are transmitted to the brain through the optic nerve. These signals make several stops on the way to the occipital cortex at the back of the brain where these signals are perceived. The anatomy of the visual system is such that signals representing objects in the right visual field of each eye are sent to the left side of the brain, and signals representing objects the left visual field of each eye are sent to the right side of the brain.

The occipital, or visual, cortex is an amazing computer that has special areas or modules that process different aspects of the visual world in different ways. For example, some areas are mainly sensitive to the borders or edges of objects in the visual field, and other areas are sensitive to motion. There are even areas in the human brain that are specialized to perceive faces! Without the brain's ability to process the raw visual data received by the eyes, people would be overwhelmed by a chaotic flux of incomprehensible stimuli.

How Vision Develops in Children

Although infants can see colors and objects well at birth, they are very nearsighted (i.e., they see things that are close to their faces well, but far-away objects are hard to see). Newborns have a strong preference for looking at faces and will briefly fixate, or focus, on a parent's face, although they do not consistently fix and follow (look at and track) objects until 3 months of age. Likewise, infants' eyes do not always move together until after 3 months of age (e.g., a newborn's eyes may occasionally cross). By 6 months of age eye movements and visual awareness are considerably improved, and between 12 and 24 months of age children show evidence of improved vision for far-away objects, although it is difficult to get an accurate assessment of how well a child sees until he or she is 3 or 4 years old, when vision can be tested using eye charts.

Testing Vision

The traditional eye chart is the gold standard for testing visual acuity (how well a child can see). Several types of visual acuity charts exist: Charts with letters are preferred for older children and adults, whereas charts with pictures and symbols can be used with younger children (who can name or match the objects they see). When a child is tested using these charts, his or her ability to distinguish objects (letters, symbols, pictures) is compared to that same ability in a person with typical visual acuity. A child with 20/20 vision can distinguish objects 20 feet away that a person with typical vision is also able to see at 20 feet; by contrast, a child with 20/40 vision can see an object at 20 feet that a person with typical vision can see at 40 feet. Eye doctors are able to use a variety of special techniques to estimate visual acuity in children who are either too young to use eye charts or unable to use these charts because of their developmental disability. They are also able to use a number of other special techniques and tests to assess other aspects of visual function and anatomy (this includes using the familiar ophthalmoscope, the optical device your child's primary doctor also uses to view the back of your child's eye).

Eye and Vision Problems in Children

Problems that children have with their eyes and vision mainly fall into one of three categories: problems related to the eyes themselves, problems with the coordinated movements of the eyes, and problems with how the brain processes visual information and regulates eye movement. These three elements work in concert to create visual experiences, so when one element is disrupted, the other two are often affected as well.

Common and Not-So-Common Problems with the Eyes Themselves

The most common eye problems that affect vision are refractive errors and astigmatism. Refractive errors, more commonly known as *nearsightedness* (*myopia*) and *farsightedness* (*hyperopia*), are problems focusing light accurately on the retina. Many people have eyes that are not perfectly round—they may be a little foreshort-

Eye Doctors

Eye doctors vary in their training and the types of evaluations and treatments they can provide. *Ophthalmologists* have completed medical school (i.e., they have an MD degree) and have had further intensive training in the medical and surgical treatment of eye disorders and visual problems. *Pediatric ophthalmologists* have had further specialty training and experience in treating eye disorders and visual problems in children. *Doctors of optometry* typically complete 4 years of specialty training after college and receive an OD (oculus doctor) degree. They screen for eye and vision problems, prescribe corrective lenses, and treat eye-specific disorders but cannot perform surgery or treat systemic diseases that may affect the eyes. An *optician* is a technician (not an eye doctor) who is trained to fill prescriptions for corrective lenses; training and certification requirements vary from state to state.

ened or a little elongated, and this results in blurred vision. *Astigmatism* refers to irregularities in the curvature of the cornea or the lens, which also can result in blurred vision. Many people who are mildly nearsighted or farsighted, or who have mild astigmatism, often do fine without any special interventions, but people with more significant problems usually need corrective lenses (glasses or contact lenses).

Less common problems with the eyes include disturbances in the structure and function of the eye. These may be present at birth or a consequence of adverse circumstances or injury. Problems with the formation of the eyes can occur during fetal development because of an underlying genetic problem or because of exposure to toxins, certain medications, or viruses that can affect eye development.

For example, a number of genetic disorders are associated with microphthalmia, or small, incompletely developed eyes. Colobomas, which are gaps or holes that can occur in several different parts of the eyes (mostly notably the iris or the retina), are also associated with several genetic conditions. Alcohol is a potent toxin that affects fetal development and that can result in several different eye and eye muscle problems, including incomplete development of the optic nerve. Fetal exposure to certain medications, such as those used for epilepsy, may adversely affect eye development and function. Congenital rubella syndrome, which is caused by fetal exposure to the rubella virus, can cause abnormalities in multiple body systems, including the eyes (fortunately the use of the rubella vaccine, which is a component of the measles–mumps–rubella vaccine, has dramatically reduced the incidence of this condition). Congenital rubella most often causes cataracts, or clouding of the lens of the eye, and microphthalmia, but it can also cause glaucoma, a condition associated with increased pressure of the fluids within the eye.

Being born prematurely creates stresses on the developing retina, resulting in abnormal growth of immature retinal blood vessels into the gelatin-like substance of the interior of the eye that gives the eye its shape (called the *vitreous humor*). In this condition, known as *retinopathy of prematurity*, scarring and subsequent contraction of the abnormal blood vessels may, in severe cases, pull the retina away from the back of the eye, causing retinal detachment. This can result in significant vision loss and even blindness. Laser treatments are used to tack down the retina when there is a high risk of detachment. Fortunately, most cases of retinopathy of prematurity are mild and resolve spontaneously without any loss of vision, but careful monitoring and close follow-up with a pediatric ophthalmologist is required.

Problems with Eye Alignment and Movement (Strabismus)

When people look at a stationary object their eyes typically work together to focus on that object, fixing steadily without any notable "jiggling." When they observe a moving object, their eyes likewise move together, in concert with head movements, to follow or track the object. Muscles attached to the outside of each eye control these movements. If a muscle is weak or has trouble working because of a problem with the nerve that controls it, the affected eye will have trouble moving together with its partner, and the eyes will be out of sync with each other. This misalignment of the eyes is called *strabismus* (see Figure 8.7). With mild strabismus the misalignment may be intermittent (e.g., may only occur when a child is tired) or may only occur when the child is looking in a particular direction. With severe strabismus the misalignment is constant. Because the brain fuses the images from each eye into a single image to provide depth perception, misalignment due to strabismus can disrupt a child's ability to see the world in three dimensions. If the brain becomes accustomed to ignoring the misaligned eye, more serious, permanent vision loss can result (see the discussion on amblyopia in the next section).

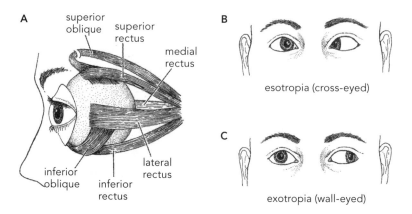

Figure 8.7. Eye muscles and strabismus. A) Muscles that attach to the outside of the eye work together to move the eye in every direction. Weakness in a muscle causes strabismus. B) In esotropia, one eye turns inward. C) In exotropia, one eye turns outward. (From Batshaw, M.L., Pellegrino, L., & Roizen, N. [Eds.]. [2007]. *Children with disabilities* [6th ed., p. 147]. Baltimore, MD: Paul H. Brookes Publishing Co.; reprinted by permission.)

Mild forms of strabismus can be treated with patching (in which the good eye is patched to force the brain to use weaker eye) or glasses. Severe forms of strabismus usually require surgical correction. Eye exercises do not seem to help strabismus, although mild strabismus may improve as a child matures.

Problems with Brain Processing and Control: Amblyopia, Cortical Visual Impairment, and Nystagmus

People use their eyes to see, but it is the brain that does the actual seeing! Likewise, eye muscles move the eyes, but the brain controls and regulates this movement. Problems in the brain can result in both vision loss and atypical eye movements, even when the eyes and eye muscles themselves are normal.

Amblyopia, or lazy eye, is an especially common brain-related form of vision loss. Amblyopia occurs when the brain prefers to use one eye over the other (it is really the brain, rather than the eye, that is lazy). It can occur for several reasons. If a child has significant misalignment of the eyes due to strabismus, her brain may become accustomed to ignoring the affected eye. This can actually result in permanent vision loss in the neglected eye, even though the eye itself is normal. Patching the good eye to force the brain to use the affected eye can prevent permanent vision loss, especially if done when a child is very young (e.g., toddler or preschool age). It is often difficult to entice a child to keep the patch on, but most children will become accustomed to it, especially when the lazy eye starts to improve. Eye drops that blear vision or glasses with one fogged or blackened lens may be alternatives to a patch in some situations. Surgical correction of strabismus may be the treatment of choice for more severe problems (although glasses and patching may still be needed after surgery).

Patching and Amblyopia

seeds Patching the good eye in a child at risk for amblyopia, especially if done at a young age, may prevent permanent vision loss.

Amblyopia can also occur when a child has significantly different vision in one eye than the other. This can occur if one eye is much more nearsighted or farsighted than the other (i.e., differences in refractive error), if one eye has much worse astigmatism than the other, or if one eye has vision loss due to some other problem (e.g., the presence of a cataract). Corrective lenses can adjust for differences in acuity due to refractive errors and astigmatism; specific treatments (e.g., surgery) and eye patching may be needed for other specific problems.

Cortical visual impairment (also known as *central visual impairment*) refers to vision loss that is due to either problems in the visual parts of the brain (especially the occipital, or visual, cortex at the back of the brain) or problems with the nerve pathways that carry signals from the eyes to the brain. In cortical visual impairment, the eyes themselves are healthy. Cortical visual impairment can be the result of brain injury due to lack of oxygen, infection, or trauma, or it may be the result of problems with brain development in the fetus.

Nystagmus is unintentional jiggling or shaking movements of the eyes. It most often involves both eyes but may be more noticeable in one eye than the other, and it is often more noticeable when the eyes are turned in a particular direction. Nystagmus has many causes. It can be the result of a problem with the brain's ability to control eye movements, it may be a side effect of certain medications, or it may be an isolated finding that runs in certain families. Nystagmus can also be the result of vision loss involving both eyes. The brain needs the feedback of constant visual input in order to make fine adjustments in eye movement from moment to moment. When that input is lacking, the brain's ability to lock in on objects in the field of vision is compromised, and coarse, jittery eye movements are the result.

Visual Impairment and Blindness

If a child can see no better than 20/70 in the best eye, even with corrective lenses, then he or she is said to be visually impaired. If a child's vision is no better than 20/200 in the better eye (again, even with correction), then he or she is said to be legally blind. Children with severely limited peripheral vision may also meet criteria for legal blindness. Blindness is most often due to problems with the retina or optic nerve. *Peripheral blindness* refers to severe vision loss due to problems with the eyes themselves; *cortical* or *central blindness* refers to severe vision loss due to problems with the optic nerves or brain. Peripheral blindness is usually irreversible, but some cases of cortical blindness may improve over time, depending on the cause of the vision loss.

Blindisms

Children with significant visual impairment or blindness may exhibit repetitive, self-stimulatory behaviors such as hand flapping, head banging, rocking, blinking, eye pressing, or head rolling. These behaviors are thought to be an attempt to provide sensory input to compensate for lost vision. Blindisms can be distinguished from the self-stimulatory behaviors associated with autism spectrum disorders by the fact that children with visual impairment alone lack the social and communication deficits associated with autism.

Children with visual impairment usually have significant functional vision, and even children who are blind may have some degree of useful vision. Educational and therapeutic interventions aim to help these children learn to take maximum advantage of their residual vision while learning to rely on the other senses to compensate for their loss of vision. Teachers of the visually impaired and orientation and mobility specialists (therapists devoted to helping people with visual impairment learn to navigate their environment) have special training and expertise in helping children with visual impairment. Using braille is a well-known method for teaching school-age children with visual impairments to read. Audio books provide an alternative means for these children to gain access to a wide variety of literature. Computerized devices (e.g., smartphones and tablet computers) have opened up an array of options for obtaining information, communicating, and controlling the environment (e.g., using computers to remotely control light switches and door locks). Some special educational programs are geared toward the needs of children with visual impairments, but this trend is counterbalanced by a strong preference to include children with visual impairments in general classroom settings with typically developing peers whenever possible (see Chapter 7).

DO YOU FEEL WHAT I FEEL?
SENSORY PROCESSING PROBLEMS IN
CHILDREN WITH DEVELOPMENTAL DISABILITIES

Marcia has always been a sensitive child. Even when she was an infant, her parents found it very difficult to comfort her. Unlike her older siblings she did not seem to like being cuddled, and her colic seemed to last the better part of her first year. Marcia is now a 4-year-old preschooler. She is bright, has wonderful language skills, and is very imaginative, but she has problems with clumsiness and coordination and she is still very sensitive. Loud noises make her cry, she does not like to get her hands messy, and she is annoyed by the tags on her clothes (which her parents now automatically remove from all new garments). She also dislikes foods that have a lumpy or slimy texture and has been known to gag at the sight of these foods. She was evaluated by an occupational therapist from her school district, who told her parents that Marcia has a sensory processing disorder.

Sensory processing disorders are a relatively recently recognized phenomenon. Child development specialists have known for many years that children with disabilities are prone to react to various sensory stimuli in unpredictable, sometimes exaggerated ways, but it was not until the early 1960s that Dr. A. Jane Ayres, an educator, occupational therapist, and neuroscientist, coined the term *sensory integration dysfunction* to characterize this ubiquitous but perplexing phenomenon. Although in theory sensory integration refers to the processing and interplay of all of the senses, in practice it relates most particularly to the feeling senses, or the sense of touch (the tactile sense), the sense of balance (the vestibular sense), and the sense of body position (proprioception).

The Feeling Senses

Like hearing and vision, the feeling senses work by taking a particular form of energy and converting it into nerve impulses that are transmitted to the brain for processing and perception. For hearing, sound energy is converted into nerve impulses in the cochlea; for vision, light energy is converted into nerve impulses in the retina. Likewise, for the feeling senses, specialized organs convert the energy associated with touch, posture, and movement into nerve impulses that the brain can process, integrate, and interpret.

The Sense of Touch (the Tactile Sense)

When an object comes into contact with the skin, people feel it because microscopic sensors (sensory receptors) embedded in the skin transmit nerve impulses to the brain by way of sensory nerves and nervous system tracks in the spinal cord. Some sensors are closer the surface than others and detect light touch, whereas some are deeper and detect presure. There are also special sensors that detect pain and heat. Depending on the type of sensation and the sensor involved, nerve impulses follow different pathways through the nervous system on the way to the brain, with many stops and way stations along the way. Each way station represents a potential point at which a nerve impulse can be modified by other signals coming into the same station, so that a signal originating at a sensor in the tip of the index finger now may "look" different to the brain than a signal originating from the same sensor 5 minutes from now. Millions of these tactile sensors

Acupuncture:
Closing the Gate on Pain?

Acupuncture, or the insertion of fine needles at strategic locations in the skin to relieve pain, is thought to work by modifying pain signals. Nerve impulses stimulated by the needle in the skin travel to the spinal cord and interrupt, or close the gate on, pain signals coming from other nerves.

are distributed across the surface of the skin, with higher concentrations located at strategic sites, such as the tips of the fingers and the surfaces of the lips. The brain does an amazing job of processing and integrating the incredibly complex information represented by these myriad signals.

The Sense of Balance (the Vestibular Sense)

When a person moves or tilts his or her head, fluid in the vestibular apparatus of the inner ear (also known as the *semicircular canals;* see Figure 8.3) is set into motion, which stimulates microscopic sensors (hair cells) that transmit signals to the brain. These signals are used by the brain to calculate head position and movement relative to gravity, providing critical information about the position and orientation of the body in space. The familiar sensation of dizziness and loss of balance that occurs when someone spins quickly and stops suddenly is caused by the unchecked flow of vestibular fluid, which creates a false and disorienting sense of persistent motion.

The Sense of Position (Proprioception)

Imagine what it would be like if, when you closed your eyes, you had no sense of where your arms or legs were or what posture your body was holding. This body sense, called *proprioception* (from the Latin *proprius,* meaning "one's own"), is mediated by millions of stretch and pressure sensors in the muscles and joints. It is a strange, unsensed sense, something that people barely notice but would miss horribly if it were suddenly taken away. There is a kind of metaphysical connection between what people think of as their sense of self and the sense of their own physical presence created in the mind's eye by proprioception.

Movement and Sensation

Movement and sensation are two sides of the same coin. Through movement the feeling senses are activated, and through sensation a frame of reference is created that provides the basis for movement. Movement creates sensation by bringing objects into contact with skin, by turning and tilting the head to activate the sense of balance, and by contracting muscles and bending joints to create a sense of body position and motion. Sensation anchors movement by providing a constant flow of feedback about the consequences of motion, allowing moment-to-moment adaptation to a changing body configuration and the changing demands of the environment. The term *sensorimotor* recognizes this seamless integration of the motor control and sensory processing systems. One cannot operate without the other.

Sensory Processing Disorders

jargon buster

Sensory Integration and Processing

Sensory integration: The registration, processing, integration, and perception of sensation

Sensory processing disorders: Specific clinically recognized forms of sensory integration dysfunction

Sensory overresponsivity: An exaggerated reaction to sensation

Tactile defensiveness: An aversive reaction to touch

Texture sensitivity: An aversion to certain food textures

Hyperacusis: An aversion to noise or particular sounds

Sensory underresponsivity: A decreased response to sensory stimuli (including pain)

Sensory-seeking behavior: The overactive pursuit of sensory stimulation

Dyspraxia: Motor planning and coordination problems associated with sensory integration dysfunction

Sensory diet: A schedule of targeted interventions that address the sensory needs of a child with a sensory processing disorder

Children vary greatly in the ways in which they register, process, and respond to sensory stimuli. For some children these responses are exaggerated to the point of being problematic for daily functioning; these children are said to have a sensory processing disorder. To understand the nature of sensory processing problems it is helpful to review the sensory processing scheme in Figure 8.1.

Many children with hearing and vision problems have trouble with the first and second steps in this scheme (e.g., a child with recurrent ear infections has a problem with sensory input; a child with a detached retina cannot convert, or transduce, light energy into nerve impulses). By contrast, children with sensory processing disorders have problems with the third and fourth steps. They receive sensory input normally and convert this input into nerve impulses as expected, but their brains process, perceive, and respond to these signals in unexpected ways.

Some children, such as Marcia, exhibit sensory overresponsivity, or exaggerated reactions to sensory stimuli. There are different forms of sensory overresponsivity. If your child is sensitive to touch, does not like the feeling of particular fabrics, hates tags on clothes, becomes distressed when her hands get messy, or hates to be barefoot, she is showing signs of tactile sensitivity or tactile defensiveness. If your child is particularly sensitive to the lumpy, chewy, stringy, or slimy aspects of certain foods, she is said to have texture sensitivities. Oversensitivity to loud noises is very common, especially among children with disabilities, and is sometimes referred to as *hyperacusis*. Other children are very sensitive to bright light, or smells, or tastes. It is not uncommon for a child with sensory overresponsivity to show exaggerated reactions to several different types of sensory stimuli.

Other children show sensory underresponsivity. Your child may react slowly or not at all to the sounds, sights, smells, or tactile sensations that would ordinarily elicit a clear or even dramatic response from most children. Sensory underresponsive children are particularly noted for their lack of response to pain. Although the pain sensors in the skin are perfectly normal, and pain signals are transmitted to the brain normally, sensory underresponsive children seem to process and perceive the sensation of pain differently, judging from their muted response to noxious stimuli. If your child has difficulty with communication skills in addition to sensory underresponsivity, you may be worried that you will not be able to tell if he is hurt or ill.

Yet another group of children are sensory-seeking children. If your child is a sensory seeker he will have a profound need for stimulation and will energetically pursue activities that provide this. Sensory seekers often love to run, jump, climb, spin, crash, wrestle, squeeze, and hug and often have trouble respecting personal boundaries in the process. Some of these children love spicy food, loud noises (mainly of their own making), and anything exciting. They get revved up and overstimulated very easily. Parents often describe their sensory-seeking child as energetic, boisterous, impulsive, fearless, intrusive, high maintenance, and easily bored.

The Chicken or the Egg, Part I:
Sensory Processing Disorders and Coordination

Children with sensory processing disorders frequently have trouble with motor skills and coordination. This makes sense given the close relationship between movement and sensation. For some children, coordination problems seem more dominant; for others, sensory processing seems to be the primary difficulty. Medical professionals tend to use the term *developmental coordination disorder* to describe developmentally based disorders of motor coordination and tend to deemphasize the role of sensory processing problems in the genesis of coordination difficulties (see Chapter 2). Therapists, especially those who work with children with sensory processing problems, tend to prefer the term *developmental dyspraxia,* or just *dyspraxia,* to describe motor coordination problems seen in children and tend to emphasize the role of sensory integration dysfunction in the emergence of these problems. In practice it is very difficult to separate the chicken from the egg when trying to determine whether motor control or sensory processing is primary difficulty for children with coordination difficulties.

The Chicken or the Egg, Part II: Sensory
Processing Disorders and Developmental Disabilities

Sensory integration dysfunction is common in children with developmental disabilities. For example, children with autism spectrum disorders exhibit every type of sensory processing disturbance described in this chapter (see Chapter 4). Children with Asperger syndrome are particularly known for having difficulties with motor coordination (dyspraxia). Children with attention-deficit/hyperactivity disorder frequently exhibit prominent sensory-seeking behavior (see Chapter 5). Children with learning disabilities and intellectual disability are also more likely than typically developing children to exhibit some degree of sensory integration dysfunction (see Chapter 6).

Controversy exists among professionals regarding the validity of sensory processing disorder as a discrete, stand-alone diagnosis. Some argue that sensory processing problems always and only exist as a component of other diagnoses. Others argue that sensory processing disorders not only exist in their own right but are frequently misdiagnosed as other conditions. For example, according to this view many children with prominent sensory-seeking behaviors are misdiagnosed as having attention-deficit/hyperactivity disorder. Still others argue that whether or not sensory processing disorders exist apart from other developmental disabilities they clearly represent an important clinical phenomenon with significant functional and therapeutic implications and that on that basis alone they should merit official recognition as a diagnosis.

Interventions for Sensory Processing Disorders

Understanding the nature of your child's sensory sensitivities, sensory deficits, and sensory needs is key to knowing how best to help him and to design useful interventions. The real-life impact of a particular sensory problem must also be considered. For example, if your child is sensitive to loud noises, it makes sense to avoid situations that you know in advance will be problematic for him. If your child is a sensory seeker, providing him with a schedule of activities that help to meet his sensory needs may help him to stay on task for other activities during the course of the day (such a schedule is called a *sensory diet*). If your child tends to be underresponsive, enlisting him in activities that are engaging, dynamic, and arousing may help him to focus on the people and activities around him.

Your child's therapist (usually an occupational therapist) may also use special interventions, such as brushing the skin with a stiff brush, that are intended to desensitize a child to stimuli he finds to be aversive. Other techniques, such as direct joint compression, deep muscle massage, and vestibular stimulation (e.g., spinning and swinging a child) can be used both as desensitization techniques and as a way of stimulating, arousing, or engaging a child's sensorimotor system and attention. Some therapists feel that these interventions may help to reprogram sensory integration processes to help the child achieve a higher level of adaptability, although research supporting this contention is lacking.

9

Special Medical Problems

Although most children with disabilities are quite healthy, they are more likely than their typically developing peers to encounter special medical problems at some point in their lives. These problems can have a significant impact on their growth and development, and can sometimes be difficult to diagnose and treat. Knowing something about these special medical problems, and knowing how to access help from the healthcare system to address these problems, is the focus of this chapter.

YOUR CHILD'S MEDICAL HOME

When your child has a disability, it is important for you to feel confident in his medical care. Your child may need medical specialty services, prescription medications, special tests and procedures, and referrals for special evaluations and interventions. When several professionals and agencies become involved in your child's care, it can be difficult to ensure adequate communication among providers and family members, and care can become fragmented. As the parent of a child with a disability, you will do your best to coordinate services and advocate for him, but you will need the support of a medical provider who knows him and your family well, sees him on a regular basis, can provide basic preventive care (well-child examinations, immunizations, and developmental and medical screening tests), and can coordinate referrals and tests while keeping the big picture in mind. Most often a primary care doctor (typically a community pediatrician or family practitioner) will serve in this capacity, providing a medical home, or base of operations for your child's medical care. In some cases your child may receive support through a special program that offers multidisciplinary care for a specific developmental disability. For example, programs for children with spina bifida, Down syndrome (DS), and cerebral palsy (CP) have developed in many metropolitan areas (especially in association with teaching hospitals and medical schools) to help coordinate complex medical care in partnership with primary care providers. In this instance the medical home is less a place than a team of people who work together to ensure coordination and continuity of care.

BASIC HEALTH CARE FOR
CHILDREN WITH SPECIAL NEEDS

Even if your child has special health care needs related to her disability, most of the basic preventive care she will require will differ little or not at all from the care provided to typically developing children. Well-child visits and examinations; screening tests for hearing, vision, and development; and blood tests to rule out conditions such as lead exposure will likely be the same for your child as for any other child. Concerns about your child's development may prompt earlier or more frequent administration of developmental screening assessments, but the tests themselves will most likely be the same as those administered to all other children (see Chapter 7).

Immunizations (vaccines) will also, with rare exceptions, be the same for your child as for any other child. Concerns were raised in the past about the possible adverse developmental effects of immunizations (especially in relation to the autism spectrum disorders). However, a wealth of scientific evidence disproves any connection between immunizations and developmental disabilities. In fact, children with disabilities have, if anything, a more compelling need for thorough immunization. Many are more prone than their typically developing peers to the devastating effects of the infections that these immunizations are designed to prevent.

Basic aspects of growth and nutrition are also in the province of your child's primary care doctor, who will track your child's progress with regular measurements of weight, height, and head circumference. This is an especially important aspect of well-child care for children with disabilities, who are more prone to growth deficiencies and excesses for a variety of reasons. The fact

Immunizations for Children with Developmental Disabilities

With rare exceptions, children with developmental disabilities should receive the same immunizations as typically developing children. Substantial scientific research *refutes* the idea that immunizations cause developmental disabilities.

that your child's doctor tracks growth parameters over time is especially critical. When a child has a growth problem, it is very often the rate of growth (which can only be determined by obtaining multiple measurements over time) rather than one particular measurement that is the key to determining the nature of the problem. For example, if a child is very short but has always been short and is growing at a normal rate, his short stature may be familial or hereditary; by contrast, if a child is very short because he has been growing at a slower than expected rate, there may be a significant underlying medical problem such as growth hormone deficiency. Likewise, if a child has a very large head (macrocephaly) but has always had a large head and the rate of head growth is normal, her large head size may run in the family or may be part of a genetic condition that is associated with macrocephaly, such as fragile X syndrome (see Chapter 11). By contrast, if an infant with spina bifida has a special shunt to drain cerebrospinal fluid (see "How Is Spina Bifida Diagnosed?" in the Appendix) and shows a sudden jump in her rate of head growth, a buildup of fluid in the brain (hydrocephalus) may have occurred because of the shunt malfunction, which will require surgical repair.

Your child's primary care doctor cares for a wide variety of common childhood ailments, including colds (upper respiratory infections), sore throat (pharyngitis), sinus infection (sinusitis), pink eye (conjunctivitis), ear infections (otitis media), stomach bug (gastroenteritis), skin rashes, allergies, and mild transient respiratory problems.

A number of chronic (long-term) health problems may also be managed by your child's primary doctor, depending on his or her level of comfort with any particular issue. For some health care conditions, he or she may choose to refer your child for consultation with a medical specialist. In some instances this may be a one-time consultation; in others the specialist may see your child on a regular basis for a particular medical concern, but your child's primary doctor will still take the lead in providing care for that concern. In still other cases the specialist may take the lead in managing a particular problem, although your child's primary doctor will still be involved as the head of the health care team, making sure that the care provided by the specialist fits into the big picture of your child's health care program.

SPECIAL HEALTH CARE ISSUES IN CHILDREN WITH DISABILITIES

This section highlights several particularly common and often challenging health care issues that frequently affect children with disabilities.

Growth and Nutrition

As mentioned previously, growth deficiencies and excesses are common concerns in children with disabilities. Obesity, a form of growth excess, has become a universal concern for all children and adults; people with disabilities are not immune to this concern, and many have special risk factors for developing obesity. For example, children with autism who take risperidone to help manage agitation and aggression often struggle with excessive weight gain due to increased appetite, a common side effect of the medication (see Chapter 10). Children with developmental coordination disorder, CP, or spina bifida may be less active than their typically developing peers, burning fewer calories through exercise and activity and thus being more prone to excessive weight gain as a consequence.

Growth deficiencies take many forms. The most common problem, inadequate weight gain, is usually due to inadequate caloric intake. Children with disabilities as a group are prone to inadequate caloric intake for a variety of reasons. Feeding problems (see Chapter 3) due to swallowing difficulties, texture sensitivities, or medical problems such as gastroesophageal reflux disease (GERD; see "Problems at the Junction: Gastroesophageal Reflux") are common causes of poor weight gain in children with disabilities. Just as some medications have icreased appetite as a side effect, other medications (including many commonly used to treat attention-deficit/hyperactivity disorder [ADHD]) can suppress appetite, with poor weight gain as a result.

Less common is the fact that some children do not grow well despite hav-

Do Not Blame Poor Weight Gain on Skinny Genes or Hyperactivity

Parents are sometimes tempted to write off poor weight gain as being due to either a hereditary tendency toward thinness or their child's high activity level. A skinny child from a skinny family still gains weight at a normal rate; children with poor weight gain, by definition, do not. Likewise, an active child will naturally compensate for the extra calories she burns through increased food intake and will only have poor weight gain if something interferes with this natural process.

ing adequate nutrition. For example, children with hormone deficiencies (e.g., growth hormone or thyroid hormone deficiencies) exhibit poor height gain, or linear growth, which usually occurs in parallel with poor weight gain. By contrast, children with poor weight gain due to inadequate nutrition usually have normal linear growth unless they have been severely malnourished for an extended period of time. Children with hormone deficiencies also usually have a normal body mass index, which is an indirect measure of body fat stores based on height and weight. By contrast, children who are overweight (because they eat too much) have an increased body mass index, and children who are underweight (because they eat too little) have a decreased body mass index.

Children with certain genetic conditions may also exhibit atypical growth patterns because in a sense their bodies are programmed to grow differently. For example, children with DS (see "Down Syndrome" in the Appendix) are usually short compared to other family members, and their growth pattern over time is unique. However, children with other genetic conditions may exhibit atypical growth as a consequence of over- or undereating. For example, children with Prader-Willi syndrome, who have unique physical features, developmental problems, and behavioral concerns, frequently become obese because of a marked tendency to overeat rather than a difference in their growth pattern.

It is possible for a child to be undernourished without being underweight; in fact, some children who are obese are actually undernourished! In addition to getting enough major nutrients, or macronutrients (proteins, carbohydrates, and fats), children must also consume a sufficient variety of foods to ensure adequate intake of essential micronutrients (vitamins and minerals). The macronutrients provide energy (calories) for growth and also provide the building blocks for constructing and maintaining body tissues and organs. Micronutrients are like the oil in an engine: They are needed to keep the body's many processes (metabolism) running smoothly. Fruits and vegetables are a particularly rich source of micronutrients.

Many children with disabilities are selective or picky eaters; children with autism spectrum disorders are particularly known for this (see Chapter 4). A lack of fruits and vegetables in the diet or inadequate intake of high-quality protein (especially if a child does not eat dairy products, meat, or fish) are frequent concerns. It is often difficult to know for sure whether a child is getting adequate nutrition; enlisting the help of a dietician, a professional who specializes in analyzing diets and offering suggestions for remediating deficiencies, can be very useful.

Tummy Trouble

Closely related to nutritional concerns are problems with the *gastrointestinal system*, which refers to the collection of organs that process the food people eat and the liquids they drink. The gastrointestinal system is organized like an assembly line. Food that is swallowed is carried down the esophagus, a tube-like organ that connects the lower throat (pharynx) to the stomach, by a wave of muscular contraction. Food passes through a muscular gateway, the gastroesophageal junction, and enters another muscular organ, the stomach, where it is churned and stomach acid and special enzymes begin the process of digestion. The partially processed food bolus is then delivered to the long, winding, snake-like small intestine, where digestion is completed and the resultant broth of nutrients is absorbed into the bloodstream. A particularly important stop along this assembly line is the duodenum, the first segment of the small intestine. Bile (manufactured in the liver and necessary for to digest fat) and enzymes (manufactured in the pancreas and necessary to digest carbohydrate and protein) are secreted into the small intestine at this point.

After the long passage through the small intestine is complete, indigestible leftovers are passed to the large intestine, where excess water is absorbed and the fecal remnants of the digestive processes are eliminated via the rectum.

Problems can occur at several points along the assembly line. Particularly common concerns for children with disabilities are problems at the gastroesophageal junction (gastroesophegeal reflux), problems in the small intestine (malabsorption), and problems in the large intestine (constipation).

Problems at the Junction: Gastroesophageal Reflux

As food moves from the esophagus to the stomach it should ideally stay in the stomach, but some people have problems with stomach contents slurping back into the esophagus—this is called *gastroesophageal reflux* (GER). A little GER occurs in everyone; in fact, the majority of infants have frequent, generally benign reflux that leads to the familiar phenomenon of spitting up. When reflux is more frequent and persistent, the acidic stomach contents can cause *esophagitis*, or significant irritation, inflammation, and erosion of the lining of the esophagus (which lacks the protective barrier against acid that the stomach has). Esophagitis may eventually lead to serious ulceration and bleeding. When GER is severe enough to affect a child's health, the child is said to have gastroesophageal reflux disease (GERD).

The exact causes of GERD are complex and not completely understood, but major contributing factors are decreased gut motility (the ability of the muscular walls of the esophagus, stomach, and intestines to move a food bolus forward) and decreased effectiveness of the muscular sphincter at the gastroesophageal junction (which acts as a one-way valve, keeping stomach contents from backing up into the esophagus). Children with disabilities, especially those with physical disabilities such as CP, are more likely to have decreased gut motility and so are more prone to GERD. Constipation, another common gastrointestinal problem in children with disabilities (see "Problems with Elimination: Constipation"), can actually aggravate GERD through a reflex mechanism that suppresses stomach motility.

The symptoms of GERD are listed in Table 9.1. The common symptoms of GERD in adults, regurgitation (the sensation of something coming back up) and heartburn, may not be evident in nonverbal children, so parents and doctors must be alert to the presence of other clues. This is especially true with children with disabilities who are more prone to GERD and may have subtle, indirect evidence of the disease. For example, children with unexplained food refusal; or apparent pain at night when lying in bed; or unexplained episodes of agitation, aggression, or self-injury may have unrecognized GERD. GERD can also affect breathing by aggravating asthma symptoms (leading to increased wheezing or coughing). Children with physical disabilities such as CP may aspirate, or breathe in, regurgitated acidic stomach contents and can develop significant lung irritation and pneumonia as a consequence.

If a mild form of GERD is suspected it may be appropriate to try treatment and observe the child's response as a way of diagnosing the disease. In many cases symptoms are unclear and special diagnostic procedures are used. Endoscopy is the gold standard: While the child is under anesthesia, a gastroenterologist (a doctor who specializes in diseases of the gastrointestinal system) inserts a tube down the esophagus and visualizes the walls of the esophagus and the stomach, taking small tissue samples along the way. Endoscopy is especially important for identifying esophageal irritation and ulcer. A pH probe study may also be considered: In this procedure a probe with a pH, or acid, detector is inserted through the nose and down the back of the throat and

Table 9.1.   The symptoms of gastroesophageal reflux disease

Recurrent regurgitation or vomiting
Wet burps
Heartburn
Discomfort or pain after meals
Discomfort or pain when lying down (especially at night)
Aggravation of asthma symptoms
Sour breath
Erosion of tooth enamel
Recurrent aspiration or pneumonia
Poor eating or weight gain
Unexplained episodes of agitation, aggression, or self-injurious behavior (in nonverbal children)

is secured so that the detector at the tip of the probe sits in the lower esophagus. Episodes of reflux are documented over several hours, and the severity of the GER can be assessed.

Treatment of GER usually includes lifestyle changes and the administration of medications that reduce stomach acid. Lifestyle changes include not lying down after eating, propping children up in bed slightly, and avoiding foods that are suspected to aggravate GER (e.g., chocolate, peppermint, cola, orange juice). Traditional antacids temporarily neutralize stomach acid and provide momentary relief, but they do not work well for persistent GER, and moreover many contain aluminum hydroxide, which should not be given to infants and young children. Medications that affect acid production are much more effective. These include medications that reduce acid production, such as famotidine (Pepcid) and ranitidine (Zantac), and those that completely stop acid production, such as omeprazole (Prilosec) and lansoprazole (Prevacid). Although many of these medications are now available in over-the-counter preparations, you should consult with your child's doctor before considering a specific treatment.

Rarely in children with intractable GER surgical interventions are considered. The most commonly used procedure is called a *Nissen fundoplication.* In this procedure a part of the stomach wall is wrapped around the base of the esophagus, creating a kind of artificial valve to restrict the movement of stomach contents back into the esophagus.

Problems with Absorption: Food Sensitivities

Children (and adults) can be sensitive to particular foods for several reasons. For example, lactose intolerance, or sensitivity to the milk sugar lactose, is very common in adults, especially those of Asian, African, or Native American ancestry. Lactose intolerance is due to a deficiency in the intestinal enzyme lactase, which breaks down lactose into simple component sugars that can be absorbed. People with lactose intolerance typical become bloated, experience abdominal discomfort, and develop flatulence and diarrhea. Special dairy products with added lactase allow individuals with lactose intolerance to consume dairy products, at least to a limited degree.

In some cases a child's immune system may react to a specific food component, typically a protein. For example, celiac disease, a fairly common and probably underdiagnosed condition, is caused by sensitivity to gluten, the major protein in wheat and several other grains. The body's immune system makes antibodies that attack gluten, causing inflammation in the small intestine and symptoms of malabsorption, such as bloating, diarrhea, abdominal pain, and poor appetite. The inflammation in the intestine causes problems with the absorption of a number of nutrients, which may result in weight loss, poor linear growth, or symptoms of vitamin deficiency. Blood tests are available to screen for celiac disease and should be considered for children who have symptoms of the disease or who are at risk for developing it (e.g., children with diabetes or hypothyroidism). Among children with disabilities, children with DS are especially prone to celiac disease (see "Down Syndrome" in the Appendix).

The Gluten-Free, Casein-Free Diet

Many parents of children with autism and other developmental disabilities experiment with diets for their children that exclude gluten (wheat protein) and casein (milk protein). Children on the gluten-free, casein-free diet do not typically have confirmed sensitivities to gluten or casein and often have none of the specific gastrointestinal symptoms associated with celiac disease or milk-protein allergy (although nonspecific gastrointestinal symptoms are often reported). The diet is based on a theory that the products absorbed as a result of digesting these proteins adversely affect brain function, and it is typically used to help with challenging behaviors and improve social responsiveness. Although some parents report positive results, research does not support the effectiveness of the diet.

Children whose blood tests screen positive for celiac disease should have an endoscopy and biopsy of the lining of the small intestine to confirm the diagnosis. Treatment involves removing from the diet all foods that contain gluten.

Some children may have true food allergies. In these cases exposure to the offending food can precipitate a full-blown allergic, and anaphylactic, reaction that causes hives, triggers breathing problems, and in some instances may be life threatening. Peanut allergies are the most common food allergy, followed by tree nut allergies, egg allergies, and milk-protein allergies. Infants may have a milk-protein sensitivity associated with formula intolerance and bloody stools, but they typically outgrow this. Blood tests and skin tests (typically administered by allergy specialists) can help pinpoint the source of a child's allergy symptoms and are often done in conjunction with testing for environmental allergies.

Problems with Elimination: Constipation

Constipation is an extremely common childhood problem and is especially prevalent among children with developmental disabilities. Children with DS, CP, and spina bifida have specific functional or neurological impairments that increase the likelihood of their developing problems with constipation (see the Appendix). The main characteristics of constipation are as follows:

- Two or fewer bowel movements per week
- Periodic episodes of incontinence (bowel accidents) after acquiring toileting skills
- Excessive stool retention
- Painful or hard bowel movements
- The presence of a large fecal mass in the rectum
- Large-diameter stools that may obstruct the toilet

Besides being associated with discomfort, anxiety, and embarrassment, constipation also aggravates or triggers other problems, such as GER (see "Problems at the Junction: Gastroesophageal Reflux") and poor appetite with food refusal and inadequate weight gain. A small number of children have organic constipation, which can be related to a specific medical or neurological condition (e.g., CP, spina bifida). Most have functional constipation, which is the result of a pattern of dysfunctional toileting that is sometimes triggered by painful bowel movements that encourage stool retention or may be the result of multiple factors, including dietary issues, lack of exercise, or difficulties with toilet training.

Although special interventions may be required for some forms of organic constipation (e.g., children with constipation due to low hypothyroidism are treated with thyroid hormone replacement), strategies used to treat functional constipation are often used to treat organic constipation as well. Treatment typically involves a clean-out phase and a maintenance phase. Children who are severely constipated typically have a large mass of stool in the rectum that is difficult or impossible to pass (this is called an *impaction*). The goal of the clean-out phase is to relieve this impaction, and this is most often accomplished with the use of rectal stimulant laxatives (e.g., rectal bisacodyl [Dulcolax]). Stimulant laxatives work by stimulating bowel motility (in other words, helping the colon to push things along). Oral stimulant medications are available but tend to cause more abdominal cramping than the rectal suppository forms. In some instances laxatives do not work and enemas are used. The clean-out phase is usually completed in 1–2 days; in rare instances, if typical treatments are ineffective, a child may be admitted to the hospital to complete the clean-out phase.

The goal of the maintenance phase of treatment is to establish regular bowel movements (at least one soft stool per day) and to normalize bowel function so that constipation does not recur. The mainstay of the maintenance phase of treatment is the use of osmotic laxatives, which work by drawing water into the bowel to help soften the stool. A number of osmotic laxatives are available; many doctors favor the use of polyethylene glycol (Miralax), which has fewer side effects than some of the other options. Dietary interventions include increasing the amount of water, fruits, vegetables, and fiber in the diet. Behavioral interventions focus on establishing a consistent toileting schedule (usually organized around having the child sit on the toilet after meals).

Recovering from Chronic Constipation Takes Time

When a child has been severely constipated for a long time, the bowel wall is stretched and distorted and becomes less effective in moving bowel contents forward. A major goal of maintenance therapy is to give the colon time to recover its function. Although dietary changes are an important part of maintenance therapy they are usually insufficient by themselves; the consistent use of laxatives is usually required to give the colon time to heal.

A Toothsome Task: Good Dental Care

Going to the dentist is perhaps not an entirely toothsome (i.e., agreeable) experience for many people, but good dental care is very important for all children and is especially relevant to the health and well-being of children with disabilities. Although the basic elements of dental care are the same for children with disabilities as for typically developing children, a number of special considerations apply to children with disabilities. For example, children with oral sensitivities may resist having their teeth brushed, and a great deal of patience and creativity is often required to find a way to accomplish this without too much wailing and grinding of teeth. Many children with disabilities have delays in acquiring daily living skills, such as brushing their teeth, and so flossing is a challenge in the best of circumstances. These difficulties all add up to the same concern: Problems with dental hygiene increase the risk of developing dental disease, including cavities (dental caries) and gum disease (periodontal disease).

Children with disabilities also have special problems related to their diagnoses. For example, some children with severe intellectual disability or autism are prone to constant teeth grinding, called *bruxism*. This results in the erosion of tooth enamel and creates an additional risk factor for the development of dental disease. Some children with CP tend to thrust their tongues against their teeth, which affects tooth position and predisposes them to problems with malocclusion (improper tooth alignment). Children with DS tend to have crowded teeth and often experience drying and bleeding of gums because of a tendency to mouth breathe. Children with epilepsy (see "Firestorm in the Brain: Seizures and Epilepsy") sometimes take medications that can cause overgrowth of the gingiva (gum tissue), which predisposes them to gum disease; and children with prolonged, severe tonic-clonic (grand mal) seizures may occasionally experience dental trauma as a consequence of a seizure episode.

Establishing Dental Care

The American Academy of Pediatric Dentistry recommends that all children have their first dental visit by 12 months of age. This is especially advisable for children with disabilities, but finding a dentist who has experience working with children and is sensitive to the needs of a child with disabilities can be challenging. The purpose of the first dental visit is mainly to get parents acquainted with the basics of good dental care and to make a plan for dental

jargon buster

Dental Terminology

Primary teeth: Baby teeth, which begin to erupt (come in) from 4 to 14 months of age and have all erupted by 2–3 years of age (total number of primary teeth: 20)

Permanent teeth: Adult teeth, which begin to erupt, pushing out the corresponding primary teeth, by 6 years; all have erupted by adolescence except for wisdom teeth, which erupt after age 17 (total number of permanent teeth: 32)

Dental caries: Cavities, or dental decay, caused by acid produced by bacteria adherent to the teeth, which breaks down tooth enamel and can eventually lead to tooth infection (dental abscess) and possible tooth loss

Periodontal disease: Gum disease caused by bacteria, resulting in inflammation of the gums (gingivitis) followed by destruction of the bony sockets that hold the teeth, leading to tooth loss

Malocclusion: The misalignment of teeth, predisposing a person to abnormal wear on tooth surfaces, increased risk of dental caries, and discomfort with chewing; malocclusion is remediated through orthodontic interventions (i.e., braces)

Bruxism: Teeth grinding

follow-up. During the toddler and preschool years dental visits should be fun rather than anxiety provoking and serve to help a child become accustomed to the potentially intimidating aspects of the dental office before more intrusive dental examinations and procedures are needed.

The special art of pediatric dentistry involves helping children to be comfortable with examinations and procedures that are inherently stressful. Humor, playfulness, special behavioral techniques, and the judicious use of sedation when needed are all part of this art. In some instances examinations and procedures must be done under full anesthesia, so it is important that your child's dentist have access to a facility that has established procedures for providing this service safely.

Dental Care at Home

The most important aspect of your child's dental care is the part that happens at home. Although it is important to encourage your child to help with dental hygiene from an early age, you should supervise the process and actively complete brushing until your child has clearly demonstrated the ability to do this on her own. A soft nylon-bristle toothbrush should be used for brushing; an electric toothbrush may be a good choice for some children and may have particular advantages in terms of preventing gum disease. Two minutes of brushing (timed with a timer!) twice a day is typically recommended. Special flossers for kids make it easier for children to manipulate floss and, like kids' toothpaste, often come in fun flavors. Fluoride in toothpaste, in municipal water supplies, and applied in the dentist's office is important for preventing cavities; your child's dentist will let you know if additional fluoride supplementation is needed if your community does not add fluoride to the water supply. Dentists also apply plastic sealants to bumpy surfaces of molars to help prevent cavities, so it is advisable to ask the dentist whether this is an option for your child.

Firestorm in the Brain: Seizures and Epilepsy

Brianna is a 4-year-old girl with left-sided spastic hemiplegia, a type of CP that causes weakness and muscle tightness mainly on one side of the body (see Chapter 2). One afternoon she seems unusually groggy and cranky after waking up from a nap. Her parents become alarmed as she seems suddenly disoriented, her speech becomes garbled, her eyes deviate toward the right side of her body, and she falls to the floor. Her right arm then stiffens as she arches her body; within a minute or so her left arm and both legs also stiffen. After another minute or so, Brianna's arms begin to jerk and relax over and over again, staying in sync with each other, while her whole body convulses, or shudders to the same rhythm. Her breathing seems erratic: She makes panting noises, she drools, and her lips turn blue. Her parents are frightened that she cannot breathe, and they call 911.

By the time the ambulance arrives about 10 minutes later the jerking movements stop, Brianna's body relaxes, and her breathing eases. Her lips are no longer blue but her skin is pale and clammy. Her parents notice that she has wet herself. Brianna sleeps on the way to the emergency room; by the time the doctor sees her she has begun to awaken. An hour later she is still a little groggy but is almost back to her usual self. The emergency room doctor tells her parents that he believes she has had a seizure.

Seizures are frightening, mysterious, and sometimes elusive events that occur as a consequence of abnormal, uncontrolled electrical discharges in the brain. Brain cells, or neurons, are like tiny batteries that store electrical energy. The controlled dis-

jargon buster

Terminology Related to Seizures and Epilepsy

Seizure: A sudden abnormal electrical discharge in the brain that is associated with atypical and involuntary movements, sensation, or experiences

Epilepsy: A condition marked by having had two or more unprovoked seizures

Status epilepticus: Seizures that do not stop spontaneously

Partial seizure: A seizure that starts in one area of the brain (also called a *focal seizure*)

Generalized seizure: A seizure that starts in the entire brain

Simple seizure: A seizure without a loss or alteration of consciousness

Complex seizure: A seizure associated with a loss or alteration of consciousness

Tonic seizure: A seizure associated with sustained muscle contraction and stiffening of the limbs

Clonic seizure: A seizure associated with intermittent muscle contraction and synchronous jerking of the limbs

Tonic-clonic seizure: A seizure with tonic and clonic phases (also called a *grand mal seizure*)

Absence seizure: A seizure associated mainly with a brief (a few seconds) loss of consciousness without prominent motor manifestations or a postictal phase (also called a *petit mal seizure*)

Myoclonic seizure: A seizure associated with very sudden, isolated bending or extending of the head and torso, sometimes involving the limbs, that may occur individually or in clusters

(continued)

charge of electrical impulses through networks of neurons in the brain is the basis of all brain function. A system of checks and balances exists in the brain to ensure that neurons and neural networks do not get out of hand: Neuronal excitation is balanced by neuronal inhibition. Seizures occur when neurons or neuronal networks become overexcited or when the balance between excitation and inhibition in the brain is compromised.

Seizures are often likened to an out-of-control fire, a kind of firestorm of electrical activity in the brain. This is an apt metaphor up to a point. Like with a fire, something has to trigger the initial blaze; and like with a fire, the likelihood that a seizure will start and spread depends on the prevailing conditions. Hot, dry, windy weather is the firefighter's nemesis; cool, wet, calm weather is his friend. Like a fire started by a wayward cigarette tossed negligently into a patch of dry grass, some seizures start through the rogue activity of specific neurons in specific areas of the brain: In this instance a seizure is said to have a focal origin, and the seizure itself is called a *par-*

tial (or *focal*) *seizure.* And like fires, seizures are more likely to occur when the climate of the brain is off balance, favoring neuronal excitation over inhibition. At a certain point the balance between these two influences tips far enough in favor of excitation that the seizure threshold is exceeded, and a firestorm of electrical mayhem ensues.

jargon buster **(continued)**

Atonic seizure: A seizure with sudden loss of muscle tone

Postictal: Describing the period after a seizure; postictal sleepiness or reduced responsiveness is associated with some types of seizure

Unlike fires, which must always start somewhere, some seizures seem to start everywhere at once, like a kind of electrical version of spontaneous combustion. Seizures that involve the entire brain from the onset are called *generalized seizures.*

And unlike fires, which tend to burn out of control as long as conditions favor their spread, seizures are usually, and fortunately, self-limited. The brain seems to have automatic mechanisms to suppress the persistence of these electrical firestorms, which usually burn themselves out after a few minutes. In those rare instances when a child has a seizure that persists unabated (beyond 15 or 20 minutes), she is said to be in status epilepticus.

Brianna's story is consistent with a partial seizure that has evolved into a generalized seizure. Her seizure starts with speech problems, eye deviation to the right side, and stiffening of the right arm. Because the left side of the brain controls the right side of the body, and also controls speech for most people, it is likely that the focus of Brianna's seizure is located somewhere in the left side of her brain. As the seizure proceeds the stiffening spreads to the rest of Brianna's body (it has secondarily generalized).

Initially Brianna's seizure manifests as stiffening of her limbs and arching of her body due to the persistent contraction of muscles driven by the firestorm in her brain—this is the tonic phase of her seizure. This is followed by the clonic phase of her seizure, during which synchronous, rhythmic muscle contractions cause jerking movements of the limbs and convulsions of the body. Because Brianna's seizure involves both a tonic and a clonic phase, she is said to have had a tonic-clonic seizure (formerly a *grand mal seizure*).

Because the rhythmic contractions of the clonic phase of a seizure involve the muscles used for breathing, distressing grunting or panting noises are heard that lead to the impression that the seizing child is choking. Seizure activity also causes changes in the autonomic nervous system, which controls basic body functions, including the flow of blood in the small vessels of the skin. When these vessels contract, blood flow is restricted, resulting in pale, sweaty skin and blueness in the lips and extremities. This contributes further to the impression that the child cannot breathe. Although her breathing is not as efficient as it normally would be, the seizing child is breathing, and as long as the seizure is self-limited there is no risk of brain damage. (Children in status epilepticus are at increased risk for brain damage if the seizure is not stopped, but the seizure must be very long—probably longer than an hour—to result in permanent damage.)

During the seizure itself Brianna is unresponsive. Seizures that are associated with a loss or alteration of consciousness are called *complex seizures;* those that are not are called *simple seizures.* Primary generalized seizures (those that start in the whole brain) are always associated with loss or alterations of consciousness, so the terms *complex* and *simple* are applied only to partial seizures. Generalized and complex partial seizures are typically (although not always) associated with a postictal state (the word *ictal* refers to the active

The Strange World of Partial Seizures

In a *simple partial seizure,* the abnormal electrical discharge stays in one area of the brain and the symptoms of the seizure relate to the function of that area. The seizure may manifest as the jerking of a body part (a motor symptom), as an odor or a taste, or as a visual or auditory hallucination (a sensory symptom, also called an *aura*). A simple partial seizure may even trigger a specific memory or emotion. If the seizure involves a larger area of the brain and consciousness is affected, then a *partial complex seizure* has occurred. The child appears slow to respond and disoriented (and may become combative because of his confusion). He may experience an aura, which is followed by odd, stereotyped movements, including blinking, gesturing, grimacing, chewing, or actions that mimic typical activities such as buttoning and unbuttoning— these are called *automatisms.* Postictal drowsiness or sleep usually follows. Because of their strange characteristics, and because they tend to occur during sleep, partial seizures are sometimes misinterpreted as night terrors.

phase of a seizure). Brianna's postictal phase is characterized by persistent sleepiness, which is a common postictal manifestation. Rarely a child may exhibit transient neurological abnormalities, such as temporary paralysis (called Todd's paralysis) as a postictal phenomenon.

Brianna's seizure would be classified as a partial complex seizure with secondary generalization because it starts as a partial (focal) seizure, involves the loss of consciousness (is complex), and spreads to the rest of the body (becomes secondarily generalized). The other main seizure types are simple partial seizures (focal seizures with no alteration of consciousness), complex partial seizures (without secondary generalization), and generalized seizures.

Generalized seizures are further divided into convulsive (those that involve abnormal, involuntary changes in muscle activity) and nonconvulsive (those that involve impaired consciousness but without abnormal movement) seizures. The tonic-clonic seizure is the classic example of a generalized convulsive seizure, but a number of other types exist, including myoclonic seizures (which involve isolated, convulsive jerks of the head and torso) and atonic seizures (sometimes called *drop seizures;* which involve the sudden loss of muscle tone).

A prime example of a nonconvulsive generalized seizure is the absence seizure (formerly a *petit mal seizure*). Sometimes called *staring seizures,* absence seizures are characterized by a very sudden, very brief (typically just 3–5 seconds) loss of consciousness. This is sometimes associated with eyelid flutters or subtle, involuntary facial movements, but more obvious atypical movements are absent. There is no postictal state, so the child snaps back to normal in an instant. A child may be in the middle of a game when the seizure occurs, and the game will be interrupted during the seizure. When the seizure is over the child may feel a sense of disorientation, or a feeling of having lost track of what he was doing, but he will typically resume his game as if nothing has happened.

Absence seizures can be tricky to diagnose and insidious in their effects. Most children who stare off or space out are not having seizures—they are usually just having trouble staying focused, or their mind has wandered, or they are distracted or simply daydreaming. Children with ADHD are particularly prone to this. However, some children with absence seizures are misdiagnosed as having ADHD. Some children with absence seizures have hundreds of seizure episodes a day and are constantly losing track of what they are doing, giving the appearance of a child who is distracted and unfocused.

There are a few key observations that help to distinguish absence seizures from typical mind wandering. Absence seizures occur at random and as equally as likely to happen during preferred and nonpreferred activities. Mind wandering occurs mainly when a child is bored or involved in a nonpreferred activity. Absence seizures occur in all settings; mind wandering tends to occur in some settings (places that are boring or distracting) more than others (places that are interesting or exciting). It is not possible to redirect or get the attention of a child in the midst of an absence seizure; a child whose mind wanders can be easily refocused by something that is sufficiently engaging. Finally, absence seizures are very brief (a few seconds), whereas the wandering mind tends to linger in its distracted state for more extended periods of time.

Complex partial seizures can also manifest as staring spells, although these seizures exhibit more obvious clues that they are seizures, including abnormal movements (sometimes odd, stereotypical movements called *automatisms* that mimic normal activities—e.g., scratching, buttoning), more obvious and prolonged alterations of consciousness, and in some instances a postictal state of sleepiness or disorientation.

Questions and Answers About Seizures and Epilepsy

The following are frequently asked questions about seizures and epilepsy.

What Is the Difference Between Seizures and Epilepsy?

Seizures are specific events associated with abnormal brain electrical discharge; a child is said to have epilepsy if he has had two or more unprovoked seizure episodes. If someone has a seizure after getting hit in the head, or as a consequence of drug use, or following a period of severe sleep deprivation, the seizure is considered to be provoked and epilepsy is not diagnosed.

Provoked seizures usually occur in isolation; an exception to this is febrile seizures (also called *febrile convulsions*), a common ailment of early childhood that runs in families. A child with febrile seizures has a generalized tonic-clonic episode that is triggered by a high fever. The episode typically lasts for just a few minutes and always involves both sides of the body equally. About one third of children with febrile seizures have more than one episode, but it is rare to have more than three episodes. Most children outgrow febrile seizures by 5 years of age. If a child has seizures with fever that last longer than usual, are associated with unusual features (e.g., one side of the body being more affected than the other), occur more than three times, or persist after 5 years of age, it may be that the febrile seizures are actually an early manifestation of true epilepsy.

In addition to the main types of epilepsy (which are associated with a single seizure type, e.g., tonic-clonic seizures, absence seizures, or partial complex seizures) epilepsy syndromes may include several seizure types or seizures that manifest in a characteristic manner. Rolandic epilepsy is the most common benign epilepsy syndrome of childhood. This condition is characterized by partial seizures that start with jerking of the tongue, face, or hands and progress to other body areas. These seizures most often occur while a child is falling asleep or waking up. This type of epilepsy, which usually starts in the early school years, is not associated with underlying brain dysfunction or developmental disability, usually resolves by adolescence, and has no associated long-term effects.

In contrast to the benign nature of Rolandic epilepsy, the myoclonic epilepsy syndromes are often difficult to treat and are frequently linked to serious underlying brain disorders with associated significant long-term neurologic dysfunction. A prime example is infantile spasms, which most often appear between 4 and 6 months. The myoclonic seizures associated with this condition are initially revealed as a deceivingly benign-appearing bend of the head and trunk that looks like a sudden, spasmodic bow. The spasms may occur one at a time or in clusters and may be associated with alterations in consciousness or lethargy, but in some instances the infant appears perfectly happy and responsive. An electroencephalograph (EEG; see "How Are Seizures Diagnosed?") shows evidence of electrical chaos in the brain in an alarming pattern known as *hypsarrythmia.* Infantile spasms are notoriously difficult to treat and often evolve into another epilepsy syndrome called *Lennox-Gastaut syndrome,* which is associated with severe intellectual disability; a regression of skills; and several different, difficult-to-control seizure types.

How Are Seizures Diagnosed?

I characterized Brianna's seizure not on the basis of a medical test but by its story—how it started, what it looked like, and how it affected Brianna. When a medical condition is diagnosed in this way it is called a *clinical diagnosis.* Seizures are diagnosed mainly by 1) how they start (things that happen that lead up to the seizure), 2) what they look like (which parts of the body they affect, how they evolve, whether they are associated with a loss of consciousness, and how long they last), and 3) what happens after they stop (postictal events, such as sleepiness). In other words, seizures are diagnosed mainly by careful observation and review of the seizure events themselves. This means that the people who actually observe the seizure (most often parents, other caregivers, and teachers) provide critical information for establishing a diagnosis. Occasionally parents are able to capture a video recording of a suspected seizure, which can be enormously helpful in making a diagnosis.

Special tests are also used to characterize seizures and the causes of seizures. An EEG is usually performed in the aftermath of a seizure and is also used to monitor the effects of treatment and the evolution of the condition over time. In this procedure small electrodes that measure electrical activity in the brain are taped to the scalp at several locations.

Your Observations Are Key to Accurately Diagnosing Seizures

Although special tests (e.g., electroencephalographs) are helpful in characterizing seizures and epilepsy, seizures are diagnosed mainly from careful observations and descriptions of the seizures themselves. Doctors rarely observe the seizures they diagnosis: They rely on parents, other caregivers, and teachers for key information. Your careful observations (ideally written down) are critical to an accurate diagnosis.

These electrodes are connected to a computer that records and displays brain wave patterns. Characteristic changes in specific areas of the brain (e.g., the hypsarrythmia pattern seen in infantile spasms) may be suggestive of a seizure focus or a specific type of seizure or epilepsy. In most instances a child will not actually have a seizure while the EEG is being recorded, but it may be possible to use special techniques to bring out a seizure or seizure-like brain wave pattern. For example, having a child hyperventilate or exposing him to flashing lights may provoke a seizure (you may be surprised to learn that video games and television shows have been known to provoke seizures in some children!). Some seizures are more likely to occur when a child is drowsy or asleep, so having the child stay up the night before an EEG may increase the likelihood that a seizure will occur (this is called a *sleep-deprived EEG*). In some cases when there is great uncertainty about whether a child is having seizures, or when the type of seizure is uncertain, an extended EEG study (typically 24 hours or more) with video and vital sign monitoring (called a *prolonged video EEG*) may be needed.

What Are the Causes of Seizures and Epilepsy?

As mentioned previously, isolated seizures may be provoked by a specific inciting event such as a blow to the head, a drug overdose, serious infection, or a brain tumor. When a child first has a seizure, special tests are usually considered to rule out specific causes. For example, if a child has fever, lethargy, and a stiff neck, he will usually have a spinal tap (also called *lumbar puncture*) to rule out meningitis, a serious infection of the membrane surfaces surrounding the brain and spinal cord. Often children who come to the emergency room with first-time seizures will have a computed tomography scan of the brain, which provides a fast but fairly detailed picture of the brain that can be used to help rule out obvious tumors, trauma, bleeding, stroke, and brain infection.

Children with recurrent seizures, or epilepsy, often undergo magnetic resonance imaging, which provides a more detailed picture of the brain than a computed tomography scan offers and can sometimes show subtle brain anomalies that may be associated with epilepsy. Other special neurological tests and blood tests may be considered on a case-by-case basis, but even after extensive testing it is not uncommon for the cause of epilepsy to be unclear.

Epilepsy occurs in about 0.5%–1% of the population. Some forms of epilepsy run in families; others seem to occur out of the blue in a single family member. In many instances a person with epilepsy has normal brain scans and blood tests, has had typical development, and has no known risk factors for seizures—this person is said to have idiopathic epilepsy (the word *idiopathic* derives from the Greek and means "one's own suffering"). In other cases a specific anomaly, such as an abnormality of brain development, is recognized as the basis for the seizures. Children with developmental disabilities as a group are at increased risk for epilepsy compared to the general population, and this is especially true of children with severe forms of intellectual disability, autism, and CP.

How Are Seizures Treated?

A child who comes to the emergency room with a prolonged seizure that does not stop on its own will receive urgent treatment with injectable antiseizure (anticonvulsant) medications. A child who has had a single, unexplained seizure without apparent cause (and who has a normal EEG, no signs of neurological compromise, and no form of developmental disability) is often not treated unless seizures recur.

A child with recurrent seizures (epilepsy) or a child who considered to be at high risk for seizure recurrence is usually treated with an antiseizure medication; the specific medication used is based on the child's age, the type of seizure, and the side effect profile of the medication being considered (see Table 9.2). The goal is to use a single medication at the lowest effective dose with the fewest possible side effects. For difficult-to-control seizures, higher dosages or the use of multiple medications is sometimes required.

All antiseizure medications have potential side effects, some of which are common and often manageable, and some of which are severe and even life threatening. Regular blood tests to monitor drug blood levels and specific body functions (e.g., blood counts and liver function tests) are needed with some medications. Some antiseizure medications (including valproate and carbamezepine) can cause birth defects and should not be taken

Table 9.2. Medications commonly used to treat epilepsy

Medication	Primary uses	Common side effects (rare/severe reactions)	Monitoring blood levels required?
Valproic acid (Depakene; Depakote)	Partial and generalized seizures	Weight gain, sedation, hair loss (blood reactions, pancreatitis, liver dysfunction)	Yes
Carbamazepine (Tegretol; Carbatrol)	Simple and complex partial seizures	Weight gain, sedation (blood reactions, dizziness)	Yes
Oxycarbamazepine (Trileptil)	Partial seizures	Fatigue, dizziness (severe skin reaction, low blood sodium)	No
Lamotrigine (Lamictal)	Partial and generalized seizures; Lennox-Gastaut syndrome	Nausea or vomiting, dizziness, sedation (severe skin reaction)	No
Levetiracetam (Keppra)	Adjunct treatment of partial and generalized seizures	Sedation, behavior changes (psychosis, depression, severe behavioral effects)	No
Topiramate (Topamax)	Partial and generalized seizures	Sedation, irritability, slurred speech, tingling in the extremities (kidney stones)	No
Ethosuximide (Zarontin)	Absence seizures	Nausea; vomiting (abdominal pain, blood reactions)	Yes

Note: Selected medications and side effects are shown here as examples (this list is *not* comprehensive). Monitoring blood tests are routinely performed for medications indicated but may be required for any medication in specific circumstances. You should consult with your child's doctor regarding other medications and to obtain more detailed information about uses and side effects.

during pregnancy unless no other treatment option is available, and then only under careful medical supervision.

Is It Possible to Stop Taking Antiseizure Medications, or Are They Needed for Life?

Although some people must take antiseizure medications for many years, or even for life, it is often possible to safely discontinue treatment. This depends on many factors, including the type of epilepsy a child has, how difficult the seizures have been to control, and whether specific risk factors (e.g., a focal brain anomaly) exist that increase the likelihood of seizure recurrence.

If these factors are favorable, and the child has been free of seizures for an extended period of time (typically a minimum of 2 years), an EEG is typically obtained. If the results are normal, the medication may be slowly weaned. The child should be monitored closely for signs of recurrent seizure activity, and in some cases follow-up EEG studies may be obtained.

Tics, Twitches, Tremors, and Twirls: Unusual Movements in Children with Disabilities

Michael is a 6-year-old boy with ADHD who has had a tendency to blink and grimace suddenly and randomly for more than a year. His primary care doctor witnessed this during a routine checkup when he was 5 years old, told his mother that Michael had a simple motor tic, and advised her to ignore it as long as it did not bother Michael. At times his tic would occur many times in a day, but there have been days or weeks when it did not appear at all. About a month ago Michael started to shrug his shoulder suddenly and randomly throughout the day, and over the past week he has started sniffing almost constantly. His mother thinks he might have seasonal allergies, but his doctor suspects that both the shoulder shrugs and sniffing may be new tics.

Wendy is a 3-year-old with autism. She loves to stare at ceiling fans and often squints, blinks, and flaps her hands repetitively while doing this. Her parents brought her to see a child neurologist because they were worried she might be having a seizure, but they were told that these movements represent self-stimulatory behavior that is often seen in children with autism spectrum disorders.

Children with developmental disabilities—and many typically developing children—exhibit unusual movements from time to time. If your child has unusual movements, you may be confused or alarmed by them. It is important to understand that in most cases these movements are benign: They cause no harm to your child, they often do not require any special treatment, and not infrequently either they resolve on their own or your child can learn to integrate them successfully into the patterns of daily life.

Unusual movements take many different forms. For example, you may notice that your child's unusual movements always follow the same pattern, involving the same parts of the body in the same way with each occurrence, or you may notice that they vary from day to day. The movements may seem disorganized and chaotic, or repetitive and rhythmical. They may occur at random, or they may happen at predictable times and in particular situations. They may seem to be at least partly under your child's control, or they may seem to have a mind of their own.

You may also find that you are able to prompt your child to stop his unusual movements (or divert his attention from them), or you may find that you cannot influence them at all. You may also notice that your child's unusual movements may wax and wane over time—some days they may seem to happen constantly, and then, inexplicably, they may disappear for weeks or months at a time.

Noticing what your child's unusual movements look like, how often and under what circumstances they occur, and whether your child seems to have any control over them will help to determine what they are, what if anything needs to be done about them, and whether they are likely to persist.

Tics, Tic Disorders, and Tourette Syndrome

Tics (the unusual movements, not the nasty insects—those are *ticks*) are very common in early childhood. Tics are sudden movements, such as a blink or a facial grimace, that are discrete (they occur one at a time) and stereotyped (they look the same each time they happen). There are two types of tics: motor tics and phonic tics. Motor tics involve movement only, most often of the head or upper body. Phonic tics involve a contraction of muscles in the vocal tract, so they are characterized in particular by the production of sound; if the vocal cords are involved, they are called *vocal tics*. Motor and phonic tics may be simple or complex; examples of each are listed in Table 9.3. In general, simple tics involve uncomplicated, sudden, nonpurposeful movements or vocalizations, whereas complex tics involve more elaborate movements that imitate or approximate purposeful actions or speech.

In contrast to some atypical movements that may be entirely involuntary, or outside of a child's control, tics can often be controlled, suppressed, or postponed, although this can be very difficult to do. In fact, one of the hallmarks of a tic is its compulsive

Table 9.3. Types of tics

Type of tic	Examples
Simple motor	Blinking, grimacing, nose twitching, repetitive eye opening, jaw clenching or opening, tensing or jerking of extremities
Complex motor	Head shaking, head or body posturing (e.g., shoulder shrugs), distorted facial expressions, tapping, waving, scratching, touching, jumping, making rude gestures
Simple phonic	Grunting, sniffing, coughing, throat clearing, clicking, hissing, barking, whistling, and making other animal sounds
Complex phonic	Sudden, sometimes explosive utterances involving words, phrases, or sentences and occasionally obscenities or profanities

quality. A tic is usually preceded by an uncomfortable sensation, feeling, or urge that only the performance of the tic itself will relieve. Like an itch that must be scratched, trying to ignore the urge to tic often increases the tension to let it go. It is not uncommon for children who are self-conscious about their tics to try to hold them back while at school, only to release the floodgates when they get home.

Occasional, isolated, transient tics are very common in early childhood. About 25% of all children have them. Most often these are simple tics, such as blinking or grimacing, that occur more or less frequently for brief periods, may wax and wane for a time, but resolve spontaneously within a few weeks or months. Children with this pattern are said to have a transient tic disorder. If tics persist beyond 12 months a child is said to have a chronic tic disorder. Chronic tic disorders may involve only motor tics or, less commonly, only phonic tics. If a child has both motor and phonics tics for more than 12 months, she is said to have Tourette syndrome.

Tourette syndrome has become associated with a vision of bizarre, socially inappropriate behavior and severe tics, including explosive swearing and obscene language and gestures. Fortunately this represents an extreme and rare manifestation of the condition. In fact, children with Tourette syndrome vary greatly in the type and severity of the tics they have. Very often the child with Tourette syndrome initially exhibits a simple motor tic that most often appears between 3 and 10 years of age. As one tic resolves another tic takes its place. Eventually the repertoire of tics will come to include phonic tics, and complex tics may enter the mix. In the earlier example, Michael has had simple motor tics for more than a year, so he can be diagnosed with a chronic tic disorder. More recently he has developed complex motor tics and has a new phonic tic. This pattern suggests that he may be in the early stages of Tourette syndrome, although he has not had the phonic tic long enough (more than 12 months) to confirm the diagnosis.

Although not a part of the diagnostic criteria for Tourette syndrome (which is based solely on the presence of motor and phonic tics for more than 12 months), the conditions that are associated with this syndrome often have a bigger impact on a child's life than the tics themselves. ADHD is especially frequent, occurring in at least 50% of children with Tourette syndrome. About one third of children with Tourette syndrome have obsessive-compulsive disorder (see Chapter 5). Learning disabilities, stuttering and other disorders of speech and language, anxiety disorders, mood disorders, oppositional defiant disorder, self-injurious behavior, and problems with explosive anger and mood regulation are all being seen with increased frequency in these children. And although the tics associated with Tourette syndrome usually decrease significantly both in frequency and in severity when a child reaches adolescence, the problems associated with the related conditions often persist.

The treatment of Tourette syndrome and other tic disorders often focuses on interventions for associated conditions such as ADHD rather than on the tics themselves. In fact, for the majority of children with tics no treatment is necessary— interventions are considered only when the tics cause significant disruption and disability. If a child is unconcerned about her tics, and they cause her no social embarrassment, then it is

Medications for Attention-Deficit/ Hyperactivity Disorder in Children with Tics

Stimulant medications used as first-line therapy for attention-deficit/hyperactivity disorder, such as methylphenidate (Ritalin, Metadate CD, Concerta), amphetamine (Adderall, Adderall XR) and lisdexamfetamine (Vyvanse), were once thought to be unsafe for children with tic disorders because they have been observed to increase tics in some children. Recent research suggests that these medications can be used safely in children with tic disorders and that the benefits of successfully treating significant attention-deficit/ hyperactivity disorder in these children outweigh the risk of aggravating tics, which may be less than previously suspected.

usually appropriate to forgo therapy. If, however, a child is very self-conscious about her tics or finds them embarrassing, distracting, and disruptive, then treatment may be indicated.

For some older children and adults a behavioral approach to treatment may be considered. This is based on the idea of teaching the person to recognize the urge to tic and learn to preempt the tic by engaging in a substitute, competing behavior.

A variety of medications can reduce the frequency and severity of tics (see Chapter 10), but it is important to recognize that no medication cures or eliminates tics, and no medication affects the likelihood that tics will persist. Medications known as typical antipsychotics, such as haloperidol (Haldol), have traditionally been used as first-line therapy, but these have significant short- and long-term side effects, and most doctors prefer starting out with medications with a more favorable side effect profile. Clonidine and guanfacine in particular can reduce tics, have relatively manageable side effects (although they can cause sedation in some children), and come in long-acting forms that are also used in treating ADHD. A new generation of atypical antipsychotics, such as risperidone (Risperdal), which are also used to treat agitation and aggression associated with autism, have a better side effect profile than typical antipsychotics and are often considered when clonidine or guanfacine are insufficiently effective. In some instances medications used to treat anxiety and obsessive-compulsive disorder, such as fluoxetine (Prozac) and sertraline (Zoloft), may reduce the occurrence of tics, perhaps by ameliorating the factors (e.g., anxiety) that tend to aggravate them.

Stereotypies: Self-Stimulatory Behaviors

Wendy, the child with autism described previously, exhibits several behaviors that are often called *self-stimulatory behaviors* (more formally they are called *stereotypies*, and more casually they are called *stims*). The hand flapping that she does when she is excited (in this example, to express her pleasure at observing a ceiling fan) is a typical example. Hand flapping is repetitive and rhythmical, and for Wendy it is both an expression of an abundance of pleasure and a source of pleasure in and of itself. The squinting and blinking that she does, although superficially similar to the blinking and grimacing associated with some simple motor tics, is clearly connected to the pleasure of looking at the spinning fan and, in some mysterious way, seems to enhance Wendy's experience of the fan.

One way to think of self-stimulatory behaviors is that they represent either 1) an effort to enhance the experience of an object or sensation (as when a child looks at, listens to, touches, smells, or licks an object in a way that seems unusual or even inappropriate); or 2) an effort to create a pleasurable experience through repetitive, rhythmic activity.

Self-stimulatory behaviors are also comforting behaviors. They often occur when a child is bored, or anxious, or overstimulated, and in each instance the child finds solace in the repetitive rhythm of the self-stimulatory activity. This tendency is by no means confined to children with disabilities. Many typically developing children exhibit these comforting and self-soothing behaviors (rocking back and forth in bed is a familiar example of this). Yet self-stimulatory behaviors do seem to occur with greater frequency and intensity in children with disabilities. Children with sensory processing disorder (see Chapter 8), autism spectrum disorder (see Chapter 5), or severe intellectual disability (see Chapter 6) are especially likely to exhibit stereotypies. Common self-stimulatory behaviors are listed in Table 9.4.

In some cases self-stimulatory behavior may become extreme and may snowball into self-injurious behavior. There is a theory that children who engage in severe self-injury (e.g., severe

Table 9.4. Common self-stimulatory behaviors

Hand flapping
Finger flicking, twirling, or repetitive crossing
Squinting
Atypical vocalizations (e.g., squealing, nonfearful screaming)
Jumping, hopping, or toe walking
Spinning
Rocking
Running back and forth or in circles
Flicking or flipping objects with the hands or fingers
Collecting objects, one in each hand
Smelling, sniffing, or licking objects
Viewing objects close up, between the fingers, through peripheral vision
Covering the ears to distort sounds
Teeth grinding (bruxism)

head banging, self-biting, self-hitting, eye gouging, skin picking) may, through their actions, cause a release of brain endorphins (morphine-like brain chemicals) that signal pleasure. So in a bizarrely counterintuitive way, these inherently painful activities may actually be self-reinforcing because of the effects they have on the pleasure centers of the brain.

Most self-stimulatory behaviors are not dangerous in and of themselves, but they can become distracting, and in some cases they may interfere with more purposeful activities. Perhaps more important, they have the potential to be socially stigmatizing—this is often a primary concern of parents. Fortunately, self-stimulatory behaviors tend to abate as children grow and mature—this is especially true of typically developing children and children with milder forms of developmental disability. Interventions are focused primarily on behavioral methods (e.g., redirection and reinforcement of competing behaviors) and social skills training to alert a child to differences between private and public behavior. Medications such as risperidone are sometimes tried to help address severe self-injurious behavior, but the results are inconsistent, and the effects of medications on milder stereotypies are even more unpredictable and often disappointing.

Other Unusual Movements in Children with Disabilities

A variety of other unusual or atypical movements is observed in children with disabilities. Tremors are fine, rapid, repetitive movements most commonly observed in the hands. Intention tremors are most commonly observed. They occur mainly when a child is engaged in an intentional, or voluntary, action, such as reaching for an object. In these instances they may represent a problem with motor planning that can occur as part of several physical disabilities, including some forms of CP and some cases of developmental coordination disorder. There is also a familial form of tremor called *essential tremor* that seems to be genetic in nature and that is not associated with developmental disability.

Tremors when one is at rest (i.e., tremors that occur all of the time and are not associated with or influenced by activity in particular) are associated with neurological disease such as Parkinson's disease in adults but are less common in children. They may occur in specific circumstances as a side effect of medication or as a reaction to a metabolic disturbance such as low blood sugar.

A variety of other unusual movements have as their hallmark the fact that they are involuntary. These include chorea (rapid, jerky movements), athetosis (slow, writhing movements), and dystonia (uncontrolled postural changes with muscle tightness). These involuntary movements mainly occur without reference to purposeful movement, although in some instances purposeful action may temporarily suppress them. Seizures (see "Firestorm in the Brain: Seizures and Epilepsy") are often associated with involuntary movements that vary in their character depending on the type of seizure. Chorea, athetosis, and dystonia in children are most often associated with extrapyramidal CP and are thought to be related to a dysfunction of deep brain structures called the *basal ganglia* (see Chapter 2).

Myoclonus is sudden, lightning-fast movements that may be isolated (discrete) or repetitive or rhythmic. Although myoclonus is mainly of interest as a manifestation of certain types of epilepsy, it can occur apart from epilepsy. For example, myoclonic jerks are often observed during sleep transitions, such as falling asleep and wakening. They occur commonly in both children with disabilities and typically developing children.

Special Health Care Needs
for Children with Down Syndrome,
Spina Bifida, and Cerebral Palsy

ote to the reader: This appendix is written for those who are interested in learning in greater detail some of the common medical concerns that occur in children with three important disability-related conditions: Down syndrome, spina bifida, and cerebral palsy. This information is presented in a more condensed format that the rest of this book, with the intention of providing a concise introduction that may serve as a springboard to further reading (including an exploration of more comprehensive discussions of these conditions listed in the Resources section at the end of this book).

Most children with developmental disabilities have fairly typical health care needs, although as a group they are more prone to difficulties with growth and nutrition; gastrointestinal complaints; dental concerns; and neurological concerns, including epilepsy and unusual body movements. Some children have specific conditions that, in addition to causing disability, lead to special health care concerns. There are in fact many such conditions, all deserving of attention, but here the focus is on three particularly important examples: Down syndrome (DS), spina bifida, and cerebral palsy (CP). These conditions are highlighted here because they are relatively common, because the health care concerns associated with them are substantial, and because each represents a different type of medical diagnosis that can lead to both disability and complex health care needs. DS is a genetic condition caused by the presence of an extra chromosome, spina bifida is a complex birth defect of the nervous system, and CP is a condition that most often results from brain damage that disrupts early brain development. Each condition is associated with a variety of developmental, sensory, and health care concerns, some of which are unique to the condition and some of which are shared by children with other diagnoses.

DOWN SYNDROME

Down syndrome is an important, common and complex genetic condition that is associated with a number of specific medical concerns, some of which manifest primarily in the newborn period, and some which are important throughout the lifespan.

What Causes Down Syndrome?

DS is the most common genetic cause of intellectual disability. It occurs in just less than 1 birth per 1,000. DS is most often caused by the presence of an extra chromosome (specifically chromosome 21). Humans typically have 23 pairs of chromosomes: One half of each pair comes from the father (via sperm cells), and the other half comes from the mother (via egg cells). DS most often happens when a glitch occurs in the creation of the egg cell so that two maternal chromosome 21s (instead of one) are combined with one paternal chromosome 21 for a total of three chromosomes (instead of the expected two)—this is why DS is also called *trisomy 21*. Mothers older than 35 years of age are particularly prone to experiencing this glitch (the technical term for which is *nondisjunction*), so their pregnancies are monitored especially closely for signs that the developing fetus may have DS.

A small number of children with DS (about 4%) have translocation Down syndrome. Like children with trisomy 21, they have extra chromosome 21 material, but instead of being present as an extra chromosome, a copy of chromosome 21 hitches a ride on another chromosome (most often chromosome 14). Although children with translocation DS and trisomy 21 DS are indistinguishable with regard to health care needs and development, the risk of recurrence is very different. A child with translocation DS may have a parent who is a carrier of a balanced translocation; that is, the parent does not have DS but carries the hybrid chromosome. If this parent passes this atypical chromosome on to future offspring, there is a higher risk of having another child with DS compared to the risk for parents with a child with trisomy 21.

About 1% of children with DS have mosaic Down syndrome. Their bodies have a mixture of typical cells (containing two chromosome 21s) and atypical cells (containing three chromosome 21s). These children may have slightly mild symptoms of DS depending on the percentage and distribution of typical and trisomy 21 cells in their body.

How Is Down Syndrome Diagnosed?

DS can be diagnosed prenatally by amniocentesis, a procedure that involves the insertion of a needle through the mother's abdominal wall into the amniotic fluid surrounding the fetus within the uterus, or womb. Fetal cells floating in the fluid can be tested for the presence of an extra chromosome 21. Another procedure, called *chorionic villus sampling*, involves taking a tissue sample from the membranes surrounding the fetus through the vagina and can be done earlier in the pregnancy. Both procedures are associated with a small but significant risk of fetal loss (miscarriage), so screening tests are performed to determine which mothers are at greatest risk for having a child with DS.

A first trimester screening procedure that incorporates maternal age, specific results from a special sonogram study of the fetus (called *nuchal translucency ultrasonography*) that assesses the neck fold of the fetus, and the results of maternal blood tests can detect DS 82%–85% of the time. A second trimester test incorporates maternal age with the results of blood tests. Putting the first and second trimester tests together, it is possible to predict DS 95% of the time. Characteristic findings on sonogram examinations (ultrasound images of the fetus obtained through the maternal abdominal wall) can also provide clues that suggest the possibility of DS.

After birth the diagnosis is based on recognizing the characteristic features of DS in the newborn (see Figure 9.1). The diagnosis is confirmed by obtaining a blood sample from the infant and testing it for trisomy 21 or translocation DS; other tests may be required to confirm a diagnosis of mosaic DS.

What Special Medical Problems May Be Evident at Birth?

Between 40% and 50% of children with DS are born with heart (cardiac) abnormalities and may require surgery to correct them. A common heart problem involves having abnormal communication between the top two chambers of the heart (the atria)

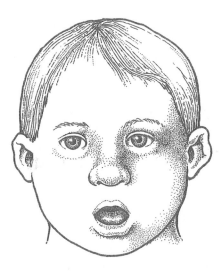

Figure 9.1. The features of Down syndrome. Characteristic facial features of children with Down syndrome include small head size; a flattening of the face and back of the head; small, low-set ears; upslanting of the eyes; skin folds on the inner corners of the eyes; a small, upturned nose; and a protruding tongue (due to the low tone of the facial muscles, not a large tongue). Other features include a single crease across the palms, short stubby fingers, a hernia of the belly button, and an exaggerated space between the first and second toes (called a *sandal gap*). (From Batshaw, M.L. [1997]. *Children with disabilities* [4th ed., p. 362]. Baltimore, MD: Paul H. Brookes Publishing Co., reprinted by permission.)

and the bottom two chambers (the ventricles)—this is called an *atrioventricular septal defect* (also called an *atrioventricular canal*). Blood rushing through the defect may cause a heart murmur that a doctor can hear with a stethoscope; the diagnosis is confirmed by obtaining an echocardiogram, an ultrasound imaging test similar to the sonogram performed during pregnancy. Surgical correction is required. A variety of other heart abnormalities may also occur, some of which require surgical correction and some of which can be monitored by a pediatric heart doctor, or pediatric cardiologist.

Some children with DS are born with duodenal atresia. In this condition the duodenum, the tube that connects the bottom of the stomach with the rest of the small intestine (see "Tummy Trouble" in Chapter 9), has formed improperly during fetal development and is closed rather than open, so food that is being digested cannot pass through. This must be corrected surgically in the newborn period. Other children may have developmental

abnormalities of the esophagus, rectum, or trachea that also require surgical correction.

Some children with DS are born with an abnormality in the
development and functioning of the lower colon, a condition
called *Hirschsprung disease,* that results in severe constipation or a
complete inability to pass stool. Surgery is required to remove the
segment of dysfunctional bowel.

Some children with DS are born with an absent or small
thyroid gland (called *congenital hypothyroidism*), and they do not
produce enough thyroid hormone, which is necessary for body
metabolism, growth, and brain development. Blood tests can determine whether a child has low thyroid hormone, and thyroid
supplements can be given when needed.

Some children with DS are born with cataracts, or clouding
of the lens of the eye. If this is detected by a child's doctor, the
child should be promptly referred to a pediatric ophthalmologist
for evaluation and treatment.

Rarely children with DS can develop leukemia, a type of
blood cancer that involves an abnormal increase in white blood
cells, which are an important part of the immune system. More
commonly newborns with DS may develop a temporary, noncan-
cerous increase in their white blood cell count; this is called *transient myeloproliferative disorder* and must be distinguished from
leukemia.

What Special Medical Problems
May Be Evident at Other Times?

A number of medical problems that affect individuals with DS
may occur at any time during the lifespan. While some problems
are more common in childhood, others may manifest for the first
time in adulthood, and some may persist throughout life.

Hypothyroidism

Children with DS are prone to developing hypothyroidism, or
low thyroid hormone production, at any time of life (the risk actually increases with age). The American Academy of Pediatrics
recommends testing for low thyroid hormone at 6 months and 1
year of age and then yearly thereafter.

Ear Infections and Hearing Loss

Children with DS are also prone to a variety of problems with their ears—especially recurrent infections and fluid accumulation—that predispose them to hearing loss. In fact, an astonishing 75% of children with DS develop hearing problems. The American Academy of Pediatrics recommends that children who do not have symptoms of ear or hearing problems have their hearing testing by an audiologist at 6 months of age, 1 year of age, and then annually once it is possible to test hearing in each ear separately.

Vision Problems

Many children with DS need corrective lenses (glasses), and some have eye muscle weakness (strabismus; see Chapter 8). Problems with jiggling eye movements (nystagmus), droopy eyelids (ptosis), and blocked tear ducts are also common. Cataracts may be present at birth (see "What Special Medical Problems May Be Evident at Birth?"). The American Academy of Pediatrics recommends that all children with DS have their first ophthalmologic exam (eye evaluation) by a pediatric ophthalmologist within the first 6 months of life, then yearly up to 5 years of age, every 2 years up to 13 years of age, and every 3 years thereafter.

Tummy Trouble

Children with DS are prone to gastroesophageal reflux (GER) and even more so to chronic constipation (see "Tummy Trouble" in Chapter 9). Celiac disease most often manifests in infancy after the introduction of products that contain wheat but can occur at any time. If a child is showing poor appetite, bloating, poor weight gain, chronic diarrhea, or persistent constipation despite treatment, blood tests should be done to screen for celiac disease.

Growth, Nutrition, and Obesity Concerns

Although some children with DS may have trouble with insufficient weight gain, as a group they are more prone to obesity. Obesity also predisposes these children to diabetes, which occurs at a higher rate in children with DS than in typically developing children. The body mass index (described in "Growth and Nutrition" in Chapter 9) is important in monitoring the trend toward obesity. Most children with DS have short stature, although their ultimate height is influenced by how tall their parents are.

Joint Laxity and Atlantoaxial Instability

Children with DS have low muscle tone and joint laxity, or looseness of the joints. A particular concern relates to the joint at the top of the spinal column in the neck called the *atlantoaxial joint*. If there is too much flexibility or give in this joint, the bones of the spinal column may press on the spinal cord within, potentially causing spinal cord damage and even paralysis (this is called *atlantoaxial instability*). This is especially likely to happen during extreme bending (flexion) or stretching (extension) of the neck (as when a child is trying to learn somersaults). The American Academy of Pediatrics previously recommended that x rays of the neck be obtained for all children with DS between 3 and 5 years of age; this recommendation has since been withdrawn because of uncertainties about the accuracy of the test. It is now recommended that all parents be counseled to be vigilant for changes in gait, changes in arm or hand use, changes in bowel or bladder function, neck pain, head tilt, or signs of weakness as possible indicators of atlantoaxial instability. A child's primary doctor should be alerted immediately to any concerns and proper steps taken, including the careful taking of x rays of the neck and prompt referral to a pediatric neurosurgeon or pediatric orthopedic surgeon experienced in treating atlantoaxial instability. Parents are also counseled about the importance of cervical spine (neck) positioning if their child with DS has anesthesia, surgery, or any special x-ray tests that might put undue stress on the atlantoaxial joint.

Obstructive Sleep Apnea

Children with DS tend to have floppy airways: When they are lying down they can have trouble keeping the air passages in the back of their throat open. This may cause interrupted breathing and snoring, nighttime wakening, and daytime sleepiness or irritability, which may be signs of obstructive sleep apnea. Obstructive sleep apnea occurs in 50%–75% of children with DS. In addition to the developmental and behavioral consequences of disrupted sleep, obstructive sleep apnea can also have significant medical consequences, including adverse effects on the heart. Evaluation by an otolaryngologist (a doctor who specializes in ear, nose, and throat problems) is warranted. Because of the difficulties in recognizing the signs of obstructive sleep apnea, the American Academy of Pediatrics recommends that all children with DS have a formal sleep study (also called a *polysomnogram*) by age 4 (see "Sleeping" in Chapter 3).

Dental Problems

Children with DS are prone to a variety of dental problems, including an increased risk of cavities, widely spaced or crowded teeth, and bruxism (teeth grinding). It is very common for children with DS to have delayed eruption of teeth, and many children have a decreased number of teeth.

Skin Problems

Children with DS seem to have sensitive skin and are more prone to developing rashes, dryness, eczema, and skin infections. They are also more likely to develop hair loss and patchy baldness, called *alopecia areata*, which is thought to occur as the result of the body's immune system attacking the hair follicles. Topical medications may help; consultation with a skin specialist (dermatologist) may be considered.

Iron Deficiency Anemia

Children with DS are at increased risk for iron deficiency anemia due to a decreased dietary intake of iron. The American Academy of Pediatrics recommends that a blood test to measure hemoglobin (a measure of anemia) be obtained annually beginning at 1 year of age.

Seizures

Children with DS are at increased risk for developing seizures. Infantile spasms (see "What Is the Difference Between Seizures and Epilepsy?" in Chapter 9) are of particular concern.

Concerns with Sexuality and Fertility

Children with DS follow the typical pattern of physical change during puberty. Females are fertile and have a 50% chance of having a child with DS themselves. Males are usually infertile, although rare exceptions have been reported.

Special Developmental, Emotional, and Behavioral Concerns

Most children with DS have mild to moderate intellectual disability. Children with DS also have a higher incidence of autism spectrum disorders; emotional difficulties, such as depression and anxiety; and behavior difficulties related to impulsivity and distractibility (these children are sometimes diagnosed with attention-deficit/hyperactivity disorder), defiant behavior, and aggression.

SPINA BIFIDA

Spina bifida is the most complex birth defect-associated condition that is compatible with life. Individuals with spina bifida, especially the most complex and severe forms, have very challenging medical problems that require a team of professionals working in concert with family members to successfully manage.

What Causes Spina Bifida?

As noted in Chapter 2, spina bifida occurs when the precursor to the spinal cord, called the *neural tube,* fails to form properly early in fetal development. Although the most obvious manifestation of this is abnormal development of the spinal cord, problems also occur in the brain. The mildest form, spina bifida occulta, occurs in about 10% of the population and affects only the vertebrae (backbone segments) that surround the spinal cord. There are no physical symptoms or signs of this; it is only seen on x ray, which reveals a small split in the bones that cover a small segment of the spinal cord. In more severe forms of spina bifida a segment of the spinal cord and the nerves that are connected to it are also involved. A sac containing spinal and nerve tissue, called a *meningomyelocele,* bulges out of the back where the split occurs (see Figure 9.2).

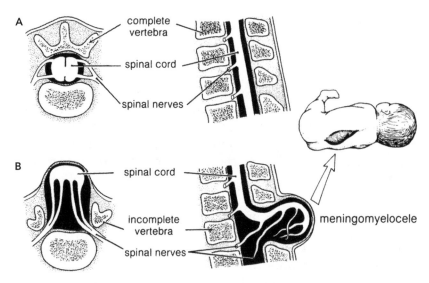

Figure 9.2. Comparing the normal spine and spina bifida. A) A cross-section and longitudinal section of the normal spine at birth, showing complete enclosure of the spinal cord and nerves within the spinal canal formed by the bony vertebra. B) In spina bifida a defect of vertebral development allows a segment of the spinal cord and associated nerves to bulge out through the skin of the back—the visible sac on the newborn's back is called a *meningomyelocele*. (From Batshaw, M.L., Pellegrino, L., & Roizen, N. [Eds.]. [2007]. *Children with disabilities* [6th ed., p. 421]. Baltimore, MD: Paul H. Brookes Publishing Co.; adapted by permission.)

In the United States about 60 children out of every 100,000 are born with meningomyelocele. Environmental, nutritional, and genetic factors all seem to play a role in this condition. An association between a dietary deficiency of folic acid during pregnancy and an increased incidence of spina bifida in offspring is an especially important discovery that has shed light on the role of maternal nutrition in the genesis of spina bifida. Fortifying foods (e.g., bread) with folic acid and taking folic acid supplements during pregnancy have reduced but not eliminated the occurrence of spina bifida. Alcohol, hyperthermia (increased maternal body temperature), and several medications, including the antiseizure medications valproic acid (Depakote) and carbamazepine (Tegretol) and the acne medicine isotretinoin (Accutane), have been associated with an increased risk of spina bifida. Girls are more likely than boys to have spina bifida, and women from certain ethnic groups (e.g., Latino women) are at higher risk than others of having an infant with spina bifida.

The degree of motor impairment and physical disability associated with spina bifida is directly related to the level of the spinal abnormality. Muscle paralysis and loss of sensation occur below the level of the lesion, so the higher on the spine the lesion occurs, the more severe the effect will be. (The motor impairments and limitations on mobility associated with lesions at each spinal level are discussed in Chapter 2.) Likewise, higher-level spinal lesions are associated with more significant and more complex brain complications, health care problems, and developmental concerns.

How Is Spina Bifida Diagnosed?

A maternal blood test for alpha-fetoprotein, usually obtained between the 16th and 18th weeks of pregnancy, is elevated when the developing fetus has an open meningomyelocele (this same test is low in mothers of children with DS). In these cases, a maternal sonogram (ultrasound image of the fetus within the uterus) is used to characterize spinal and brain anomalies. Moreover, an amniocentesis is performed to collect amniotic fluid (the liquid that bathes the fetus within the womb) to test for elevated alpha-fetoprotein and other proteins associated with meningomyelocele. (Chromosome testing is also performed to rule out rare genetic conditions that are sometimes associated with spina bifida.)

What Special Medical Problems May Be Evident at Birth?

When meningomyelocele is identified prenatally, plans are usually made to have the delivery at a medical center that specializes in the care of newborns with spina bifida and other complex medical needs. Infants are typically delivered by cesarean section to avoid additional damage to the exposed spinal cord that could occur during their passage through the birth canal. Newborns with meningomyelocele usually receive routine care in the delivery room and nursery, but special care is taken to cover and protect the protruding sac of spinal and nerve tissue from contamination, and antibiotics are administered to prevent infection. The sac must be surgically closed within 72 hours of birth to prevent serious infection and to forestall further damage to adjacent healthy areas of the spinal cord.

Although the spinal abnormality associated with meningomyelocele is apparent at birth, further evaluation is required to identify associated problems of the brain, back, legs, and internal organs. An ultrasound or magnetic resonance image of the brain is obtained to look for brain abnormalities, especially hydrocephalus (a buildup of fluid in the brain) and Chiari II malformation (see "What Are the Functional and Health Care Consequences of the Brain Anomalies in Spina Bifida?"). The identification of hydrocephalus in a newborn with spina bifida is especially important. Hydrocephalus occurs when the normal drainage of the ventricles (the fluid-filled spaces in the central area of the brain) is obstructed. As the ventricles enlarge, the newborn's head also enlarges (as determined by measures of head circumference) because his skull bones are not yet fused together. Eventually the increased pressure associated with the ballooning ventricles will cause brain damage. The problem is treated surgically with the placement of a shunt, or a special tube that diverts cerebrospinal fluid (the fluid that fills the ventricles and bathes the surfaces of the brain) from the ventricles to drain elsewhere in the body, most often the space in the abdomen between the abdominal wall and the internal organs called the *peritoneal space* (see Figure 9.3). The surgery is performed by a neurosurgeon, a doctor who specializes in the surgical treatment of brain and spinal cord problems.

A newborn with spina bifida is also evaluated by an orthopedic surgeon, a doctor who specializes in the treatment of muscle and bone problems, who evaluates deformities of the spine (e.g., an exaggerated inward curving of the lower spine called *kyphosis*) and limbs (e.g., club foot, in which the foot is stuck with the toes pointed down and the foot turned and curved inward). In some cases early surgical correction is considered. Blood tests and ultrasound images of the kidneys are also obtained to rule out abnormalities of kidney anatomy or function. A special test (called a *voiding cystourethrogram*) is performed to check for a backup of urine from the bladder into the kidneys. If this urinary reflux is observed, the child is usually placed on prophylactic antibiotics to prevent serious kidney infection.

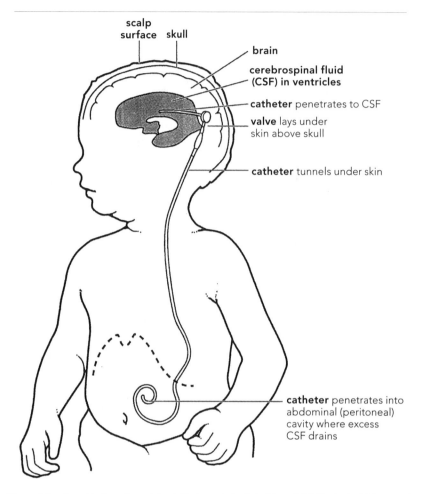

scalp
surface   skull

brain

cerebrospinal fluid
(CSF) in ventricles

catheter penetrates to CSF

valve lays under
skin above skull

catheter tunnels under skin

catheter penetrates into
abdominal (peritoneal)
cavity where excess
CSF drains

Figure 9.3.   A ventriculoperitoneal shunt. Hydrocephalus (a buildup of fluid in the brain) is treated surgically with the placement of a ventriculoperitoneal shunt, a system of tubes and valves that drains cerebrospinal fluid from the ventricles in the brain to the peritoneal cavity in the abdomen. (From Dormans, J.P., & Pellegrino, L. [1998]. *Caring for children with cerebral palsy: A team approach* [p. 88]. Baltimore, MD: Paul H. Brookes Publishing Co.; reprinted by permission.)

What Are the Functional and Health Care Consequences of the Spinal Malformation in Spina Bifida?

Many of the most challenging aspects of managing the rehabilitation and medical concerns associated with spina bifida are a direct or indirect consequence of the primary spinal malformation that defines the condition.

Motor Impairments

As previously noted, the level of the spinal cord malformation is directly correlated with the motor impairment and functional limitations associated with spina bifida (these are discussed in Chapter 2).

Spine and Limb Deformities

Children with spina bifida commonly have deformities of the spine, such as scoliosis (a sideways curvature of the spine) and kyphosis (an exaggerated inward curvature of the spine). They are also prone to developing contractures, which represent permanent shortening of muscles and tendons with associated fixed deformities of the limbs (especially in the legs and feet). Bracing, therapy, and surgery are often required to address these problems.

Loss of Sensation and Skin Ulcers

Loss of sensation occurs below the level of the spinal cord lesion, so children with spina bifida cannot sense pain in those areas of the body. Skin ulcers, called *decubitus ulcers* or *decubiti,* tend to form at pressure points that usually occur at bony prominences in the lower back, buttocks, feet, and ankles. These can be difficult to treat and sometimes require hospitalization. Preventive care involves constant vigilance and a diligent routine of pressure-relieving movements and postural adjustments (e.g., shifting positions every few minutes while seated in a wheelchair).

Bladder and Bowel Dysfunction

Most children with spina bifida have bladder and bowel dysfunction. Bladder dysfunction occurs as a consequence of 1) problems storing urine or 2) problems emptying urine. A special concern is the combination of a tight sphincter at the outlet of the bladder and increased tone of the walls of the bladder itself, which creates pressure that can cause backup or reflux or urine into the kidneys. Kidney infections and chronic kidney damage that ultimately lead to life-threatening renal failure may occur as a consequence.

To relieve the pressure of the urine and aid in the development of urinary continence, parents and children are taught to use catheters to drain the bladder regularly; the procedure is called *clean intermittent catheterization.* Clean intermittent catheterization usually starts when the child is between 3 and 5 years of age and is done every 2–4 hours. Most children can learn to catheterize themselves by 8 years of age. Regular monitoring of urinary function using a variety of special tests is supervised by a urologist, a doctor with special expertise in the diagnosis and management of bladder disorders. If clean intermittent catheterization is unsuccessful, special surgical procedures are sometimes considered to improve urinary continence and to provide more reliable urine drainage and pressure relief.

Bowel dysfunction due to inadequate emptying of the colon and loss of sensation frequently results in constipation. In addition to the typical strategies for addressing constipation (see "Tummy Trouble" in Chapter 9), special catheters are often used to allow for the regular administration of enemas as part of a bowel program. If conventional methods are unsuccessful, surgical placement of a tube through the abdominal wall into the colon may be considered. This allows for the direct flushing of fluids to completely evacuate the bowels.

Tethered Spinal Cord

In a child with spina bifida the spinal cord ends lower in the spinal column than it does in other children, and it may adhere to adjacent tissues so that as the child grows, the spinal cord gets stuck rather than shifts freely within the spinal column. This tethering of the spinal cord results in a variety of problems, usually in the form of some type of functional regression. Symptoms include increasing leg weakness, muscle atrophy, loss of sensation, decreased leg reflexes, the formation of new decubitus ulcers, regression of walking skills, pain in the back or legs, regression in bladder or bowel function, and rapid worsening of orthopedic problems such as foot and back deformities. Magnetic resonance imaging may help in diagnosing tethered spinal cord but is not conclusive; careful recognition of changes in function is key to the diagnosis. A neurosurgeon will typically be consulted and may recommend surgery to release the tethered spinal cord.

Some children with spina bifida can develop pockets of fluids within the spinal cord itself (this is called *syringomyelia,* or *syrinx* for short). This can happen anywhere along the spinal cord, resulting in neurological compromise that can cause symptoms similar to those of a tethered spinal cord or a Chiari II malformation (see "Chiari II Malformation"), depending on the location of the syrinx.

Sexual Dysfunction

Children with spina bifida experience the same changes associated with puberty and adolescence that other children experience, but because sexual sensations and function are mediated by nerves from the lower spinal cord (close to the nerves that control bladder and bowel function), most experience some degree of sexual dysfunction. This affects females and males differently. Females have decreased sensation in the genitalia but have normal fertility, although pregnancies can be high risk, especially in women with significant spinal deformities. Males experience decreased sensation as well, may have trouble achieving and maintaining an erection, and may not be able to ejaculate. Despite these challenges, many adults with spina bifida are able to successfully integrate sexual activity and intimacy into their lives, and many options exist for addressing fertility problems in those who wish to have families.

What Are the Functional and Health Care Consequences of the Brain Anomalies in Spina Bifida?

While the spinal anomaly associated with spina bifida is its most defining characteristic, the brain anomalies associated with this condition are equally important in determining functional outcomes and as the basis for several medical concerns.

Hydrocephalus and Shunt Failure

The shunts used to treat hydrocephalus work well, but they are unfortunately prone to failure. Shunt infection or mechanical problems with disconnected tubing, blockage or kinking of the tubing, or valve dysfunction can all lead to shunt failure and the symptoms of progressive hydrocephalus. These include head-ache, irritability, lethargy, vomiting, double vision or eye devia-tion, increased head circumference or bulging fontanel (soft spot) in infants, decline in attention skills and academic work in older children, and changes in mood or personality. X rays of the shunt and computed tomography scans are used to assess whether the shunt needs to be repaired or replaced; fluid samples may be extracted directly from the shunt to test for signs of infection. Ventriculitis, or infection of the ventricles, is a potentially life-threatening consequence of shunt infection that can cause fur-ther motor and cognitive impairment above and beyond that as-sociated with a child's spina bifida.

Chiari II Malformation

The Chiari II malformation occurs in the majority of children with spina bifida. Just as the spinal cord sits lower in the spinal canal in these children, lower parts of the brain (including part of the brainstem, a structure that ends where the spinal cord begins and is important in the regulation of vital functions such as breathing) are displaced downward through the hole at the base of the skull into the upper part of the spine in the neck.

The normal flow of cerebrospinal fluid within and over the surfaces of the brain is restricted in the region affected by the Chiari II malformation: In this way the anomaly is thought to be a key factor in the high rates of hydrocephalus in children with spina bifida. If these brain structures are further compromised—as, for example, when a child has worsening hydrocephalus (which cre-ates downward pressure) or a tethered spinal cord (which creates downward pull)—breathing difficulties, hoarseness of the voice, trouble swallowing, episodes of apnea (interrupted breathing), and weakness of the arms may ensue. Surgical decompression in-volving the removal of segments of bone in the upper spine may be required to relieve these symptoms.

Strabismus

Strabismus refers to problems with eye muscle weakness and eye movement (see Chapter 8). About 20% of children with spina bifida experience some degree of strabismus. Early referral to a pediatric ophthalmologist (eye doctor) is recommended for all children with spina bifida.

Epilepsy

Seizures and epilepsy occur in about 15% of people with spina bifida. These are most often generalized tonic-clonic seizures (see "Firestorm in the Brain: Seizures and Epilepsy"). Seizures may be a symptom of shunt infection or malfunction, so care should be taken to consider this possibility in a child with a first-time seizure or a child who experiences worsening seizures despite previously having good seizure control.

Learning Disabilities and Attention-Deficit/Hyperactivity Disorder

Children with spina bifida generally demonstrate average to low-average results on IQ tests (i.e., they do not typically have intellectual disability), but they are prone to attention-deficit/ hyperactivity disorder and learning disabilities (see Chapters 5 and 6, respectively). Verbal cognitive and learning skills tend to be strong, and visuospatial, visual-motor, and nonverbal problem-solving skills may be weak. Nonverbal learning disability and math learning disability are particularly common. Most children with spina bifida are able to function in typical classroom environments with appropriate support under an individualized education program (see Chapter 7).

Precocious Puberty

Puberty that starts before 8 years of age in girls or 9 years of age in boys is defined as early or precocious puberty. Children with spina bifida (especially girls) experience precocious puberty more frequently than do typically developing children. This is thought to be a consequence of the brain anomalies associated with spina bifida (children with more severe forms of CP also have an increased incidence of precocious puberty). Although children with precocious puberty experience an early growth spurt, their ultimate height tends to be shorter than expected. Children who show signs of early pubertal development should be evaluated by an endocrinologist, a doctor who specializes in growth and hormonal disorders, to determine the best course of action to address these concerns. For example, the use of medications that delay the onset of puberty may be considered.

Other Health Care Concerns

Obesity is a major health care concern for many children, and it is a particularly common problem among children with spina bifida. A vicious cycle of decreased activity leading to weight gain, which makes movement more difficult, which begets further weight gain, results in significant health and functional consequences. In some cases obesity is the difference between being able to walk and being completely reliant on a wheelchair. Implementing a diet and exercise program is easier said than done but can have a critical impact on a child's quality of life.

Lack of mobility also leads to decreased bone density (because bones are strongest when they are used) and an increased risk of fractures. In addition to encouraging exercise, parents should pay attention to their children's dietary intake of key nutrients—especially calcium and vitamin D.

For unknown reasons many children and adults with spina bifida develop an allergy to latex. Symptoms may be mild, such as a runny nose, itchy eyes, or skin rash, but some individuals can have a life-threatening allergic reaction. Every effort should be made from birth to avoid exposure to products that contain latex to forestall the development of a latex allergy.

CEREBRAL PALSY

The causes and types of CP are discussed in detail in Chapter 2. This discussion focuses on health care concerns and on special interventions for the management of the motor control and muscle tone impairments associated with CP.

What Are Some of the Main Health Care Concerns for Children with Cerebral Palsy?

Health care concerns for children with CP are quite variable. In general, children with milder forms of CP (especially spastic diplegia [which affects mostly the legs] and hemiplegia [which affects one side of the body more than the other]; see Chapter 2) have good health and in many instances have similar health care requirements as their typically developing peers. By contrast, children with more severe forms of CP (e.g., spastic quadriplegia [which affects the entire body]) are much more prone to an array of health care concerns and medical complications.

Growth, Nutrition, and the Digestive Tract Concerns

Children with severe CP frequently have trouble eating as a consequence of motor control difficulties. If a child cannot finger feed or use utensils, she may be dependent on others to feed her, or if she is able to feed herself, she may tire quickly and not get enough to eat. If a child also has trouble coordinating the complex movements involved with swallowing, she may develop an aversion to food or drink (see Chapter 3) out of fear that she will choke (these types of swallowing difficulties are referred to as *dysphagia*). Children with CP are also more prone to GER and constipation (see "Tummy Trouble" in Chapter 9) and will not eat well if these conditions are unrecognized or inadequately treated.

Parents and doctors sometimes speculate that poor weight in children with CP is due to increased metabolism, or the burning of extra calories as a consequence of having spastic or rigid muscles. In most cases this is not correct. In fact, research suggests that children with CP, particularly the more severe forms, actually burn fewer calories than expected because of their reduced mobility. The bottom line is that children with CP who have trouble gaining weight do so because they are undernourished.

The primary interventions for addressing feeding difficulties focus on identifying the main contributing factors (e.g., swallowing difficulties, GER, constipation) and providing therapy and medical interventions to address these concerns. A special feeding and swallowing assessment may be performed by a speech-language pathologist with special expertise in swallowing difficulties. The assessment may include special x-ray studies that allow for a detailed analysis of the swallowing mechanism and assess the risk of aspiration (food and drink going into the lungs). A feeding program that involves special feeding techniques, the use of adapted utensils, and attention to posture and body position will then be tailored to a child's particular needs.

If major concerns persist regarding inadequate caloric intake, a feeding tube may be considered. If a tube is needed temporarily, a nasogastric tube can be placed into the nose and directed down the back of the throat and into the stomach. If a more permanent tube is needed, a gastrostomy tube is often used. In this case a small opening is created in the abdominal wall, and the tube is inserted directly into the stomach. A syringe or pump delivers liquid food into the stomach through the tube. In some cases feeding tubes are placed into the small intestine rather than the stomach; this is usually done to avoid aggravating GER.

Unlike children with severe CP, many children with mild forms of CP are actually prone to obesity because they get insufficient exercise and tend to have a relatively sedentary lifestyle.

Asthma and Aspiration

Children with CP seem to be more prone to asthma than other children. This is especially true of children who were born prematurely and children with GER (GER may aggravate asthma through reflex mechanisms). Children with severe CP may also be prone to aspiration. Aspiration occurs when food, drink, saliva, or stomach contents (with severe GER) are inadvertently misdirected down the windpipe (trachea) into the lungs. This causes irritation and inflammation in the lungs, aggravating asthma symptoms, and is also a cause of serious lung infection, or pneumonia. Interventions focus on preventing the causes of aspiration. In rare cases of severe risk of aspiration a tracheotomy may be considered. In this procedure an opening is made at the base of the neck and a small breathing tube is inserted directly into the trachea, thereby bypassing the upper airway.

Vision Problems

Children with CP, like children with spina bifida, are prone to strabismus, or problems with uncoordinated movement of the eyes, and also have increased problems with visual acuity. Some children with severe CP have cortical visual impairment (see Chapter 8). Early contact with an ophthalmologist and annual eye examinations are recommended.

Hearing Problems

Children with CP are at increased risk for hearing loss for a variety of reasons. Even if a child passes a newborn hearing screening, it is advisable for him to have regular, formal audiologic assessments beginning as soon as developmental concerns become apparent.

Skin Ulcers

Children with severe CP who are relatively immobile are prone to developing skin ulcers, or decubitus ulcers, at pressure points and bony prominences. Although they are able to sense pain (unlike children with spina bifida, who are prone to decubiti because of a loss of sensation), these children lack sufficient independent mobility to regularly adjust their body position and posture and are dependent on their caregivers to do this for them.

Dental Problems

Children with CP have an increased risk of dental caries and periodontal disease (see "A Toothsome Task: Good Dental Care" in Chapter 9) because of difficulties maintaining hygiene and, in some instances, the effects of other medical problems such as GER with regurgitation. Children with CP especially have trouble with malocclusion (improper tooth alignment) and often require orthodontic interventions.

Drooling

Many children with severe CP have significant problems with drooling because of poor oral motor control. This can pose substantial challenges for hygiene and represent a significant barrier to social integration. Interventions include behavior-based approaches and biofeedback procedures. Medications, particularly glycopyrrolate, can reduce the production of saliva. Injections of botulinum toxin A, or Botox, into salivary glands can also reduce the flow of saliva for several weeks before the effects wear off. In particularly severe cases that do not respond to other therapies surgery directed at permanently reducing saliva production may be considered.

Urinary Dysfunction

Children with CP frequently have problems with urination caused by hypertonia (tightness and overactivity) of the muscles in the bladder wall and the sphincter muscles that control the outflow of urine. Special studies assessing bladder function may be warranted; consultation with a urologist is often helpful in determining the nature of the problem and the best treatment options.

Epilepsy

Approximately 40% of children with CP develop seizures. Children with more severe cognitive and physical disability are especially prone to epilepsy. Partial epilepsy is the most common type of seizure activity observed in children with CP and is especially common in children with spastic hemiplegia who have seizures.

What Are the Main Orthopedic Concerns for Children with Cerebral Palsy?

Orthopedic care refers to activities and interventions that focus on facilitating the function of the musculoskeletal system (the body's system of muscles and bones) and remediating impairments of that system. It is a central concern for all children with CP. Children with CP experience abnormal stresses across various joints in their arms, legs, hips, and back as a consequence of unbalanced muscle contraction, restricted motion due to muscle tightness (hypertonia), or exaggerated motion due to muscle looseness (hypotonia). These stresses have short- and long-term consequences for the functioning of these joints, which must be monitored closely. When a child is first recognized as having signs of CP, she should be evaluated by an orthopedic surgeon or other health professionals experienced in the orthopedic care of children with CP.

Hip Dislocation

Children with CP (especially those with spastic diplegia and quadriplegia) are prone to displacement of the head of the femur (thigh bone) from its place in the hip joint because of an imbalance of muscle forces across this joint. This is especially related to tightness of the muscles on the inside of the thigh, called the *adductor muscles,* which tend to pull the legs together in a scissoring motion. When the head of the femur is partially displaced, hip subluxation has occurred. When the head of the femur is completely displaced from the hip socket, hip dislocation has occurred. Hip subluxation is has no obvious symptoms and can only be identified by x ray. It can usually be treated successfully with a straightforward surgical procedure called an *adductor tenotomy* (see Figure 9.4). Abnormal motion and pain in the hips signals complete dislocation, which requires a more complex and less consistently successful surgical repair. Identification of hip subluxation before it advances to full dislocation is therefore a high priority for preventive care and one of the major reasons to refer a child with CP to an orthopedic surgeon as early as possible (ideally during infancy, even if the diagnosis is only suspected).

Contractures

A child with CP who has tight muscles will initially have a normal range of motion around the joints that those muscles serve, but over time the muscles may become permanently shortened and limited in their motion. This results in a restriction of movement at the joint called a *contracture.* For example, a young child with tight calf muscles who walks on his toes may be able to keep his feet flat when standing still, but over time his ankles will become stuck with the toes pointed down and he will be up on his toes even when standing still. Sometimes the development of contractures can be slowed through physical therapy, exercise, or bracing or through injections with botulinum toxin A (see "Botulinum Toxin [Botox]"), which temporarily weakens tight muscles. However, once contractures have developed, surgery is required to correct the resulting deformity.

Scoliosis

Scoliosis, or curvature of the spinal cord, is another consequence of the imbalance of muscle forces in CP. Mild scoliosis is sometimes treated with bracing. Surgery involves the use of rods and wires to hold the spine straight. An effort is made to postpone scoliosis surgery until after the adolescent growth spurt. Because

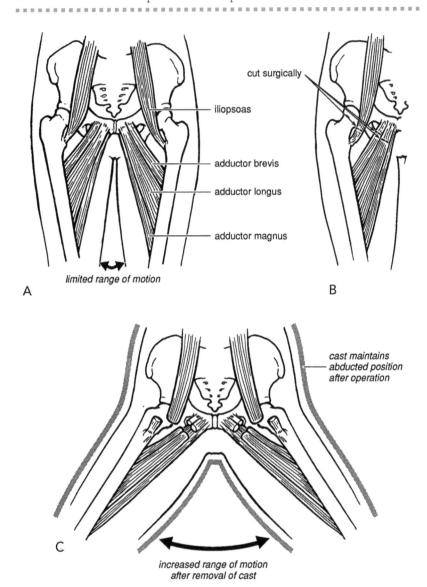

Figure 9.4. Adductor tenotomy. A) Tight adductor muscles on the inside of the thigh cause scissoring and predispose the child to hip dislocation. B) Cutting selected muscle fibers relieves the tension on the hip joint. C) Casting the child's hips in a frog-leg position for 6–8 weeks after surgery improves hip's range of motion and prevents hip dislocation. (From Batshaw, M.L., Pellegrino, L., & Roizen, N. [Eds.]. [2007]. *Children with disabilities* [6th ed., p. 403]. Baltimore, MD: Paul H. Brookes Publishing Co.; reprinted by permission.)

the spine is still growing rapidly prior to the growth spurt, a more extensive and invasive surgical procedure is required in younger children to adequately stabilize the spine.

Special Interventions for the Treatment of Spasticity and Dystonia

In addition to therapy, bracing, and orthopedic procedures—which are directed mainly toward maintaining function and remediating the orthopedic complications of CP—several special medical and surgical treatments have been used to directly address the underlying spasticity and dystonia (two forms of muscle tightness) associated with CP.

Medications

Three medications—baclofen, dantrolene, and diazepam—have been used to reduce spasticity. Diazepam (Valium) is most often used on a short-term basis to reduce muscle spasms after surgery. Dantrolene works directly on muscles to reduce muscle tone but is associated with liver toxicity. Baclofen works on the spinal cord to influence reflex mechanisms that contribute to muscle tone and spasticity. Side effects of the oral form of the medication include sedation, confusion, balance problems, and nausea. Baclofen can also be administered directly into the cerebrospinal fluid surround the spinal cord (this is referred to as *intrathecal baclofen therapy*). In this procedure a catheter that is connected to a disk-shaped pump implanted below the skin of the abdomen is threaded into the spinal canal. The pump contains a reservoir for baclofen and is programmable, so the exact amount of medication delivered can be precisely controlled. Although the baclofen pump has the advantage of being able to deliver medication to its exact target (the spinal cord), this type of therapy has been associated with many side effects and complications.

Botulinum Toxin (Botox)

Botox (botulinum Toxin A) is well known as a cosmetic treatment to reduce facial wrinkles, but it has also become important in the treatment of a number of neurological conditions, including CP. The drug is injected directly into muscles affected by spasticity and works by blocking signals from the nervous system to these muscles. This results in a temporary weakening and "loosening" of the treated muscles, which are then more amenable to physical therapy and bracing. The effects of the drug typically last for

3–6 months, after which the injections may be repeated. The treatment is most often administered by orthopedic or rehabilitation specialists, has become an important alternative to medications, and may in some cases postpone or prevent the need for orthopedic surgery.

Selective Dorsal Rhizotomy

Selective dorsal rhizotomy is a special surgical procedure that can reduce spasticity in the legs. In this procedure a neurosurgeon cuts selected nerves exiting the spinal cord, interrupting the reflex circuits that contribute to spasticity. This procedure is used most often in individuals with severe spasticity who do not walk but whose high muscle tone makes positioning and daily care very challenging.

Stereotactic Encephalotomy

Stereotactic encephalotomy is special neurosurgical procedure that involves the surgical disruption of tracts within the brain that contribute to the dystonia (severe rigidity and distorted postures) associated with some of the extrapyramidal forms of CP (described in Chapter 2, these are rare forms of CP associated with fluctuating muscle tone, rigid posturing, and involuntary movements). It is mainly reserved for individuals with particularly severe dystonia that has been resistant to all other interventions.

10

Medications

Medications come in many different forms and have many different uses. Most, if not all, people have used prescription and nonprescription (over-the-counter) medications at times, and most have given their children medications for ear infections, colds, or other common ailments. Some medications have their primary effect on specific infectious agents. For example, antibiotics disable or kill bacteria, and antiviral and antifungal agents disable or kill their respective targets. Other medications work by affecting a specific body system or process. For example, certain inhaled medications used for asthma target the respiratory system and act to open constricted airways. Several types of medications are discussed in Chapter 9 as they relate to the treatment of specific medical problems associated with developmental disabilities. In many instances the decision to use a medication is fairly straightforward, as when a child's pediatrician prescribes an antibiotic for an ear infection or an antihistamine for allergy symptoms. In other instances, especially those involving the use of medications that affect mental functions, emotion, and behavior (known as *psychotropic medications*), the decision process is much more complex and is often fraught with uncertainty and anxiety for parents and doctors alike.

TO MEDICATE OR NOT TO MEDICATE

Consider Abby and Eddy, two children who are struggling—one at school and one at home.

Medications

Medication (medicine): A substance used to treat disease or relieve pain

Drugs: Substances used as medications or used for illicit purposes (i.e., illegal drugs)

Prescription medication: A drug prescribed by a licensed medical practitioner

Over-the-counter medication: A medication that does not require a prescription

Psychotropic medications: Medications that primarily affect the central nervous system, with potential effects on mental function, cognition (information processing, memory, attention, etc.), motor performance, emotions, and behavior

Approved use (indication): A use of a medication for a specific diagnosis or condition that has been given official approval by the Food and Drug Administration based on adequate experience and research

Off-label use: A use of a medication that is not officially approved by the Food and Drug Administration but is based on the clinical experience of individual practitioners or groups of professionals

PROBLEMS AT SCHOOL

Abby is an 8-year-old girl who was diagnosed with attention-deficit/hyperactivity disorder (ADHD) at age 6. She is smart, friendly, and likable and is not disruptive to her classmates, but she has struggled in school because of her distractibility and restlessness. A thorough psychoeducational assessment has shown no signs of a learning disability, but Abby is falling behind her peers academically, and her teachers and parents agree that her ADHD is the main reason for this. Abby now has an individualized education program and receives appropriate support in the form of classroom accommodations and modifications to tests and homework assignments, and a special education teacher works with Abby to reinforce academics and to help her improve her organizational skills. Yet despite these interventions Abby is still struggling. Her pediatrician has suggested a trial of medication to help her focus at school, but Abby's parents are very worried about potential side effects and say that they do not want medications to make Abby into a zombie. They say that they will only consider medications as a last resort.

PROBLEMS AT HOME

Eddy is an 8-year-old boy with an identified learning disability who is receiving appropriate educational support. Although Eddy is doing well at school, his behavior at home has been a concern. He has become increasingly defiant, especially with his mother, and is prone to angry outbursts, especially when he does not get his way. His mother is glad but also frustrated that Eddy's teacher has seen none of this behavior. She asks Eddy's pediatrician whether a medication could be prescribed to control Eddy's behavior. The pediatrician asks about the situation at home and learns that the parents have recently separated. The pediatrician feels uncomfortable prescribing a medication and confesses being uncertain whether it is even appropriate to use one in this situation. She suggests counseling instead, but Eddy's mother replies in frustration that she has already tried this, that it did not work, and that something has to be done.

Abby's parents and Eddy's mother represent the bookends in the debate about medications. At one end are parents who are strongly opposed to the use of psychotropic medications under any circumstances or who would only consider using them as a last resort. At the other end are parents who are hoping for a quick fix for their child's behavior or school problems and look to medications as a kind silver bullet. Most parents fall somewhere in between these two extremes. They worry about putting their child on a medication and fret about possible side effects, but they also want to keep an open mind about any intervention that may help their child.

Primary care doctors and other medical practitioners also fall on a spectrum

There Are No Silver Bullets or Quick Fixes

Medications may be helpful, but they are not a cure-all for a child's social, behavior, or emotional difficulties. They should be used as part of a comprehensive strategy that includes educational, behavioral, habilitative, and counseling interventions.

with regard to the use of psychotropic medications. Some are uncomfortable using any of these medications; others use them liberally and perhaps in some instances without sufficient consideration of other, nonmedication options. Again, most medical practitioners fall somewhere in the middle of these two extremes. They consider and prescribe medications for specific conditions and selected people based on their level of experience and comfort and tend to refer families to specialists when uncertainties arise.

The fact is that psychotropic medications are controversial, and honest differences of opinion do exist with regard to their appropriate use, especially with children. This chapter takes the perspective that each parent and medical practitioner must come to his or her own conclusions about these medications. These conclusions should be based on a rational consideration of the known facts regarding the use of these medications, including the potential benefits and risks of their use, and an understanding of how a particular medication may help (or hinder) a particular child based on his or her developmental and behavioral concerns.

HOW DO PSYCHOTROPIC MEDICATIONS WORK?

Psychotropic medications affect cognitive functions, emotions, and behavior mainly by influencing the activity of brain chemicals called *neurotransmitters.* A quick review of the geography of the nervous system will help to explain how this works.

The nervous system is actually composed of two main parts: the central nervous system (which includes the brain and spinal cord) and the peripheral nervous system (which includes nerves that carry signals to and from all areas of the body). The brain is the main target of psychotropic medications. The brain is like an orchestra with many different sections. These sections have different parts, or functions, that must work together smoothly to make music. Most brain functions, such as those that regulate breathing, heart rate, blood pressure, and hormonal responses, happen automatically and without a person being aware of them. Many brain functions, such as those that involve strong emotional responses, including aggression or fear, are based on automatic processes that are at least partially subject to conscious modification (e.g., people can learn to suppress, though not eliminate, fight-or-flight responses). Other brain functions, such as those that control body movement and conscious thought, are under voluntary control, although even these have a basis in automatic brain processes (e.g., people do not typically think much about walking once they have learned how to do it).

At a microscopic level the brain is composed of a complex network of cells called *neurons* (see Figure 10.1). The wiring of the brain is composed of short and long tentacle-like processes that connect neurons to one another. These processes are called *dendrites* (which receive input signals from other neurons) and *ax-*

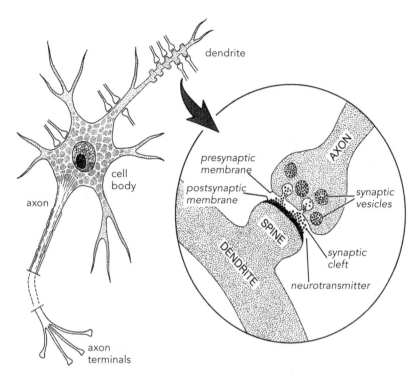

Figure 10.1. Neurons, synapses, and neurotransmitters. Neurons ("brain cells") have 3 main parts— a cell body, dendrites (input fibers), and axons (output fibers). At the point of contact between one neuron's axon and another's dendrite is a small gap called a synapse. Neurotransmitters are chemical substances that cross the synapse, and are influenced by psychotropic medications. (From Batshaw, M.L., Pellegrino, L., & Roizen, N. [Eds.]. [2007]. *Children with disabilities* [6th ed., p. 197]. Baltimore, MD: Paul H. Brookes Publishing Co.; reprinted by permission.)

ons (which send output signals to other neurons). Neurons do not actually make direct contact with each other, however: A tiny gap called a *synapse* separates the end of one axon from its target neuron. Like a person jumping across a small creek, something has to "leap" across a synapse to keep a nerve impulse moving forward; that something is a neurotransmitter. There are many different neurotransmitters in different parts of the brain, and each has a special role. For example, the neurotransmitters dopamine and norepinephrine are important in the functioning of those parts of the brain involved in attention and impulse control; and the neurotransmitter serotonin is important in areas of the brain that regulate emotions and basic functions such as sleeping, eating, and sexual behavior. Medications that affect the availability and activity of these neurotransmitters can therefore potentially influence those brain functions. For example, many medications used for ADHD are thought to affect the dopamine and norepinephrine systems, whereas many medications used for anxiety and depression are thought to affect the serotonin system.

In truth, experts really only have a rudimentary idea of exactly how psychotropic medications actually work; these drugs are judged more on their observable effects in real people than on their theoretical effects in the brain. Stated differently, although scientists know something about the pharmacological effects of these medications (how they work on various body systems such as the nervous system), the clinical effects of the medications (how they affect observable symptoms in real people) are of primary concern to doctors and parents. Some of the known clinical effects of psychotropic medications commonly used in children with developmental disabilities are listed in Table 10.1.

Yet the question remains: Why should you, or why should you not, use these types of medications in children with developmental disabilities?

Table 10.1. Medications: Primary and secondary uses

Type of medication (Examples)	Primary uses	Secondary uses	Side effects
Stimulants Methylphenidate (Ritalin, Metadate CD, Concerta) Dextroamphetamine (Dexedrine) Amphetamine (Adderall XR) Lisdexamfetamine (Vyvanse) Dexmethylphenidate (Focalin, Focalin XR)	Inattention, distractibility, impulsivity, and hyperactivity associated with ADHD[a]	Inattention, distractibility, impulsivity, and hyperactivity associated with developmental disorders other than ADHD	Decreased appetite, weight loss, insomnia, mood changes, anxiety, increased tics (common), increased seizures in epileptic children (rare)
SNRIs Atomoxetine (Strattera)	Inattention, distractibility, impulsivity, and hyperactivity associated with ADHD[a]	Inattention, distractibility, impulsivity, and hyperactivity associated with developmental disorders other than ADHD	Stomachache, anxiety (common); liver dysfunction (rare)

Type of medication (Examples)	Primary uses	Secondary uses	Side effects
Alpha2-agonists Clonidine (Catapres, Kapvay) Guanfacine (Tenex, Intuniv)	Inattention, distractibility, impulsivity, and hyperactivity associated with ADHD (Intuniv, Kapvay, and clonidine)[a] Tics associated with Tourette syndrome[a]	Impulsivity and hyperactivity associated with developmental disorders other than ADHD (short- and long-acting forms), sleep onset, aggression, agitation (often when used in conjunction with other medications)	Sedation, decreased blood pressure, fainting, increased blood pressure if stopped suddenly
SSRIs Fluoxetine (Prozac) Sertraline (Zoloft) Escitalopram (Lexapro)	Major depressive disorder in older children and adolescents (fluoxetine, escitalopram)[a] Obsessive-compulsive disorder in school-age children and adolescents (fluoxetine, sertraline)[a]	Anxiety, obsessive-compulsive symptoms, and dysthymia (chronic depressed or negative mood) in children with a variety of developmental disabilities; behavioral adaptability	Behavioral activation (agitation, restlessness), appetite and sleep changes, suicidal ideation in adolescents and young adults
Atypical antipsychotics Risperidone (Risperdal) Aripiprazole (Abilify)	Agitation, aggression, autistic disorder in school-age children and adolescents[a] Bipolar disorder and schizophrenia in older children and adolescents[a]	Agitation, aggression, mood instability, obsessive-compulsive symptoms, tics, severe disruptive behavior, self-injurious behavior associated with a variety of developmental disabilities	Increased appetite and weight gain, metabolic syndrome (increased blood sugar, increased lipids and bad cholesterol), short-term neurological side effects, possible long-term neurological side effects (tardive dyskinesia)
Mood stabilizers Valproate (Depakote) Lamotrigine (Lamictal) Topiramate (Topamax)	Seizures and epilepsy[a] Mood instability associated with severe aggression (autistic disorder)	Mood instability associated with developmental disabilities other than autism Bipolar disorder in adults, off-label uses in children with mood disorders (valproate and lamotrigine)	Most can cause sedation and possible adverse cognitive effects; varied adverse effects on multiple organ systems are medication specific

Sources: Myers (2007); Myers and Johnson (2007).

Key: CD, controlled delivery; ADHD, attention-deficit/hyperactivity disorder; XR, extended release; SNRI, selective norepinephrine reuptake inhibitor; SSRI, selective serotonin reuptake inhibitor.

[a]Indication approved by the Food and Drug Administration.

WHY USE MEDICATIONS?

The simplest answer to this question is that medications can help. Although medications are not always appropriate or useful, in specific instances they can be of dramatic benefit to specific children. This is especially true if a child has little control over his symptoms. For example, children with severe ADHD, especially when they are younger, have great difficulties with impulse control. With constant prompting from adults they may be able to control themselves for brief periods of time, but they revert back to their baseline impulsiveness when these external supports are removed. These children tend to elicit negative responses from those around them, and over time they may develop a reputation for being bad; tragically, these children then begin to think of themselves as bad. They have little ability to learn self-control because, ironically, their lack of impulse control interferes with their ability to learn these skills. Years of research on ADHD has shown that medications that improve impulse control and attention may be the single most helpful intervention for improving function and outcomes in such children.

Medications may also support other interventions. For example, children with developmental disabilities are more prone to problems with anxiety and depression than other children, and efforts to provide counseling and educational interventions may be hampered by their underlying emotional state. In these situations medications should only be considered if the child is under the care of a qualified mental health professional, but in specific circumstances the introduction of the right medication may powerfully facilitate the efficacy of the child's primary, nonmedical interventions.

WHY NOT USE MEDICATIONS?

Taking medication is not always, or even usually, the most appropriate response to the varied behavior and emotional problems that occur in children with developmental disabilities. There are several reasons for this.

Medications Do Not Teach

Medications may have specific or general effects on aspects of behavior and emotion, but they never teach a child more appropriate or adaptive ways of responding to other people or to their own feelings and reactions. Medications may facilitate the learning process in some instances, but they can never replace that process.

Medications Are Not Appropriate for Many Types of Behavior and Emotional Problems

Most behavior difficulties in children are specific to a particular circumstance and are influenced by antecedents (events that trigger the behavior) and consequences (events that follow the behavior). For example, telling a toddler "no" when she wants to put a fork in an electrical outlet may trigger a tantrum, and the attention that she then receives from her siblings who suddenly appear to witness her outburst may tend to reinforce and prolong the tantrum and increase the likelihood that a similar reaction will occur in the future. Using behavior measures (e.g., redirecting the toddler, paying attention to appropriate safe behavior, using time-out strategies for unsafe behavior) would be the most appropriate way of dealing with the situation; using medication interventions would be very inappropriate.

Other behavioral concerns represent deficits in social skills or coping strategies, and the most appropriate interventions for dealing with these involve teaching and reinforcing those skills. Many emotional difficulties are most appropriately addressed through counseling. In these instances using medications may represent a way of avoiding rather than addressing the underlying problem.

Medications May Mask Other Problems

Many children are subject to stressful and sometimes abusive situations at home or at school, and problematic behavioral and emotional reactions are a common and understandable response to these adverse circumstances. A child who suddenly refuses to go to school may be having a problem with a bully on the playground at recess; a child who has become increasingly distracted at school may have recently experienced a parental separation. Placing the first child on a medication to reduce defiance or the second child on a medication to increase attention would be inappropriate and would tend to distract attention from the underlying cause of the behavior changes.

Likewise, medications may mask or distract attention from a medical problem that is causing behavior changes. For example, a nonverbal child with autism may experience an increase in agitation and aggression as a consequence of an unrecognized toothache. Treating that child with an atypical antipsychotic such as risperidone may reduce aggression temporarily, but the primary problem has been missed. Similarly, a child with obstructive sleep apnea may be inattentive at school because he is tired (see Chapter 3). Treating this child with a medication for ADHD would also be inappropriate.

Medications Have Side Effects

All medications have potential side effects, although not all children experience them. In general the wider the range of cognitive, behavioral, and emotional effects a medication has, the broader its range of potential side effects. Short-term side effects are those that occur only when the child is taking a medication and would be expected to disappear when the medication is discontinued. Long-term side effects are those that result from prolonged use of a medication and that may not resolve when the medication is discontinued.

The Effects and Side Effects of Psychotropic Medications

In general the more positive or beneficial effects a psychotropic medication has (presumably because of the range of effects it has on brain function), the more likely it is to have side effects and the less predictable its long-term effects will be.

Common side effects (e.g., appetite and sleep changes, dry mouth, upset stomach) tend to be mild and occur with many different types of medication. Other side effects may be severe; these may be associated with a class of medications or may be specific to a medication. Medications that have frequent, severe, or life-threatening side effects should never become available for prescription; when severe side effects become known after a medication has become widely available, the medication should immediately be removed from the market. Most psychotropic medications rarely have severe side effects, but all the same these effects must be recognized, and in some cases the Food and Drug Administration (FDA) has affixed black box warnings to specific medications or classes of medication to highlight particular concerns. However, it is important to recognize that a medication with a black box warning is not necessarily more dangerous or does not necessarily have worse side effects than a medication without such a warning.

Some side effects of a medication may be well known, but some may only be suspected, and in some instances they may be unknown (especially those for newer medications). Many psychotropic medications have been studied and used mainly in adults, and the potential side effects in children may not be well known. The potential benefits of a medication must always be carefully weighed against the potential for harm, and this can sometimes be a difficult calculation, especially when the child is young.

CHOOSING A MEDICATION: APPROVED VERSUS OFF-LABEL USES

When a pharmaceutical company develops a new drug it must test that drug (generally in animals first and then in humans) and must provide adequate evidence of the safety and efficacy of the drug before it is approved for use by the FDA. When the FDA approves a specific medication it generally does so with a specific population and a specific use, or indication, in mind. For example, fluoxetine (Prozac) is approved for use in adults with major depressive disorder, obsessive-compulsive disorder, bulimia nervosa (an eating disorder), panic disorder, premenstrual dysphoric disorder, or a depressive form of bipolar disorder. After its initial approval for use in adults, it was subsequently approved for use in children 8–18 years of age with major depressive disorder and in children 7–17 years of age with obsessive-compulsive disorder. For many psychotropic medications a similar pattern applies: Medications are initially researched and approved for use in adults and then researched and approved for use in children. Medications for ADHD are a notable exception: Most are researched and approved for use in children before approval is extended to use them in adults.

Medications are used off label when a drug that has been approved by the FDA is prescribed to a different population or for a different indication than that for which it is officially approved. For example, after its approval by the FDA fluoxetine was only prescribed for its approved uses in adults, but its use in clinical practice was gradually expanded to include adolescents and older children (it was prescribed off label). After a time adequate experience and research existed to allow the approval of fluoxetine for use in older children and adolescents major depressive disorder and obsessive-compulsive disorder (these have now become approved uses). The medication is still often used in clinical practice off label for other indications (e.g., treating severe anxiety in a child with Asperger syndrome).

Although medical practitioners tend to feel most comfortable prescribing medications for their approved uses, in many instances off-label uses may be appropriate. The principle that applies when one is trying to determine whether an off-label use of a medication is appropriate is referred to as *standard of care*. The *standard of care in*

Black Box Warnings

Black box warnings are warnings associated with specific medications or groups of medications that the Food and Drug Administration has determined may have rare but potentially life-threatening side effects. The following are examples of black box warnings relevant to psychotropic medications discussed in this chapter:

Increased risk of suicidality: Increased risk of suicidal thoughts, gestures, and attempts in children, adolescents, and young adults. Associated with all selective serotonin reuptake inhibitors and some atypical antipsychotic medications, including aripiprazole (Abilify) and the attention-deficit/hyperactivity disorder (ADHD) medication atomoxetine (Strattera).

High abuse potential, dependency: Risk of abuse and dependence on drugs, especially in individuals with a history of drug abuse. Associated with all stimulant ADHD medications.

Cardiovascular adverse events and sudden death: Potentially life-threatening cardiac events (generally associated with misuse of medications, particularly in individuals with preexisting cardiac conditions). Associated with some stimulant ADHD medications, including dextroamphetamine/amphetamine (Adderall XR) and lisdexamfetamine (Vyvanse).

(continued)

medicine refers to those diagnostic and treatment practices that are accepted by the medical community based on the collective experience of many practitioners and the evidence provided through research. Medical practitioners strive to base their diagnostic and treatment practices on the best evidence available; a major challenge with regard to the use of psychotropic medications in children is that very often adequate research is lacking. The standard of care is therefore by necessity an evolving and dynamic entity rather than a set of black-and-white rules or guidelines and must be responsive to changes in knowledge of medications and the conditions they treat.

jargon buster

(continued)

Medication-specific black box warnings: Many medications, including several anticonvulsant mood stabilizers, have warnings that are specific to the drug. For example valproate (Depakote) has warnings for severe liver and pancreatic toxicity and possible teratogenic effects (effects that disturb fetal development in pregnant women taking the medication). Lamotrigine (Lamictal) has warnings for the development of a severe, potentially life-threatening rash (called *Stevens-Johnson syndrome*).

MEDICATIONS BY DIAGNOSIS

FDA-approved medications are usually linked to specific recognized diagnoses. The process of research and evaluation that leads to approval is based on the supposition that a recognizable population of individuals with a particular diagnosis experience a specific set of (hopefully beneficial) effects when using a particular medication. ADHD and autism spectrum disorders are prime examples of specific diagnoses for which specific medications have received FDA approval.

Approved Medications for Treating Attention-Deficit/Hyperactivity Disorder

ADHD is a major exception to the general rule that most medications are approved for use in adults before they are approved for use in children. Methylphenidate (Ritalin), a psychostimulant,

Controlled Substances

Some psychotropic medications (e.g., psychostimulant medications used to treat attention-deficit/hyperactivity disorder) have the potential to be misused and abused and have thus received the designation *controlled substance*. These drugs are regulated by the Food and Drug Administration and the Drug Enforcement Agency, and special rules apply regarding the prescription of these medications.

was approved for use in children with ADHD in 1957 (ADHD was called *minimal brain dysfunction* at the time). Shortly thereafter dextroamphetamine (Dexedrine) was also approved. In the 1970s pemoline (Cylert) was approved (for what was now called *hyperkinetic disorder of childhood*), but it has since been abandoned because of concerns about its toxic effects on the liver. In the 1980s ADHD finally got its current name, and in the 1990s a new form of amphetamine (Adderall) received FDA approval. The use of these medications increased considerably after the publication of a landmark study in 1999 (the Multimodal Treatment Study of ADHD) that provided strong evidence that these medications are very effective for treating the primary symptoms of ADHD, especially when combined with psychosocial treatments (behavioral interventions and counseling), and that they work better than psychosocial interventions alone. Since 2000 several long-acting (extended release) forms of psychostimulant medications have been introduced (e.g., Adderall XR, Concerta, Focalin XR, Vyvanse), as have several nonstimulant medications (e.g., atomoxetine [Strattera], extended release guanfacine [Intuniv], extended release clonidine [Kapvay]). Most practitioners use long-acting psychostimulants as the first line of therapy and tend to use other medications (including nonstimulants) as second- or third-line therapies.

Approved Medications for Treating Autism

Two medications, risperidone (Risperdal) and aripiprazole (Abilify), are FDA approved to treat irritability and aggression associated with autism. These drugs belong to a class of medications known as *atypical antipsychotics*—*atypical* to distinguish them from the older generation of typical antipsychotics (e.g., haloperidol, or

Haldol) and *antipsychotic* referring to the use of these medications in treating the thought disorders associated with schizophrenia. Atypical antipsychotics have come to be used widely in adult and child psychiatry because they have a range of potentially beneficial effects and uses (both approved and off label) in treating disorders of thought, mood, and behavior. The successful off-label use of atypical antipsychotic medications for the treatment of severe agitation and aggression in children with autism eventually led to an accumulation of research evidence demonstrating that risperidone and aripiprazole are effective and generally safe (although concerns for both short- and long-term side effects do exist). These drugs are therefore approved for use in children and adolescents with autism (ages 5–16 years for risperidone and 6–17 years for aripiprazole).

MEDICATIONS BY TARGET SYMPTOM

Very often psychotropic medications are prescribed to target a symptom or symptoms rather than to treat a specific diagnosis. In some cases this relates to the FDA-approved use of a medication (e.g., the treatment of impulsivity associated with ADHD), but often it represents an off-label use of the medication. In these instances less is known about the potential benefits (or side effects) of the medication, although in individual instances the benefits may be substantial. Specific target symptoms may be particularly associated with specific diagnoses (e.g., impulsivity with ADHD) but will also occur frequently in other developmental disorders.

Target symptoms are sometimes categorized as internalizing (relating to symptoms that have primarily an emotional expression; e.g., anxiety, depression, or obsessions) or externalizing (relating to symptoms that have primarily an outward, behavioral expression; e.g., hyperactivity). Other medication targets (e.g., insomnia) may relate to a lack of something rather to a positive symptom or may represent a mix of emotional and behavioral features. The relationship between target systems and the types of psychotropic medications used to treat them (as well as the overlapping effects of these medications) is illustrated in Figure 10.2.

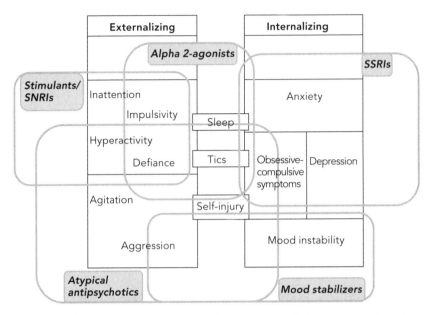

Figure 10.2. Medications by target symptoms. The overlapping effects of psychotropic medications are shown. (*Key:* SNRI, selective norepinephrine reuptake inhibitor; SSRI, selective serotonin reuptake inhibitor.)

GENERAL CONSIDERATIONS WHEN CHOOSING A MEDICATION

Given the fact that psychotropic medications overlap significantly in the symptoms they may potentially treat, deciding which medication to use for a specific child can be complicated and confusing. A fair amount of trial and error may be needed to find a good medication match. The following general guidelines can inform the decision-making process:

All other things being equal, choose a medication with fewer side effects. For example, a number of medications can potentially affect impulsivity, but some will have more possible side effects than others.

Give priority to medications that are FDA approved for a specific use. In general medications that have been approved for a specific use in a specific diagnosis have more evidence to support their safety and efficacy than medications that are used off label.

Consider medications that treat the primary symptoms associated with the specific disability. For example, using stimulant medications to treat impulsivity and distractibility associated with ADHD may also improve other symptoms, such as aggression and defiant behavior.

Avoid polypharmacy whenever possible. Polypharmacy is an informal term used to describe the practice of prescribing multiple medications. Although in some instances using a combination of medications may work best for a particular child, it is generally preferable to keep the number of medications to a minimum, and ideally one.

Start low and go slow. This applies to many if not most psychotropic medications. Side effects are less likely to occur if a low starting dose is used and the dose is gradually increased to an optimal or target level. (This is very different from the use of some medications, such as antibiotics used to treat infections, in which it is important to use the optimal or therapeutic dose from the beginning.) Likewise, many psychotropic medications should be weaned (reduced gradually) rather than stopped abruptly to avoid side effects.

Consider a medication trial and have a follow-up plan. It is generally advisable to think of the start of using any psychotropic medication as a trial period during which observations are made to determine whether the medication is beneficial and to identify side effects. Having a follow-up plan, which usually involves telephone contacts and scheduled medical visits with the prescribing doctor, is key to a successful medication trial and even more important to the ongoing management of medication use. Follow-up medical visits usually involve reviewing symptoms and side effects, checking vital signs (e.g., blood pressure) and growth parameters (especially weight), and obtaining monitoring blood tests.

11

Why Did This Happen?
The Causes of Disability

Vincent was born on a bright, unseasonably warm morning in late April. Contractions began in the wee hours of the morning, Vincent's mother's water broke at 4 a.m., his parents hurried to drop his 4-year-old sister with a family friend, and Vincent was born within minutes of his mother's arrival at the hospital. He had come a week before his due date, and in the delivery room things happened so quickly that there was no time to hook his mother up to the usual monitoring equipment that would let the doctors and nurses track the progress of the labor. The delivery was precipitous: One moment his mother felt the urge to push, and the next Vincent was in the hands of the obstetrician, who luckily was on hand, having just attended another delivery.

Vincent did not cry right away. The obstetrician used a bulb syringe to suction his nose and mouth and propped an oxygen mask next to Vincent's face as he lay on his back with his head turned to one side under a warming light. Although Vincent was quiet (his parents anxiously awaited his first lusty cry) he had a good heart rate, vigorous movements, and fair muscle tone. His skin was mostly a bright, healthy pink except for a tinge of blue in his hands and feet. Vincent was still having a little trouble breathing 20 minutes after the delivery. He made little grunting sounds with each breath, his nostrils flared, and the skin between his ribs retracted inward with each inspiration. Vincent's pediatrician had arrived to evaluate Vincent, and she told his anxious parents that he probably had some retained amniotic (fetal) fluid in his lungs and that this could cause a temporary difficulty with breathing. They would monitor Vincent in the special care nursery for a few hours and then transfer him back to the general nursery once his breathing problem resolved.

Eight hours later Vincent's breathing was still labored and he still needed supplemental oxygen, which was delivered via a small tube that circled his head and released a steady stream of oxygen through two small holes positioned beneath his nose. A chest x ray showed overinflation of the lungs and a "fuzzy" background on the x-ray film. Vincent's pediatrician explained that this is consistent with a condition called *transient tachypnea of the newborn*. She was not surprised by this finding, which she said is common in infants with retained amniotic fluid. Vincent's x ray also showed a small pneumothorax, or pocket of air between the right lung and chest wall that represented air that had escaped his overinflated lungs. His pediatrician was more concerned about this. She explained that a pneumothorax is a less common complication of transient tachypnea of the newborn and sometimes requires the surgical placement of a chest tube to relieve the pressure of the escaped air.

Vincent's parents were understandably frightened, especially by the pneumothorax and the prospect of a chest tube, but over the next 24 hours Vincent's breathing improved, a repeat x ray demonstrated resolution of the pneumothorax, Vincent's supplemental oxygen was discontinued, and he was able to transfer to the general nursery. Breast feeding was difficult at first, but by the time he was discharged from the hospital with his mother 4 days after he was born Vincent was breathing fine and feeding like a champ.

Years later Vincent was diagnosed with a mild form of autism. His parents diligently researched Vincent's diagnosis on the Internet and found a confusing array of opinions regarding the possible causes of autism. Medical experts seemed to favor the idea that autism spectrum disorders, as well as several other developmental disorders, are mainly based on genetic factors, but Vincent's family had no history of developmental problems at all. Vincent's pediatrician recommended genetic screening tests, but they all came back normal. In reviewing the results of these tests, she told Vincent's parents that in many instances the causes of developmental disabilities are just unknown. They had trouble accepting this. Although his pediatrician reassured them otherwise, Vincent's parents could not help but wonder whether the events surrounding his birth may have had something to do with his disability. They requested a magnetic resonance imaging scan of the brain to look for evidence of brain damage.

WHY?

When your child has a disability, it is natural to wonder why it happened. Most parents are scared that they may somehow be to blame either because of something they did or did not do during the pregnancy or because of something they did or did not do in raising their child properly. Or they may blame themselves for passing on the wrong genes to their child (as if any one has control of their genes!).

In other instances parents may feel motivated to identify an external cause for their child's disability. Perhaps something in the environment is to blame. Perhaps a toxin, or virus, or allergen, or something in the diet is responsible. Or perhaps the disability is the result of an adverse reaction to a vaccine, or an antibiotic, or some other medical treatment.

Even more commonly parents worry that a problem at birth may be to blame for their child's disability. Giving birth to a child is an emotional rollercoaster ride even in the best of circumstances; parents remember every small detail connected with their child's birth, especially if something went wrong. In fact most births do not go exactly as expected, and most parents can recall some aspect of their child's birth that was concerning if not harrowing. When children grow and develop as expected, parents can look back on these birth events with equanimity and humor, but when unexpected disabilities emerge they naturally flash back to these events and consider them with sudden suspicion.

For many parents the main motivation for wanting an answer to the "why" question is the underlying assumption that if you know the cause of a problem, you will be in a better position to treat or fix it. This way of thinking is at the heart of modern medicine. If someone has an infection, the doctor has to know the likely cause of the infection so that she can treat it with the right antibiotic. If someone has a heart attack, the doctor needs to do imaging studies to check the coronary arteries and blood tests to check cholesterol levels so that he can treat the problem and hopefully prevent future recurrence. If someone develops seizures, the doctor does tests to determine the type so as to aid in the selection of an anticonvulsant medication and orders brain imaging studies to rule out specific causes of seizures, such as a brain tumor that might require surgery or chemotherapy. So if a child is diagnosed with autism, or intellectual disability, or cerebral palsy, or any of the other developmental disabilities, doctors hope that if they can get to the root of the problem, they will be in a better position to help that child.

Finally, for many parents a major motivation for answering the "why" question is the concern that they might have another child with a similar disability or that the disability may somehow run in the family. This is especially true when there are concerns about a possible genetic basis for a disability. The complexities of hereditary and the ambiguities involved in interpreting the results of genetic tests can make the pursuit of these answers a less than straightforward proposition. Genetics specialists (medical geneticists and genetic counselors in particular) are often needed to help parents sort through the quagmire of genetic information.

NATURE, NURTURE, AND THE NEVER-ENDING DEBATE

From time immemorial, philosophers and scientists (and just about everyone else) have debated the relative contribution of nature (the stuff people are born with) and nurture (things that happen to them) in determining who and what individuals are. This debate has extended to the discussion of the causes of developmental disabilities.

The story of this debate in the annals of autism research is particularly instructive. Leo Kanner, an Austrian American psychiatrist working at The Johns Hopkins University, first described cases of autism in the 1940s. He speculated about a possible connection between inadequate parenting and autism. This idea took hold, and through much of the mid-20th century autism was thought to be caused by emotional deprivation due in particular to inadequate mothering. The term *refrigerator mother* came to refer to emotionally impoverished mothers incapable of nurturing their offspring. This coincided with the dominant belief that infants were born as blank slates and that their personalities and destinies were primarily a function of the quality of their early relationships and home environment.

Although the refrigerator mother theory of autism was soundly disproved in subsequent research, the idea of inadequate parenting as the basis of developmental disability persists. Part of the reason for this is the reasonable assumption that who people are has something to do with how they are raised. It is certainly true that growing up in a loving, stable home environment is a major advantage and that growing up in a stressful, neglectful, unstable home environment is a major disadvantage. It is much less certain how upbringing affects basic aspects of a person's personality, character, and intelligence. Studies of identical twins separated at birth have yielded surprising insights into the relative contributions of parenting and genetics on these traits. Despite major differences in home environments, the twins in these studies grow up to have surprisingly similar interests, attitudes, temperamental qualities, and abilities and make surprisingly similar choices in selecting careers and spouses.

So genetics seems to play a major role in determining who people are and what they will become; rather than being blank slates individuals are born with a kind of blueprint for the person they will become. Some have gone so far as to say that genetics is destiny! In discussions of nature versus nurture, most experts argue that genes and environment make an equal contribution to who people are and what they become.

Likewise, most experts allow for the importance of both genes and environment in the genesis of developmental disabilities, although the concept of environment in this instance is quite different from the social environment described above. When people say that their personalities and character are determined by their environment, they usually mean that their families, friends, towns, countries, and cultures have something to do with who they are. They are thinking of the social and cultural environment and about relationships. In the days when the refrigerator mother theory of autism was in vogue, psychological and social elements of the environment were thought to be the basis for many developmental disabilities. Now when people talk about the environment as it relates to health and disability, they are usually thinking of the air people breathe, the water they drink, the food they eat, and bad things such as toxins and pathogens that lurk in the shadows, waiting to inflict harm. They are thinking of the physical environment.

The pendulum has swung back and forth between times when theories of development and disability biased toward nature are in vogue and when theories biased toward nurture are favored. It has become popular, and perhaps safe, to fall back on the notion of interaction. People like to say that development, personality, and disability are a function of the interaction between genetics and environment, between the stuff individuals are born with and things that happen to them. Yet most of the time what is meant by the term *interaction* is a bit vague. The term suggests that genetic and environmental factors commingle in some mysterious way to produce the developmental and disability outcomes seen in real life (see Figure 11.1). In truth, saying that genes and the environment interact is sometimes a cover for uncertainty and a reminder that humility is warranted given all that is not understood about the causes of disability.

GENES, BRAINS, AND THE STUFF PEOPLE ARE BORN WITH

Everyone has heard of DNA. It is in the news, it is at the heart of many crime and investigation dramas, and the famous double helix even shows up as a fashionable necklace accessory. Most

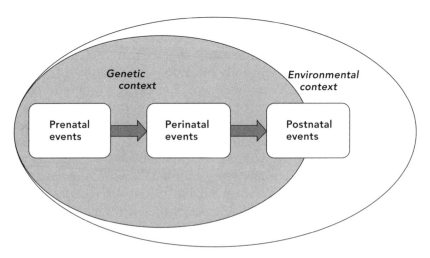

Figure 11.1. Genetics versus environment. Genetic factors have a powerful influence on development and disability, especially in the early stages of life. Environmental factors are potentially important throughout life and interact with genetic factors, especially during the prenatal phase of development.

people have also heard of genes. People get half of their genes from their mother and half from their father, and genes have something to do with the color of a person's eyes, how tall he or she is, and how good he or she is at learning and doing certain things. DNA is the stuff of life, the secret code, the blueprint. Genes are the inheritance, the library of traits handed down from one generation to the next. It all gets a little vague from there.

And then there is the brain. The brain is the great mystery, the seat of intelli-

Genetics 101

jargon buster

DNA (deoxyribonucleic acid): The molecule that contains the genetic code

Chromosomes: Packages of DNA that contain multiple genes; humans have 23 pairs of chromosomes, numbered 1–22, plus the sex chromosome pair (XX for females, XY for males)

Genes: Segments of DNA that contain the code for specific proteins

Proteins: Molecules that form the structure and machinery of the cell

Cells: The microscopic building blocks of all of the organs of the body

gence and personality, the master controller of basic body functions, the mover of muscles, the repository of memory and instinct, the source of emotion and inspiration, the place where consciousness rises and unconscious processes surge in the depths. It is not much to look at, the convoluted surface having the appearance of a slimy cauliflower, but looks are not everything. It is beautiful in its inner workings and in its startling complexity, and it is central to an understanding of developmental disability. When one thinks of disorders of learning and cognition, or contemplates the basis of motor coordination problems, or considers the mysteries of autism, one necessarily invokes the brain and questions what has gone wrong in its workings to have resulted in these conditions. When a child has a disability it is natural to first consider the possibility that something disturbed or injured the child's brain. But it is important to understand that much of how the brain works has to do with how it got put together in the first place, and DNA and genes are key to this understanding.

Simply put, the brain is made of stuff, and DNA and genes provide the blueprint for how that stuff gets put together. Like all of the organs of the body, the brain is composed of microscopic cells (see Figure 11.2). Cells are composed mostly of water sur-

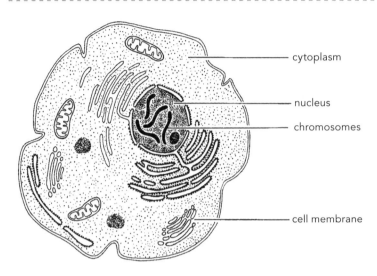

cytoplasm

nucleus

chromosomes

cell membrane

Figure 11.2. The cell. The cell membrane defines the outer boundary of the cell. The nucleus contains the chromosomes, which are packages of DNA and genes. The cytoplasm contains many structures (organelles) that perform the various the functions of the cell. (From Batshaw, M.L., Pellegrino, L., & Roizen, N. [Eds.]. [2007]. *Children with disabilities* [6th ed., p. 4]. Baltimore, MD: Paul H. Brookes Publishing Co.; adapted by permission.)

rounded by a thin cell membrane that defines the outer boundary of the cell. The interior of the cell is a labyrinth of strange and wonderful objects with many varied functions. One of these objects is the centrally located nucleus. The nucleus contains chromosomes, which are packages of DNA. Each person has 23 pairs of chromosomes; one member of each pair comes from the mother, and the other from the father. Twenty-two of the 23 chromosome pairs are called *autosomal chromosomes* and are the same in males and females. The 23rd chromosome pair includes two *sex chromosomes*, so called because they determine sex. Females have two X chromosomes, and males have one X chromosome and one Y chromosome.

Each chromosome contains thousands of genes, which are segments of DNA that encode specific proteins. Protein is the basic structural material of the cell. If DNA is the blueprint, proteins are the building materials that make up the walls and floor, electrical system, plumbing, and machinery of the cell. If there is a problem with the blueprint, or if there is a mistake in the construction process, the final product (the brain and the other organs and structures of the body) may have structural or functional problems.

When it comes to how the brain gets put together, the situation is a bit more complicated than just saying that DNA provides the blueprint for the brain, and if the blueprint is good, and the construction process follows the blueprint, the brain will work the way it should. Although it is true that the genetic code provides for the basic structure of the brain, the connections within the brain are continuously adjusted and molded by experience (see Figure 11.3). Brain cells begin to make connections with one another (called *synapses*) during fetal life, and the number of these connections increases dramatically during early childhood, reaching a peak by about 8 years of age. It seems that nature provides people with more connections than they need: The number of synapses decreases slowly beginning in adolescence through a

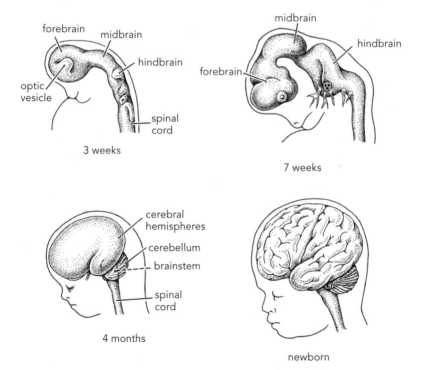

Figure 11.3. Brain development. In the early stages of embryonic development the brain and spinal cord develop from a tube-like structure that becomes segmented. The forebrain develops into the cerebral hemispheres, the midbrain develops into the brainstem, and the hindbrain develops into the cerebellum. The brain has achieved its basic shape by 4 months gestation. (From Batshaw, M.L., Pellegrino, L., & Roizen, N. [Eds.]. [2007]. *Children with disabilities* [6th ed., p. 28]. Baltimore, MD: Paul H. Brookes Publishing Co.; reprinted by permission.)

process of pruning—people keep the connections they use, and those that are less useful disappear. Although the net number of connections decreases with age, individuals are able to make new connections throughout life, and through the processes of learning they continuously strengthen connections and reshape networks of neurons in response to the challenges of daily life. Genes continue to be active participants in this process. They direct the machinery of the cells from moment to moment in response to the demands of the environment. So DNA is both architect and foreman: As architect, DNA provides the blueprint for the basic structure of the body and brain, and as foreman it continues to provide direction and support in response to the vagaries of life as one grows and develops.

Genes, Heredity, and Developmental Disability

Some developmental problems seem to run in families (see Table 11.1). For example, it is not at all uncommon for a child with attention-deficit/hyperactivity disorder (ADHD) to have a parent who confesses to having had similar difficulties with inattention, distraction, and impulsiveness as a child. Similarly, many people with dyslexia and other learning disabilities can point to siblings, parents, grandparents, aunts and uncles, or cousins with similar challenges. If a child has autism, he or she is much more likely to have siblings with some form of autism spectrum disorder and, more broadly, is more likely to have siblings with other developmental disorders besides autism (e.g., speech and language disorders are more common in such families). Not uncommonly, family members of a child with autism may have traits associated with autism without showing other characteristics

Table 11.1. Developmental disorders that tend to run in families

Attention-deficit/hyperactivity disorder

Dyslexia

Other learning disabilities (e.g., language-based learning disability, math learning disability)

Asperger syndrome

Other autism spectrum disorders (e.g., high-functioning autism)

Developmental coordination disorder

Mild intellectual disability

required for a diagnosis of autism. The parents of children with Asperger's syndrome are more likely than the parents of other children to have a background in the natural sciences, engineering, or mathematics. What is surprising is that there also seems to be an increased tendency toward psychiatric disorders such as bipolar disorder and schizophrenia in families of individuals on the autism spectrum.

Heredity refers to the passing of traits from parent to child, from one generation to the next, and involves literally thousands of different physical and functional characteristics. Eye and skin color, height, and facial features are common examples of hereditary traits. Although some traits may relate to the action of a single gene, most result from the cooperative interaction of multiple genes. For example, eye color is influenced by more than a dozen different genes, including separate specific genes for brown, green-blue, and brown-blue eye color located on different chromosomes. Likewise, developmental disorders that tend to run in families, either in their full form or as traits or tendencies, are probably associated with the effects of multiple genes. In some instances specific forms of a gene, called *alleles*, are discovered to be associated with particular developmental disorders in certain families, but it is usually not possible in these cases to say with certainty that a particular form of a gene is the cause of a person's disability. Genetic testing in these instances would not prove that a person has a particular developmental disability or that a certain gene variant is the cause of a previously diagnosed developmental disability.

Genes, Mutations, and Genetic Anomalies

Some developmental problems seem to happen out of the blue. For example, a child may have autism or a severe intellectual disability, but there is no family history of similar problems. Or in some cases a developmental disability does run in the family but in a very specific pattern. It may show up only in males on the maternal side of the family. Or it may occur only among the siblings of a particular set of parents but is absent in the extended family tree. Or it may occur in each generation of a family, with some family members exhibiting the condition and others not, in a striking, all-or-nothing pattern. In some cases

The Inheritance of Single Gene Traits

Some genetic traits are determined by single genes. In the mid-1800s, Gregor Mendel, a scientist and Augustinian friar, first discovered how these traits are transmitted from parents to offspring. *Autosomal traits* are determined by genes on one of the 22 autosomal chromosomes; *sex-linked traits* are determined by genes on the X chromosome. Some traits are dominant, whereas others are recessive. Genes for dominant traits overrule genes for recessive traits, so if one parent contributes a dominant gene for a trait and the other a recessive gene, only the dominant trait will be expressed in the offspring. Two genes—one from each parent—are required for a recessive trait to be expressed. *Autosomal dominant* and *autosomal recessive traits* are expressed in both males and females; *sex-linked recessive traits*, because they are determined by genes on the X chromosome, are usually expressed only in males. (Females do not express sex-linked traits but can pass one on to their sons; in this case, the females are considered carriers of the trait.)

the developmental disability is associated with telltale physical traits, such small or big head size, unusual birthmarks, growth problems, unusual facial features, or anomalies of the limbs or organs.

These types of observations seem to suggest that the disability is a consequence of something unusual or unexpected. If heredity (the passing of traits from one generation to the next) is likened to the usual lineup of television programs that one might watch on a particular evening, then these out of the blue situations would be the genetic equivalent of breaking news or a severe weather alert. They interrupt the regularly scheduled programming within the genetic scheme of a family, suggesting that something unexpected has happened to create conditions favorable to the genesis of a disability.

Unexpected genetic changes are often referred to as *mutations*. In the broadest sense a mutation can be defined as any type of genetic change, although most often doctors use the word *mutation* to mean a genetic change that has important real-life consequences. Some of the most important types of genetic change are listed in Table 11.2. A familiar example of genetic change is Down syndrome. Most individuals with Down syndrome have an extra chromosome number 21 (Down syndrome is also called *trisomy 21* for that reason). In addition to several characteristic physical traits and medical concerns, individuals with Down syndrome usually have mild to moderate intellectual disability and are more

Table 11.2. Genetic changes that can cause developmental disabilities

Extra or missing chromosomes
Duplications or deletions of groups of genes
Changes (mutations) of the DNA within specific genes
Disorders of gene expression or regulation

prone to autism spectrum disorders than people without Down syndrome (see Chapter 9).

Another less familiar but important cause of developmental disability is a condition known as *fragile X syndrome.* In this condition a DNA change occurs in a gene on the X chromosome (one of the sex chromosomes). Boys with this genetic change have characteristic physical features (e.g., a large head and prominent ears), but these features are relatively subtle, especially in early childhood. Most have mild to moderate intellectual disability, and like individuals with Down syndrome, boys with fragile X syndrome seem to be more prone to having autism spectrum disorders than the general population. Girls with fragile X syndrome tend to be less severely affected. They often lack the physical traits associated with fragile X syndrome and tend to have milder developmental disabilities, such as learning disability, or in some cases show no signs of disability. (Girls are thought to be more mildly affected because they have an extra X chromosome with unchanged DNA that can counterbalance the deleterious effects of the fragile X mutation.) Because fragile X syndrome is relatively common, and because mildly affected or unaffected girls may pass the mutation on to their children without realizing it, there is often some urgency associated with identifying this condition.

There are in fact literally thousands of known genetic conditions. Although individually most of these conditions are rare, collectively they are more common than people typically suspect. Recognizing and diagnosing a specific genetic condition can be challenging. Doctors must be alert to the clues in an individual's physical, developmental, and family profile in order to recognize that a genetic diagnosis may be possible.

Genetic Testing

Some genetic conditions can be tested for, but others cannot. Among genetic conditions for which testing exists a wide variety of tests are available. Most are blood tests, although some genetic testing is done on tissue samples (skin and muscle biopsies are most frequently used). Some genetic tests screen for unsuspected genetic problems in newborns. Some are tests that involve looking at chromosomes under a microscope to observe their number and structure. Many tests involve a direct analysis of DNA for specific anomalies in specific genes. Some tests hone in on the products of gene activity. The number and types of genetic tests is increasing exponentially, and the situation will only become more confusing and complicated as more genetic discoveries are made. It is therefore not possible, practical, or desirable to try to test a child for everything when a genetic problem is suspected; good judgment must be used to determine which tests are most likely to yield useful results.

THINGS THAT HAPPEN: PREGNANCY, BIRTH, AND BEYOND

Every pregnancy is different, and every birth is different. First-time parents especially are often surprised by the discrepancy between what they have heard and read the process of having a child would be like and what it actually is like. It is usually exciting, often nerve racking, and occasionally frightening. Although things do not always go exactly as expected, the vast majority of children are carried to term and delivered successfully. In rare instances adverse events or circumstances that occur during pregnancy (the prenatal period), at the time of birth (the perinatal period), or after birth (the postnatal period) can disturb the development or functioning of the nervous system and other body systems, resulting in or contributing to various forms of developmental disability.

Pregnancy and Prenatal Events

Human gestation typically lasts about 9 months, or 40 weeks, and is divided into three trimesters. The events of the first trimester are particular dramatic. The trimester begins with the implantation of the embryo (which is little more than a hollow ball of cells) in the wall of the uterus and ends with a recognizably human-looking fetus whose major organ systems and body plan are established. The most dramatic phases of brain development also occur during the first trimester and into the beginning of the second trimester. Brain cells (neurons) proliferate wildly so that by the end of this period people have the maximum number of brain cells they will ever have! The familiar shape and structure of the brain is also established by about 4 months gestation. It is during this early period of rapid development that the genetic plan for the brain and nervous system unfolds, and it is also during this period that the plan is most vulnerable to disruption. Disturbances that occur later in the pregnancy tend to have less dramatic effects, although these may still contribute to the development of disability.

Prenatal Infections

Mothers frequently have colds and other minor viral illnesses during pregnancy that are benign and have no impact on their developing child. However, specific, less common infections are known to cause significant injury to the developing fetus and brain. The classic example of this is rubella, or German measles. A mother who contracts the rubella virus develops mild systems (mainly a rash and fever), but the virus can wreak havoc on the developing fetus, affecting multiple organ systems and causing vision and hearing impairment, poor brain growth with small head size (called *microcephaly*), and significant developmental disability, including intellectual disability (formerly *mental retardation*) and autism. Fortunately this condition, called *congenital rubella syndrome,* has become quite rare since the rubella vaccine was introduced in the late 1960s.

Infections of greatest concern include cytomegalovirus, toxoplasmosis, varicella (chickenpox), herpes simplex, and HIV. Cytomegalovirus is actually a very common infection; most people are exposed to it as children, have minor or no symptoms, and develop protective immunity. Mothers who have insufficient immunity may contract the infection with minimal or no symptoms. If this occurs early in pregnancy, significant fetal malformation, microcephaly, and intellectual disability may result. If the infection occurs later in the pregnancy, progressive hearing loss but not intellectual disability may result. Fortunately only a small fraction of fetuses exposed to cytomegalovirus develop problems.

Toxoplasmosis is a rare illness passed from cats to humans that can cause vision problems, hearing impairment, and intellectual disability in affected fetuses. If used early in the pregnancy, drugs can limit the adverse impact of this infection.

The varicella (chickenpox) virus can disturb the development of the limbs and facial structures and occasionally affects brain development. A common childhood illness in the past, chickenpox is now the target of a vaccination that is routinely administered to children in the United States. Maternal immunity due to previous infection or vaccination protects the fetus from the varicella virus.

The herpes simplex virus does not typically infect the developing fetus. Rather, infants born to mothers with chronic vaginal herpes infections can contract the virus while passing through the birth canal. Generalized herpes simplex virus in a newborn can cause brain injury and subsequent intellectual disability. Infants of mothers with known vaginal herpes are usually delivered by cesarean section to reduce the risk of infection.

HIV, or the AIDS virus, can pass to the fetus late in pregnancy; it does not affect early fetal development, but the infected newborn is at risk for developing AIDS in early childhood. The administration of antiviral drugs to mothers during pregnancy combined with delivery by cesarean section has greatly reduced the incidence of neonatal HIV infection.

In the case of these infections, the fetus is infected directly by an agent such as a virus. In some instances bacteria may infect the membranes surrounding the fetus within the uterus; this is called *chorioamnionitis.* Although the fetus itself is not infected, chorioamniotis predisposes the mother to premature labor and has been linked with an increased risk of cerebral palsy, especially in infants born prematurely.

Environmental Toxins (Teratogens)

Teratogens are toxic substances or energy sources that have adverse effects on fetal development. The possible effect of environmental toxins on the developing brain has been the subject of considerable controversy; substances of particular concern include heavy metals (e.g., lead, mercury), pesticides, and by-products of manufacturing (e.g., polychlorinated biphenyls, dioxins). High-dose exposure to lead can result in death or severe brain injury; lower dose exposure results in milder but significant effects on cognition and behavior. Mercury is a known neurotoxin, but the effects of environmental and other forms of mercury in the genesis of disability are uncertain. Pregnant women are generally advised to avoid fish, such as tuna and salmon, that have relatively high concentrations of mercury. A form of mercury known as thimerosal, which is used as a preservative in some vaccines, has been the subject of particular controversy as a possible cause of autism. Although subsequent research has not supported this claim, thimerosal has been removed from childhood vaccines. Polychlorinated biphenyls and dioxins may have adverse effects on attention, memory, and information processing and may also adversely affect endocrine (hormone) function. High-dose exposure to pesticides (as well as herbicides and fungicides) in occupational settings has been associated with disturbances in cognition and peripheral nerve function. The effect of lower levels of to exposure to pesticides, particularly on the fetus, is unclear.

Alcohol, Substance Abuse, and Tobacco

Ethanol, the form of alcohol present in wine, beer, and liquor, is a known and serious teratogen (toxin). It particularly affects early fetal development. The full range of effects is observed in fetal alcohol syndrome and includes poor fetal growth; small head size; facial, limb, and eye anomalies; and a variety of developmental and psychiatric problems, including ADHD, learning disability, intellectual disability, mood disorders, and disruptive behavior disorders. Many children exposed to alcohol during fetal development exhibit the developmental and behavioral features of fetal alcohol syndrome but may lack some or all of its physical characteristics. The variable effects of alcohol on the fetus have been characterized variously by the terms *fetal alcohol effects, fetal alcohol spectrum disorder,* and *alcohol-related neurodevelopmental disorder.* Even small amounts of alcohol used occasionally during pregnancy may have adverse effects on the fetus, so women are counseled to abstain entirely from drinking alcohol if they are pregnant or planning to become pregnant.

Significant concerns exist regarding the effects of different substances (illicit drugs) and tobacco on the developing fetus.

Cocaine and methamphetamine may cause the constriction of fetal blood vessels, which may result in limb and intestinal abnormalities. Heroin and methadone use during pregnancy causes a serious withdrawal state in the newborn characterized by irritability, low blood sugar, and seizures, although physical malformations have not been linked to their use. Marijuana and tobacco use during pregnancy has been associated with low birth weight and prematurity. The long-term effect of prenatal exposure to these substances on learning, memory, attention skills, and behavior is uncertain, but enough evidence exists to suggest that they cannot be considered safe.

Medications

Most over-the-counter and prescription medications are thought to be safe for use during pregnancy, although it is advisable to avoid unnecessary medication use (especially early in pregnancy) and to check with a doctor or pharmacist about the safety of specific medications. A number of medications and classes of medications are known fetal teratogens. Several anticonvulsant medications (medications used to treat epilepsy), including phenytoin (Dilantin), valproate (Depakote), and carbamazepine (Tegretol), have been associated with developmental delay and disability and with malformations of the face, limbs, and spine. The prescription acne medicine isotretinoin (Accutane) and the psoriasis medication etretinate (Tegison) have been associated with face and brain malformations. Several anticancer drugs, which work by killing rapidly dividing cancer cells, can cause fetal loss or malformation by attacking the rapidly dividing cells in the human embryo. The infants of mothers who have taken these medications during pregnancy are not always affected adversely; higher doses, using multiple medications (e.g., taking several anticonvulsant medications together), and using medication during the early stages of pregnancy are associated with an increased likelihood of malformations and subsequent developmental problems. Thalidomide, which was used to treat pregnancy-related nausea in the 1950s, was pulled from the market when it was linked with severe limb abnormalities in exposed fetuses. It has been reintroduced on a limited basis (with rigorous precautions and restrictions) for the treatment of a rare type of cancer and certain neurological conditions.

Radiation

The possible effects of low-dose radiation exposure (e.g., that which is used for medical x rays) on the developing fetus are unknown. Pregnant women exposed to massive doses of radiation associated with the atomic bomb blasts in Japan during World War II experienced an increase in miscarriages, premature birth, and infants born with small head size and intellectual disability. Because of the uncertainties regarding the effects of standard x rays and computed tomography scans (which use substantially higher levels of radiation than simple x rays), it is generally advisable to avoid these tests during pregnancy when possible. Magnetic resonance imaging (MRI) scans and sonograms use magnetism and high-frequency sound waves, respectively, to create images. Because they do not use radiation, their use is preferred during pregnancy.

Maternal Diabetes

The fetuses of women with chronic diabetes or pregnancy-associated diabetes (known as *gestational diabetes*) are at increased risk for malformation of the heart, spine, and limbs. In the newborn period infants of diabetic mothers often need treatment for low blood sugar. Women who have poor control of their blood sugar during pregnancy are more likely to have infants with malformations, and this poor control is also associated with an increased risk of later developmental disability.

Birth and Perinatal Events

Problems that occur around the time of birth are of frequent concern for parents of children who are later diagnosed with a disability. Being born too soon (prematurity) and problems with the birth process itself are of particular concern.

Prematurity

Infants are considered to be premature if they are born prior to 37 weeks, or about 8 months gestation; *extreme prematurity* refers to infants born prior to 28 weeks, or about 7 months gestation. There are many reasons why infants are born prematurely. Premature delivery is more likely to happen to very young women (especially teenagers) and to women older than 35. Women who are pregnant with multiples (twins or triplets), women who have previously delivered prematurely, and women with certain abnormalities of the uterus or cervix are at particular risk for delivering prematurely. Certain maternal infections increase the likelihood of premature delivery, as do risk factors related to lifestyle, including drug, alcohol, or tobacco use; poor prenatal care; poor maternal weight gain during pregnancy; and socioeconomic disadvantage.

A variety of stresses and medical complications related to prematurity account for an increased incidence of developmental problems and developmental disability in infants born prematurely. Bleeding in the brain (intraventricular hemorrhage) and the disruption of blood supply to key areas of the brain (periventricular leukomalacia) are associated with subsequent cerebral palsy (see Chapter 2). Eye problems affecting the retina (retinopathy of prematurity) lead to vision loss and in some cases blindness (see Chapter 8). Serious infections and medical problems related to nearly all of the major organ systems, including the lungs, intestines, liver, kidneys, and blood, can have direct and indirect effects on the vulnerable, immature brain of the premature infant. Even premature infants who are spared serious medical complications may be adversely

jargon buster

Birth and Its Complications

Preterm labor: Labor that occurs before 37 weeks' gestation

Premature rupture of membranes: Early rupture of membranes that surround the fetus (when the water breaks); associated with premature delivery and increased risk of intrauterine infection

Preeclampsia: A condition characterized by increased maternal blood pressure and edema (swelling) with protein in the urine; if untreated, preeclampsia progresses to eclampsia/toxemia

Eclampsia/toxemia: A condition characterized by severely increased maternal blood pressure with edema, protein in the urine, maternal seizures, and compromised delivery of oxygen to the fetus

Placenta previa: Placement of the placenta over the uterine outlet

Placental abruption: Detachment of the placenta from the uterine wall

Umbilical cord prolapse: Delivery of the umbilical cord ahead of the infant; can result in compromised delivery of oxygen to the infant during the birth process affected by the stresses of leaving the protected environment of the womb for a world of sights, sounds, and sensations for which they are insufficiently prepared. A range of outcomes from intellectual disability and autism to subtler problems with learning, attention skills, and emotional and behavioral regulation occur with increased frequency in children born prematurely than those born at full term. The most obvious disabilities are recognized in early childhood, but subtler disabilities may not be apparent until the child is school age.

Problems at the Time of Birth

Infants undergo a dramatic transition at the time of birth. Within the protected environment of the uterus, the soon-to-be-born infant has all of his or her needs provided for through the placenta and umbilical cord. The placenta is an amazing organ that serves as the interface between the mother's circulation and the infant's. Within the placenta, oxygen and nutrients pass from the mother's bloodstream to the infant's, and waste products pass from the infant's bloodstream to the mother's. The umbilical cord carries oxygen and nutrients from the placenta to the infant's heart (via the umbilical vein) and carries waste products from the infant's body back to the placenta (via two umbilical arteries). Blood is routed through the unborn infant's heart through a special opening (the foramen ovale) and a special blood vessel (the ductus arteriosus). The special pathway that blood follows through the fetal heart is called the *fetal circulation.*

At and immediately after birth a dramatic change in the infant's blood circulation takes place. Now the infant's own organ systems must take over the functions of the placenta. The lungs must supply oxygen and get rid of carbon dioxide, and the liver and kidneys must process and rid the body of other waste products. The gastrointestinal tract will digest and absorb nutrients into the infant's circulation. A dramatic change in blood flow within the heart and its large blood vessels must occur to accommodate these changes. In particular, the blood pressure within the circulation of the lungs must decrease so that blood can flow freely into the lungs, and the foramen ovale and ductus arteriosus must close. If these events do not occur smoothly, and especially if there is an extended period during which placental blood flow is compromised before the infant has a chance to switch over to the newborn circulation pattern, the infant's brain may be compromised as a result of an insufficient supply of oxygen and nutrients.

The mother also experiences dramatic changes during labor and delivery. Chemical signals between the fetus and the mother trigger contractions of the uterus, which are followed by a rupturing of the membranes surrounding the fetus. This rupturing releases the amniotic fluid (the fluid surrounding the fetus)—this is what is meant by saying that a mother's "water has broken." Premature rupture of membranes occurs when these membranes break too early in the labor process, or even before labor is fully under way, and can be associated with infections of the uterus (chorioamnionitis; see "Prenatal Infections") and premature delivery. Some women (especially those who are pregnant for the first time) experience an elevation in blood pressure associated with body swelling (edema) and protein in the urine. This is called *preeclampsia;* if it progresses to eclampsia (severely elevated blood pressure, maternal seizures, and compromised placental blood flow), both the mother and the infant are at significant risk. The best treatment for preeclampsia is delivering the infant, which is accomplished by inducing labor (to speed up the natural labor process) or performing a cesarean section.

The most concerning events that occur at the time of delivery are those that compromise the function of the placenta (see Figure 11.4) and umbilical cord. Placenta previa occurs when the placenta, which is usually located at the upper pole of the uterus, instead sits over the exit of the uterus, blocking passage of the infant during labor and resulting in bleeding and compromising the infant's oxygen supply. Placental abruption (detachment of the placenta from the uterine wall) is especially worrisome—it can result in significant blood loss for the mother and significantly compromised delivery of oxygen and nutrients to the unborn infant. Umbilical cord prolapse, or the delivery of the umbilical cord ahead of the infant, can severely compromise blood flow from the placenta to the infant through persistent compression of the umbilical cord. Like placental abruption, umbilical cord prolapse can result in significant neurological injury if not recognized and treated immediately.

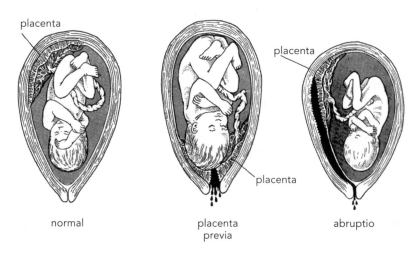

Figure 11.4. The placenta and labor. Normally the placenta lies at the upper pole of the uterus. In placenta previa it blocks the uterine outlet (birth canal). In placental abruption (abruptio placentae) it becomes dislodged from the uterine wall, resulting in maternal bleeding and compromised blood flow to the infant. (From Batshaw, M.L., Pellegrino, L., & Roizen, N. [Eds.]. [2007]. *Children with disabilities* [6th ed., p. 41]. Baltimore, MD: Paul H. Brookes Publishing Co.; reprinted by permission.)

Infants who experience significant stress during the birthing process due to problems such as lack of oxygen, very long labor, maternal diabetes, or increased maternal blood pressure may pass their first bowel movement (called *meconium*) before they are born. In some instances, meconium is breathed (aspirated) into the lungs and can cause lung irritation, pneumonia, and breathing problems that require oxygen and sometimes mechanical breathing (ventilator) support in the newborn period. Meconium is actually seen at many births and is typically suctioned from the infant's mouth and throat, causing no problems. Most cases of meconium aspiration resolve without any long-term consequences, but in rare, severe cases meconium aspiration syndrome results in delayed transition of fetal circulation to normal infant circulation, causing persistent oxygen deprivation and increased risk of neurological damage.

Birth asphyxia is a term that is often used to describe compromised delivery of oxygen to an infant during the birth process. It has the unfortunate connotation of oxygen deprivation through choking or compression of the infant's windpipe, which rarely happens and is almost never the cause of neurological injury.

Hypoxic-ischemic encephalopathy (HIE) is an overly technical but more accurate term that characterizes lack of oxygen delivery (hypoxia) and blood flow (ischemia) to the infant around the time of birth resulting in neurological dysfunction (encephalopathy) and possible brain injury.

HIE is suspected in newborns who show evidence of significant neurological compromise during the first 48 hours of life. The Apgar score is a widely used rating of the health and vigor of a newborn; infants with low Apgar scores beyond 5 minutes after birth are at increased risk for long-term neurological compromise. Infants who experience significant HIE are likely to require close monitoring in a special care nursery and show signs of neurological abnormality such as poor muscle tone and lack of responsiveness to stimulation. Seizures that occur in the immediate newborn period are a particularly strong indicator of neurological compromise. Newborns who have good Apgar scores after 5 minutes, good responsiveness to stimulation, good muscle tone, and a lack of seizure activity and who are able to go to the hospital's general nursery within the first 24 hours after birth do not show evidence of HIE and are unlikely to have long-term neurological compromise due to birth-related events.

The Apgar Score

The Apgar score is a rating of an infant's health and vigor immediately after birth. Scores are typically obtained at 1 and 5 minutes after birth and are composed of five components (skin color/complexion, pulse rate, response to stimulation, muscle tone, and breathing). Each component is scored 0, 1, or 2; total scores of 0–3 are critically low, scores of 4–6 are fairly low, and scores of 7–10 are normal. Low scores at 1 minute that recover by 5 minutes are reassuring and are usually associated with good outcomes; scores that are persistently low beyond 5 minutes are associated with increased risk of neurological injury.

The Birth Process: Some Common Concerns

There are many misunderstandings and misconceptions about the relationship between events surrounding the birth process and their relationship to subsequently identified developmental disabilities. The following are frequent concerns of many parents.

1. *Lack of oxygen at birth:* Lack of oxygen at birth (HIE) is actually a rare cause of disability and is usually associated with

clear signs of neurological injury in the newborn period (e.g., seizure activity), abnormalities on brain imaging studies, and subsequent cerebral palsy. Even among children with cerebral palsy, less than 10% of cases can be attributed to HIE.

2. *Prolonged labor:* Although a source of fetal stress, prolonged labor is a relatively common occurrence and is not by itself a cause of long-term neurological problems (unless it is associated with other conditions, e.g., placental abnormalities).

3. *Umbilical cord wrapped around the neck:* The umbilical cord often becomes draped or wrapped around the infant's neck during the delivery, raising concerns about choking and asphyxia. However, as mentioned previously, this is almost never the cause of a lack of oxygen in newborns.

4. *Not crying right away:* Although crying in the delivery room is one of the signs of infant health and vigor, it is not the only sign. The Apgar score provides a more complete assessment of the condition of a newborn.

5. *Birth injury:* Actual birth injury (trauma at birth) is an extremely rare cause of disability. Many infants, especially those who are the products of a first pregnancy, those who undergo prolonged labor and delivery, or those who require forceps or vacuum extraction to assist the delivery process, show temporary deformation of the skull with associated discoloration, subcutaneous bleeding (hematomas), and bruising. Fortunately the newborn's skull is designed to be very compliant, and these sometimes scary-looking changes in the newborn's appearance resolve quickly and are rarely associated with any underlying brain injury.

Beyond Birth: Postnatal Events

Although the ordinary events of life and the type of upbringing people have had can surely affect how they grow and develop as individuals, it is relatively rare that a specific event or set of circumstances that occurs after birth can be identified as the cause of a specific developmental disability. However, there are important exceptions to this general statement.

Infections

Serious infections, especially those that involve the nervous system or those that are body-wide (systemic) and compromise vital functions such as blood pressure, can cause long-term disability in survivors. Infants and young children are especially vulnerable to such infections. Meningitis is an infection of the meninges, or coverings of the brain and spinal cord, and can be caused by viruses or bacteria. Vaccines protect against some forms of bacterial meningitis. Encephalitis is an actual infection of the brain; this is fortunately a rare type of infection, but it can and does occur. Newborns and young infants are more vulnerable to infections leading to encephalitis than older children and adults (e.g., to herpes virus infections involving the brain). Encephalitis can result in significant and long-term brain damage. Both meningitis and encephalitis are associated with sensorineural hearing loss (see Chapter 8).

Toxins

As mentioned in "Environmental Toxins (Teratogens)," lead is a neurotoxin and has well-documented negative effects on development, especially cognitive development and aspects of behavior control and attention. Exposure to other potential neurotoxins, such as mercury, is suspected of having negative consequences on development, although these effects have been more difficult to document.

Severe Neglect or Emotional Deprivation

Children are remarkably resilient, and although abuse and neglect certainly leave long-lasting emotional scars, it takes extraordinary levels of neglect and emotional deprivation to cause disability. Classic studies done in the mid-20th century of children raised in orphanages with few responsive caregivers documented severe adverse effects on children's cognitive and emotional development, especially if the children were not given an opportunity to form an emotional attachment with a primary caregiver during the early months of life.

Traumatic Brain Injury

Brain injury as a consequence of accident or abuse can result in significant neurological injury and subsequent disability. Functional outcomes tend to relate to the timing of the injury. For example, if a young child (particularly one younger than 3 years of age) sustains a significant traumatic brain injury that causes long-term impairment of motor skills, the pattern of disability that results will be consistent with cerebral palsy. Children who sustain significant brain injury after about age 8 tend to demonstrate a profile of motor and cognitive deficits similar to that seen in adults with traumatic brain injury. Traumatic brain injury has also been associated with significant long-term cognitive impairments, especially ones related to memory function and behavioral regulation.

Near-Drowning

Near-drowning and other injuries that result in significant brain hypoxia (lack of oxygen) can have devastating long-term neurological consequences that are often significantly worse than those associated with traumatic brain injury.

Medical Conditions Associated with Neurological Compromise

Rare medical conditions that have a specific neurological component, such as brain tumors and bleeding or clotting disorders that result in stroke, can result in significant disability. Other rare conditions such as cystic fibrosis (a genetic disorder that causes chronic respiratory and gastrointestinal problems) and several forms of congenital heart disease (due to abnormalities of the heart that are present at birth) that have systemic (body-wide) effects are known to be associated with learning and cognitive difficulties.

A number of inborn diseases, known collectively as *metabolic disorders,* are routinely screened for in newborns. Many of these have specific treatments to prevent or reduce the risk of long-term disability. For example, hypothyroidism (low thyroid hormone) may be identified at birth. If left untreated it may result in severe intellectual disability, but if treated one would expect a child to have typical cognitive skills.

Other metabolic conditions are caused by a lack or insufficiency of proteins called *enzymes* that control the chemical reactions that allow cells and tissues to extract energy from foods and carry on other vital life processes. For example, phenylketonuria

(PKU) is a relatively common metabolic disorder that is characterized by the lack of an enzyme that is key to breaking down phenylalanine, a component of protein. (Phenylalanine is also present in diet sodas containing the sweetener aspartame, and a warning for individuals with phenylketonuria is printed on these products.) When phenylalanine accumulates in the body it has a number of toxic effects, especially on the brain and nervous system. Treatment involves strictly limiting protein in the diet and in some cases using special medications that help the body process phenylalanine. If left untreated phenylketonuria typically results in significant intellectual disability with brain injury and seizures. If it is treated, individuals have typical general intellectual ability and are free of seizures but are still at risk for subtler learning problems. Outcomes correlate with how well blood levels of phenylalanine are controlled.

WHAT IS KNOWN AND UNKNOWN ABOUT THE CAUSES OF DEVELOPMENTAL DISABILITIES

Although Vincent, the boy described at the beginning of this chapter, had significant breathing difficulties shortly after birth, he had a good Apgar score at 5 minutes, he did not show signs of neurological compromise in the newborn period, and he recovered quickly once his breathing problems resolved. His pediatrician was fairly convinced that his autism was not related to these birth events, but she did agree to order a magnetic resonance imaging scan of Vincent's brain, which was normal.

Vincent's parents were still concerned about missing an underlying medical problem that might be treatable, and they were also concerned about the risk of recurrence (the likelihood of having other children with autism). The pediatrician referred Vincent to a medical geneticist (a medical doctor with special expertise in genetic disorders). The geneticist reviewed the results of previous testing, including the magnetic resonance imaging of the brain, the chromosome analysis (karyotype) ordered by Vincent's pediatrician, and the results of the newborn metabolic screen, all of which were normal. The geneticist carefully reviewed Vincent's medical history and also asked many detailed questions about the family history, paying special attention to members of the extended family with genetic problems or developmental disorders. Although there was no family history of autism, several family members had speech difficulties in early childhood, learning problems (especially ones related to reading), and suspected obsessive-compulsive disorder. Finally, the geneticist completed a detailed physical examination, looking for clues such as special birthmarks; particular facial features; abnormalities of the hands, feet, and genitals; or growth discrepancies, all of which may be associated with specific genetic disorders. Vincent's examination was normal.

The geneticist ordered additional tests, including a DNA test for fragile X syndrome, another DNA test known as a *chromosome microarray* (a general survey of all of the chromosomes that may detect subtle abnormalities missed by a standard chromosome test), and additional blood and urine tests to screen for metabolic disorders. All of these tests were normal. He counseled Vincent's parents that many children with autism do not have an identifiable cause or genetic abnormality to explain their disability. He also agreed with Vincent's pediatrician that the events at birth did not explain his autism. He indicated that statistically speaking, families with one child with an autism spectrum disorder have about a 5%–10% risk of having another child with autism spectrum disorder, and about a 10%–15% chance of having another child with some type of developmental problem.

Many families have an experience similar to Vincent's family in their attempts to identify the cause of their child's disability. Doctors typically start by looking for clues in the medical history, in family history, and on the child's physical examination that will help them to focus subsequent testing. Because there are so many possible causes of developmental disabilities, it is necessary to narrow the scope of investigation, testing for disorders with the highest probability of occurrence given the disability being considered. When specific clues are lacking, some broad generalizations can help to guide the evaluation process. For example, children with cerebral palsy are more likely to have identifiable brain abnormalities associated with their disability, so it often makes sense to begin the process of investigation by obtaining brain imaging studies (e.g., an MRI scan). Children with severe to profound intellectual disability or severe autism (especially if it is associated with intellectual disability) often undergo tests that focus on identifying genetic abnormalities. Children with more common, milder developmental disabilities such as developmental language disorder, learning disability, ADHD, developmental coordination disorder, and the milder forms of autism spectrum disorder frequently do not show evidence of an identifiable brain or genetic anomaly. In many cases (especially for children with learning disorders and ADHD) doctors will forgo detailed testing entirely, making exceptions when specific aspects of the history or physical examination prompt them to consider a particular diagnosis.

It would be fair to say that although experts know a lot about the types of things that cause developmental disabilities in general, they still have a great deal of difficulty identifying the cause of developmental disabilities in specific instances. And it is very often the case that even when the cause of a child's disability is known, that knowledge may have relatively little impact on what can be done to help that child. Even when a child has a very well known condition such as Down syndrome (see Chapter 9), only broad generalizations can be made about the disability characteristics of the condition. Children with Down syndrome vary a great deal from one another (as do all children), and their specific strengths and weakness, temperamental characteristics, and personality traits must form the primary basis for determining appropriate interventions.

Does Knowing the Cause of a Disability Help Your Child?

Although knowing the cause of your child's disability may be very important for determining if you or other family members are at risk for having other children with similar disabilities, this knowledge may have little effect on the educational and therapeutic interventions you choose for your child.

Postscript

The Volunteer in Your Garden

*A*nyone who has tended a garden for more than a year or two knows that there will always be surprises. Besides the unpredictability of knowing how your tomatoes, cucumbers, zucchini, or beans will turn out from one year to the next there are the occasional unexpected incursions of the denizens of nature who decide that your garden should become an annex of their natural habitat. Some of these incursions actually are, or should be, predictable. A gardener who knows that there are rabbits or deer in the neighborhood is merely being foolish if he or she does not put up a proper barrier to deter their likely interest in a particular crop.

Then there are the real surprises. Some readers will judge me as naïve, but I was quite taken aback when, a few years ago, I discovered that chipmunks have a remarkable fondness for tomatoes. The first evidence of this was the discovery of low-lying fruit with large chunks missing, which I at first took to be evidence of a larger creature that had happened by and decided on an impromptu snack. Then one day I spotted a cheerful-looking chipmunk skittering across our deck with a grape tomato stuffed in his mouth and the incriminating remains of several previously enjoyed tomatoes scattered in his wake. Although guides to garden pests offer advice about removing chipmunks from one's garden, this was never an option for me. My children were acquainted with this particular pest, whom they had named Cookie and adopted as an accidental pet,

347

and as I was informed that the incursion in question was in fact not his upon my garden but mine upon his yard, I was forced to concede his superior claim. I have since decided that the lost produce should be considered a form of taxation or tribute rightly owed to the liege lord of our yard.

Less dramatic but no less significant incursions are of the botanical variety. Weeds are an unavoidable fact of life for every gardener, and as every gardener knows, due diligence is required to keep the local vegetation from taking over. I have adopted a preemptive strategy in this battle, using raised garden beds and landscape fabric in an attempt to give my vegetables an advantage over the native flora (and not insignificantly to minimize the need for me to get down on my hands and knees and join the fight).

But still the weeds often get the upper hand. One year early in my gardening career I relaxed my vigilance, and the weeds breached the first lines of defense, establishing a tenacious foothold in and around my plants. As I got to work retaking lost ground and reclaiming control I came across a wayward, slightly pathetic-looking plant that somehow seemed un-weed-like. My first instinct was to pull it up, but curiosity stayed my hand, and I let it grow, just to see what it was. Within a few weeks it revealed itself to be a tomato plant, presumably the progeny of the prior season of gardening, perhaps attributable to Cookie's perennial efforts at tomato redistribution. I called my dad, who was the acknowledged master of gardening in my family (and whose wisdom, advice, and humor I now greatly miss). He told me that I most likely had a volunteer, the gardening term for a plant that comes up on its own rather than being deliberately planted by a gardener. He said that a volunteer tomato plant may not produce fruit of the same quality as its parent plant and sometimes yields no fruit at all, but occasionally a volunteer will produce a new and tasty variety of tomato that a farmer will deliberately perpetuate.

I decided to let it grow. It never got very big and only produced a few undersized tomatoes, but they were by far the juiciest, sweetest, tastiest tomatoes that have ever come from my garden.

When you first discover that your child has a disability you may feel like the gardener who has completely lost control to the weeds and the pests, which threaten your hopes for a hopeful, happy, and fruitful life for your child and for your family. But as so many parents have told me in my years working with children with disabilities, though the first surprises are often unpleasant and unwelcome, very often happier surprises are in store. You may have a volunteer growing in your midst, and although the fruits of any life are inherently unpredictable, you may discover, as so many parents do, that your child will bring unexpected joy and sweetness into your life. It may not be the life you planned (for your child or for yourself), but as many parents discover it is a life full of unexpected beauty despite the many obstacles and frustrations that come with raising a child with a disability.

I hope you have found encouragement in these pages to trust yourself and your instincts when you suspect that your child has a disability, and I encourage you to trust that you will be able to help your child grow, thrive, and be fruitful. In the process you may discover things about yourself as well. Being a parent changes everyone, and being the parent of a child with a disability, though uniquely challenging, can be uniquely rewarding as well. I have been amazed and humbled by the resourcefulness, wisdom, and good humor of so many parents of children with disabilities, who have taught me to see their children with special needs as being truly special—and not just because of their needs. Parents like you are a resource for the rest of us, helping us individually and collectively to understand the value of every child and every person regardless of their ability or disability. As a society we are gradually becoming more aware of the fundamental arbitrariness of these words, and we are slowly and painfully coming to the realization that disability is more about the artificial restrictions created by society than about any inherent deficiency of individuals.

So do your best to clear away the weeds, water and tend your garden, and let your volunteer grow. My wish for you is that you find joy in the process and surprise in the outcome. And I hope you will come to believe that of all people, you are exactly the right person for the job—because you are.

Resources

GENERAL INFORMATION

Child Development and Developmental Disabilities

Batshaw, M.L., Pellegrino, L., & Roizen, N.J. (2007). *Children with disabilities* (6th ed.). Baltimore, MD: Paul H. Brookes Publishing Co.

Brazelton, T.B. (2006). *Touchpoints: Birth to 3: Your child's emotional and behavioral development.* Cambridge, MA: Da Capo Lifelong Books.

Dixon, S.D., & Stein, M.T. (2006). *Encounters with children: Pediatric behavior and development.* St. Louis, MO: Mosby.

Ages and Stages: Birth to 12 months

http://www.extension.iastate.edu/Publications/PM1530A.pdf
Find information about the physical, mental, emotional, and social development of children between birth and 12 months of age on this web site.

**American Academy of Pediatrics Section
on Developmental and Behavioral Pediatrics**

http://www.dbpeds.org
Information for professionals and parents on various aspects of developmental disabilities can be found here.

Child Development Institute

http://www.childdevelopmentinfo.com
The Child Development Institute is a web site for parents on child development, parenting, child psychology, teenagers, health, safety, and learning disabilities.

KidsHealth

http://kidshealth.org
KidsHealth offers a wide variety of information pertaining to child health issues.

Zero to Three

http://www.zerotothree.org
Zero to Three promotes the healthy development of infants and toddlers.

Coping with Developmental Disability

Beach Center on Disability

http://www.beachcenter.org
Beach Center on Disability is a research and training center that disseminates information about families with members who have developmental disabilities.

The Center for Universal Design

http://www.ncsu.edu/project/design-projects/udi/
The Center for Universal Design provides publications and information for parents and professionals concerning accessible housing design and financing issues. It also makes referrals to local organizations.

Children's Disabilities Information

http://www.childrensdisabilities.info
This is a support site for parents that contains articles, lists of books, and web links.

The Compassionate Friends

http://www.compassionatefriends.org
The Compassionate Friends is a national and worldwide organization that supports and aids parents in the positive resolution of the grief experienced upon the death of a child and fosters the physical and emotional health of bereaved parents and siblings.

Easter Seals

http://www.easter-seals.org
Easter Seals is a nonprofit community-based health agency dedicated to increasing the independence of people with disabilities, especially those with autism. The web site offers a range of quality services, research, and programs.

Exceptional Parent

http://www.eparent.com
Exceptional Parent is a magazine published since 1971 that provides straightforward, practical information for families and professionals involved in the care of children and young adults with disabilities; many articles are written by parents.

**Family Village: A Global
Community of Disability-Related Resources**

http://www.familyvillage.wisc.edu
Family Village offers a wealth of links to a wide variety of disability-related resources.

Family Voices

> http://www.familyvoices.org
> Family Voices is a national grassroots clearinghouse for information and education concerning the health care of children with special health needs.

Federation for Children with Special Needs

> http://www.fcsn.org
> The Federation for Children with Special Needs offers parent-to-parent training and information.

National Organization on Disability

> http://www.nod.org
> The National Organization on Disability promotes the acceptance and understanding of the needs of citizens with disabilities through a national network of communities and organizations. It also facilitates the exchange of information regarding resources available to people with disabilities.

Parent to Parent USA

> http://www.p2pusa.org
> On this web site, state and local chapters provide one-to-one, parent-to-parent support by matching trained parents with newly referred parents on the basis of their children's disabilities and/or family issues they are encountering or have encountered.

Sibling Support Project

> http://www.siblingsupport.org
> Sibling Support Project is a national program dedicated to the interests of brothers and sisters of people with special health and developmental needs.

CHAPTER 1:
WHEN YOUR CHILD HAS TROUBLE TALKING

Agin, M.C., Geng, L.F., & Nicholl, M.J. (2003). *The late talker: What to do if your child isn't talking yet.* New York, NY: St. Martin's Press.

Feit, D., & Feldman, H.M. (2007). *The parent's guide to speech and language problems.* New York, NY: McGraw-Hill.

Williams, A.L., McLeod, S., & McCauley, R.J. (2010). *Interventions for speech sound disorders in children.* Baltimore, MD: Paul H. Brookes Publishing Co.

Apraxia—KIDS

> http://www.apraxia-kids.org
> Information on verbal apraxia can be found here.

National Center for Stuttering

http://www.stuttering.com/homepag.htm
The National Center for Stuttering provides information and supports research on stuttering.

Speech and Language Development in Infants and Young Children

http://members.tripod.com/Caroline_Bowen/devel1.htm
Information on speech and language development and interventions are available on this web site.

Speech Therapy Activities

http://www.speechtx.com
Find free, printable speech-language activities for speech-language pathologists and parents on this web site.

CHAPTER 2:
WHEN YOUR CHILD HAS TROUBLE WALKING

Cerebral Palsy

Miller, F., & Bachrach, S.J. (2006). *Cerebral palsy: A complete guide for caregiving.* Baltimore, MD: The Johns Hopkins University Press.

Cerebral Palsy—Neurology Channel

http://www.healthcommunities.com/cerebral-palsy/children/overview-of-cerebral-palsy.shtml
This web site provides information about cerebral palsy, including types, causes, treatments, risk factors, complications, and prognosis.

CPParent

http://www.cpparent.org
CPParent provides general information about cerebral palsy, its causes, and some treatments. It contains a dictionary to help parents better understand medical terms they may hear.

My Child with Cerebral Palsy

http://www.cerebralpalsy.org
This web site offers an array of information and resources for parents of children with cerebral palsy.

United Cerebral Palsy

http://www.ucp.org
United Cerebral Palsy provides direct services to children and adults with cerebral palsy, including medical diagnosis, evaluation and

treatment, special education, career development, counseling, social and recreational programs, and adapted housing.

Developmental Coordination Disorder

Kurtz, L.A. (2008). *Understanding motor skills in children with dyspraxia, ADHD, autism, and other learning disabilities: A guide to improving coordination.* London, England: Jessica Kingsley Publishers.

Bright Futures at Georgetown University

http://www.brightfutures.org/physicalactivity/issues_concerns/10.html
A helpful summary of developmental coordination disorder and suggested resources is available at this web site.

CHAPTER 3:
WHEN YOUR CHILD HAS
TROUBLE WITH DAILY LIVING SKILLS
Daily Living Skills (General)

Baker, B.L., & Brightman, A. (2004). *Steps to independence: Teaching everyday skills to children with special needs* (4th ed.). Baltimore, MD: Paul H. Brookes Publishing Co.

Ling, J. (2010). *I can't do that! My Social Stories to help with communication, self-care and personal skills.* Thousand Oaks, CA: Sage Publications.

Feeding and Nutrition

Williams, K.E., & Foxx, R.M. (2007). *Treating eating problems of children with autism spectrum disorders and developmental disabilities: Interventions for professionals and parents.* Austin, TX: PRO-ED.

American Dietetic Association

http://www.eatright.org
The American Dietetic Association provides general information on diet and nutrition.

ComeUnity's Resources for Feeding and Growth of Children

http://www.comeunity.com/premature/child/growth/resources.html
Links to recommended parent discussion lists, articles, and hospitals/institutions that offer feeding therapy can be found on this web site.

Dysphagia Resource Center

http://www.dysphagia.com
The Dysphagia Resource Center offers links to resources on swallowing and swallowing disorders.

New Visions

http://www.new-vis.com
New Visions provides education and therapy services to professionals and parents working with children with feeding, swallowing, oral-motor, and prespeech problems.

Sleep

Durand, V.M. (1998). *Sleep better! A guide to improving sleep for children with special needs.* Baltimore, MD: Paul H. Brookes Publishing Co.

Ferber, R. (2006). *Solve your child's sleep problems.* New York, NY: Fireside Books.

Toileting

Wolraich, M., & Tippins, S. (2003). *American Academy of Pediatrics guide to toilet training.* New York, NY: Bantam Books.

CHAPTER 4:
WHEN YOUR CHILD HAS
TROUBLE WITH SOCIAL SKILLS

Autism Spectrum Disorders (General)

Notbohm, E. (2005). *Ten things every child with autism wishes you knew.* Arlington, TX: Future Horizons.

Notbohm, E., & Zysk, V. (2010). *1001 great ideas for teaching and raising children with autism or Asperger's.* Arlington, TX: Future Horizons.

Powers, M.D. (2000). *Children with autism: A parent's guide.* Bethesda, MD: Woodbine House.

Sicile-Kira, C. (2004). *Autism spectrum disorders: The complete guide to understanding autism, Asperger's syndrome, pervasive developmental disorder, and other ASDs.* New York, NY: Berkeley Publishing Group.

Thompson, T. (2007). *Making sense of autism.* Baltimore, MD: Paul H. Brookes Publishing Co.

American Academy of Pediatrics—Autism

http://www.aap.org/healthtopics/autism.cfm
This web site provides information on autism for parents and doctors from the American Academy of Pediatrics.

Autism Society

http://www.autism-society.org
The Autism Society of America is a national, grass-roots organization devoted to improving the lives of those affected by autism.

Autism Speaks

http://www.autismspeaks.org
Autism Speaks is a national organization devoted to disseminating information and promoting research on the autism spectrum disorders.

Families for Early Autism Treatment

http://www.feat.org
Families for Early Autism Treatment is an organization in California dedicated to promoting scientifically proven, best outcome treatment for children with autism (related organizations in various states are called Families for Effective Autism Treatment).

National Center on Birth Defects and Developmental Disabilities (NCBDDD): Autism Information Center

http://www.cdc.gov/ncbddd/autism/index.htm
This web site has a unique feature: It links to the Autism Spectrum Disorders Kids' Quest (http://www.cdc.gov/ncbddd/kids/autism.html), a series of informative sites provided by the NCBDDD for the purpose of educating children about developmental disabilities.

Asperger Syndrome

Attwood, T. (2008). *The complete guide to Asperger's syndrome.* London, England: Jessica Kingsley Publishers.

Attwood, T., & Grandin, T. (2006). *Asperger's and girls: World-renowned experts join those with Asperger's syndrome to resolve issues that girls and women face every day!* Arlington, TX: Future Horizons.

Baker, J. (2005). *Preparing for life: The complete guide for transitioning to adulthood for those with autism and Asperger's syndrome.* Arlington, TX: Future Horizons.

Bashe, P.R., & Kirby, B.L. (2005). *The OASIS guide to Asperger syndrome: Advice, support, insight, and inspiration.* New York, NY: Crown Publishers.

■■■

Faherty, C., & Mesibov, G.B. (2006). *Asperger's...What does it mean to me? A workbook explaining self awareness and life lessons to the child or youth with high functioning autism or Aspergers, structured teaching ideas for home and school*. Arlington, TX: Future Horizons.

Myles, B.S., & Southwick, J. (2005). *Asperger syndrome and difficult moments: Practical solutions for tantrums, rage, and meltdowns*. Shawnee Mission, KS: AAPC Publishing.

Ozonoff, S., Dawson, G., & McPartland, J. (2002). *A parent's guide to Asperger syndrome and high-functioning autism: How to meet the challenges and help your child thrive*. New York, NY: Guilford Press.

**OASIS@MAAP—The Online Asperger
Syndrome Information and Support Center**

http://www.aspergersyndrome.org/
This web site provides information about Asperger syndrome and other autism spectrum disorders, and links to resources.

Social Skills

Baker, J. (2001). *Social skills picture book: Teaching communication, play and emotion*. Arlington, TX: Future Horizons.

Baker, J. (2006). *The social skills picture book: For high school and beyond*. Arlington, TX: Future Horizons.

Baker, J., & Myles, B. (2003). *Social skills training for children and adolescents with Asperger syndrome and social-communication problems*. Shawnee Mission, KS: AAPC Publishing.

Gray, C. (1994). *Comic strip conversations: Illustrated interactions that teach conversation skills to students with autism and related disorders*. Arlington, TX: Future Horizons.

Gray, C. (2010). *The new Social Story book*. Arlington, TX: Future Horizons.

Gray, C., & White, A.L. (2002). *My Social Stories book*. London, England: Jessica Kingsley Publishers.

Howlin, P., Baron-Cohen, S., & Hadwin, J.A. (2011). *Teaching children with autism to mind-read: The workbook*. New York, NY: Wiley.

Loomis, J.W. (2008). *Staying in the game: Providing social opportunities for children and adolescents with autism spectrum disorders and other developmental disabilities*. Shawnee Mission, KS: AAPC Publishing.

McGinnis, E. (2011). *Skillstreaming in early childhood: A guide for teaching prosocial skills*. Champaign, IL: Research Press.

McGinnis, E. (2011). *Skillstreaming the adolescent: A guide for teaching prosocial skills*. Champaign, IL: Research Press.

McGinnis, E. (2011). *Skillstreaming the elementary school child: A guide for teaching prosocial skills*. Champaign, IL: Research Press.

Myles, B.S. (2004). *The hidden curriculum: Practical solutions for understanding unstated rules in social situations.* Shawnee Mission, KS: AAPC Publishing.

CHAPTER 5:
WHEN YOUR CHILD HAS TROUBLE BEHAVING

Attention-Deficit/Hyperactivity Disorder

Barkley, R.A. (2000). *Taking charge of ADHD: The complete, authoritative guide for parents.* New York, NY: Guilford Press.

Hallowell, E.M., & Ratey, J.J. (1994). *Driven to distraction: The experience and treatment of attention deficit disorder in children and adults.* New York, NY: Pantheon Books.

A.D.D. WareHouse

http://www.addwarehouse.com
This web site is a resource for clinicians, parents, teachers, adults, and students to order by mail books, games, videos, and other materials related to attention-deficit/hyperactivity disorder.

Attention Deficit Disorder Association

http://www.add.org
The Attention Deficit Disorder Association is a national organization that provides education, research, and public advocacy that is especially focused on the needs of adults and young adults with attention-deficit/hyperactivity disorder.

Children and Adults with Attention-Deficit/Hyperactivity Disorder

http://www.chadd.org
This web site is a support group for parents of children with attention disorders.

Behavior and Temperament

Baker, J. (2008). *No more meltdowns: Positive strategies for managing and preventing out-of-control behavior.* Arlington, TX: Future Horizons.

Barkley, R.A. (2006). *Understanding the defiant child.* New York, NY: Guilford Press.

Greene, R.W. (2010). *The explosive child: A new approach for understanding and parenting easily frustrated, chronically inflexible children.* New York, NY: Harper.

Kristal, J. (2005). *The temperament perspective: Working with children's behavioral styles.* Baltimore, MD: Paul H. Brookes Publishing Co.

Phelan, T.W. (1995). *1–2–3 magic: Effective discipline for children 2–12.* Glen Ellyn, IL: Child Management.

Porter, L. (2008). *Young children's behavior: Practical approaches for caregivers and teachers* (3rd ed.). Baltimore, MD: Paul H. Brookes Publishing Co.

Tymchuk, A.J. (2006). *The health and wellness program: A parenting curriculum for families at risk.* Baltimore, MD: Paul H. Brookes Publishing Co.

CHAPTER 6:
WHEN YOUR CHILD HAS TROUBLE LEARNING

Intellectual Disability

The Arc

http://thearc.org
The Arc is a national advocacy organization that works on behalf of individuals with intellectual disabilities and their families. It has more than 1,000 state and local chapters.

President's Committee for People with Intellectual Disabilities

http://www.acf.hhs.gov/programs/pcpid/index.html
This web site provides information about the mission and activities of the President's Committee for People with Intellectual Disabilities.

Learning Disability

Joshi, R.M., Treiman, R., Carreker, S., & Moats, L.C. (2008–2009). How words cast their spell: Spelling is an integral part of learning the language, not a matter of memorization. *American Educator, 32*(4), 6–16, 42, 43. Available from http://louisamoats.com/Assets/How .Words.Cast.Their.Spell.pdf

Lavoie, R.D. (2005). *It's so much work to be your friend: Helping the child with learning disabilities find social success.* New York, NY: Simon & Schuster.

Levine, M.D. (2002). *A mind at a time.* New York, NY: Simon & Schuster.

Levine, M.D. (2003). *The myth of laziness.* New York, NY: Simon & Schuster.

Shaywitz, S.E. (2003). *Overcoming dyslexia: A new and complete science-based program for reading problems at any level.* New York, NY: Alfred A. Knopf.

International Dyslexia Association

http://www.interdys.org
The International Dyslexia Association is a nonprofit organization devoted to helping individuals with dyslexia and their families and communities.

LD Online

http://www.ldonline.org
Resources on learning disabilities for parents, students, teachers, and other professionals can be found at LD Online.

Learning Disabilities Association of America

http://www.ldanatl.org
This web site provides information about learning disabilities and resources available nationally through the Learning Disability Association of America.

National Center for Learning Disabilities

http://www.ld.org
This web site provides information about learning disabilities.

National Reading Panel

http://www.nationalreadingpanel.org/
This web site includes a summary of scientific research on dyslexia and effective reading instruction with information for parents.

CHAPTER 7:
WHEN YOUR CHILD NEEDS EXTRA HELP

Early Intervention, Special Education, and Family Support

Cutler, B.C., & Pratt, S. (2010). *You, your child, and "special" education: A guide to dealing with the system* (Rev. ed.). Baltimore, MD: Paul H. Brookes Publishing Co.

Wood, K.I., & Youcha, V. (2009). *The ABCs of the ADA: Your early childhood program's guide to the Americans with Disabilities Act.* Baltimore, MD: Paul H. Brookes Publishing Co.

Building the Legacy: IDEA 2004

http://idea.ed.gov and http://idea.ed.gov/explore/view/
This web site offers comprehensive information about the Individuals with Disabilities Education Improvement Act (IDEA) of 2004 (Public Law 108-446) Part C, which funds and regulates early intervention services for infants and toddlers with disabilities and their families.

Kid Source

http://www.kidsource.com
Information on early intervention is available at Kid Source.

National Association of Private Special Education Centers (formerly the National Association of Private Schools for Exceptional Children)

http://www.napsec.org
This web site provides information about the receiving special education support in private special education settings.

PACER Center (Parent Advocacy Coalition for Educational Rights)

http://www.pacer.org
The PACER Center provides education and training to help parents understand special education laws and obtain appropriate school programs for their children.

Parent Educational Advocacy Training Center

http://www.peatc.org
The Parent Educational Advocacy Training Center is a professionally staffed organization that helps parents to become effective advocates for their children with school personnel and the educational system.

Recreation and Sports

American Association of Adapted Sports Programs

http://www.aaasp.org
The American Association of Adapted Sports Programs is a clearinghouse of information, programs, and activities related to sports and athletic activities for people with disabilities.

Disabled Sports USA

http://www.dsusa.org
Disabled Sports USA provides year-round sports and recreational opportunities to people with orthopedic, spinal cord, neuromuscular, and visual impairments through a national network of local chapters.

Girl Scouts

http://www.girlscouts.org
Girl Scouts is open to all girls ages 5–17 (or kindergarten through Grade 12). This organization runs camping programs, sports and recreational activities, and service programs and incorporates children with disabilities into general Girl Scout troop activities. See also their book *Focus on Ability: Serving Girls with Special Needs.*

International Committee of Sports for the Deaf

http://www.deaflympics.com
A history of the accomplishments of deaf athletes and links to regional confederations and technical delegates throughout the world can be found on this web site.

Little League Baseball, Challenger Division

http://www.littleleague.org/learn/about/divisions/challenger.htm
This online resource provides information and opportunities for boys and girls with disabilities to experience the emotional development and fun of playing Little League baseball.

National Center on Physical Activity and Disability

http://www.ncpad.org
The National Center on Physical Activity and Disability encourages and supports people with disabilities who wish to increase their overall level of activity and participate in some form of regular physical activity.

National Sports Center for the Disabled

http://www.nscd.org
The National Sports Center for the Disabled provides therapeutic recreation programs designed for individuals with disabilities who require adaptive equipment and/or special instruction. The organization offers summer and winter programs and has some scholarships.

Special Olympics

http://www.specialolympics.org
Special Olympics is the largest organization to provide year-round sports training and athletic competition for children and adults with intellectual disabilities and certain other significant cognitive impairments. Local, state, and national games are held throughout the United States and in more than 150 countries; world games are held every 4 years.

Wheelchair & Ambulatory Sports USA

http://www.wsusa.org
This is the web site for the governing body of various wheelchair athletics, including swimming, archery, weightlifting, track and field, table tennis, and air weapons.

Yoga for the Special Child

http://www.specialyoga.com
Yoga for the Special Child is an organization devoted to promoting the use of yoga for children with special needs and developmental disabilities.

CHAPTER 8:
VISION, HEARING, AND
SENSORY PROCESSING PROBLEMS

Visual Impairment

American Association for Pediatric Ophthalmology and Strabismus

http://aapos.org
This web site provides resources for patients and families regarding frequently asked questions of ocular conditions and is also a resource for locating a pediatric ophthalmologist in your area.

American Foundation for the Blind

http://www.afb.org
The American Foundation for the Blind offers services and resources for individuals with visual impairment.

American Printing House for the Blind

http://www.aph.org
The American Printing House for the Blind is a nonprofit publishing house for people with visual impairments.

**Lighthouse International (formerly the
National Association Visually Handicapped)**

http://www.lighthouse.org
Lighthouse International provides information and resources for people who have visual impairments.

National Braille Association

http://www.nationalbraille.org
The National Braille Association is devoted to promoting the use of braille for people who have visual impairments.

National Federation of the Blind

http://www.nfb.org
The National Federation of the Blind provides advocacy services for individuals with visual impairments.

National Library Service for the Blind and Physically Handicapped

http://www.loc.gov/nls
The National Library Service for the Blind and Physically offers free braille and audio materials to eligible borrowers by mail.

Prevent Blindness America

http://www.preventblindness.org
Prevent Blindness America is an organization devoted to preventing blindness through the provision of screening services, advocacy, training, and the promotion of research into the causes of blindness.

United States Association of Blind Athletes

http://www.usaba.org
The United States Association of Blind Athletes is an organization devoted to providing opportunities for participation in sports for individuals with vision impairment.

Hearing Impairment

Centers for Disease Control and Prevention—Hearing Loss in Children

http://www.cdc.gov/hearingloss
Comprehensive information about hearing loss can be found on this web site.

Described and Captioned Media Program

http://www.dcmp.org/
This program provides government-sponsored distribution of open-captioned materials to eligible institutions, individuals, and families.

Hands and Voices

http://www.handsandvoices.org
Hands and Voices is a nationwide nonprofit organization that is a parent-driven, parent/professional collaborative group dedicated to supporting families and their children who are deaf or hard of hearing, as well as the professionals who serve them.

Hearing Loss Association of America

http://www.shhh.org
The Hearing Loss Association of America is a national organization for people with hearing loss dedicated to the dissemination of information, advocacy, and promotion of research on hearing loss prevention and intervention.

Helen Keller National Center for Deaf-Blind Youths and Adults

http://www.hknc.org/
The Helen Keller National Center for Deaf-Blind Youths and Adults is devoted to enabling people who are deaf-blind to live and work in the community of their choice.

International Hearing Society

http://ihsinfo.org/IhsV2/Home/Index.cfm
This web site provides information on how to proceed when hearing loss is suspected.

Laurent Clerc National Deaf Education Center

http://clerccenter.gallaudet.edu/infotogo
The Laurent Clerc National Deaf Education Center web site is a comprehensive resource related to the educational, linguistic, social, and emotional development of children who are deaf or hard of hearing.

National Consortium on Deaf-Blindness

http://www.nationaldb.org/
The National Consortium on Deaf-Blindness provides technical assistance for children who are blind-deaf, and to disseminate information about deaf-blindness.

National Institute on Deafness
and Other Communication Disorders

http://www.nidcd.nih.gov/
The National Institute on Deafness and Other Communication Disorders is devoted to promoting research to improve the lives of people with communication disorders.

Sensory Processing Disorders

Kranowitz, C.S. (2005). *The out-of-sync child: Recognizing and coping with sensory processing disorder.* New York, NY: Perigee.

Sensory Processing Disorder Foundation

http://www.sinetwork.org/index.html
Sensory Processing Disorder Foundation promotes knowledge, awareness, and recognition of sensory processing disorder.

CHAPTER 9:
SPECIAL MEDICAL PROBLEMS

General Information

American Academy of Pediatrics, American Academy of Family Physicians, and American College of Physicians, Transitions Clinical Report Authoring Group. (2011). Supporting the health care transition from adolescence to adulthood in the medical home. *Pediatrics, 128,* 182–200. Available from http://aappolicy.aappublications.org/cgi/content/abstract/pediatrics;128/1/182?rss=1

Rubin, I.L., & Crocker, A.C. (2006). *Medical care for children and adults with developmental disabilities* (2nd ed.). Baltimore, MD: Paul H. Brookes Publishing Co.

National Center for Medical Home Information

http://www.medicalhomeinfo.org/how/care_delivery/
This web site provides tools and protocols that can assist with the coordination of care for children with chronic conditions.

Cerebral Palsy

See the resources in "Chapter 2: When Your Child Has Trouble Walking."

Dental

American Academy of Pediatric Dentistry

http://www.aapd.org
This web site provides information for parents and professionals on dental health in children.

National Institute of Dental and Craniofacial Research

http://www.nicdr.nih.gov
The National Institute of Dental and Craniofacial Research is a division of the National Institutes of Health devoted to improving dental health through education, training, and research.

Special Care Dentistry Association

http://www.SCDonline.org
The Special Care Dentistry Association is an international organization of oral health professionals and other individuals who are dedicated to promoting oral health and well-being for people with special needs.

Down Syndrome

Pueschel, S.M. (2001). *A parent's guide to Down syndrome: Toward a brighter future* (Rev. ed.). Baltimore, MD: Paul H. Brookes Publishing Co.

Association for Children with Down Syndrome

http://www.acds.org
The Association for Children with Down Syndrome offers information and referral services, including a free list of publications.

Down Syndrome: Health Issues

http://www.ds-health.com
This web site provides information regarding health issues in children with Down syndrome.

National Down Syndrome Congress

http://ndsccenter.org
The National Down Syndrome Congress provides information, advocacy, and support.

National Down Syndrome Society

http://www.ndss.org
The National Down Syndrome Society advocates for the value, acceptance, and inclusion of people with Down syndrome.

Epilepsy

Epilepsy Foundation

http://www.epilepsyfoundation.org/
The Epilepsy Foundation provides information and promotes research on epilepsy.

International League Against Epilepsy

http://www.ilae-epilepsy.org
The International League Against Epilepsy exists to disseminate knowledge about epilepsy, promote research, education and training, and improve services and care for people with epilepsy.

Spina Bifida

Spina Bifida Association

http://www.sbaa.org
The Spina Bifida Association is an organization devoted to enhancing the lives of people affected by spina bifida.

Tics and Tourette Syndrome

National Tourette Syndrome Association

http://www.tsa-usa.org
The National Tourette Syndrome Association promotes awareness and offers support for individuals and families affected by Tourette syndrome.

CHAPTER 10: MEDICATIONS

Myers, S.M. (2007). The status of pharmacotherapy for autism spectrum disorders. *Expert Opinion on Pharmacology, 8,* 1579.

Myers, S.M., & Johnson, C.P. (2007). Management of children with autism spectrum disorders. *Pediatrics, 120,* 1162.

Wilens, T.E. (2009). *Straight talk about psychiatric medications for kids.* New York, NY: Guilford Press.

Drug InfoNet

http://www.druginfonet.com
Information about drugs, diseases, and pharmaceutical manufacturing as well as links to related sites can be found at Drug InfoNet.

CHAPTER 11:
WHY DID THIS HAPPEN?
THE CAUSES OF DISABILITY

Family Empowerment Network

http://www.fammed.wisc.edu/fen
Family Empowerment Network is a national nonprofit organization that exists to empower families affected by fetal alcohol syndrome and other drug-related birth defects through education and support.

GeneTests

http://www.ncbi.nlm.nih.gov/sites/GeneTests/
GeneTests is a free resource on medical genetics information developed for physicians, health care providers, researchers, and the public.

Genetic Alliance

http://www.geneticalliance.org
Genetic Alliance is an international organization of families, health professionals, and genetic organizations dedicated to enhancing the lives of individuals living with genetic conditions.

Genetics Home Reference

http://ghr.nlm.nih.gov
Genetics Home Reference provides consumer-friendly information about the effects of genetic variations on human health.

March of Dimes

http://www.marchofdimes.com
The March of Dimes awards grants to institutions and organizations for the development of genetic services, perinatal care in high-risk pregnancies, prevention of premature delivery, parent support groups, and other community programs.

Premature Baby, Premature Child

http://prematurity.org
This web site was created by parents of children who were born prematurely and who had developmental issues.

Index